THIS
LAND
IS...

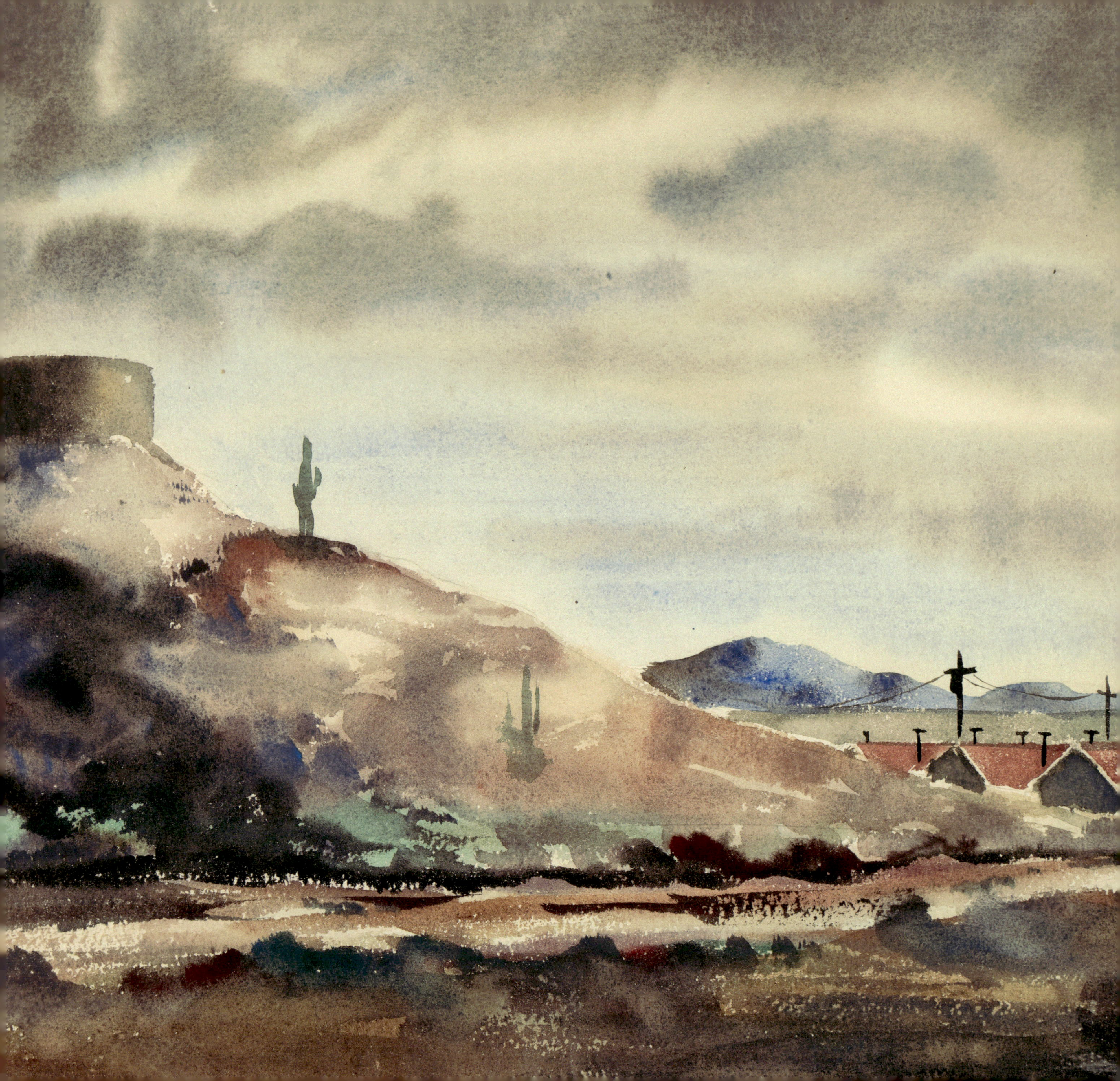

THIS LAND IS...

Edited by
Josh Garrett-Davis and
Linde B. Lehtinen

THIS LAND IS...

Edited by
Josh Garrett-Davis and
Linde B. Lehtinen

Field Notes on American Ground

The Huntington
San Marino, California

Distributed by the University of Pennsylvania Press

Contents

Roots

Uprootings

Amendments

Edge Effects

Disturbances

Regenerations

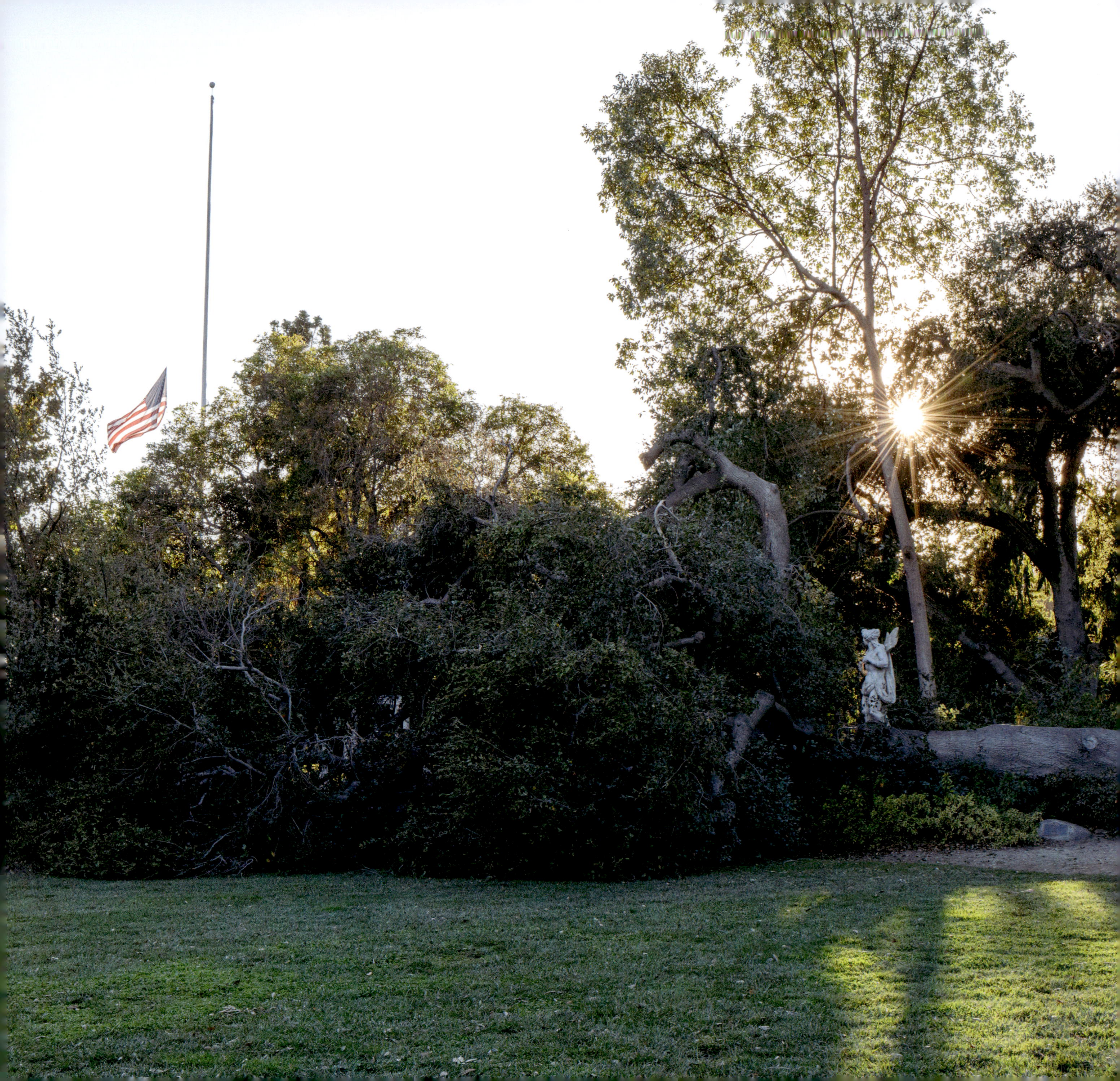

President's Foreword

From California to the New York Island . . .
This land was made for you and me.
—Woody Guthrie, "This Land Is Your Land"

El Segundo Boulevard, Palos Verdes Hills, Hermosa Beach, Santa Monica Pier. The ghost of Spanish-haunted English in the City of the Angels.
—Dana Gioia, "On Being Translated into Spanish"

Manhattan is a Lenape word.
—Natalie Diaz, *Postcolonial Love Poem*

This photograph shows a fallen Coast Live Oak (*Quercus agrifolia*) on the North Vista of The Huntington. The oak was uprooted in the windstorm of January 7–8, 2025, which fueled the Eaton and Palisades Fires. Flags were at half-staff that month to mourn the death of former President Jimmy Carter, who was elected months after the US bicentennial in 1976. The European sculpture in the middle of the foliage, which depicts the allegory of Truth, was carved in limestone by an unknown artist in the late seventeenth or early eighteenth century. Amid the devastation, the sun peeks through the trees, suggesting more hopeful times ahead, and a sapling sprouted from one of the oak's acorns is now more than six feet tall. Photograph by Dana Barsuhn, January 15, 2025.

During the US bicentennial in 1976, the 200th anniversary of the Declaration of Independence, I watched tall ships cruising down the Hudson River from a friend's balcony in New York City. After the turmoil of both the Vietnam War and Watergate, the procession on the Hudson felt therapeutic, a moment of healing. On the occasion of the semiquincentennial, The Huntington's *This Land Is . . .* offers insight and inspiration amid another tumultuous period in American history. From my home in California, I am honored to introduce this volume, which brings together contributions from a wide range of writers, scholars, artists, botanists, and educators who offer meditations on the theme of land and its relationship to history and culture. Edited by curators Josh Garrett-Davis and Linde B. Lehtinen, this collection of essays attests to the centrality of land in forming our personal, as well as national, memories.

From The Huntington's vantage point on the West Coast, far removed from the original thirteen colonies that dominate the American historical imagination, we have used our library, art, and botanical collections to refresh colonial themes and reflect more generally on land as both common and contested ground. We propose new ways of completing the phrase *This Land Is . . .* , which serves as both the title of this book and a yearlong program of activities.

That phrase borrows from Woody Guthrie's classic credo on place and belonging in America, "This Land Is Your Land," written in 1940 after Guthrie hitchhiked across the country to New York City. Guthrie thought of the song as an alternative to Irving Berlin's wildly popular "God Bless America." Guthrie's lyrics revealed not only the magnificence of the American landscape but also the disparate experiences that shape the sense of belonging among the many groups that inhabit this land.

Historically, the land is a palimpsest that reflects layers of possession and dispossession. The word "palimpsest" literally refers to "a manuscript or piece of writing material on which the original writing has been effaced to make room for later writing but of which traces remain." The concept has particular resonance for The Huntington's observance of this anniversary, which reveals traces of the American past that are hiding in plain sight or overlooked. These layers deepen our understanding of place and displacement across time. The two epigraphs above that accompany the lines from Guthrie suggest that languages, too, are palimpsests, "from California to the New York Island."

In January 2025, devastating wildfires and winds scarred Southern California, the land, and our communities. Traces of this tragedy will endure for generations. It is our hope that the disastrous displacements will give way to the rejuvenation of our land and the rebuilding of our local communities, despite the lasting memory of loss. There is no greater reminder that this land—yours and mine—is terribly precious—and binds people together. The land is a limited resource we all need for survival. It has shaped our past and will shape our future.

Shiva Temple from west of Horn Creek
Morning sun of December 20 1966
35mm Kodachrome #20 by Butchart

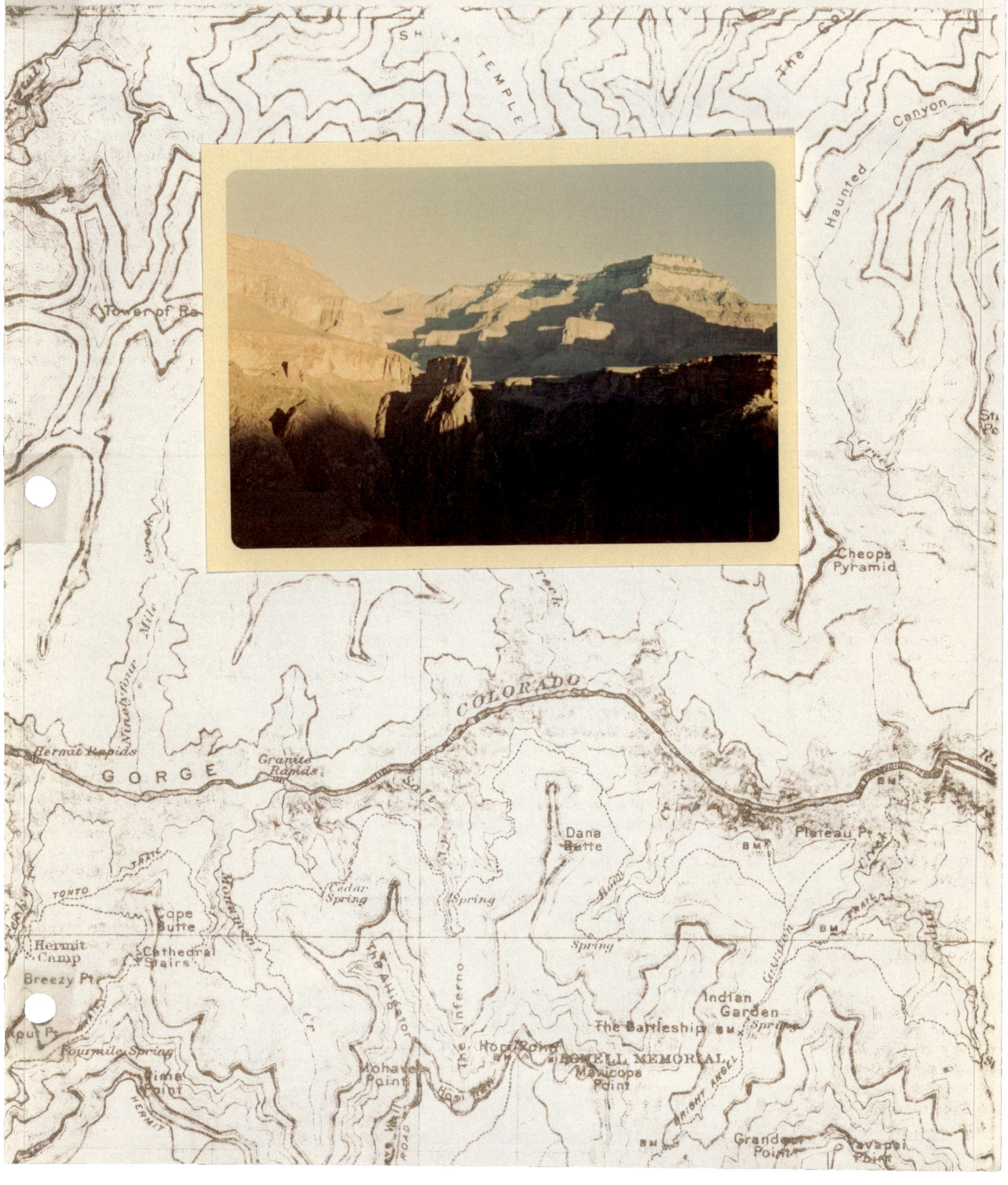

Introduction

Field Notes

On the back of a printed document, the secretary of the New York Provincial Congress handwrites the names of county representatives convening to vote in July 1776 on an important declaration. . . .

A songwriter in a Midtown Manhattan hotel in 1940 crosses out his title as he perfects the lyrics for what will be an American anthem. . . .

A Japanese American artist mixes watercolors to render a mountaintop water tank in the Arizona desert, creating an image of somber beauty amid the injustice of World War II incarceration. . . .

A novelist rides the bus through the multilayered urban landscape of 1990s Los Angeles to capture details regarding environment and society, highlighting key phrases and words in her notebook as she imagines the coming century. . . .

Each of these moments produced a record, a memory, an American field note. In the strictest sense, field notes consist of close observations that allow for the writer's later reflection and interpretation, as with George Washington's measurements for a survey near his Mount Vernon estate as he expanded the property in the 1780s (fig. 2).[1] Botanists use field notes to collect information about the natural world and even to preserve specimens. Artists employ drawings to render form and light through the study of nature. Surveyors rely on their experiences in the field to construct maps and delineate boundaries. Often handwritten, these records invite us to consider the actions used to produce them, whether measuring, wandering, excavating, or tracking changes over time.

A more expansive definition of field notes encompasses photographs, poetry, essays, maps, sketches, and impressions of nascent ideas. The contributions to this book are far more refined and crafted than field notes. But they

Figure 1
Otis R. Marston, page from "Grand Canyon Views; Colorado River: Miles 89.5–92.6 Below Lee's Ferry." 11 × 8½ in. Photograph by John Harvey Butchart, "Shiva Temple from west of Horn Creek," 1966. Chromogenic print. Otis R. Marston Papers, The Huntington.

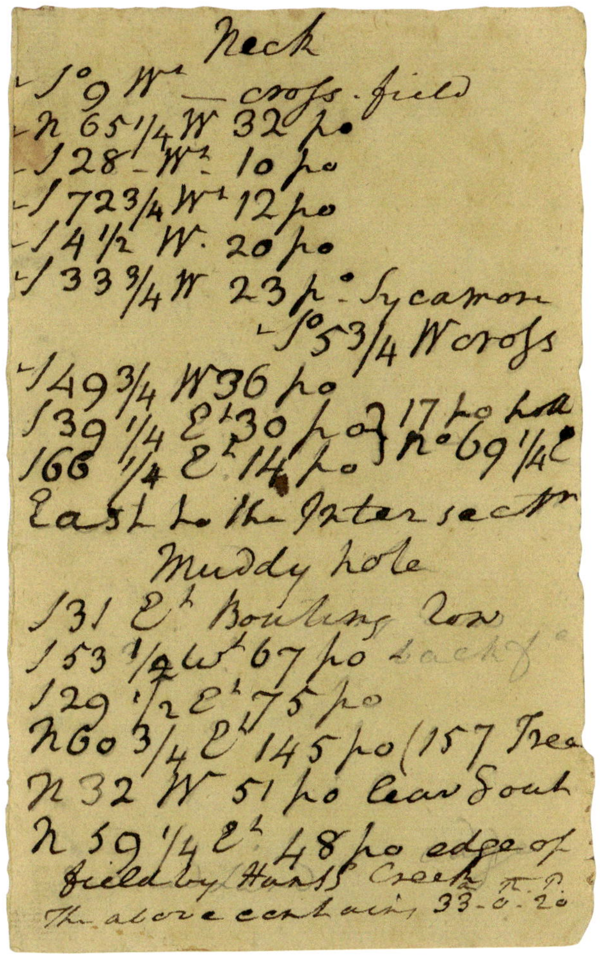
Neck
S 9 W — cross. field
N 65 1/4 W 32 po
S 28 W 10 po
S 72 3/4 W 12 po
S 4 1/2 W 20 po
S 33 3/4 W 23 po Sycamore
S 53 3/4 W cross
S 49 3/4 W 36 po
S 39 1/4 E 30 po
S 66 1/4 E 14 po N 69 1/4 E
East to the Intersection
Muddy hole
S 31 E Bowling Row
S 53 1/2 W 67 po
S 29 1/2 E 75 po
N 60 3/4 E 145 po (157 Tree
N 32 W 51 po leav South
N 59 1/4 E 48 po edge of field by Hunts Creek
The above contains 33-0-20

Figure 2
George Washington, "Field Notes for Survey of Mount Vernon," ca. 1784–89. George Washington Collection, The Huntington, Purchased by Henry E. Huntington, HM 74696.

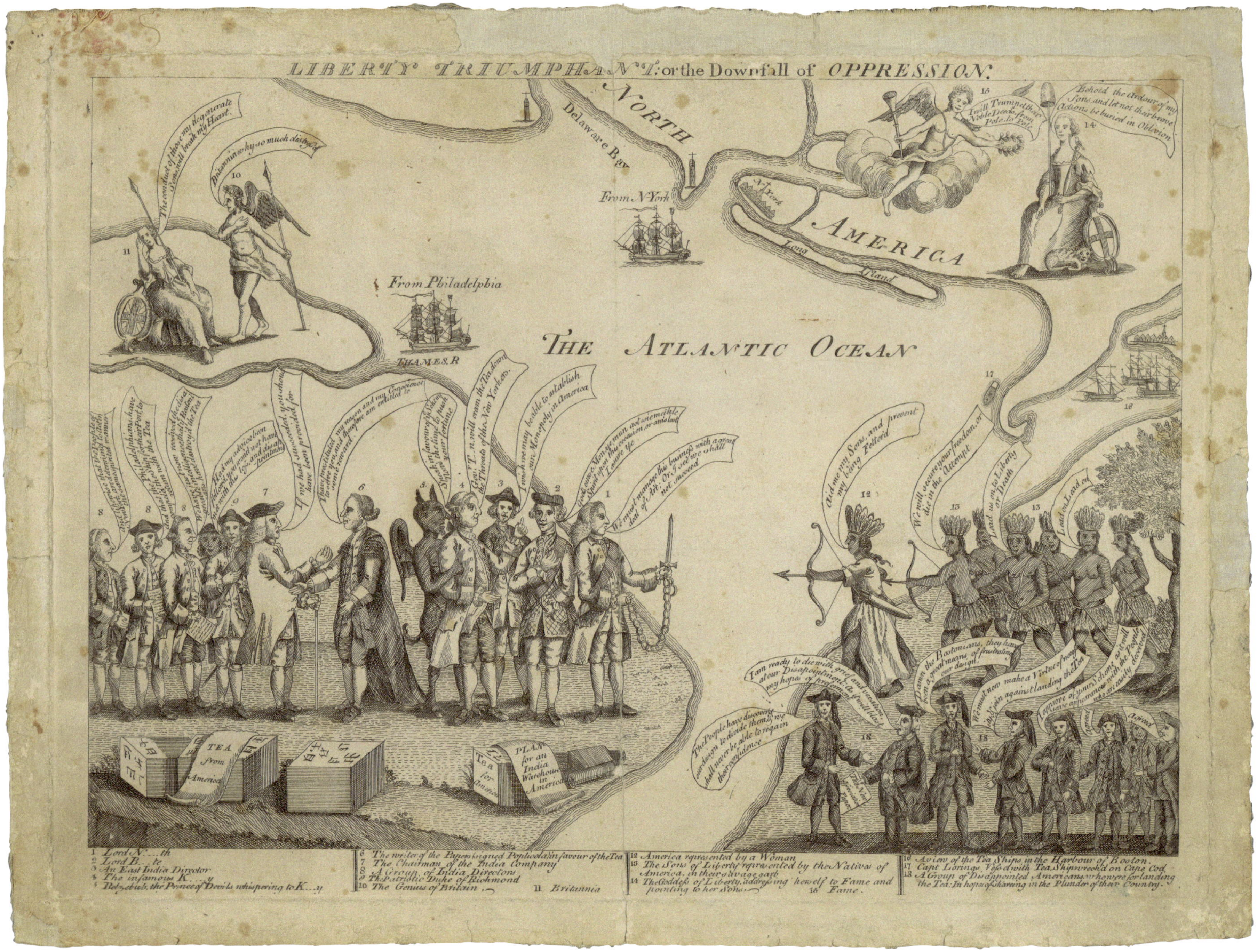

Figure 3
Henry Dawkins, *Liberty Triumphant; or the Downfall of Oppression*, ca. 1773. Engraving, 11 × 17 in. The Huntington, priAPC 0001.

offer firsthand observations on land and history across many parts of the vast and complicated land we now call America. They take many forms: essays, an interview, a comic book–style story, and poetic combinations of image and text. These are grouped into six categories, each of which grafts a physical or ecological phenomenon onto the cultural-historical meanings of the same term: Roots, Uprootings, Amendments, Edge Effects, Disturbances, and Regenerations. Together, these branches provide a guiding framework for the volume and its related exhibition, explored in the essay that follows.

This does not pretend to be a comprehensive survey or appraisal of the territory of the United States as the nation commemorates its semiquincentennial in 2026. Rather, the title *This Land Is . . . : Field Notes on American Ground* emphasizes its ellipsis and the practice of producing field notes to signal a more provisional, open-ended approach to the nation's geography and peoples.

Roots

In American culture, roots evoke the past, family trees, and a sense of belonging to a particular place. Roots music is an earthy sound, often connected to the Southeast and the African, European, and Indigenous traditions that converged there. Roots also suggest the hidden and unseen below the surface. And *Roots: The Saga of an American Family*, the seminal novel by Alex Haley based on his own family history, was dedicated as a "birthday offering to my country" when it was released in 1976, the year of the nation's bicentennial. Haley's epic begins around 1750 in The Gambia, West Africa, as the mother of the protagonist, Kunta Kinte, carefully plants her "onions, yams, gourds, cassava, and bitter tomatoes," with ancestral prayers that the seeds will "take strong roots and grow."[2]

The United States has formally designated July 4, 1776, as its origin point, its root. But in the natural world, most roots are branching and tangled. Well before the drawn-out War of Independence (1775–83), other turning points might be designated as origins, from before 1492 to the battles of Lexington and Concord. The broadside political cartoon *Liberty Triumphant; or the Downfall of Oppression* (ca. 1773) depicts the Boston Tea Party in 1773, in which the Sons of Liberty, dressed as Mohawk people, dumped tea into the harbor to protest taxes (fig. 3). In his diary, John Adams called this unruly protest "so bold, so daring, so firm, intrepid and inflexible" as to be "an Epocha in History"—a turning point or root.[3]

Yet the Declaration of Independence—and in particular, the Fourth of July—has come to stand in for the entire process of establishing popular sovereignty. The Huntington's collection holds an early copy of the Declaration of Independence, printed by John Holt and dated July 9, 1776; it is annotated by John McKesson, secretary of New York's Provincial Congress. It records a chaotic moment, as 150 British ships bearing some 11,000 troops sailed into New York Harbor, and the congress retreated to White Plains to vote on separating from Great Britain. McKesson used the reverse side of his copy of the document to tally the unanimous support of the representatives, and he continued to use it for notes throughout July (fig. 4, foldout in back inside cover). This "field note" imbues the official moment of origin with the stages of revision, revealing the messy, multiauthored reality of history.[4]

The Declaration of Independence begins with the famous affirmation of the people's "unalienable rights" to "Life, Liberty, and the Pursuit of Happiness." While primarily a justification for severing ties with Great Britain, owing to the king's political and financial "abuses and usurpations," the text does include one major grievance related

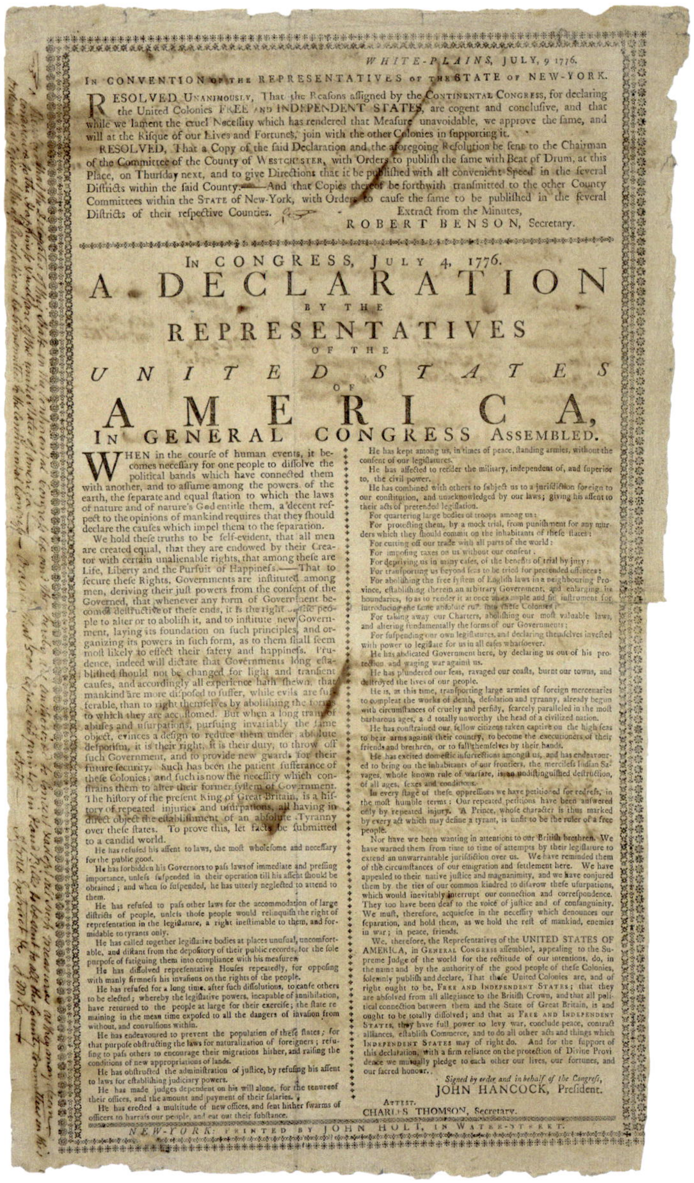

WHITE-PLAINS, JULY, 9 1776.

IN CONVENTION OF THE REPRESENTATIVES OF THE STATE OF NEW-YORK.

ROBERT BENSON, Secretary.

IN CONGRESS, JULY 4, 1776.

A DECLARATION BY THE REPRESENTATIVES OF THE UNITED STATES OF AMERICA, IN GENERAL CONGRESS ASSEMBLED.

JOHN HANCOCK, President.

CHARLES THOMSON, Secretary.

NEW-YORK: PRINTED BY JOHN HOLT, IN WATER-STREET.

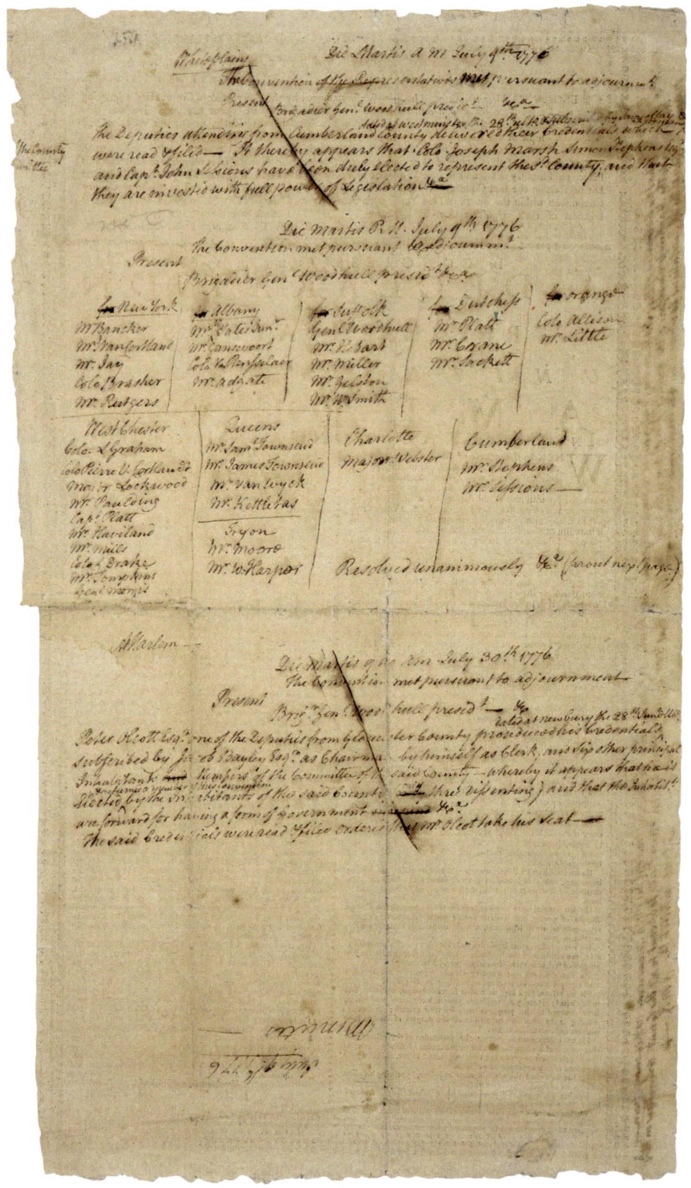

Figure 4
Broadside of Declaration of Independence with manuscript annotations by John McKesson (recto and verso), July 1776. Printed by John Holt, 20½ × 12½ in. The Huntington, Purchased by Henry E. Huntington, 1920, 81684.

Figure 5
Woody Guthrie, "This Land Is Your Land" original handwritten lyrics, February 23, 1940. Courtesy of the Woody Guthrie Archives.

Figures 6 and 7
C. F. Martin & Co., Model 000-18 guitar owned and inscribed with "This Machine Kills Fascists" by Woody Guthrie, 1936. Spruce, mahogany, celluloid, ebony, and mother-of-pearl. Courtesy Museum of Pop Culture, Seattle, WA.

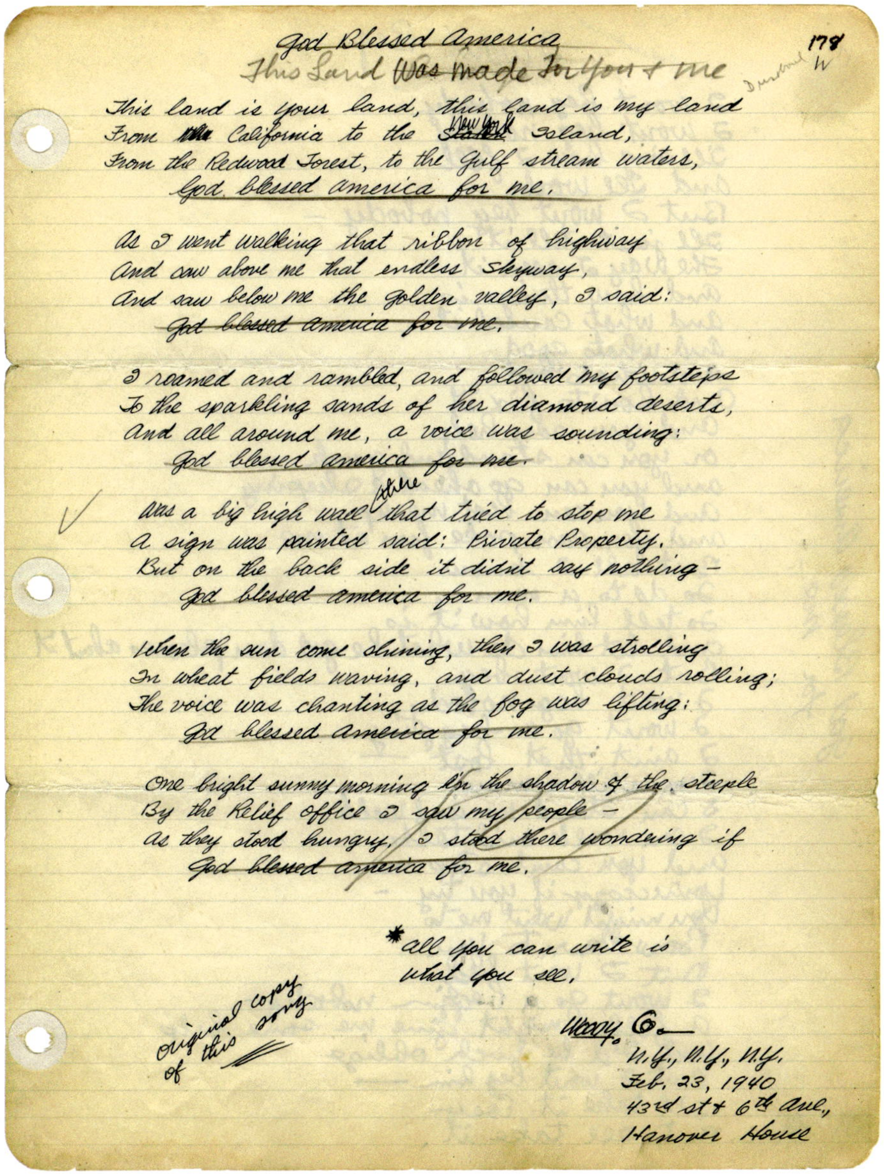
~~God Blessed America~~ 178
~~This Land Was made for You & me~~

This land is your land, this land is my land
From ~~the~~ California to the ~~Staten~~ New York Island,
From the Redwood Forest, to the Gulf stream waters,
God blessed america for me.

As I went walking that ribbon of highway
And saw above me that endless skyway,
And saw below me the golden valley, I said:
~~God blessed america for me.~~

I roamed and rambled, and followed my footsteps
To the sparkling sands of her diamond deserts,
And all around me, a voice was sounding:
~~God blessed america for me~~

Was a big high wall there that tried to stop me
A sign was painted said: Private Property,
But on the back side it didn't say nothing—
~~God blessed america for me.~~

When the sun come shining, then I was strolling
In wheat fields waving, and dust clouds rolling;
The voice was chanting as the fog was lifting:
~~God blessed america for me.~~

One bright sunny morning in the shadow of the steeple
By the Relief office I saw my people—
As they stood hungry, I stood there wondering if
~~God blessed america for me.~~

*all you can write is
what you see.

original copy
of this song

Woody G.
N.Y., N.Y., N.Y.
Feb. 23, 1940
43rd st & 6th ave.,
Hanover House

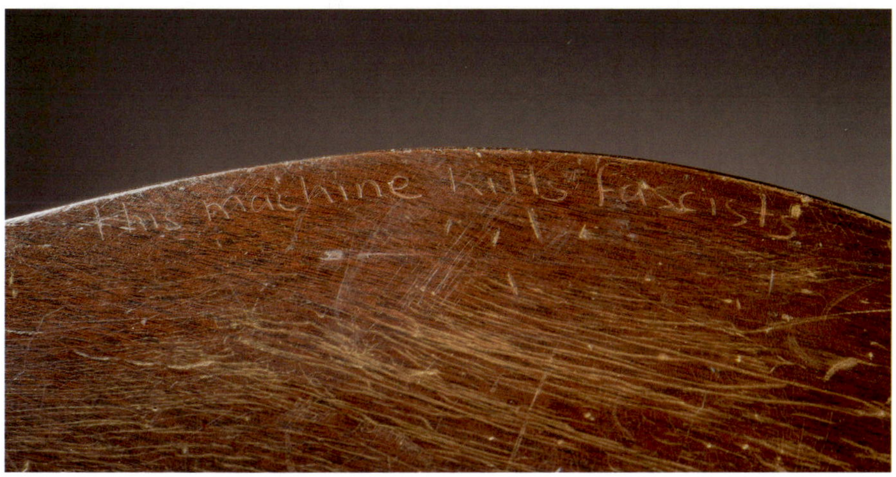

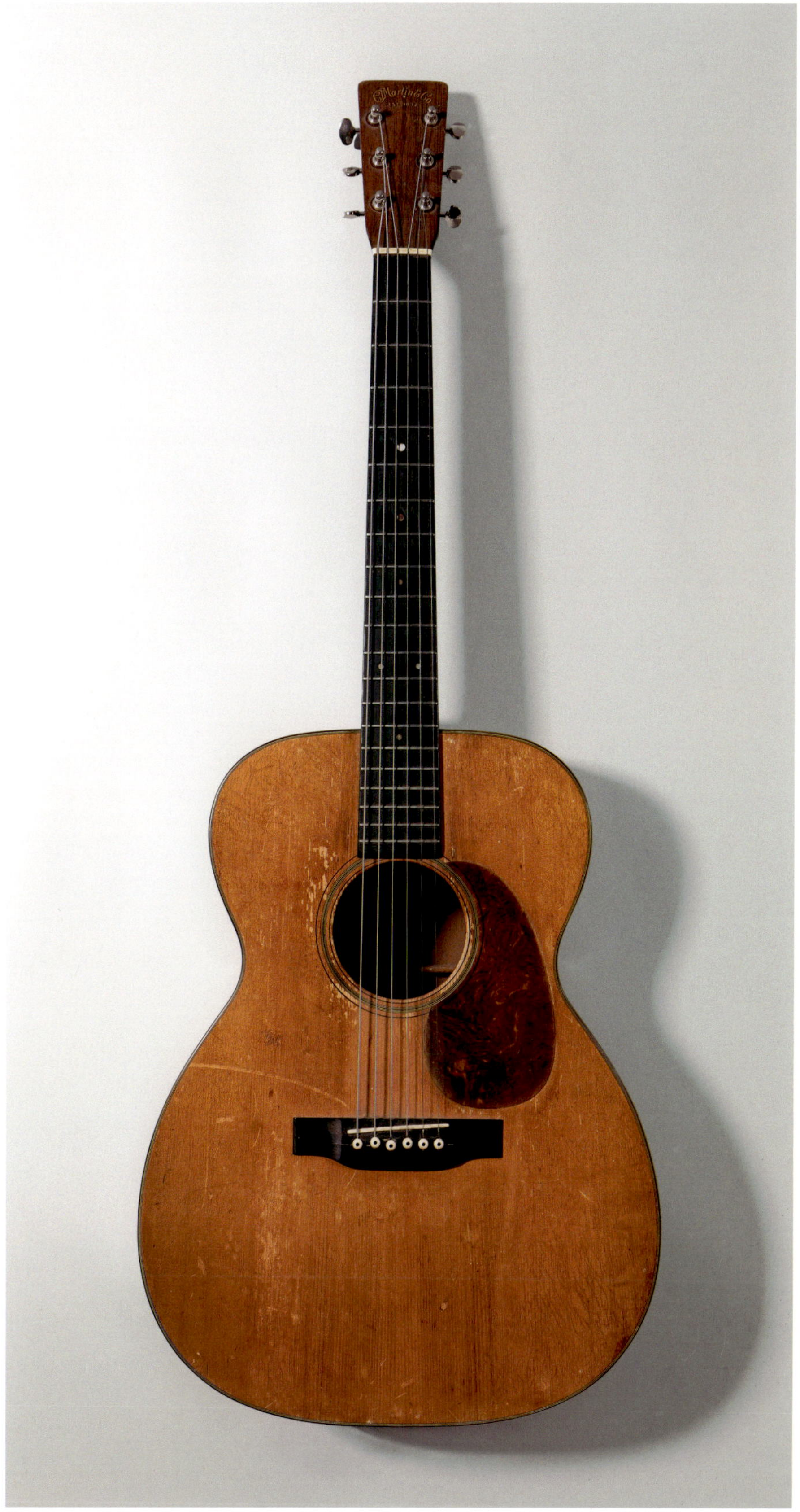

to land: "He"—that is, King George III—"has endeavoured to prevent the population of these states; for that purpose obstructing the laws for naturalization of foreigners; refusing to pass others to encourage their migrations hither, and raising the conditions of new appropriations of lands." This refers to the 1763 Royal Proclamation, which prohibited settlement on Indigenous lands west of a line drawn along the Appalachian Mountains and a subsequent treaty line. The king had also rescinded each colony's right to determine naturalization policies for new immigrants. But the nascent nation had already speculated—historically and financially—on expanding westward. These words point to a tension at the root of the country: Happiness for some meant dispossession for others.

A much later American declaration, the lyric sheet for "This Land Is Your Land" (1940) by songwriter Woody Guthrie, also bears the marks of revision (fig. 5). At some point, Guthrie changed the name of his masterpiece from "God Blessed America" to "This Land Was Made for You and Me" and reversed an earlier decision to end each verse with "God blessed America for me." The draft includes two politically pointed verses, including one that mocks a painted sign reading "Private Property." "But," the stanza continues, "on the back side it didn't say nothing." Guthrie invites us to look at the other side of the sign, to question its assertion. As a rambling troubadour, he joined refugees in camps and boxcars and grew suspicious of the notion of private property as enshrined in American law and culture. Coincidentally, the 1776 Declaration printing and Guthrie's manuscript were both created on Manhattan Island: one "New-York: Printed by John Holt, in Water-Street," and the other "N.Y., N.Y., N.Y. / Feb. 23, 1940 / 43rd St. + 6th Ave., / Hanover House."

During World War II, Guthrie began inscribing his guitars with the legend "This Machine Kills Fascists," believing

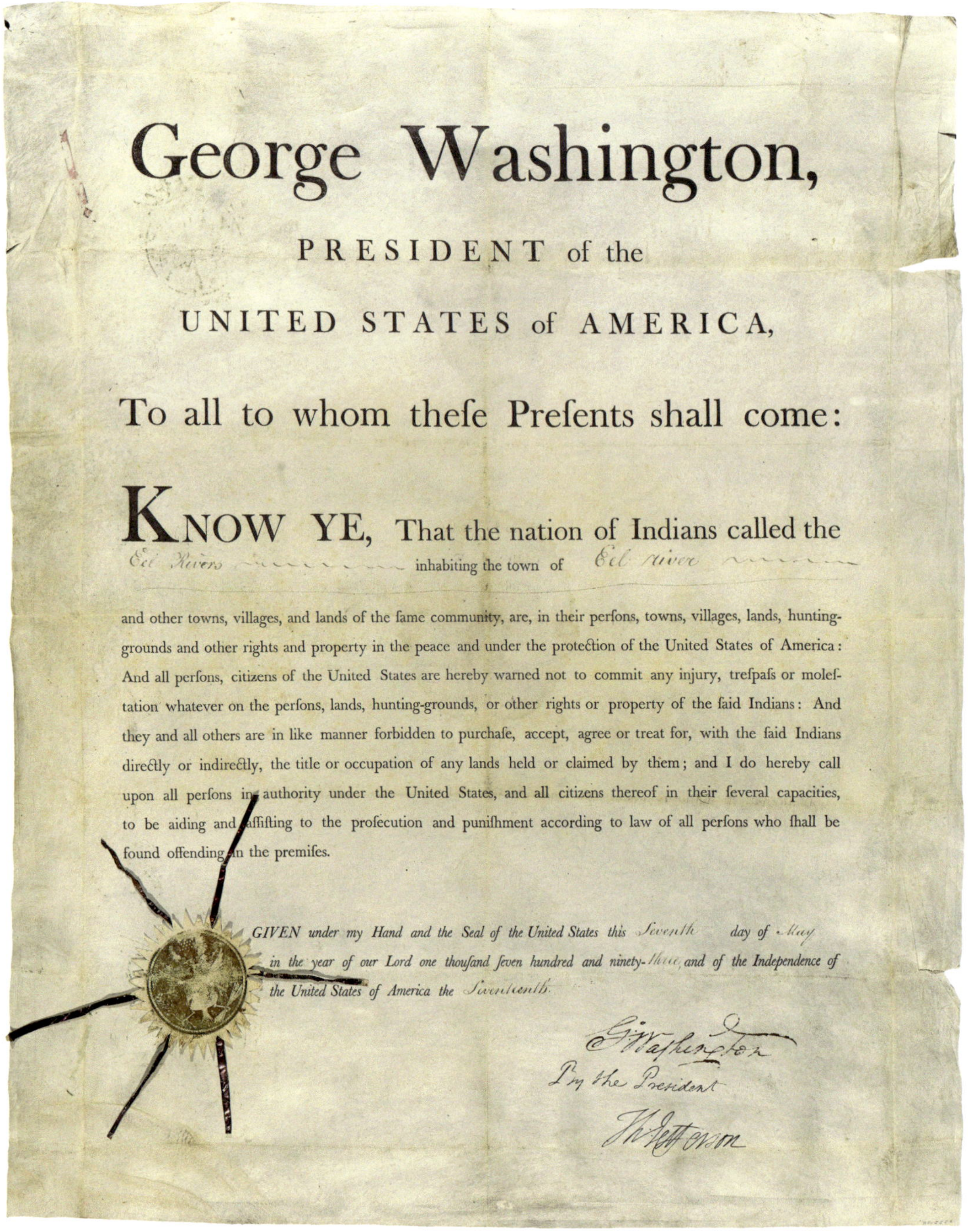

George Washington,

PRESIDENT of the

UNITED STATES of AMERICA,

To all to whom theſe Preſents shall come:

KNOW YE, That the nation of Indians called the Eel Rivers inhabiting the town of Eel river and other towns, villages, and lands of the ſame community, are, in their perſons, towns, villages, lands, hunting-grounds and other rights and property in the peace and under the protection of the United States of America: And all perſons, citizens of the United States are hereby warned not to commit any injury, treſpaſs or moleſtation whatever on the perſons, lands, hunting-grounds, or other rights or property of the ſaid Indians: And they and all others are in like manner forbidden to purchaſe, accept, agree or treat for, with the ſaid Indians directly or indirectly, the title or occupation of any lands held or claimed by them; and I do hereby call upon all perſons in authority under the United States, and all citizens thereof in their ſeveral capacities, to be aiding and aſſiſting to the proſecution and puniſhment according to law of all perſons who ſhall be found offending in the premiſes.

GIVEN under my Hand and the Seal of the United States this Seventh *day of* May *in the year of our Lord one thouſand ſeven hundred and ninety-*three *and of the Independence of the United States of America the* Seventeenth.

Go: Washington

By the President

Th: Jefferson

Figure 8
George Washington, Letter of Protection to the Nation of Indians called the Eel Rivers, May 7, 1793. 27½ × 22⅛ in. George Washington Collection, The Huntington, Purchased by Henry E. Huntington, 1920, mssGW HM 5550.

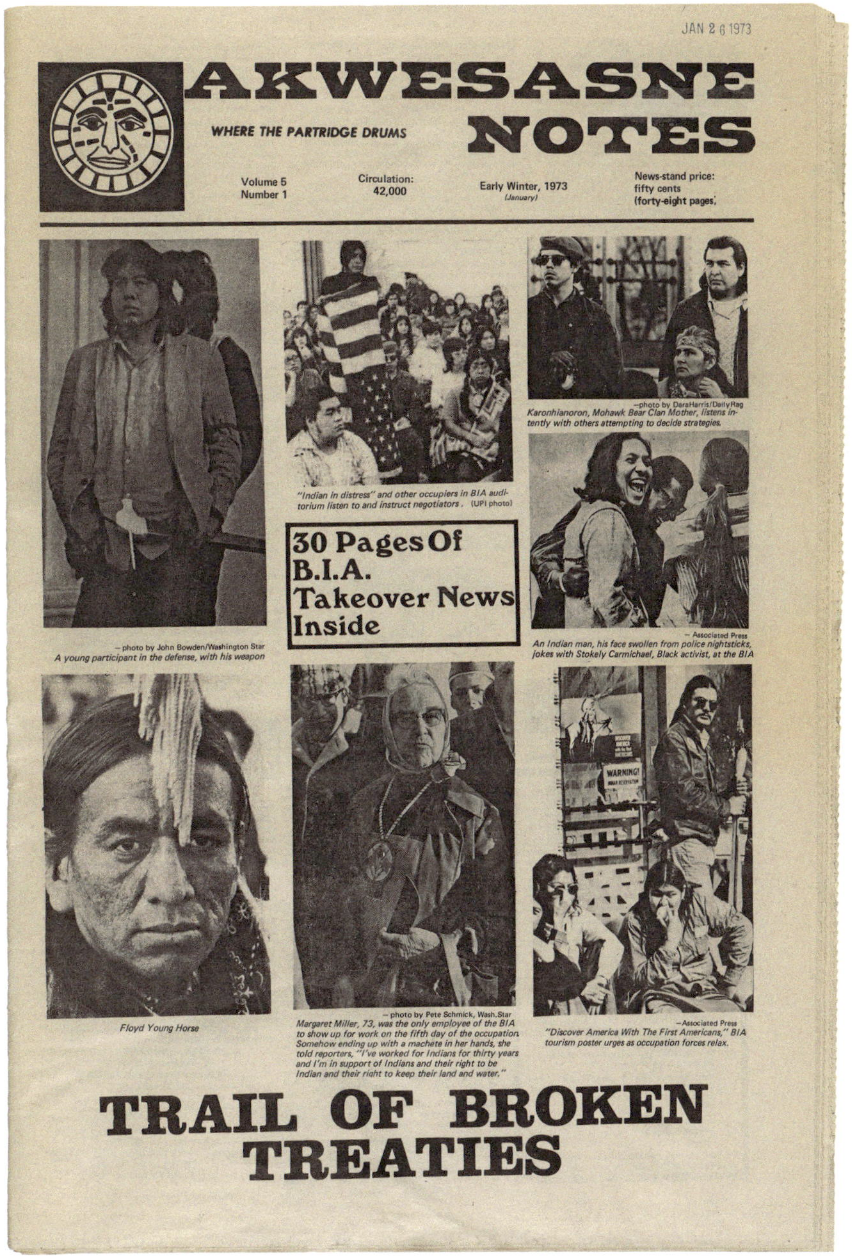

JAN 2 6 1973

AKWESASNE NOTES

WHERE THE PARTRIDGE DRUMS

Volume 5
Number 1

Circulation:
42,000

Early Winter, 1973
(January)

News-stand price:
fifty cents
(forty-eight pages;

"Indian in distress" and other occupiers in BIA auditorium listen to and instruct negotiators. (UPI photo)

—photo by DaraHarris/DailyRag
Karonhianoron, Mohawk Bear Clan Mother, listens intently with others attempting to decide strategies.

30 Pages Of B.I.A. Takeover News Inside

— photo by John Bowden/Washington Star
A young participant in the defense, with his weapon

— Associated Press
An Indian man, his face swollen from police nightsticks, jokes with Stokely Carmichael, Black activist, at the BIA

Floyd Young Horse

— photo by Pete Schmick, Wash.Star
Margaret Miller, 73, was the only employee of the BIA to show up for work on the fifth day of the occupation. Somehow ending up with a machete in her hands, she told reporters, "I've worked for Indians for thirty years and I'm in support of Indians and their right to be Indian and their right to keep their land and water."

—Associated Press
"Discover America With The First Americans," BIA tourism poster urges as occupation forces relax.

TRAIL OF BROKEN TREATIES

Figure 9
Akwesasne Notes, special issue on the "Trail of Broken Treaties," Early Winter (January) 1973, front page. The Huntington, 195321.

that music could defeat oppression. He scratched the message on the reverse side of his 1936 Martin, a field note of sorts, like McKesson's copy of the Declaration (figs. 6, 7). While Guthrie changed guitars frequently, using them like pens or tools, this rare survivor attests to the many, often revolutionary, fields through which he roamed.

Uprootings

Uprooting a plant may kill it, or move it to a place where it will thrive. In classic histories of immigration, newcomers were described as "uprooted" or "transplanted" once they arrived in the United States.[5] Some newcomers uprooted themselves voluntarily to seek opportunity; others fled persecution or famine; and others, like Kunta Kinte in *Roots*, were forced onto slave ships. Migration is a continual feature of the American experience. Even, for example, the Diné (Navajo Nation)—which retains more than seventeen million acres of its traditional homeland, Dinétah—endured the Long Walk and removal for four years during the 1860s, as well as forced separation from their children, who were sent to federal boarding schools to be assimilated (see "Seeds," p. 63).

Such uprooting was not new. During George Washington's first term as president, Euro-American settlers streamed beyond the limits set by Great Britain's 1763 treaty into the Indigenous lands south of the Great Lakes, which the settlers called the "Northwest," today's Ohio and Indiana. Britain had ceded its sovereignty over these lands in 1783, but the many Indigenous nations of the region—Lenape (Delaware), Shawnee, Myaamia (Miami), Illinois, Anishinaabe, and others—had not. These groups formed a confederacy to resist American intrusion. In the 1790s, a mix of warfare and treaty-making characterized the region.

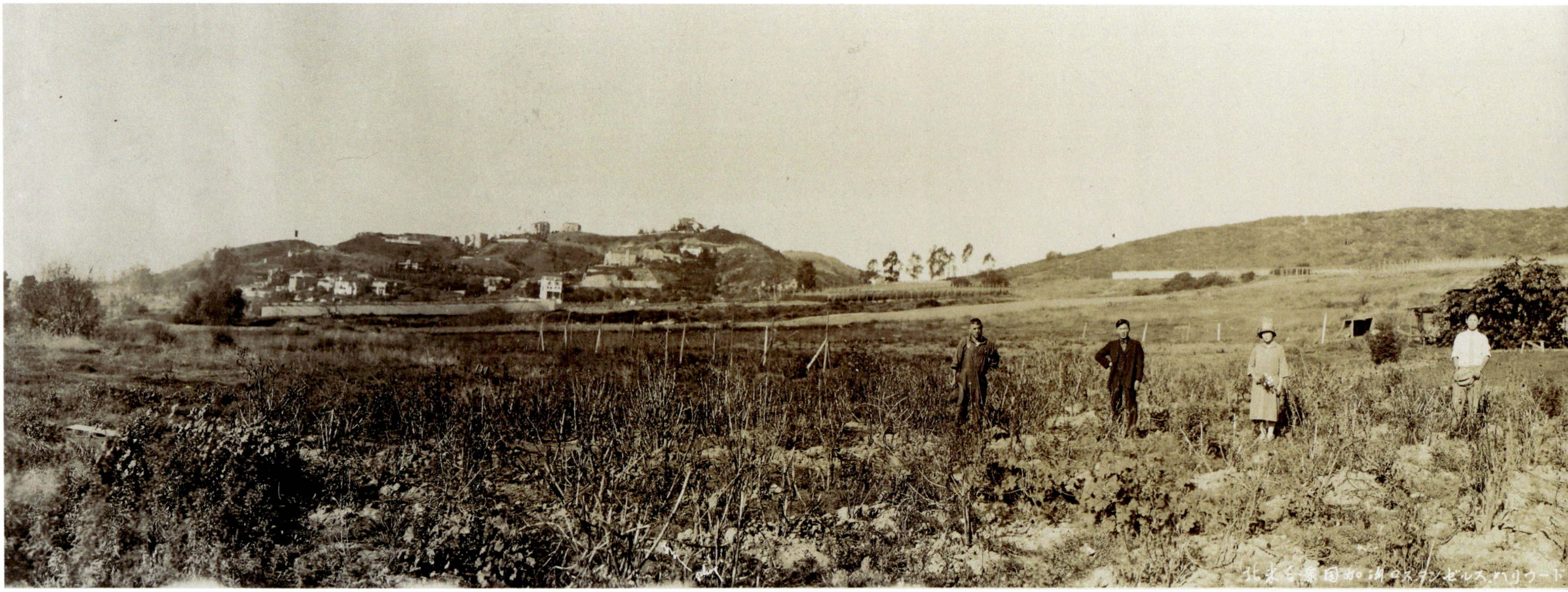

A large-scale letter of protection for a Myaamia nation called the Eel River Indians, signed by Washington and US Secretary of State Thomas Jefferson in 1793, was one of many nation-to-nation documents that reveal the resistance and negotiation in the trans-Appalachian West (fig. 8). The Myaamia and others secured smaller land bases and annuities in Indiana following the 1795 Treaty of Greenville, but after half a century more of settlement, most of the Myaamia nation agreed under threat of more violence to be uprooted in 1846 to Kansas and then to what is now Oklahoma, about 150 miles northeast of Okemah, where Guthrie would be born in 1912.

The US government made hundreds of treaties with Native nations until 1871 but often failed to honor its commitments. In the late twentieth century, Red Power activists organized the Trail of Broken Treaties, a series of caravans that drove from the West to Washington, DC, in the fall of 1972 (fig. 9). Traveling west to east against the flow of US expansion, inverting the American flag as a distress signal, and rechristening the Bureau of Indian Affairs building as the Native American Embassy, these activists challenged the inevitability of Indigenous dispossession and removal. Among their demands was to restore more than one hundred million acres to Native Americans, a process advocates today call "Land Back," which, in some cases, has begun to occur.

Some Americans have experienced cycles of rooting and uprooting. The Kuromi family moved to Southern California from Shimane Prefecture, Japan, in the first decade of the twentieth century. By 1917, they held a lease to a flower farm in the Los Feliz neighborhood northeast of Hollywood, just down the hill from what is now the Griffith Park Observatory. In a panoramic photo taken in 1928, members of the Kuromi family stand proudly amid rows of chrysanthemums, carnations, and ranunculus (fig. 10). "The flower growers in many other areas envied us," Aiko Alice (Kuromi) Ito recalled in a 1993 interview, "because this Hollywood area was free of pollution and was just the right climate to grow."[6] Aiko's father, Harue Kuromi, was even known as the "Sweet Pea King."

In 1942, when President Franklin Roosevelt issued Executive Order 9066 authorizing the incarceration of

Figure 10
The flower farm run by the Kuromi family. Pictured from left to right: Torataro Kuromi, unknown, Ichie Kawakami, Isao Kuromi, unknown, Aiko Alice Kuromi, unknown, Hitoshi "Yoke" Kuromi, Kiyo Kuromi, Isamu "Ise" Kuromi, Harue Kuromi, Fumiye Kawakami, Mikio Kawakami, and "Johnny" Kawakami. Paris Photographic Studio, *At Hollywood, Los Angeles, CA, USA. Operated by the Kuromi Family of the Shimane Prefecture*, 1928, printed later. Gelatin silver print, 10 × 44 in. Arthur Ito Papers, The Huntington, Gift of James A. Ito and Paul N. Coman.

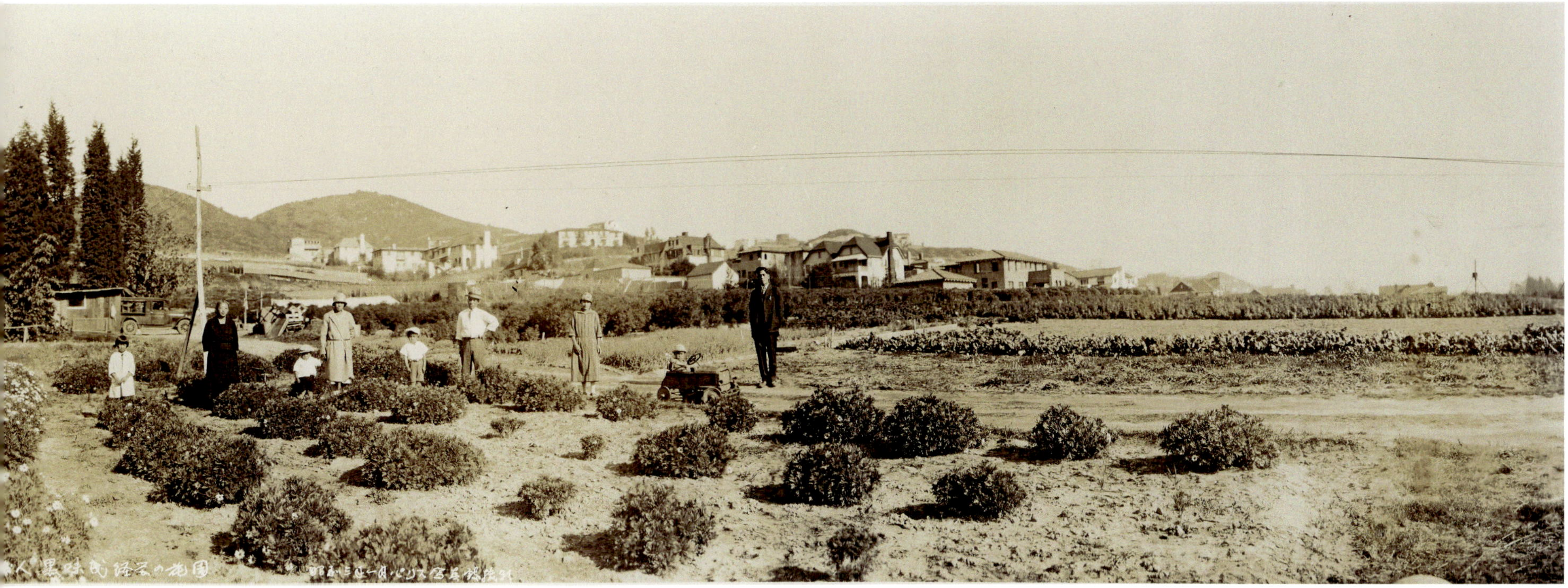

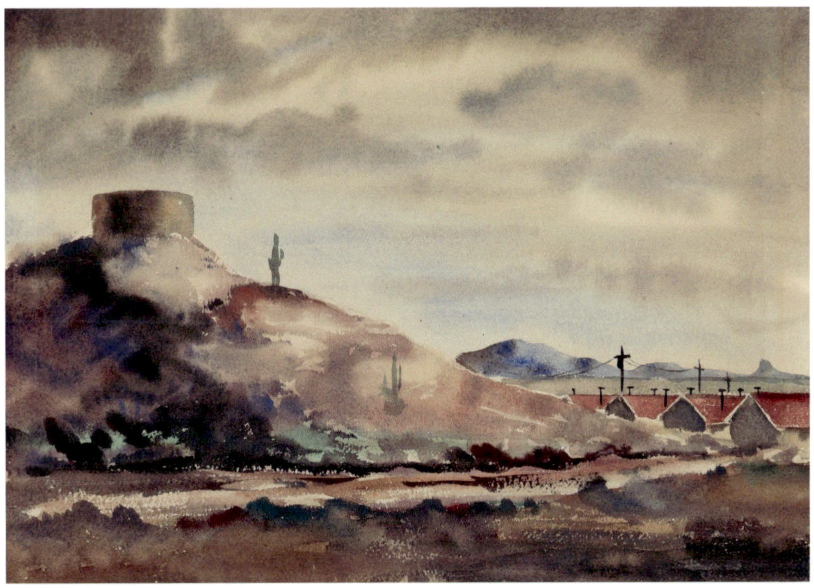

Figure 11
Unidentified artist, Water tank and barracks at the Gila River Relocation Center, Arizona, 1944. Watercolor and graphite on paper, 15½ × 21 in. Arthur Ito Papers, The Huntington, Gift of James A. Ito and Paul N. Coman.

people of Japanese descent, the Kuromi family was forced to uproot, first to the horse stalls of the Santa Anita Assembly Center and then to the Gila River Relocation Center on the Gila River Indian Reservation in Arizona. (The tribal government did not give permission for the concentration camp to be located on their land.) Artifacts that remain from this period include a comic-style map of the camp (see p. 69) and a somber watercolor drawing of the Arizona landscape (fig. 11). Ito's mother, Kiyo Kuromi, carved flowers in the ends of wooden fruit crates, maintaining a connection to the family business.

When the Kuromi family returned to Hollywood after the war, their farm equipment had been stolen, and their landlord delayed restoring access to the land. In Ito's words, they "started from scratch" and managed to operate the flower farm until they lost their lease in 1961. These layers of opportunity and loss, uprooting and resilience, injustice and removal, echo others' experiences of American lands.

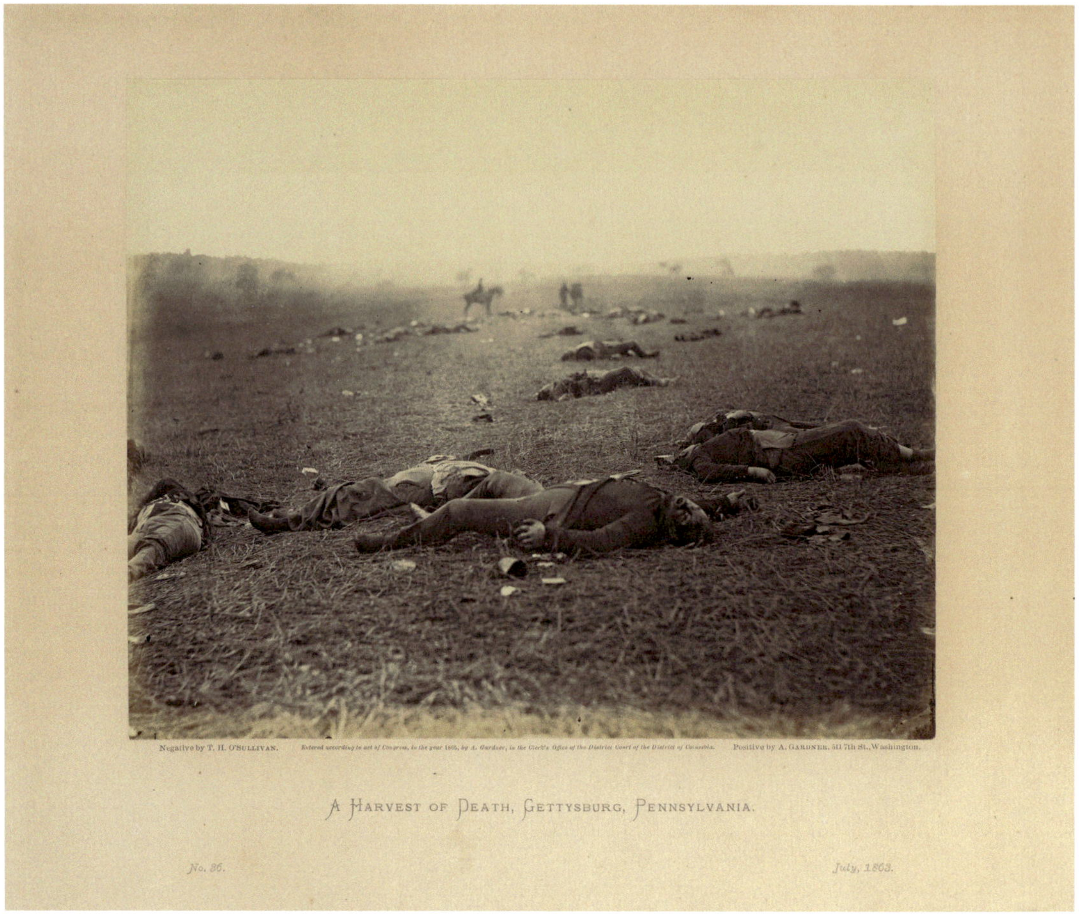

Figure 12
Timothy O'Sullivan, "A Harvest of Death, Gettysburg, Pennsylvania," 1863. Albumen print in Alexander Gardner, *Gardner's Photographic Sketch Book of the War*, vol. 1 (Philp and Solomons, 1866). The Huntington, 352125.

Amendments

From an ecological perspective, an amendment is a substance, such as compost, added to the soil to improve its physical or chemical properties. The act of amending can also aim to correct mistakes, as in personal conduct or in written laws and contracts. As a foundational document, written and signed in 1787, the US Constitution was designed to provide structure but also to be malleable. As shown by its twenty-seven amendments, the process of revising and improving can be fraught and protracted.

The trauma and scars of the American Civil War reflect some of these multiple meanings of amendment. One of the most visceral images of the grim aftermath of the Battle of Gettysburg in July 1863 depicts a horrific scene of land forever changed, as the decaying bodies of soldiers lie strewn across a hazy field. The photograph by Timothy O'Sullivan was printed and published by Alexander Gardner for his *Photographic Sketch Book of the War* in 1866, and titled "A Harvest of Death, Gettysburg, Pennsylvania" (fig. 12). This image conveys different senses of harvest, as the bodies are stripped of belongings, including shoes, and are soaked by the rain. Cemetery and garden become one as the dead slowly decompose back into the soil. The accompanying description, "Here are the dreadful details! Let them aid in preventing such another calamity falling upon the nation," aims to spare future generations this level of bloodshed and conflict.[7] Earlier in 1863, President Abraham Lincoln had issued the Emancipation Proclamation, declaring all enslaved persons "forever free." The Thirteenth

Figure 13
James Carter Beard, *The Fifteenth Amendment*, 1870. Hand-colored lithograph, 20½ × 25¾ in., printed by Thomas Kelly. Jay T. Last Collection of Politics and Social Issues Prints and Ephemera, The Huntington, priJLC_POL_002657.

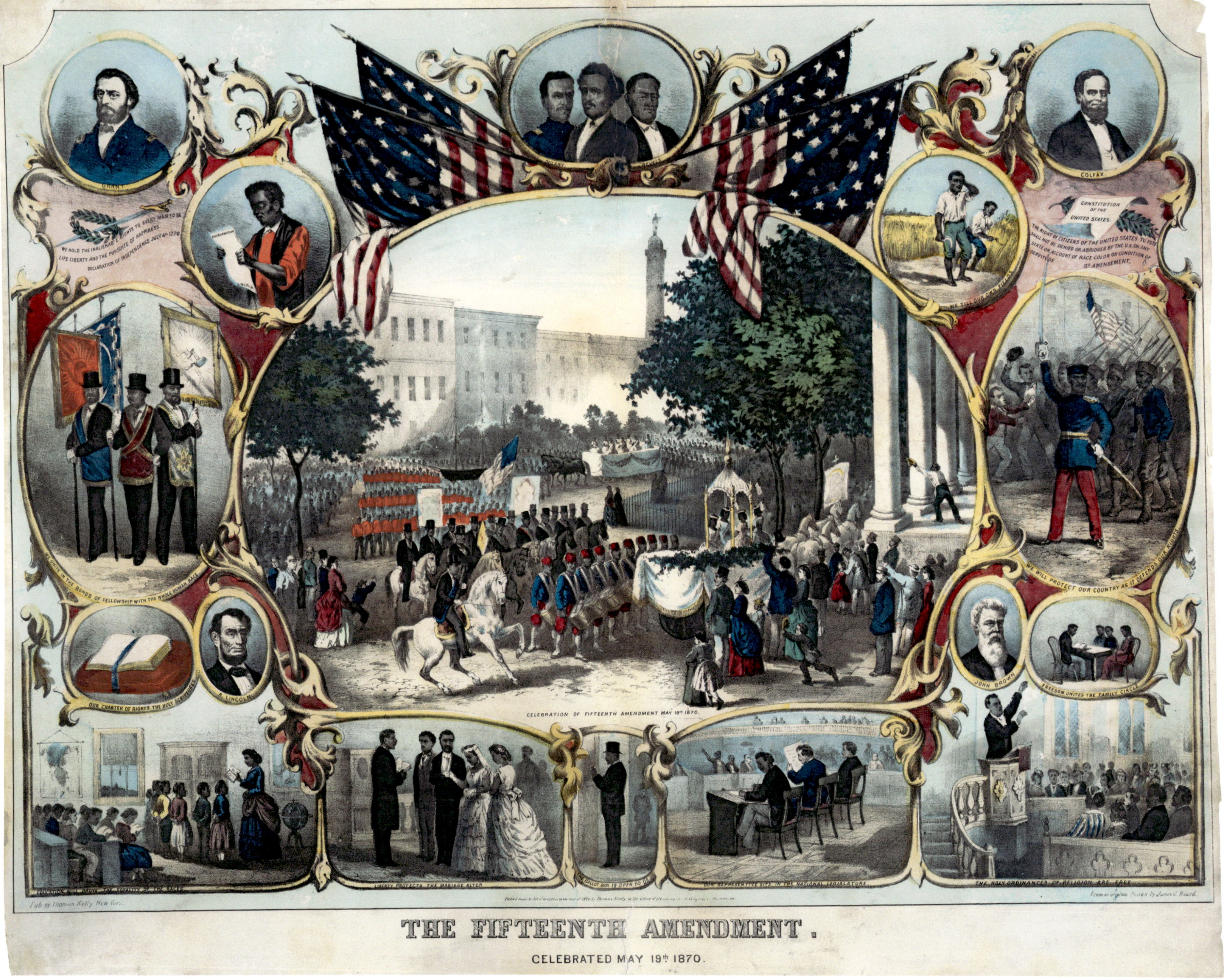

THE FIFTEENTH AMENDMENT.

CELEBRATED MAY 19th 1870.

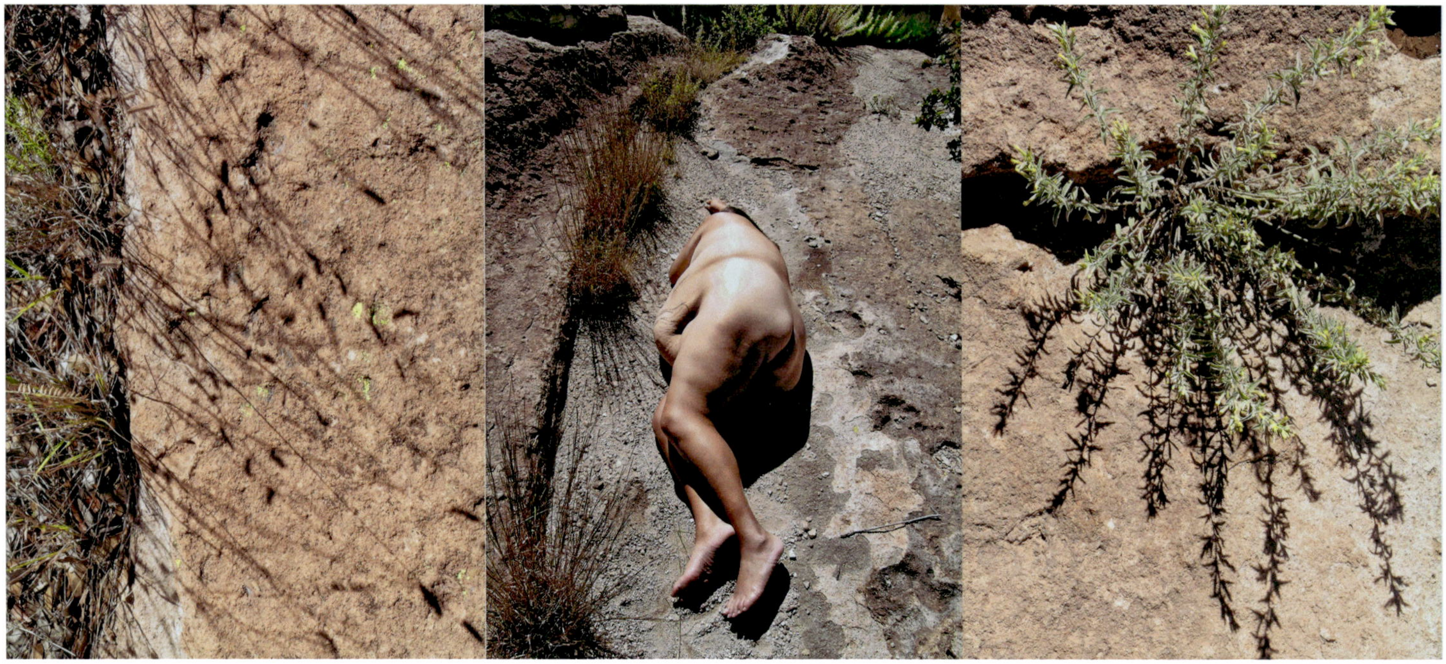

Figure 14
Laura Aguilar, *Grounded #118*, 2006–7, printed 2018. Inkjet print, 17 × 22 in. The Huntington, Gift of the Laura Aguilar Trust of 2016, 2022.3.1.2.

Amendment to the Constitution, abolishing slavery, was passed by Congress on January 31, 1865, and then ratified by the states by the end of the year. The Thirteenth, Fourteenth, and Fifteenth Amendments, known as the Reconstruction Amendments (another allusion to both land and culture rebuilt), granted citizenship and voting rights to formerly enslaved people (but, for the latter, only to men) and laid the groundwork for civil rights legislation nearly a century later (fig. 13).

Deep ties to the land and the ongoing processing of grief resonate in the work of Chicana lesbian artist Laura Aguilar. Throughout her career, Aguilar intervened in the Western landscape to shed light on underrepresented communities in Los Angeles. Her marginalized identity shaped her approach to using her own body as a kind of monument that signified strength and resistance. *Grounded* (2006–7), the final series of nude self-portraits in nature she completed before her death in 2018, places Aguilar within the desert of Joshua Tree National Park amid grasses and California fuchsia plants, as if merging with the earth beneath her (fig. 14). Aguilar felt a profound connection to Joshua Tree's rich colors and vast terrain and even requested that her ashes be scattered there.

The American poet Walt Whitman likewise navigated belonging as a queer individual, writing about nature, democracy, and the body. His experimental masterwork, *Leaves of Grass*—which he self-published on July 4, 1855, and continued to revise and expand until his death—was considered transgressive for its rhythmic language concerning spirituality, sexuality, and class. Its physical structure kept evolving; as soon as one edition was published, Whitman would first regroup and add to the poems, treating the printed book as a manuscript to be edited and republished. What began as a volume of twelve poems eventually became a compendium of close to four hundred. The title itself is a pun on "leaves"—the leaves (or pages) of the book are like blades of grass pushing out of American soil. He even designed the foil stamping on the first cover to resemble sprouting roots (fig. 15). And in a manuscript page for the poem "To Other Lands," drafted for the 1860 edition, he offered his poems to other nations as definitive expressions of America's "self-poised democracy" (fig. 16).

Perhaps Whitmanic in spirit are the accretions of Otis Reed "Dock" Marston, river runner and historian of the Grand Canyon and the Colorado River Basin. The materials he obsessively gathered in the field, spanning centuries

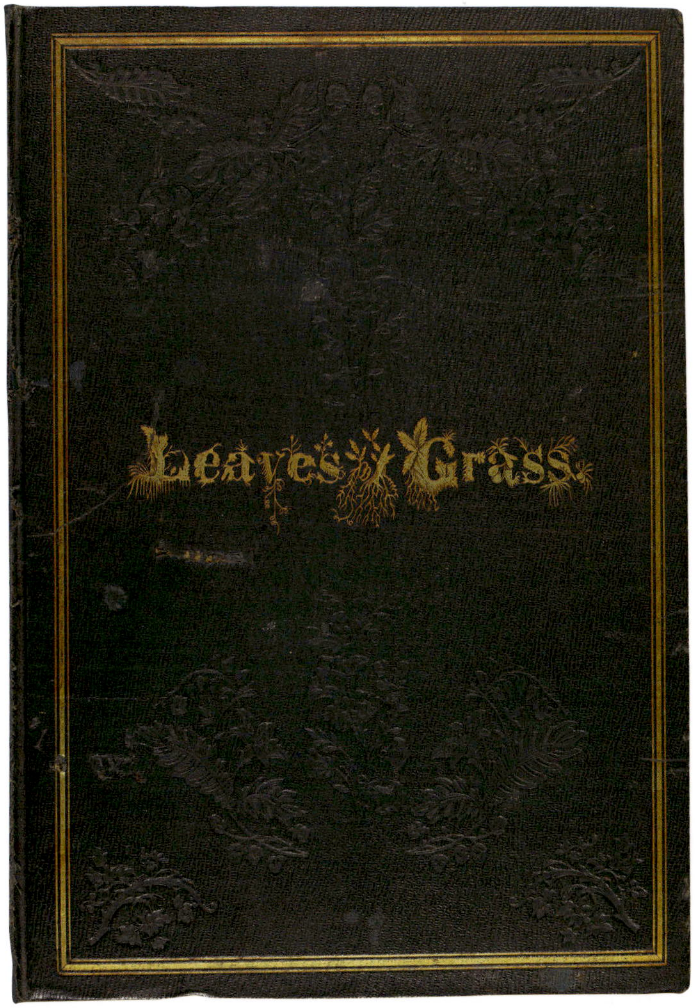

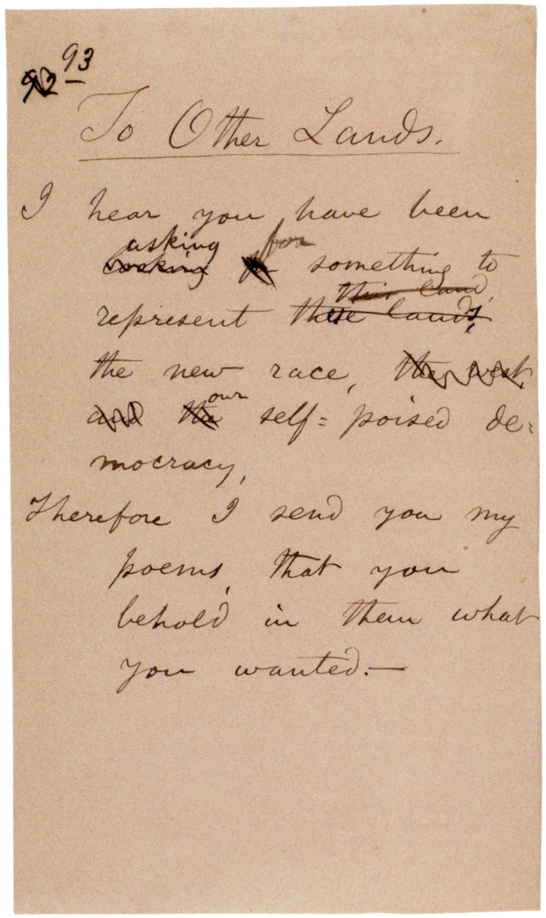
93
To Other Lands.
I hear you have been
asking for something to
represent
the new race,
our self-poised de-
mocracy,
Therefore I send you my
poems that you
behold in them what
you wanted.—

Figure 15
Walt Whitman, *Leaves of Grass*, 1st ed. (Published by the author, 1855). The Huntington, 110374.

Figure 16
Walt Whitman, "To Other Lands" (published as one of the Inscriptions, "To Foreign Lands"), manuscript, ca. 1860. The Huntington, HM 11204.

of data, aim to chronicle every section of the 1,450-mile Colorado River and to reflect the geology, water issues, tourism, film industry, and Indigenous cultures of that area. Marston had intended to write a history of the early river runners and track the changes over time to this environment. Some 250 binders contain photographs joined with maps, journal notes, and diagrams from various sources and vantage points (see fig. 1 on p. 8). This mode of amassing and reassembling materials, especially around a river that flows and shifts, reveals the intimate ties between the act of archiving and the journey through the landscape itself. In 2025, the Tribal Council of the Colorado River Indian Tribes approved a resolution giving legal personhood to the river, a new type of amendment that recognizes the rights a living waterway could hold under an expanded conception of laws and citizenship.

Edge Effects

Edge effects occur when two or more distinct ecosystems share an area—for example, the margin of a forest and a meadow. These points of intersection often show a higher rate of biodiversity. This phenomenon also applies to interactions among communities and cultures where physical zones of land converge. These shared edges can be divisive and perilous but can also nurture new forms of cultural identity and biological richness. Structures such as dams, pipelines, fences, and checkpoints delineate borders and control access to land and the movement of people.

Borders are delineated through various mechanisms, including surveying—the act of determining points on the land surface by taking measurements. The practice of surveying in the seventeenth and eighteenth centuries helped define the notion of private property. Washington and Jefferson were both surveyors, and their drawings included physical features, property lines, distances measured, compass directions, and detailed observations (see fig. 2 on p. 9; see also p. 145). In 1620, the English clergyman and mathematician Edmund Gunter designed a sixty-six-foot chain, made to be slung over the shoulder and moved easily, with one hundred links as the standard instrument for measuring distance. It was used in combination with a theodolite or compass to record direction. In the Shenandoah Valley, Native Americans called the surveyor's compass a "land stealer"—they recognized line drawing as a step toward dispossession.[8] Frontier surveying required

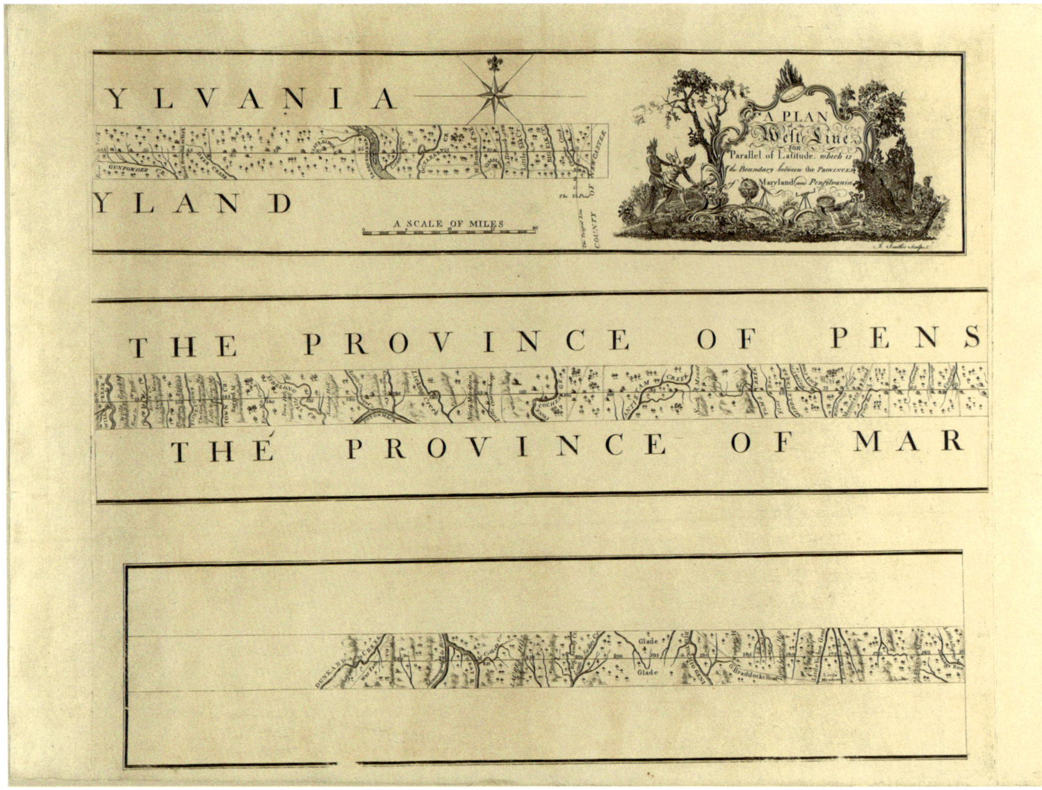

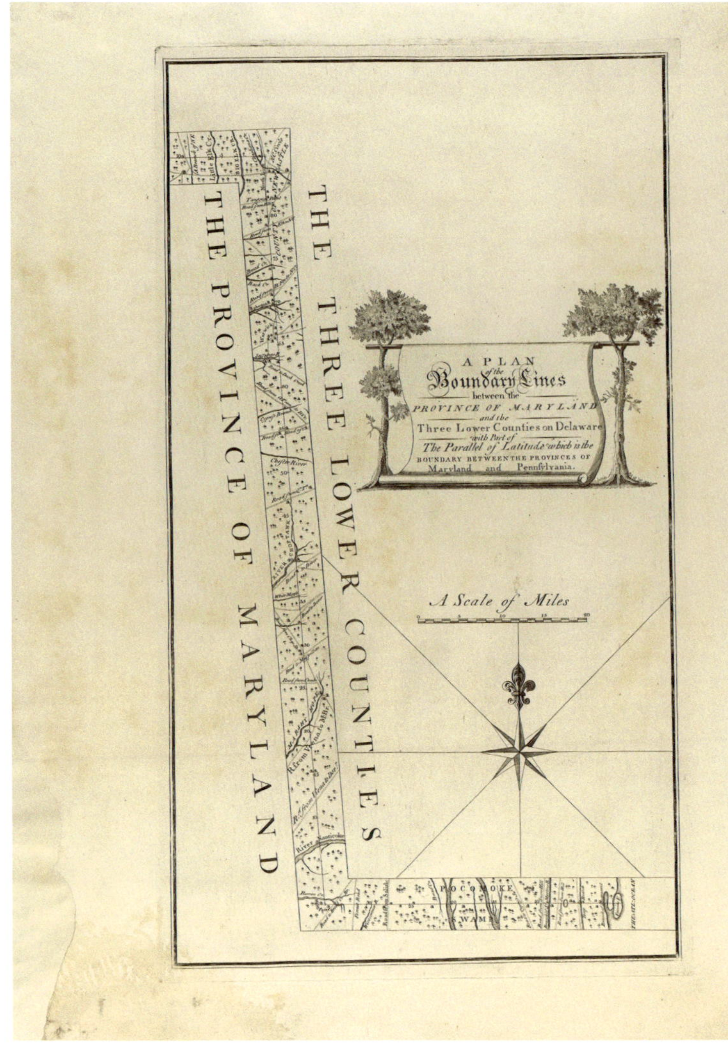

clearing sight lines, in the process destroying ecological systems and plant life.

Early American surveying is the subject of *Mason & Dixon* (1997) by Thomas Pynchon, a fictionalized account of the exploits of Charles Mason and Jeremiah Dixon in establishing the line between Pennsylvania and Maryland from 1763 to 1767 (fig. 17). One of the novel's most incisive lines underscores the disruption and moral complexity of laying claim to land, as a character warns: "'Surveying a Property Line, that may be one thing,—clearing and marking a Right Line of an Hundred Leagues, into the Lands of Others, cannot be a kindly Act.'"[9] Pynchon emphasizes the chaotic, perplexing, and clumsy process of defining and claiming land, thereby critiquing the consequences of this act.

These attempts to mark lines and impose artificial boundaries play out most visibly through maps, which serve as symbols of power. Nearly a century later, in a map from 1853, pink, blue, and green lines indicate different proposed locations for the US-Mexico border across "disputed territory," a status that remains so today (fig. 18). The annexation of Texas in 1845, the Treaty of Guadalupe Hidalgo in 1848, and the Gadsden Purchase in 1854 expanded the landholdings of the United States and altered its border with Mexico. In the process, US surveyors and commissioners were also hired to observe, collect, and record the natural features of the environment, essentially "contouring the nation."[10]

The mechanisms of surveying, including diagrams, maps, and tables, were soon joined by the technology of photography. Between 1850 and 1890, government surveys revealed the inextricable connections between Westward Expansion and the Civil War and Reconstruction. Timothy O'Sullivan, who had documented Gettysburg, served as the official photographer of the War Department's Geological Exploration of the Fortieth Parallel from 1867 until 1869. He joined Army Engineer Lt. George M. Wheeler on his 1871 Western expedition, and two years later, he embarked with Wheeler again as part of the effort to map the territory west

Figure 17
These 1768 strip maps, engravings of the original manuscript maps made by Charles Mason and Jeremiah Dixon, were too large for printers to fit on a single sheet. *Plan of the boundary lines between the province of Maryland and the Three Lower Counties on Delaware*, 1768. Engraving by James Smither and Henry Dawkins, printed by Robert Kennedy, Philadelphia, 21½ × 30 in. each. The Huntington, 479000.

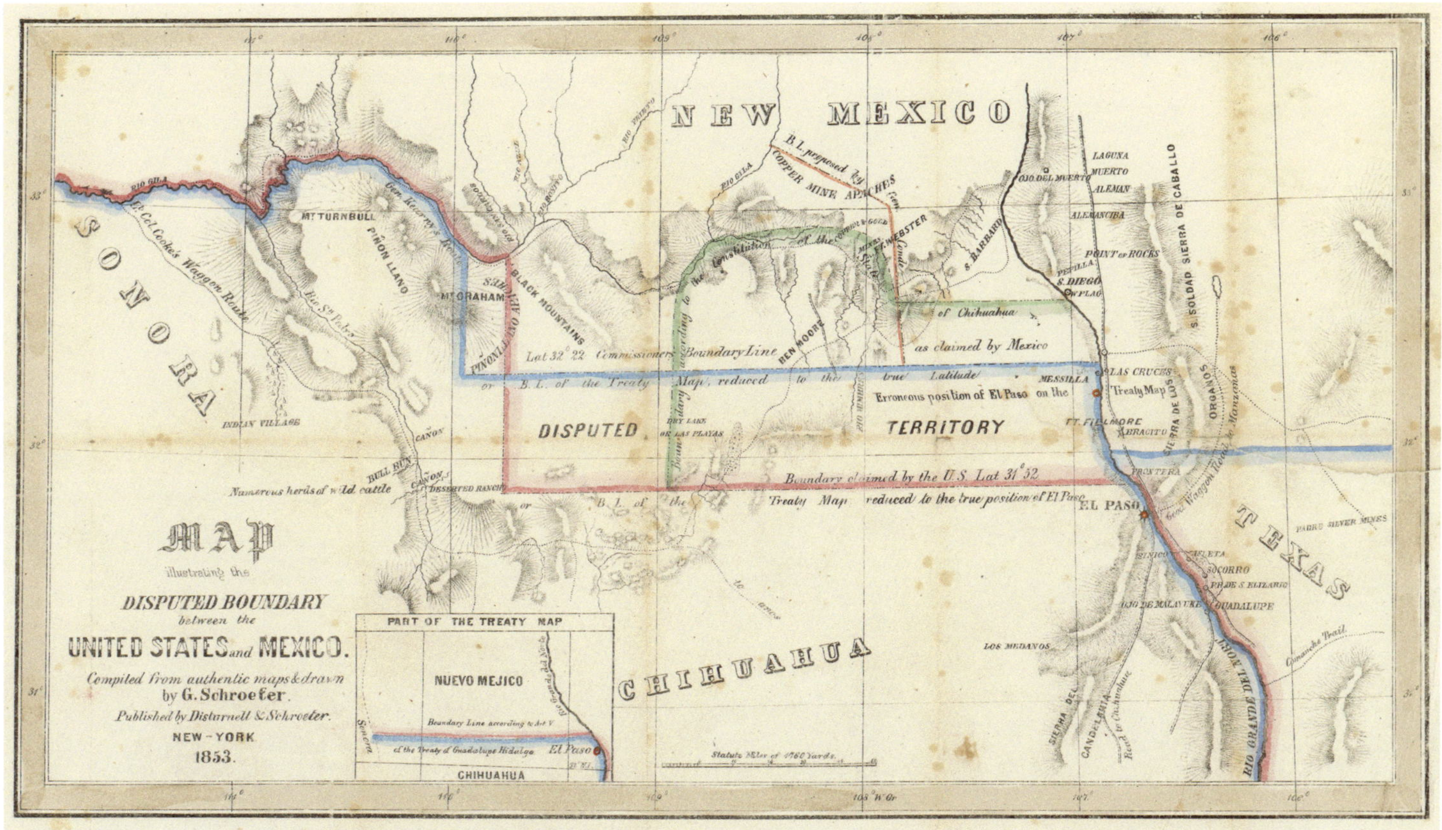

Figure 18
G. Schroeter, *Map Illustrating the Disputed Boundary Between the United States and Mexico*, 1853. Hand-colored map by Disturnell & Schroeter, 10½ × 18⅛ in. The Huntington, Library Purchase, 1931, 41433.

of the 100th meridian (roughly where the Texas Panhandle meets Oklahoma). O'Sullivan took wet-plate photographs using both large-format and stereoscopic cameras, primarily depicting mining towns, military forts, camp scenes, and geological formations.

Moving from intimate views to distant landscapes, while conveying a sense of scale, was critical. In "Historic Spanish Record of the Conquest, South Side of Inscription Rock, [New Mexico]," O'Sullivan treats the photograph like a map that orients the viewer and reveals the literal imprint of conquest past and present (fig. 19).[11] The inclusion of a ruler beneath the Spanish inscription, which O'Sullivan has made more visible by cutting back the yucca plant below, marks yet another claim to this site.

In response to the early photographic surveys, the California artist William Camargo has recast such colonial landscapes in a series called *Origins & Displacements* (2018–23) (fig. 20). In these protest pictures, he intentionally hides his face behind handwritten signs about gentrification, immigration, forced labor, and police brutality experienced by Latinx people in Southern California, particularly in his hometown of Anaheim. These declarations convey information regarding local histories as much as they comment on the broader occupation and surveillance of the borderlands. "This Area Will Gentrify Soon" reads the sign in one photograph, as Camargo stands in front of a fenced-off construction site. It is paired with a still life from his mother's bedroom, where icons of the Virgin Mary and Jesus Christ hang above a dresser that holds recycled lotion jars and her son's soccer medals. Camargo employs the nineteenth-century albumen printing process for its sepia tones, evoking the layered histories entwined in these spaces and alluding to the politics of Brown communities. Similar to Aguilar's use of her own body within the landscape, Camargo stands in for displaced populations at the borders and edges.

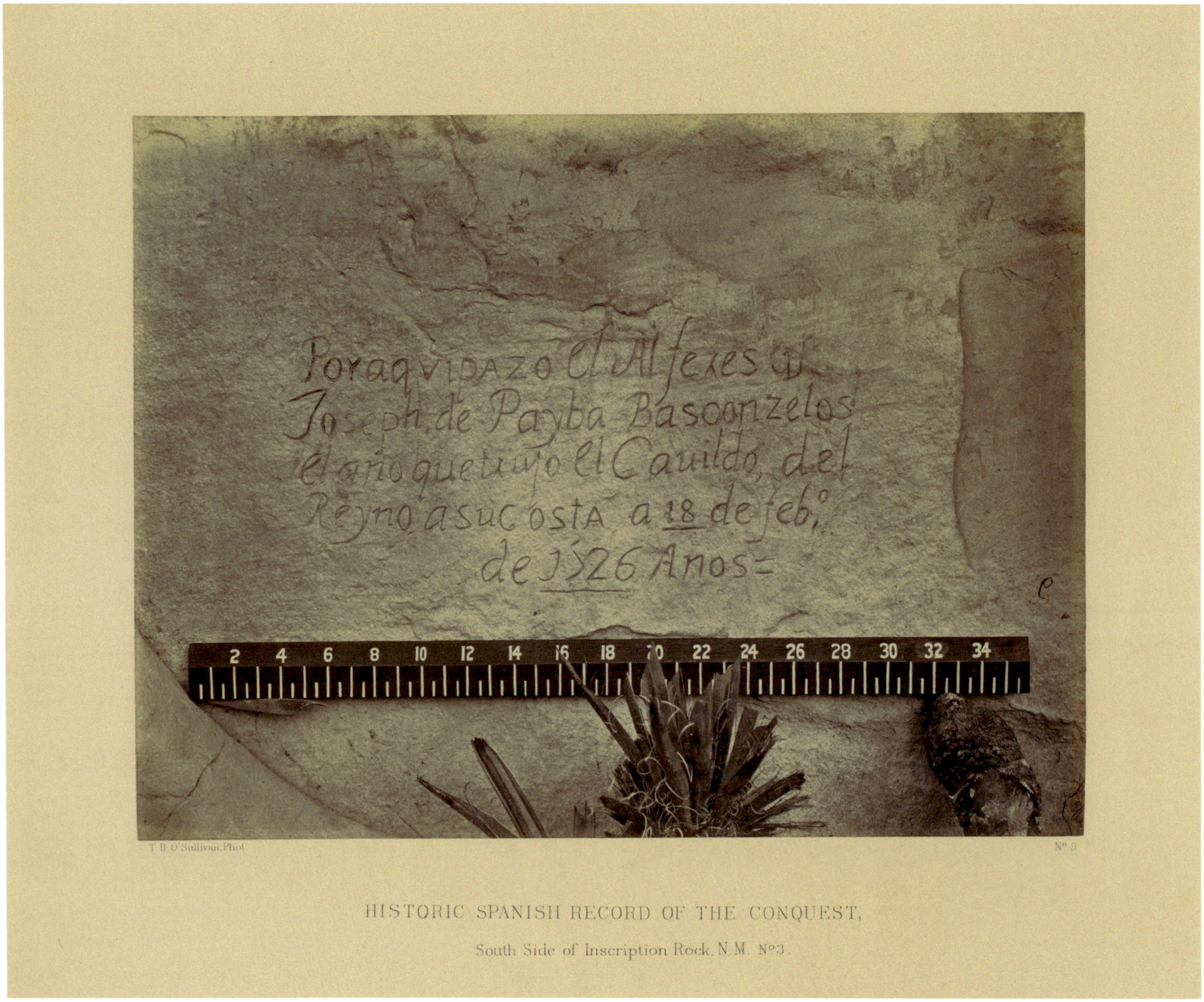

Figure 19
The carved inscription in Spanish translates to: "There passed by here the Lieutenant Don Joseph de Payba Basconzelos the year that he brought the council of the realm, at his expense, on the 18th of February of the year 1726." Timothy O'Sullivan, "Historic Spanish Record of the Conquest, South Side of Inscription Rock, N.M.," 1873, in *Geographical Surveys West of the 100th Meridian (U.S.)*, 1871–73. Albumen print, 15½ × 19¾ in. The Huntington, 278614.

Disturbances

Disturbances to the environment can include tilling, burning, logging, or other disruptions to the land, though not always in a negative sense. Any revolution, by definition, brings disturbance to a society. The American colonies' War for Independence was the start of a broader Age of Revolutions, followed by those in France, Saint-Domingue (Haiti), and most of Latin America. These national revolutions joined countless smaller revolts and efforts toward sovereignty led by Indigenous nations, enslaved peoples, settlers, and more. These battles for self-rule connect to others, literally in some cases and, in others, as parallel struggles for life, liberty, and the pursuit of happiness. In particular, France's essential military aid to the American colonists derived partly from its richest colony in the Caribbean, the brutal slavery regime of Saint-Domingue. The subsequent French and Haitian Revolutions spurred the sale of the vast Louisiana Territory to the United States in 1803.

The 1939 opera *Troubled Island* points to connections between the experiences of Black Americans and the Haitian Revolution. William Grant Still composed the score, and Langston Hughes wrote the libretto (with uncredited contributions from Verna Arvey, Still's wife). The work offers an epic retelling of the life of Jean-Jacques Dessalines, who reigned as the first emperor of Haiti in 1804–6, after the Black and enslaved masses there overthrew the French

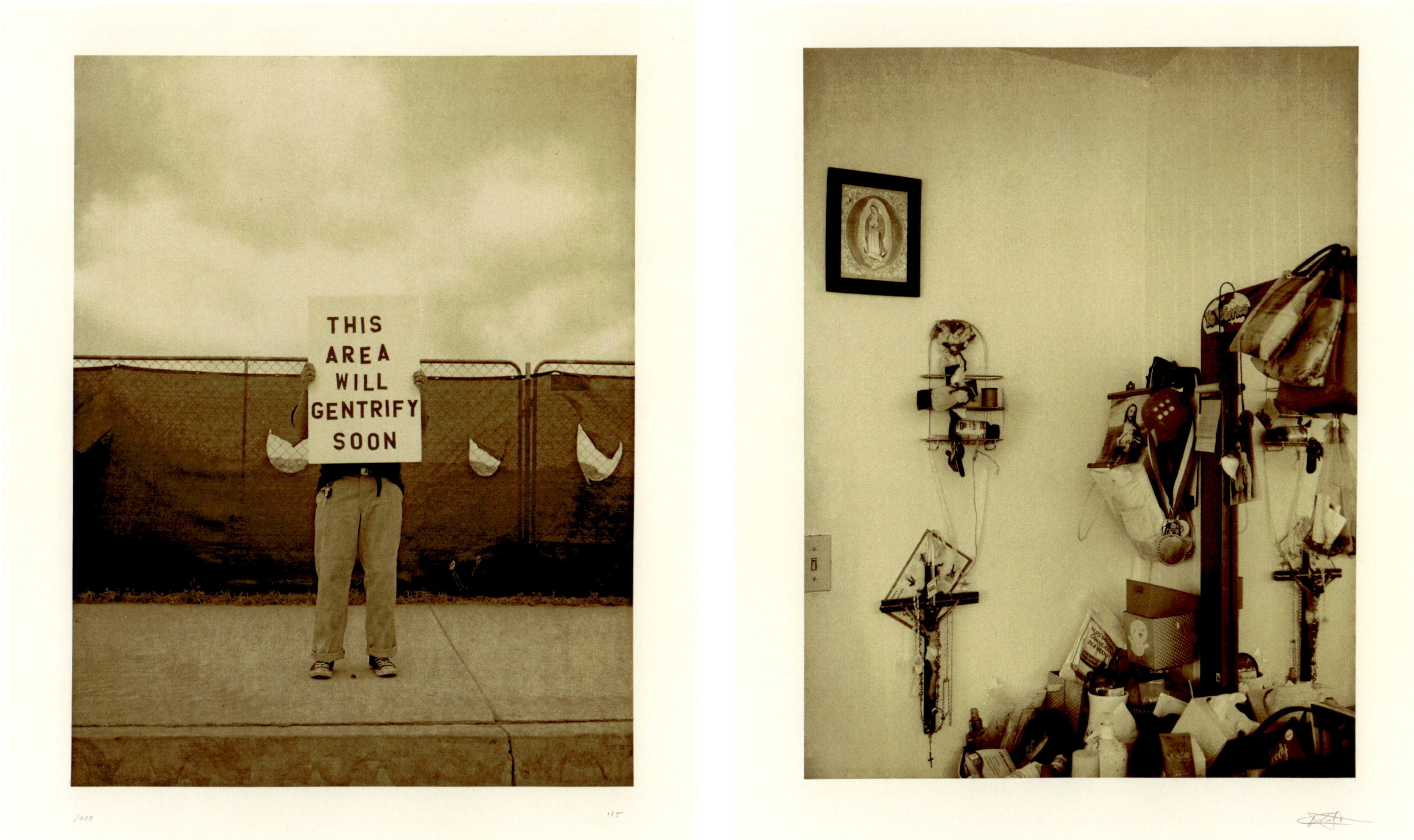

Figure 20
William Camargo, *Origins & Displacements IV*, diptych, 2022. Albumen prints, 23⅞ × 20 in. each. Printed and published by The *f*/Ø Project. The Huntington, photCL 707.

Empire. Across three acts, Dessalines travels from plotting the revolt to occupying the throne in an ostentatious and exploitative style to being assassinated.

Amid this tragic arc, the African-born elder Martel offers his voice of hope in an aria: "A world I dream where black or white, / Whatever race you be, / Will share the bounties of the earth / And every man is free."[12] Hughes first wrote the text of this aria, "I Dream a World," in a draft of the script and then published it as a poem, one of his most iconic verses. It resounds as another American declaration—but also a voice of disturbance and protest amid World War II and the growing civil rights movement. Hughes's language of dreams likely inspired Martin Luther King Jr.'s "I Have a Dream" speech in 1963.[13]

In 2002–3, the Los Angeles artist Noni Olabisi (with assistance from Charles "Boko" Freeman) created a mural based on *Troubled Island* at the William Grant Still Arts Center in the West Adams neighborhood. Olabisi painted the mural in urgent red and black hues, bringing the disturbance of a distant revolution to contemporary Los Angeles. The 90-foot mural displays the disturbing brutality of Saint-Domingue's slavery system, with Black women and men chained, whipped, and shackled. (The form of the feet, according to Olabisi's son, Oronde Spears, took inspiration from rapper Ice Cube's 1991 album cover for *Death Certificate.*) On the right side of the mural, Dessalines stands in profile, dressed in the uniform of a French military officer. At the center, the story is riven by lightning, and William Grant Still stands conducting his opera. An additional portrait of Still is anointed with a yellow spiritual "eye," which Olabisi likened to "the light of the soul, power within, the spirit realm" (fig. 21).

John McKesson's copy of the Declaration stems from a time when Manhattan, too, was a "troubled island," struggling for liberty. Haiti followed. A century later, an archipelago of "troubled islands" became parts of the United States' empire, as territories or outposts without the legal rights of states. In the Pacific and the Caribbean, Hawai'i, the Philippines, Cuba, Puerto Rico, and other islands all fell under American dominance in the 1890s and were presented to the US public as "Our New Possessions" (fig. 22). In time, they would find different fates, as states or semiautonomous territories, or they would gain independence. After the United States seized the Philippines from Spain in 1898, the revolutionary leader Emilio Aguinaldo waged a war of independence against the new power, declaring in a letter, "¡VIVA la República Filipina!" Calls for freedom would continue to spring from episodes of resistance.

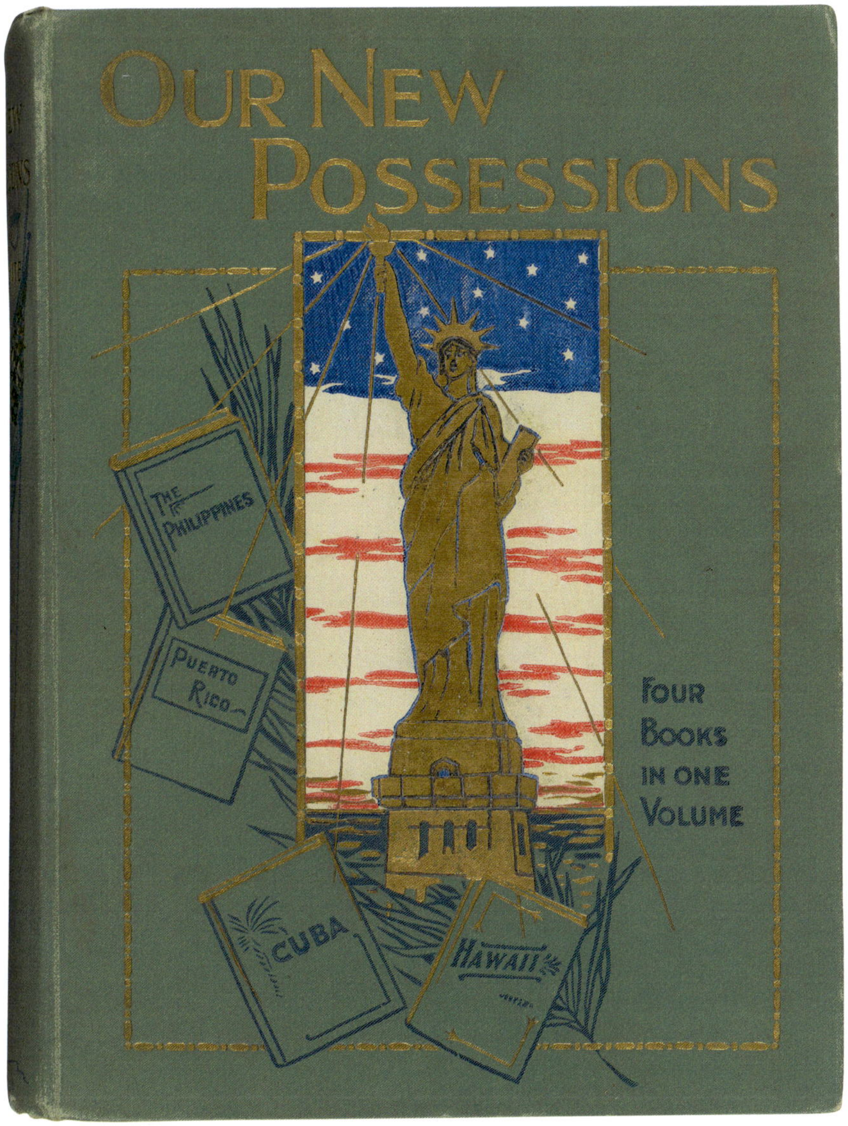

Figure 22
Trumbull White, *Our New Possessions: A Graphic Account, Descriptive and Historical, of the Tropic Islands of the Sea Which Have Fallen Under Our Sway* (Syndicate Publishing, 1898). The Huntington, Gift and purchase of Thomas V. Lange, 485664:317.

Regenerations

In nature, regeneration can follow disturbance, as when new shoots grow after a wildfire. Human caretakers use regenerative practices as well: fortifying soil with compost, planting cover crops, or looking to Indigenous traditions for stewarding the land. The physical and psychological ruins left after wars, massacres, and devastation can foster new forms of life and regrowth through acts of repair, whether small, symbolic gestures or broader reparations for historical injustices. Connecting to the environment as a regenerative space can conjure metaphysical relationships to land that generate spiritual or prescient visions.

Seeds contain the potential for many forms of growth and expression but remain dormant until activated by their environment. During the Civil War, the young artist Harriet F. Bailey decorated and mailed plum pits, apple seeds, and a pumpkin seed from Wisconsin to her uncle John Siperly, a soldier serving in the war (fig. 23). These tiny artworks would have playfully spilled out of the envelope in which they were held, accompanied by news from home. For recruits from rural areas, seeds were a vestige of the familiar and a reminder of place, generating joy and smiles amid the bleak landscape of war. One of Bailey's letters includes ink drawings of leaves and a flower, which she misspells as "phlougher," possibly a play on the word "plougher," to make another direct link to land and agriculture.

More than a century later, the novelist Octavia E. Butler conceived of the religion Earthseed as a means of renewal. Lauren Olamina, the protagonist in *Parable of the Sower* (1993) and *Parable of the Talents* (1998), develops this belief system to help a group navigate a postapocalyptic California. She looks to change as a path forward and emphasizes that all forms of life can be transplanted and adapted to different conditions. Olamina founds a community that she names "Acorn," informed by Indigenous knowledge about edible plants. At one point in the narrative, she conducts a funerary rite to honor those lost to violence in this turbulent civilization, burying their remains and planting acorns in the ground. This communion with the land is guided by Earthseed's teachings, with the ultimate hope to "take root among the stars."[14] A prolific notetaker, Butler penned phrases and words and went back over them with fluorescent markers to plot out key elements for many of her novels. One vibrant page reads: "More Heat & dust & thirst & stench & misery & Fire." Other "Mores" include sharing, Hispanics, racism, sickness, death, and high tech (fig. 24). These are Butler's version of field notes, crafted from direct observations as she navigated the diverse Los Angeles metropolis.

The desert of the Coachella Valley—a hundred miles east of Butler's Pasadena home—holds a delicate ecosystem adapted to arid conditions. To newcomers from wetter climes, its stark landscapes can inspire not only fear but also awe and introspection. After the painter Agnes Pelton moved to Cathedral City in 1932, she found California's "rare and solitary places" to be a refuge where she could cultivate her "inner vision."[15] Born in Germany and raised in New York, Pelton traveled the familiar artistic path to New Mexico before finding an even more transcendent place to paint works that weave together figurative elements of nature with cosmic abstractions. Her work *Passion Flower* from around 1945 blooms from calligraphic vines winding out of a cool miasma. It evokes a rebirth or resurrection that joins spiritual and botanical planes—consonant with Earthseed (fig. 25).

Just west of Cathedral City among the wind farms of greater Palm Springs, four young boys sprint toward the viewer in the photograph *Evolvers* by Cara Romero (Chemehuevi) (fig. 26). They are perhaps ancestors, time travelers, or spirit beings from a homeland northeast of the photograph's setting, wearing buckskin-breech clouts, feather regalia, and aviator glasses. Using her nephews as performers, Romero digitally stitches together the pictures and heightens the hues of land and sky to suggest a futuristic universe. *Evolvers* is part of her 2019 series *Jackrabbit, Cottontail, and Spirits of the Desert*, six billboards that brought Indigenous past and future into the present of the Desert X arts biennial. The cinematic panorama affirms the vibrancy of ancient stories—rich with humor and wisdom—and the enduring ties between Indigenous people and the land, generation after generation. The turbines that sprout from the land evoke a generation of a different sort, of cleaner energy and sustainable technology.

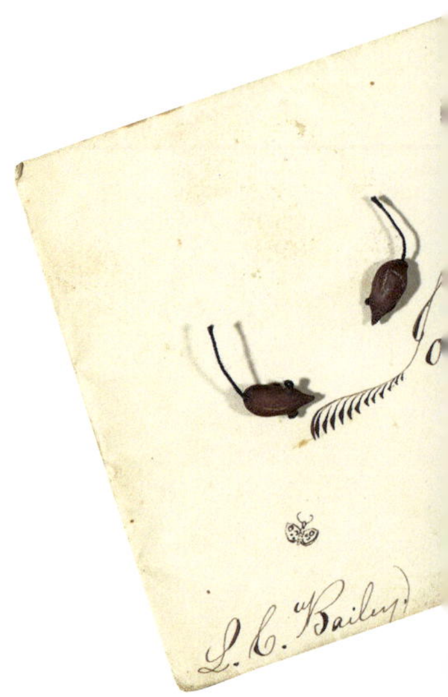

Conclusion

On January 17, 1993, a great Pasadena oak on the grounds of The Huntington collapsed during a severe rainstorm. Over its 250-year lifespan, this tree had quietly witnessed the rise and fall of empires, nations, owners, and caretakers, whose traces remain on the land now designated as The Huntington. As a tender sapling in the eighteenth century, it existed alongside Indigenous peoples known today as the Gabrielino-Tongva or Kizh Nation, who likely tended their own ancestral oak groves amid the dense chaparral landscape. In 1771, when Spanish Franciscans founded the nearby San Gabriel Mission, this tree continued to thrive, fostering an ecosystem through its foliage, bark, and acorns, even as colonial Spain dramatically transformed the area with cattle and new forms of agriculture. Through Mexican independence in 1821 and US statehood in 1850, this native species, also known as Engelmann oak *(Quercus engelmannii)*, endured different disputes and landowners, as well as rapid population growth. In 1903, Henry E.

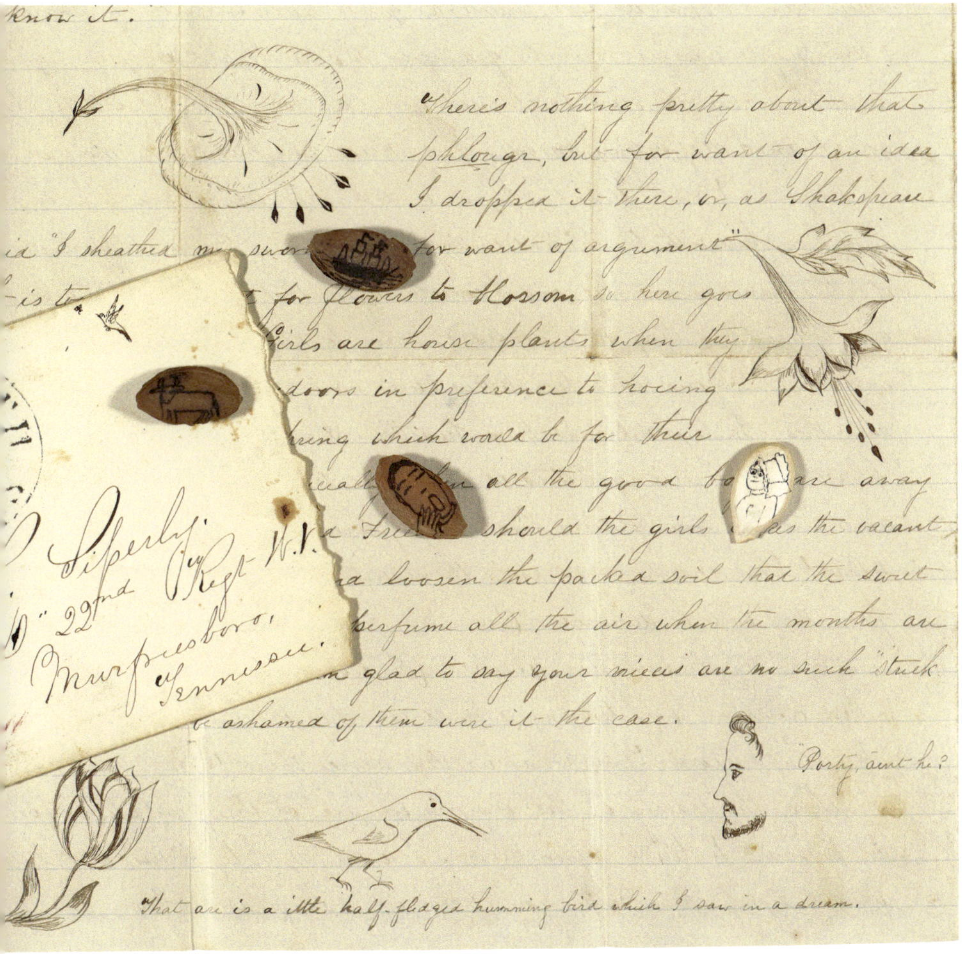

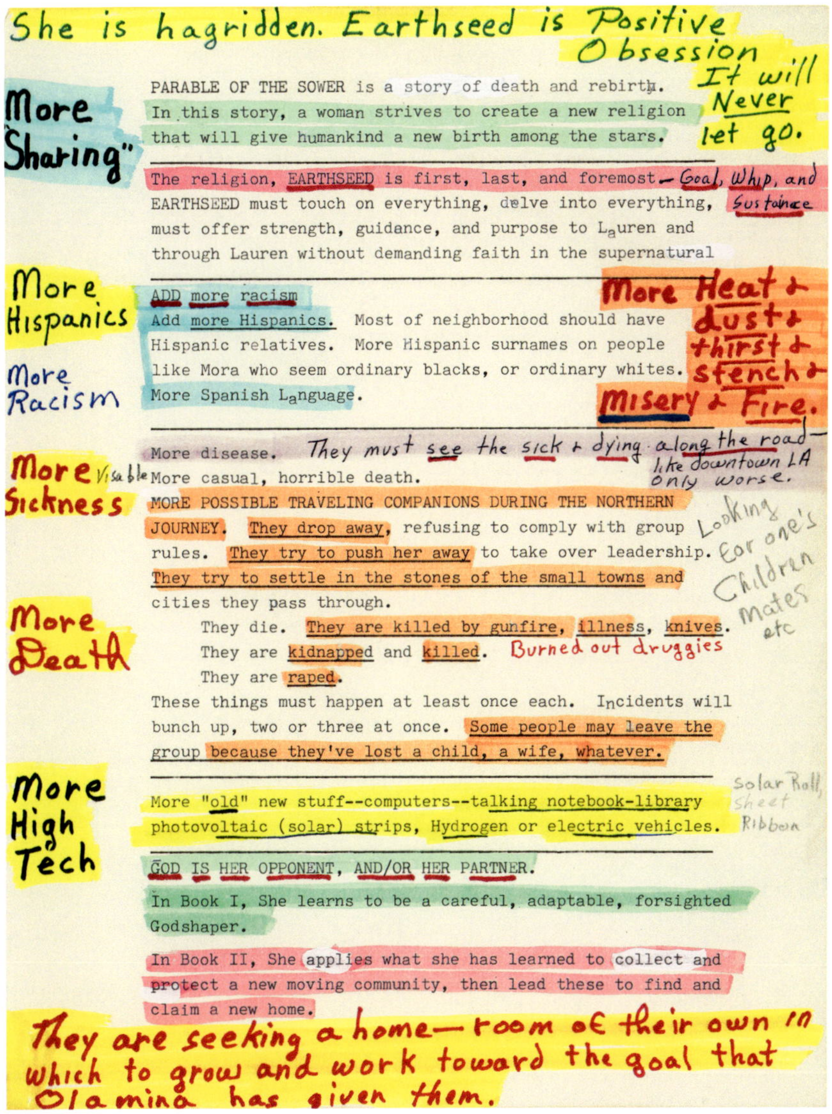

She is hagridden. Earthseed is Positive Obsession

More "Sharing"

PARABLE OF THE SOWER is a story of death and rebirth. In this story, a woman strives to create a new religion that will give humankind a new birth among the stars. It will Never let go.

The religion, EARTHSEED is first, last, and foremost—Goal, Whip, and Sustenance EARTHSEED must touch on everything, delve into everything, must offer strength, guidance, and purpose to Lauren and through Lauren without demanding faith in the supernatural

More Hispanics

More Racism

ADD more racism
Add more Hispanics. Most of neighborhood should have Hispanic relatives. More Hispanic surnames on people like Mora who seem ordinary blacks, or ordinary whites. More Spanish Language.

More Heat & dust & thirst & stench & Misery & Fire.

More Visable Sickness

More disease. They must see the sick & dying along the road—like downtown LA only worse.
More casual, horrible death.
MORE POSSIBLE TRAVELING COMPANIONS DURING THE NORTHERN JOURNEY. They drop away, refusing to comply with group rules. They try to push her away to take over leadership. They try to settle in the stones of the small towns and cities they pass through.

Looking for one's Children mates etc

More Death

They die. They are killed by gunfire, illness, knives.
They are kidnapped and killed. Burned out druggies
They are raped.
These things must happen at least once each. Incidents will bunch up, two or three at once. Some people may leave the group because they've lost a child, a wife, whatever.

More High Tech

More "old" new stuff--computers--talking notebook-library photovoltaic (solar) strips, Hydrogen or electric vehicles.

Solar Roll, Sheet Ribbon

GOD IS HER OPPONENT, AND/OR HER PARTNER.

In Book I, She learns to be a careful, adaptable, forsighted Godshaper.

In Book II, She applies what she has learned to collect and protect a new moving community, then lead these to find and claim a new home.

They are seeking a home—room of their own in which to grow and work toward the goal that Olamina has given them.

Figure 23
Harriet F. Bailey, letter to her uncle John Siperly with artwork on plum pits, pumpkin seed, and apple seeds, 1862–64. John R. Siperly Papers, The Huntington, Gift of Craig P. Knapp and Rachel R. McCallister.

Figure 24
Octavia E. Butler, notes for *Parable of the Sower*, ca. 1989. Octavia E. Butler Papers, The Huntington, Gift of the Estate of Octavia E. Butler, mssOEB 1705.

Huntington purchased the San Marino Ranch where this tree stood tall, and in 1919 established a 96,000-square-foot library with underground storage built right beside it, level with the tree's root system. What remains of this majestic tree is a cross section of its trunk. Visible rings record its growth patterns and its responses to the environment—a living archive (fig. 27). This oak bears a scar indicating a severe fire, and the thickness of its rings reveals periods of drought and flooding. During the preservation process, the tree slab split in sections, and the cracks were sutured with wooden pieces to help hold it together. It was then displayed to the public for many years in the Botanical Center.

Tree relics, or "cookies," like this often appear in national parks to illustrate historical chronologies and the age of the tree. For example, a giant redwood cross section at Muir Woods National Monument, cut down in 1930, has key moments marked on its rings, including the Magna Carta in 1215, Columbus's arrival in America in 1492, and the Declaration of Independence in 1776. But American history cannot be distilled to a single timeline or linear path.

The oak tree's 250 rings form a chronology but also suggest a sort of "field note" history. The slab embodies all the terms that orient this book: Originally rooted on the site, it was uprooted through a natural disturbance, altered and amended over time; it grew at the edges of Indigenous and settler histories, between institutional and garden space; and it has been repurposed for later generations. Tree rings, by their very multiplicity, evoke a host of unseen events and actions that have yet to be identified.

Uncovering these hidden, erased, or overlooked stories is a revelatory way to explore the relationships between people and land. This is especially true in the current moment, when narratives are often jarringly nonlinear and when scholars have recognized, more than ever, how

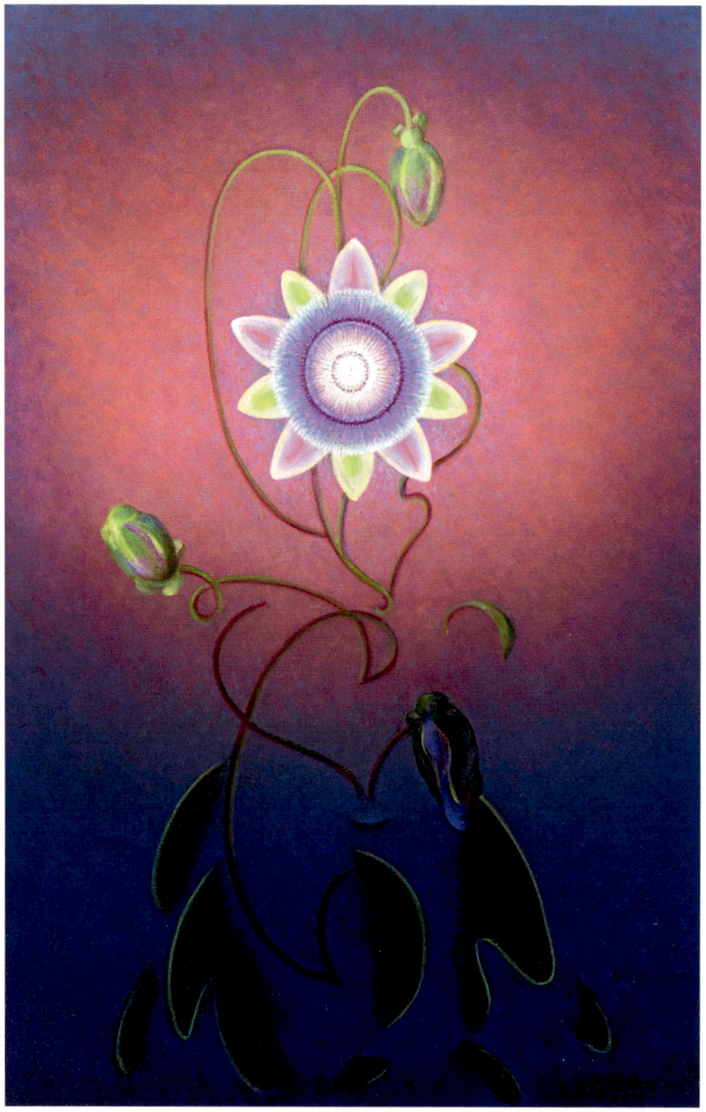

Figure 25
Agnes Pelton, *Passion Flower*, ca. 1945. Oil on canvas, 24 × 16 in. The Huntington, Purchased with funds from the Virginia Steele Scott American Art Acquisition Fund, 2016.26.

Figure 26
Cara Romero, *Evolvers*, 2019. Inkjet print, 37 × 119 in. The Huntington, Purchased with funds from The Philip and Muriel Berman Foundation, 2025.17.

multisided American history has been, from long before 1776 to the present day.

This Land Is . . ., like Alex Haley's *Roots*, is a sort of birthday offering to the country. This collection of field notes rings out in the musical sense of *notes*, including Guthrie's "This Land" and Still and Hughes's "I Dream a World," as well as many others. In Whitman's "Song of Myself," the primary poem in *Leaves of Grass*, he famously wrote, "Do I contradict myself? / Very well then. . . . I contradict myself: / (I am large. . . . I contain multitudes)."[16] He spoke of himself as embodying the nation—a generous yet hubristic impulse in an era of expansion and conquest. O'Sullivan and Gardner composed a wartime lamentation with lens and light; Romero uses the same tools in a song of resilience and renewal.

Like *Leaves of Grass*, the American story remains in constant revision and amendment, one more draft in a long-running archive that resists any attempt by an author, editor, or institution to bind it between two covers.

Josh Garrett-Davis is the H. Russell Smith Foundation Curator of Western American History at The Huntington. He is the author of What Is a Western? Region, Genre, Imagination *(2019).*

Linde B. Lehtinen is the Philip D. Nathanson Senior Curator of Photography at The Huntington. She has contributed to several exhibition catalogues and journal articles on American photography.

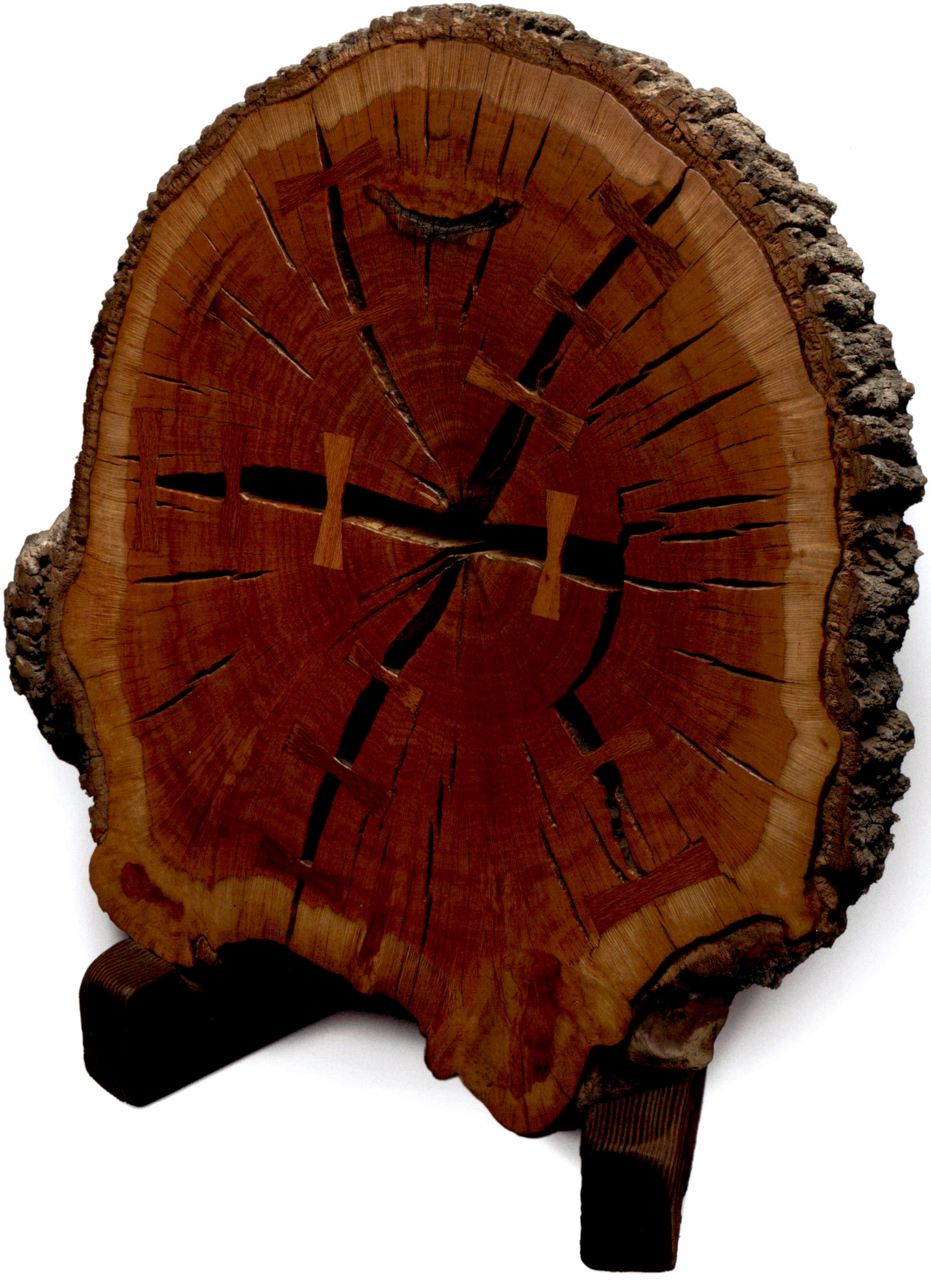

Figure 27
Cross section of Pasadena oak tree *(Quercus engelmannii)* with at least 250 rings, ca. 1740–1993. Preserved, repaired, and finished by Andrew Mitchell. Botanical Study Collection, The Huntington. Photograph by Dana Barsuhn with Travis Flack.

1. Washington's field notes do not speak to the role of enslavement at Mount Vernon. For a list of the people he enslaved around this time, see George Washington Papers, Series 4, General Correspondence: George Washington, April, Taxable Property in Truro and Fairfax Parishes including slaves, April 1788, Manuscript/Mixed Material, https://www.loc.gov/item/mgw436127.

2. Alex Haley, *Roots: The Saga of an American Family* (Doubleday, 1976), dedication, 7–8. The book's massive popularity, and the genealogy boom that followed, comprised a strong branch of the bicentennial to accompany the occasion's ephemeral parades and fireworks.

3. John Adams diary, December 17, 1773, in *Diary and Autobiography of John Adams*, vol. 2, *Diary 1771–1781*, ed. L. H. Butterfield (Harvard University Press, 1961), 86.

4. For more on the broadside, see Olga Tsapina, "'Conducive to the Happiness & Welfare of the United States of America': The Broadside of the Declaration of Independence at The Huntington Library," *American Historical Review* (forthcoming).

5. See, for instance, Oscar Handlin, *The Uprooted: The Epic Story of the Great Migrations That Made the American People* (Little, Brown, 1951); John Bodnar, *The Transplanted: A History of Immigrants in Urban America* (Indiana University Press, 1987).

6. Aiko Alice (Kuromi) Ito, interview by Amy Kitchener, August 3, 1993, transcript, Shades of L.A. Interview Project, Los Angeles Public Library, https://www.exhibits.lapl.org/shadesofla/alice-ito.

7. Alexander Gardner, *Gardner's Photographic Sketch Book of the War*, 2 vols. (Philp & Solomons, 1865–66), vol. 1, plate 36. See also Martha A. Sandweiss, *The Girl in the Middle: A Recovered History of the American West* (Princeton University Press, 2025), 89–94, in which she speculates about Gardner's authorship of the *Sketch Book* and suggests that it could have been written by others.

8. Warren R. Hofstra, *The Planting of New Virginia: Settlement and Landscape in the Shenandoah Valley* (Johns Hopkins University Press, 2004), 21.

9. Thomas Pynchon, *Mason & Dixon* (Henry Holt, 1997), 573.

10. See Celeste R. Menchaca, "Building a Border: The Material Transit of Scientific Labor," *Western Historical Quarterly* 56, no. 1 (2025): 21–41.

11. This section of carved sandstone is located at what is now El Morro National Monument in New Mexico.

12. William Grant Still, libretto by Langston Hughes, *Troubled Island: An Opera in Three Acts* (Leeds Music, 1949), 9. See also Judith Anne Still and Lisa M. Headlee, eds., *Just Tell the Story: Troubled Island* (Master-Player Library, 2006).

13. When Hughes was called before the US Senate on suspicion of communist sympathies in 1953, he planned to end his testimony with this verse—although he ultimately chose to leave it out. See Arnold Rampersad, *The Life of Langston Hughes*, vol. 2, *1914–1967 I Dream a World*, 2nd ed. (Oxford University Press, 2002), 215. See also W. Jason Miller, *Origins of the Dream: Hughes's Poetry and King's Rhetoric* (University Press of Florida, 2015), 142–59.

14. Octavia E. Butler, *Parable of the Sower* (Four Walls Eight Windows, 1993), quoted in Kaitlin Smith, "Acorns and Octavia: Imagined Futures in Earthseed's Fruiting Bodies," *Orion* (Winter 2022), https://orionmagazine.org/article/octavia-butler-acorn-earthseed-series.

15. Agnes Pelton, Guggenheim application, 1932, quoted in Elizabeth Armstrong, "Agnes in the Desert," in *Agnes Pelton: Desert Transcendentalist*, ed. Gilbert Vicario (Phoenix Art Museum, 2019), 57.

16. Walt Whitman, *Leaves of Grass* (Published by the author, 1855), 55.

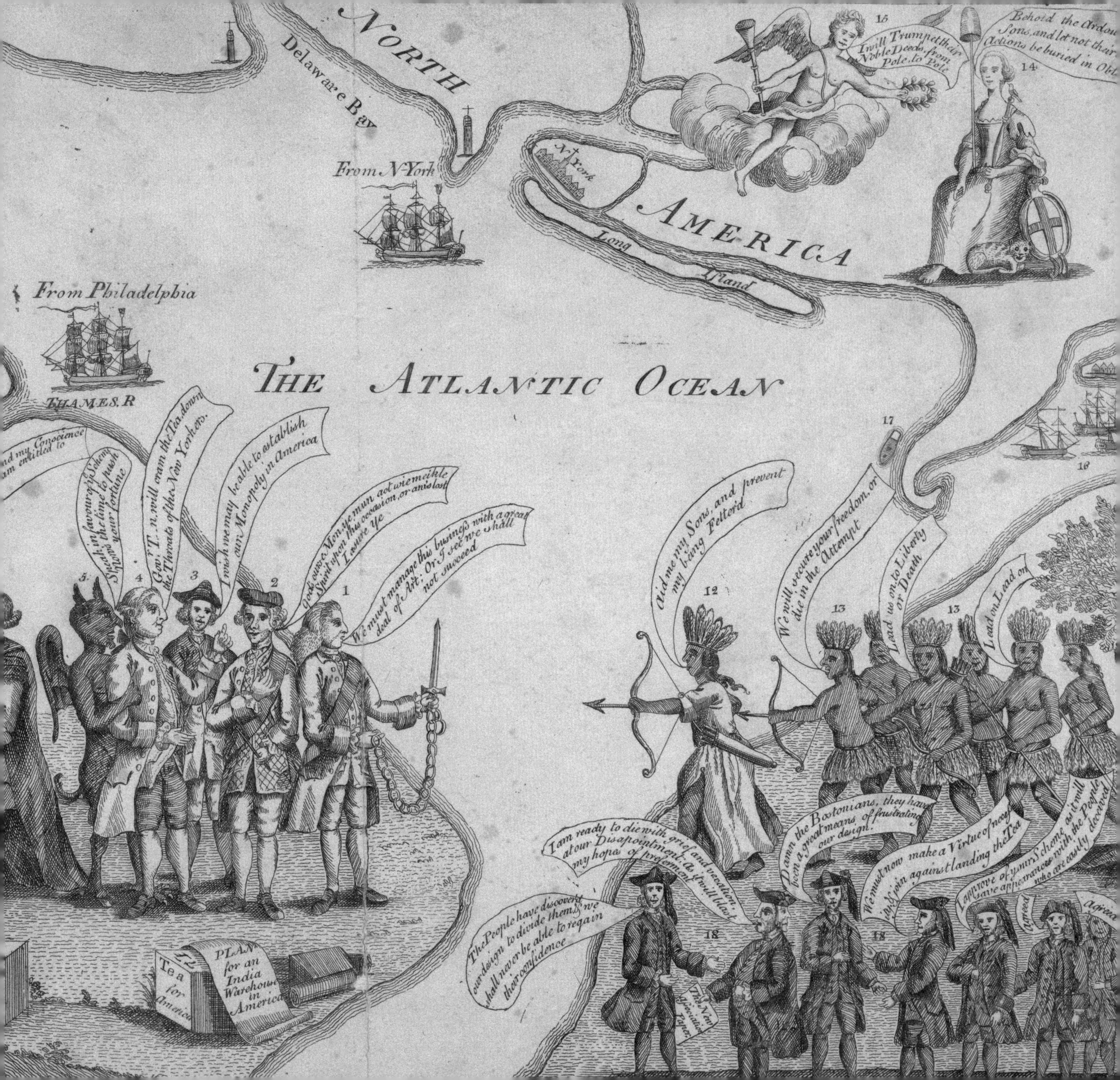

NORTH
Delaware Bay
From N. York
N. York
AMERICA
Long Island
15
I will Trumpet their Noble Deeds, from Pole to Pole
Behold the Ardou Sons, and let not their Actions be buried in Obli
14
From Philadelphia
THAMES. R
THE ATLANTIC OCEAN
17
16
nd my Conscience am entitled to
5
Speak in favour of ye Scheme Now's the time to push your fortune
4
Gov. r T...n will cram the Tea down the Throats of the New Yorkers.
3
I wish we may be able to establish our Monopoly in America
2
God's curse Mon, ye mun act wie meikle Spirit upon this occasion, or a'n's lost I assure ye
1
We must manage this business with a great deal of Art; Or I see we shall not succeed
12
Aid me my Sons, and prevent my being Fetter'd
13
We will secure your freedom, or die in the Attempt
Lead us on to Liberty or Death
13
Lead on Lead on
I am ready to die with grief and vexation at our Disapointment: As it will blast my hopes of preferment
Damn the Bostonians, they have been a great means of frustrating our design.
We must now make a Virtue of necessity & join against landing the Tea
I approve of ye Scheme as it will save appearances with the People who are easily deceived
Agreed
Agree
The People have discover'd our design to divide them & we shall never be able to regain their confidence
18
18
The New Association Paper
12 Tea for America
PLAN for an India Warehouse in America

Roots

Roots are a direct connection to the earth. Plant networks sustain life by their ability to pull nutrients from the soil, bringing unseen resources to the surface. An underground, interconnected system offers stability to an individual plant or a community. Just as plants are anchored by their roots, American history is rooted in contested American land. Members of the nation draw on treaties, documents, and myths to organize a foundational identity. However, the nation's roots extend beyond a singular narrative to tell a range of intricately woven histories of a time prior to 1776. Physical roots offer a reminder of the buried stories; unearthing them allows alternative views to emerge.

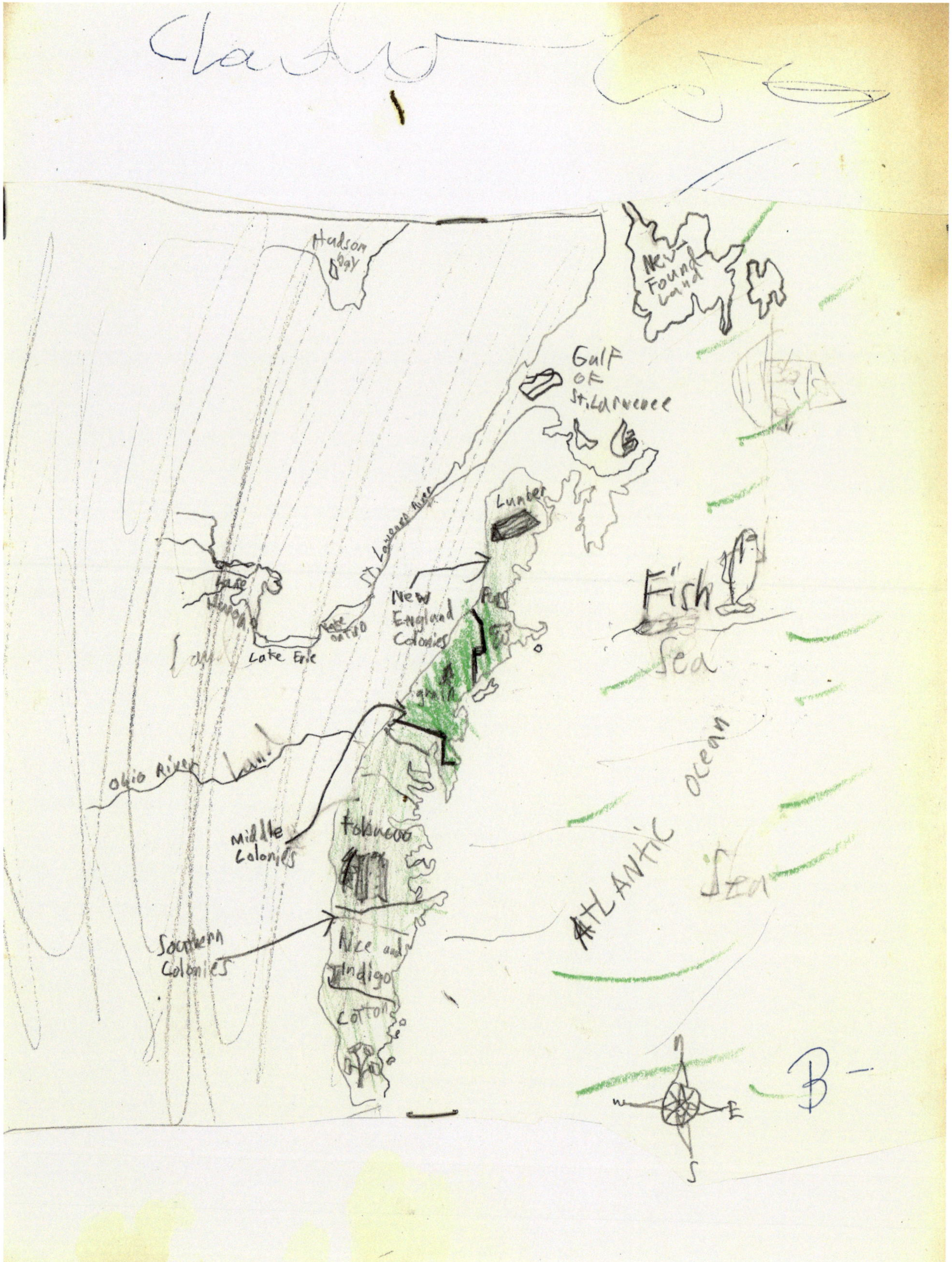
Hudson Bay
New Found Land
Gulf of St. Lawrence
Lumber
New England Colonies
Lake Erie
Fish
Sea
Ohio River
Middle Colonies
Tobacco
Atlantic Ocean
Sea
Southern Colonies
Rice and Indigo
Cotton
N
W
E
S
B-

Points of Origin

Mapping the Peoples of Early America

As far as American Revolutionaries were concerned, the population of the continent in 1783 ranged along the Atlantic coast from the St. Marys River in Georgia to the St. Croix River in Maine and extended inland a few hundred miles. The region is familiar to schoolkids today—as it was to me in 1976—as the thirteen original states. The states became "original," as in "the first," when lawmakers began debating how to admit other states to the Republic in 1784.[1] And they became "original," as in "the origin" of the United States, through the cumulative work of hundreds of history books, Fourth of July parades, and the centennial and bicentennial celebrations of the Declaration of Independence.

Considering the broader continental history, the thirteen states were neither first nor foremost, even as they rightly hold pride of place in the political history of the United States. Contrary to the foreshortened perspective of the British colonists, the North American continent stretches well past the boundaries of the thirteen states, and its history extends far deeper in time. My third-grade map unintentionally exposes the limitations of adopting a truncated view of American history (fig. 1). I made it at Edison Elementary School (now Thomas Edison Charter Academy) in San Francisco's Mission district, barely a half mile from Mission Dolores, the Spanish outpost established on Ohlone territory three months after the Declaration of Independence. My elementary school map does not encompass the Pacific coast, let alone the trans-Mississippi West, and I filled what little area I pictured west of the Appalachians with cursory pencil scrawls, a third grader's equivalent to "these lands entirely unknown."

A half century later, I have sought to improve upon my earlier effort by mapping the human population north of the Rio Grande decade by decade, starting in 1500 (fig. 2). This admittedly imprecise overview of North America plots six million people—the middle ground between high and low scholarly estimates—and illustrates that American origins precede 1776. (The abrupt edge at the present-day US-Mexico border reflects limits imposed by time and feasibility.)

Even from this satellite perspective, a few crude patterns emerge. Indigenous Americans, like other peoples around the world, preferred living near waterways. Though they survived in the extreme environments of the frigid far north and the parched Great Basin, they flourished in much greater numbers in temperate regions, such as the Mississippi Valley and Chesapeake Bay areas. Not surprisingly, they avoided the treacherous slopes and rugged peaks of the Sierras and the Rockies.

The map reveals a diversity of peoples in 1500. In the Los Angeles Basin, the Tongva (Gabrielino) harvested resources from the rich marine environment. Along the Missouri River, Plains villagers, the ancestors of today's Mandan, Hidatsa, and Arikara nations, cultivated corn, as did Pueblo peoples along the middle Rio Grande. Far to the north, Cree families hunted and fished along the shores of the Hudson Bay. And in the Virginia Tidewater, Algonkian-speaking Powhatans, the very same people who watched Jamestown colonists disembark in 1607, grew corn and gathered shellfish in coastal waters. One of their villagers would play a starring role as Pocahontas in the mythologized origin story of the thirteen colonies.

Two hundred years later, in 1700, the continent north of the Rio Grande remained predominantly Indigenous (fig. 3). A voyager on a three-thousand-mile trek up the Pacific coast from the San Diego Bay to the Aleutian Islands would not have encountered a single colonist. Striking out east from the San Francisco Bay, the traveler would have met only Indigenous Americans for hundreds, if not thousands, of miles, depending on the exact route.

Figure 1
Perfunctory map of early America, for which the author received a B- in third grade, ca. 1976. Courtesy of the author.

But there were now signs of change. The Indigenous population had dropped by perhaps 40 percent, the cumulative toll of Old World diseases such as smallpox and measles and other damages wrought by colonialism. Still, in most regions European outposts remained few and far between. The Spanish had established a presence in Pueblo country on the middle Rio Grande a century earlier. The colony counted approximately three thousand Spanish subjects living in the homelands of nearly ten thousand Indigenous Americans. Further north, in the Great Plains, European technologies such as guns and horses, if not yet Europeans themselves, were spreading through the region. Still further northward, traders on the shores of the Hudson Bay operated a brisk business with Cree and Assiniboine hunters, exchanging guns, Brazil tobacco, and other foreign goods for beaver pelts. A few outmanned and far-flung French forts dotted the shores of the Great Lakes, and French *habitants* were densely settled on the banks of the St. Lawrence River. Along the Atlantic coast, from the Carolinas to New England, British colonists and enslaved African peoples had carved out a series of populous colonies poised for rapid growth. North of the Rio Grande, the combined African and European population numbered about 250,000.

By the era of the Revolutionary War, Europe's imperial powers had encircled but not yet conquered the continent (fig. 4). Beginning in 1769, the Spanish planted a series of missions and presidios up the California coast, isolated and weak outposts, barely visible on the map, that would nonetheless have an outsized impact on Indigenous communities. Likewise, the Russians established a toehold in Alaska, a legacy still evident in the presence of the Russian Orthodox Church in the region. More broadly, in the seventy-five years since the beginning of the century, the colonial population had exploded by a factor of ten. For the first time, the 2.5 million Africans and Europeans north of the Rio Grande outnumbered the estimated 2.4 million Indigenous peoples, who were now a minority in their own homeland.

Despite this profound demographic shift, when the thirteen original states declared their independence in 1776, Native peoples remained a majority and the sole inhabitants across vast expanses, the tens of thousands of square miles hidden behind my third-grade pencil scrawls or simply not part of my elementary school assignment. The colonial exports pictured on that partial map tell only one story among many across the continent. The extent of the "thirteen original states" does not define the extent of early American history, and even while the United States commemorates Revolutionary legacies, it is worth keeping in sight other origin stories as well.

Claudio Saunt is the Richard B. Russell Professor in American History, Regents' Professor, and Co-Director of the Center for Virtual History at the University of Georgia. He is the author of four books, the most recent of which is Unworthy Republic, *and has developed several online projects, including Invasion of America, Pox Americana (with Elizabeth Fenn), and NativeGround.org, which maps in depth and detail the Cherokee families who lost their homes in the 1830s.*

1. Virginia Delegates to Benjamin Harrison, Nov. 1, 1783, Congressional Series, vol. 7, *The Papers of James Madison Digital Edition*, ed. J. C. A. Stagg (University of Virginia Press, Rotunda, 2010); "Report of the Committee," Mar. 1, 1784, Main Series, vol. 6, *The Papers of Thomas Jefferson Digital Edition*, ed. James P. McClure and J. Jefferson Looney (University of Virginia Press, Rotunda, 2008–2024).

Figure 2
Map showing human population north of the Rio Grande in 1500. ArcGIS. Courtesy of the author. Map by author.

Figure 3
Map showing human population north of the Rio Grande in 1700. ArcGIS. Courtesy of the author. Map by author.

Figure 4
Map showing human population north of the Rio Grande in the era of the American Revolution. Courtesy of the author. Map by author.

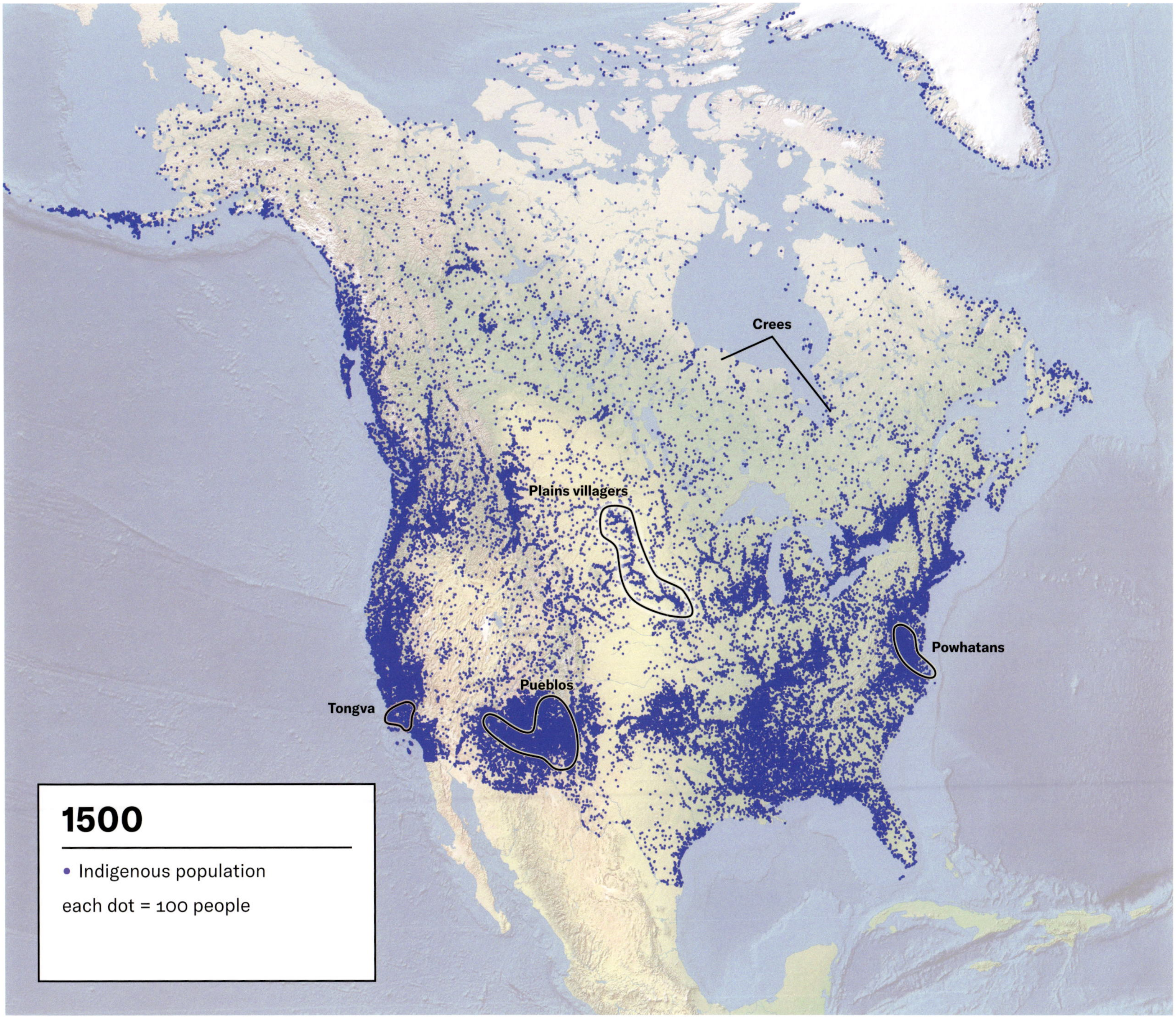
Crees
Plains villagers
Powhatans
Pueblos
Tongva
1500
• Indigenous population
each dot = 100 people

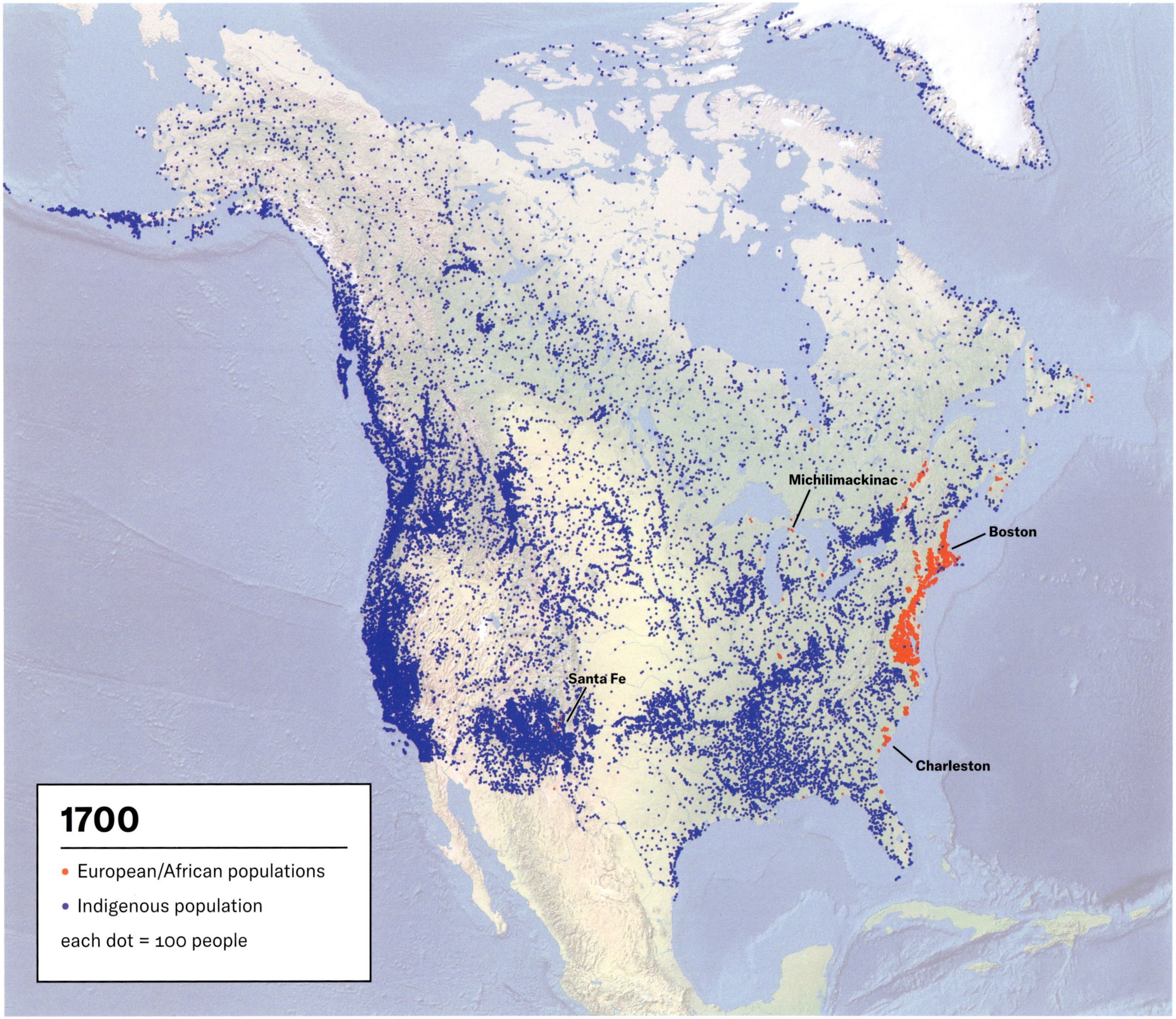
Michilimackinac
Boston
Santa Fe
Charleston
1700
European/African populations
Indigenous population
each dot = 100 people

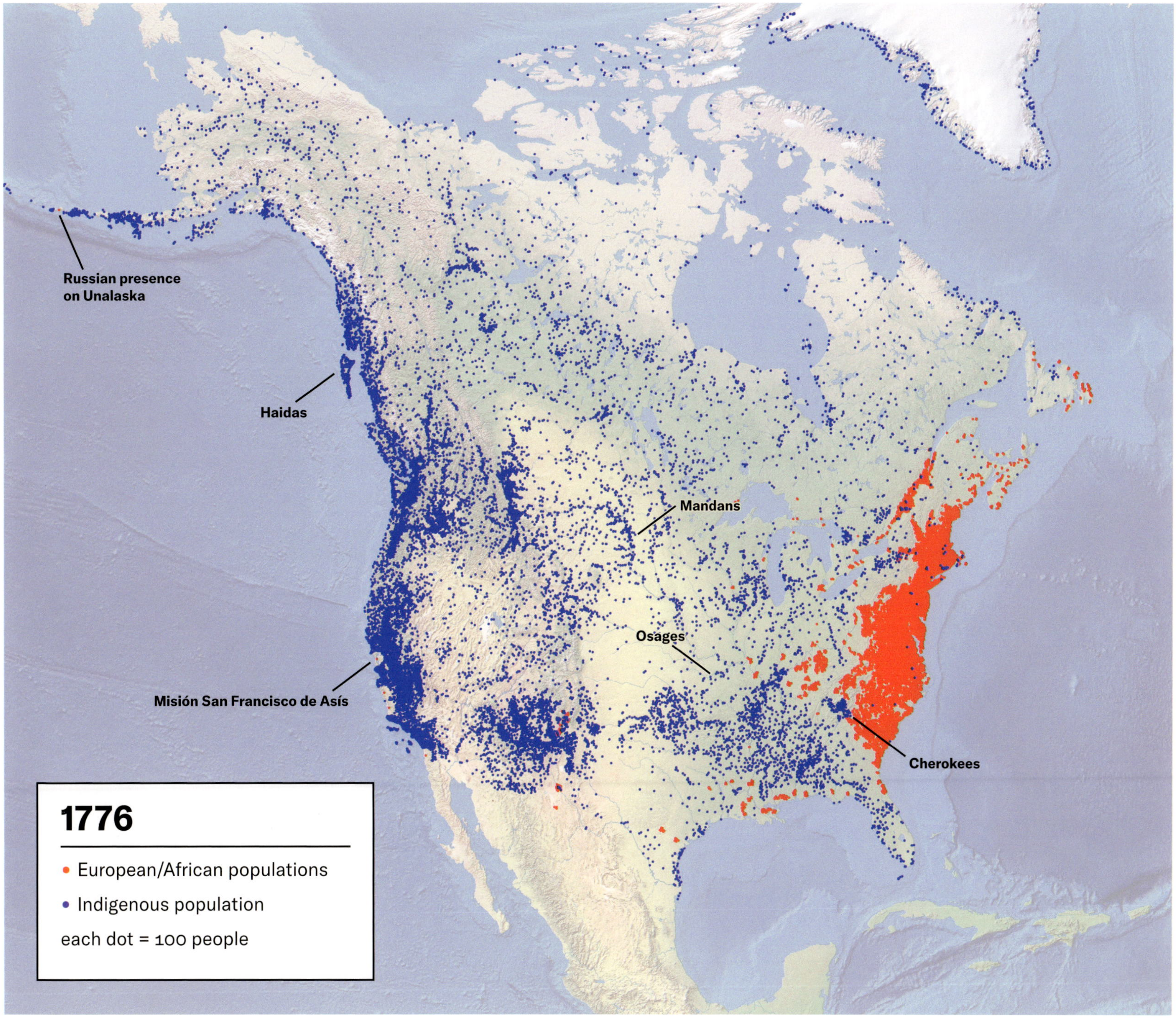
Russian presence
on Unalaska
Haidas
Mandans
Osages
Misión San Francisco de Asís
Cherokees
1776
European/African populations
Indigenous population
each dot = 100 people

e 6th

Whereas the Enemies of the United States have endeavoured by every artifice in their power to possess the Indians in general with an opinion that it is the design of the States aforesaid to extirpate the Indians, and take possession of their Country. To obviate such false suggestions the United States do engage to guarantee to the aforesaid Nation of Delawares and their heirs, all their territorial rights (in the fullest and most ample manner as it hath been bounded by former treaties, as long as they the s Delaware Nation shall abide by, and hold fast the chain of friendsh now entered into. And it is further agreed on between the contracting Parties that should it for the future be found conducive for the mutual intere of both Parties to invite any other Tribes who have been friends to the interest the United States to join the present Confederation, and to form a State whereof the Delaware Nation shall be the head, and have a representat in Congress, provided nothing contained in this Article to be considered a conclusive until it meets with the approbation of Congress. And it is al the intent and meaning of this article that no protection in countenance sh be afforded to any who are at present our Enemies by which they might escap the punishment they deserve.

timony whereof the Parties have hereunto set their hands & Seals at For

"History is complicated, violence is simple"

Lenape Reflections on the American Revolution

The murder of Chief White Eyes. The destruction of Lenape villages. The massacre at Gnadenhütten. A century-long forced removal over twelve hundred miles from their ancestral homelands. These critical events are part of the price the Lenape paid for supporting the American Revolution by signing the Treaty of Fort Pitt in 1778. The Huntington Library holds a contemporary copy of the treaty, which was the first treaty that US officials signed with a Native Nation *and* the first to be broken (fig. 1). On the occasion of the semiquincentennial of the Declaration of Independence, the Fort Pitt Treaty reminds us that the United States was founded on the betrayal of the Lenape people and the usurpation of Lenape homelands.

From time immemorial, Lenape communities lived throughout Lënapehòkink, their homelands, which encompass eastern Pennsylvania, New Jersey, Delaware, parts of New York, Connecticut, and Maryland. The Lenape were a significant sovereign force politically, culturally, and economically, with over a century of experience trading and treating with European powers before the American nation was even an idea. Escalating land dispossessions and violence forced most of the Lenape into Ohio territory by the mid-eighteenth century. The so-called Walking Purchase of 1737 played a critical role in their removal. The sons of William Penn (founder of the British colony of Pennsylvania) executed various deceptions to steal more than a million acres of retained Lenape lands in eastern Pennsylvania. Lenape leaders would repeatedly cite this injustice as motivation for their alliance with the French in the French and Indian War and ongoing attacks on British settlements (fig. 2).

At the outbreak of the Revolutionary War, Lenape leaders tried to remain neutral—a difficult feat, given that most Native Nations in the Ohio territory were allied with the British. Lenape leader Koquethagechton (Chief or Captain White Eyes) diligently pursued means to secure the lands they now occupied. White Eyes was instrumental in establishing the Fort Pitt Treaty, which he signed on September 17, 1778, along with Lenape leaders Gelelemund (Captain John Killbuck Jr.) and Captain Pipe. The Revolutionaries realized that a Lenape alliance was crucial for combating British-allied Native Nations and securing safe passage through Ohio to attack Fort Detroit. In return for their support, the Lenape were promised goods, protection, and—most significantly—the opportunity "to form a state whereof the Delaware Nation shall be the head, and have representation in Congress."[1]

The United States never upheld its end of the treaty. Two months after the signing, White Eyes joined the expedition to take Fort Detroit and was murdered by an American militiaman. American officials tried to cover up his murder by claiming he died of smallpox. In 1779, George Washington launched his campaign to destroy Haudenosaunee villages, with the assistance of General John Sullivan, General James Clinton, and Colonel Daniel Brodhead. Brodhead's troops marched through western Pennsylvania, looting and burning Lenape and Seneca villages. In 1781, Brodhead attacked the Lenape capital, Goschachgünk (Coshocton, Ohio)—previously a refuge for US-allied Lenape.[2]

On March 8, 1782, while searching for provisions at their abandoned village site in Gnadenhütten, Ohio, a cohort of Christianized Moravian Lenape were captured by American militiamen. Ignoring Lenape appeals that they were pacifist and neutral in the Revolutionary conflict, the Americans voted to execute every one of them in cold blood, including the elderly and infants. At least sixty-two Lenape men and women and thirty-four children were brutally slain. They sang hymns as they were forced to watch each other die.[3] The murderers "were not satisfied with

Detail of the Fort Pitt Treaty (fig. 1).

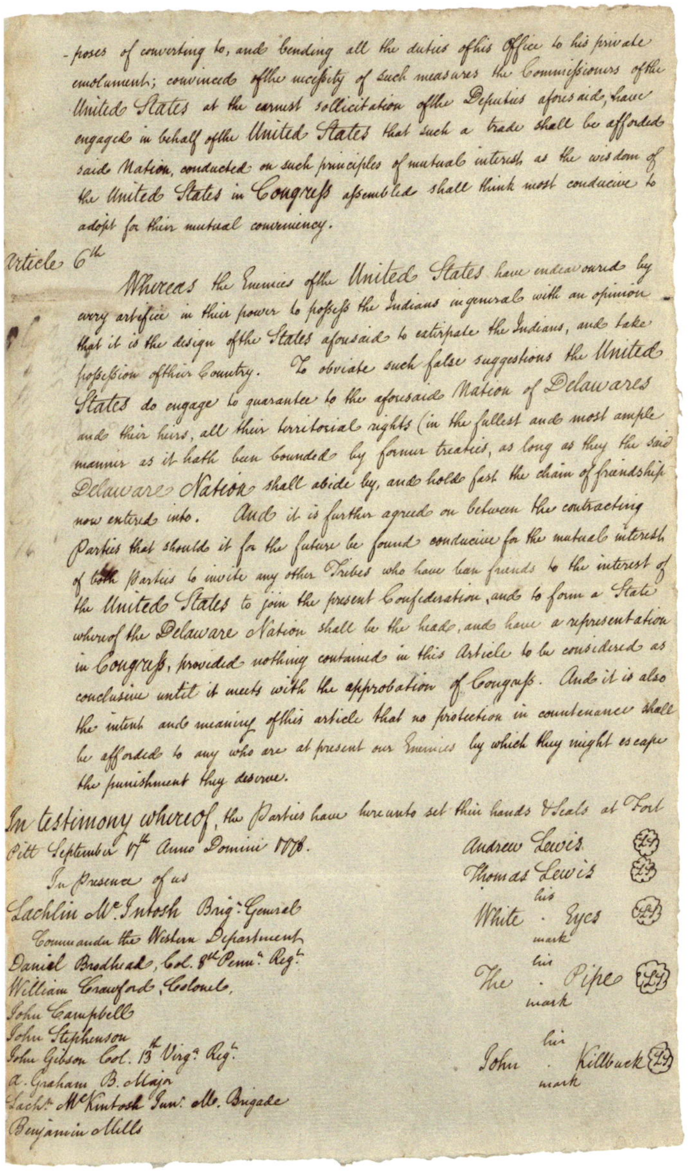
-poses of converting to, and bending all the duties of his Office to his private
emolument; convinced of the necessity of such measures the Commissioners of the
United States at the earnest sollicitation of the Deputies aforesaid, have
engaged in behalf of the United States that such a trade shall be afforded
said Nation, conducted on such principles of mutual interest as the wisdom of
the United States in Congress assembled shall think most conducive to
adopt for their mutual conveniency.

Article 6th

Whereas the Enemies of the United States have endeavoured by
every artifice in their power to possess the Indians in general with an opinion
that it is the design of the States aforesaid to extirpate the Indians, and take
possession of their Country. To obviate such false suggestions the United
States do engage to guarantee to the aforesaid Nation of Delawares
and their heirs, all their territorial rights (in the fullest and most ample
manner as it hath been bounded by former treaties, as long as they the said
Delaware Nation shall abide by, and hold fast the chain of friendship
now entered into. And it is further agreed on between the contracting
Parties that should it for the future be found conducive for the mutual interest
of both Parties to invite any other Tribes who have been friends to the interest of
the United States to join the present Confederation, and to form a State
whereof the Delaware Nation shall be the head, and have a representation
in Congress, provided nothing contained in this Article to be considered as
conclusive until it meets with the approbation of Congress. And it is also
the intent and meaning of this article that no protection in countenance shall
be afforded to any who are at present our Enemies by which they might escape
the punishment they deserve.

In testimony whereof, the Parties have hereunto set their hands & Seals at Fort
Pitt September 17th Anno Domini 1778.

In Presence of us

Lachlin McIntosh Brigr. General
Commander the Western Department
Daniel Brodhead, Col. 8th Penna. Regt.
William Crawford, Colonel,
John Campbell
John Stephenson
John Gibson Col. 13th Virga. Regt.
A. Graham B. Major
Lachn. McIntosh Junr. Mr. Brigade
Benjamin Mills

Andrew Lewis (L.S.)
Thomas Lewis (L.S.)
White his mark Eyes (L.S.)
The his mark Pipe (L.S.)
John his mark Killbuck (L.S.)

simply destroying their lives, but disfigured the dead and dying bodies in a horrible manner."[4]

"History is complicated, violence is simple."[5] This evocative sentiment from the historical graphic novel *Ghost River*—which remembers related colonial violence against the Indigenous Conestoga people near Lancaster, Pennsylvania, in 1763—bears repeating. Lenape motivations behind the signing and later refuting of the Fort Pitt Treaty are unsurprisingly complex in a chaotic time.[6] Still, the consequences of this treaty underscore the ease with which Americans enacted and justified horrific violence against the Lenape people.

Lenape leaders acted in good faith under their agreements but were repeatedly betrayed. The Fort Pitt Treaty exposes the way in which the United States recycled tactics used by earlier Dutch and British colonizers across Lenape homelands: Exploit the Lenape for resources and sovereign support; trap the Lenape into untenable positions between warring colonial powers; make ambiguous promises that would not be upheld; and finally remove them from the physical and political landscape. This structure of dispossession is the ongoing pattern referred to as "settler colonialism." The fact that the first treaty the United States made with a Native Nation was immediately broken provides critical context for understanding the broader legacy of ongoing US colonialism. The United States would continue to employ similar tactics across Indian Country.

Over the following century, the Lenape suffered further fractures of family, land, and cultural and political ties, as more than twenty broken treaties and removals forced them farther from their ancestral homelands and promised lands in Ohio. When US-sanctioned violence and removals could not eradicate Indigenous people, later policies were established to steal Indigenous children from their families, confine them to boarding schools, and outlaw their languages, religions, and cultures—another form of genocide.

Figure 1
"Articles of Agreement and Confederation Made and Entered into . . . in Behalf of the United States of North America . . . and the Delaware Indian Nation" (Fort Pitt Treaty), September 17, 1778. 13½ × 8¼ in. The Huntington, Purchased by Henry E. Huntington, HM 3974.

Figure 2
Nicholas Scull, map of the fork of the Delaware River, ca. 1735. 11⅞ × 14⅝ in. The Walking Purchase Collection, The Huntington, Purchased by the Library Collectors' Council, 2020.

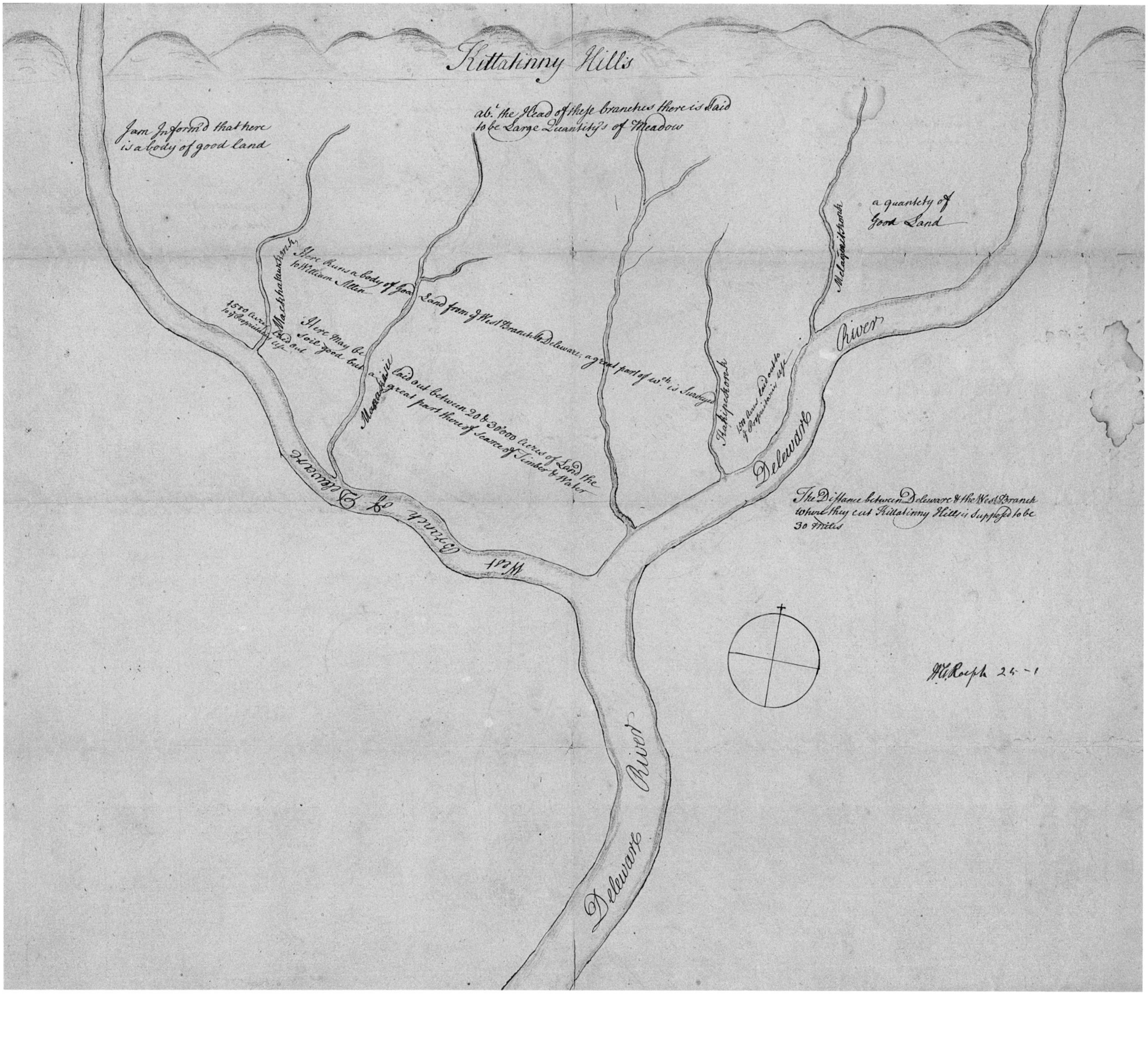

Kittatinny Hills
I am Informd that here is a body of good land
abt. the Head of these branches there is Said to be Large Quantitys of Meadow
a quantety of Good Land
Mackhackamack
Here Runs a body of Good Land from ye West Branch to Deleware, a great part of wch is Surveyed to William Allen
Here May be laid out between 20 & 30000 Acres of Land the Soil good but a great part there of Scarce of Timber & Water
1500 Acres laid out to ye Proprietary use
Hakipekonk
1500 Acres laid out to ye Proprietarys use
Melagamitkonk
Deleware River
West Branch of Deleware
The Distance between Deleware & the West Branch where they cut Kittatinny Hills is Supposed to be 30 Miles
Deleware River

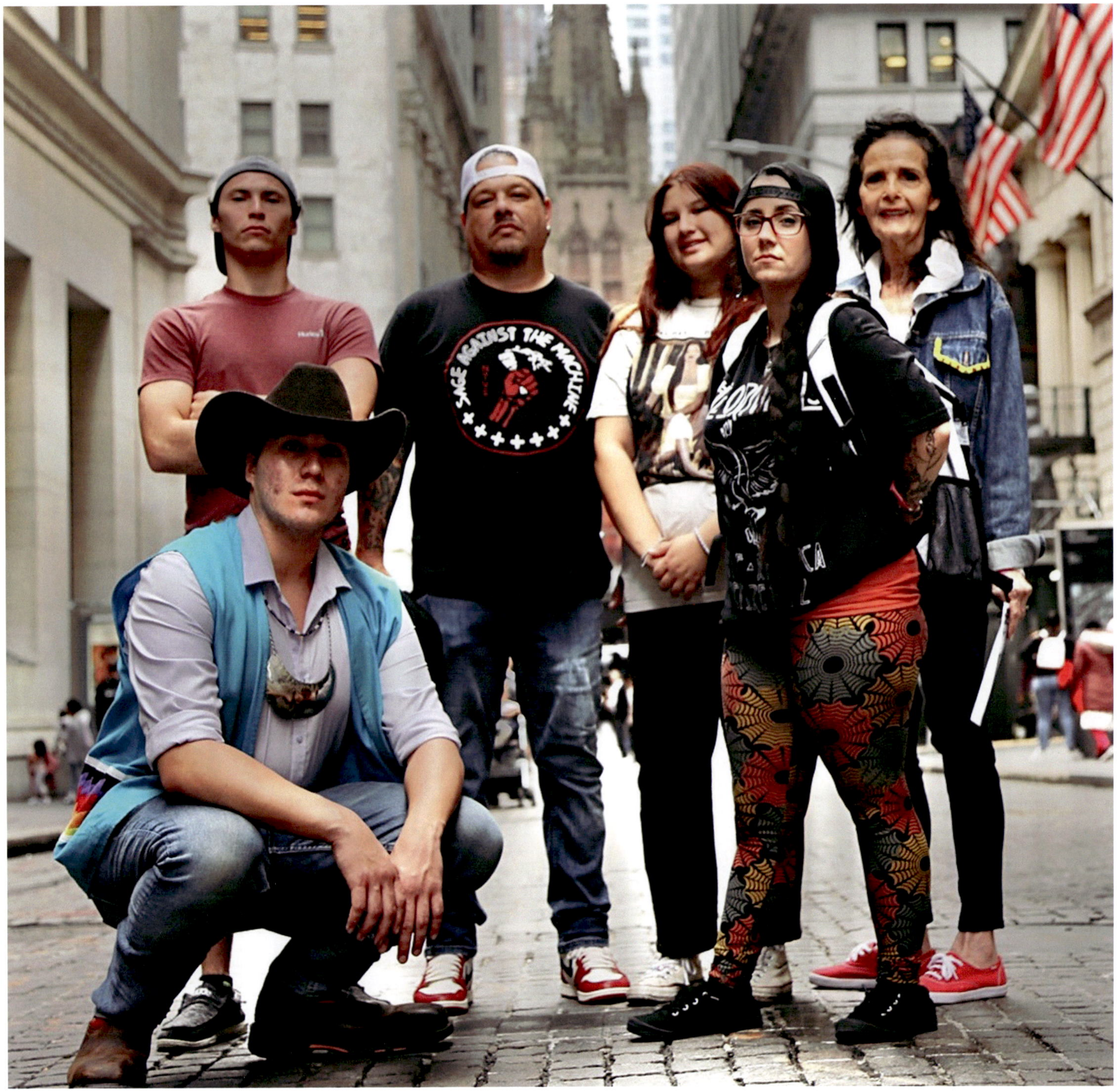

Figure 3
This image shows a Lenape group on New York's Wall Street. Alicia Rezendes notes that they stand "in defiance of the wall once built to keep our Lenape people out. The wall marked the beginning of our forced removal from our ancestral lands. This photograph is a representation of the survival, resilience, and strength of generations of Lenape making our way back to our homelands." Alicia Rezendes, *Lënapehòkink Ktàpi* (You are here in the land of the Lenape), 2023. Digital photograph, 8½ × 10 in. Courtesy of Alicia Rezendes, Turkey Clan, Delaware Tribe of Indians.

Lenape people survived and fiercely protected their sovereignty. They exist today in three US federally recognized Nations—Delaware Tribe of Indians (Bartlesville, OK); Delaware Nation (Anadarko, OK); and Stockbridge-Munsee Community (Bowler, WI)—and in three First Nations in Ontario, Canada: Eelūnaapèewii Lahkèewiit or Delaware Nation at Moraviantown; Munsee-Delaware Nation; and Delaware First Nation of the Six Nations of the Grand River.

Two hundred and fifty years ago, the Lenape endured the rise of yet another empire laying claim to their homelands, betraying their friendship, and massacring their families. Today, the legacy of Lenape resilience and sovereignty lives on as their Nations continue to fight to preserve and protect their language, culture, and rights to self-determination (fig. 3). Despite settler-colonial efforts to eradicate them from this land, the Lenape and their sacred ties to their homelands remain strong.

Jeremy Johnson is the Cultural Education Director and an enrolled citizen of the Delaware Tribe of Indians based in Bartlesville, Oklahoma. He is Lenape, Shawnee, and Peoria. Before his current role, he served as Assistant Chief of the Delaware Tribe. Mr. Johnson is a lifelong educator who worked for over eighteen years as a middle school and high school English teacher and coach. He is committed to preserving and revitalizing Lenape culture and language for the future generations of his Tribe.

Katelyn Lucas serves as the Historic Preservation Officer for Delaware Nation (Anadarko, OK) and manages their extension office in the Lenape homelands of eastern Pennsylvania. Ms. Lucas is a PhD candidate at Temple University (Philadelphia, PA), specializing in early American and Native American Literatures. Her dissertation traces the evolution and implications of Lenape representation in American literature from colonial captivity narratives to contemporary American fiction.

1. From Article 6 of the "Treaty with the Delawares," signed at Fort Pitt on September 17, 1778, between Andrew and Thomas Lewis, on behalf of the United States, and Captain White Eyes, Captain John Killbuck Jr., and Captain Pipe, on behalf of the Delaware Nation, https://americanindian.si.edu/nationtonation/treaty-with-the-delawares.html.

2. Colin G. Calloway, *The American Revolution in Indian Country: Crisis and Diversity in Native Communities* (Cambridge University Press, 1995), 37–38.

3. John Heckewelder, *A Narrative of the Mission of the United Brethren Among the Delaware and Mohegan Indians* (McCarty & Davis, 1820), 313–28; *Diary of David Zeisberger, a Moravian Missionary Among the Indians of Ohio* (Robert Clarke & Co., 1885), 80–83, https://ia600209.us.archive.org/26/items/diaryofdavid01zeisrich/diaryofdavid01zeisrich.pdf.

4. Gnadenhuetten Monument Society, *A True History of the Massacre of Ninety-Six Christian Indians, at Gnadenhuetten, Ohio, March 8th, 1782* (Printed at the Ohio Democrat Office, 1870), 10, https://www.loc.gov/item/02014421/.

5. Lee Francis 4, Weshoyot Alvitre, and Will Fenton, *Ghost River: The Fall and Rise of the Conestoga* (Red Planet Books and Comics, 2019).

6. On May 10, 1779, Delaware Nation leaders addressed Congress in Princeton, New Jersey, and implied that the Fort Pitt Treaty had been "falsely interpreted to them and contained Declarations and Engagements they never intended to make or enter into." See the "Address from the Delaware Nation, 10 May 1779," *Founders Online*, National Archives, https://founders.archives.gov/documents/Washington/03-20-02-0361. Original source: *The Papers of George Washington*, Revolutionary War Series, vol. 20, *8 April–31 May 1779*, ed. Edward G. Lengel (University of Virginia Press, 2010), 414–18.

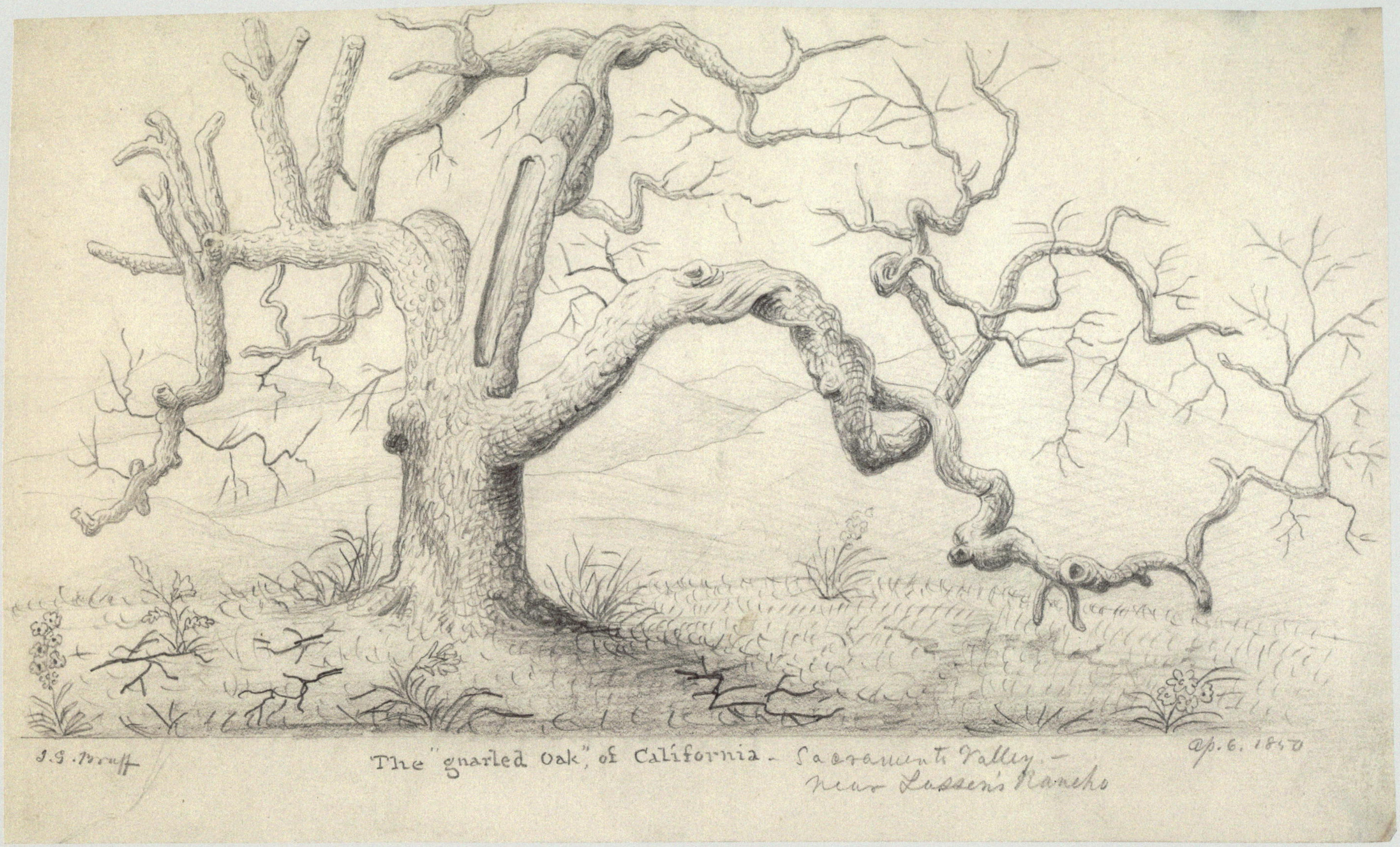

Figure 1
Joseph Goldsborough Bruff, "The 'Gnarled Oak' of California," April 6, 1850. Graphite on paper, 6 × 9½ in. The Huntington, Purchased by Henry E. Huntington, 1919, HM 8044 (150).

The National Tree

In the vast and tattered tapestry of North America's forests, the oak tree stands as an ecological, economic, and cultural symbol of resilience. From the East's sprawling temperate deciduous forests to the Southwest's oak-piñon-juniper woodlands to California's sun-soaked evergreen scrublands, oaks define many American landscapes. Despite a tumultuous history, there are thousands of individual oaks across the United States over 250 years old, with roots deeper than the nation itself.

The long evolutionary journey of oaks is a testament to their adaptability. For over 50 million years, these trees have diversified into more than 400 species worldwide, with about 90 of them native to the United States. Oaks constitute North America's most dominant woody plant genus in both biomass and species richness. Their resilience, even in poor habitats, arises from symbiotic relationships with mycorrhizal fungi, which help their roots absorb nutrients from the soil; their hard, long-lasting wood; and their tannin-rich leaves, which deter herbivores. They sustain myriad wildlife species, sheltering and nourishing birds, insects, and fungi in webs whose complexity is still being discovered.

Centuries before highways and subdivisions crisscrossed and dotted the continent, Indigenous communities relied on acorns as a staple food source. This specialized nut made by all oaks, bearing hundreds of different names in Indigenous languages, is rich in high-quality proteins, fats, and carbohydrates. At one time, acorns constituted the primary daily caloric intake for more than three-quarters of all Native Californians.

Like so many iconic trees in the American landscape, oaks have not escaped the demands of a commercial economy. With settlers came waves of deforestation, and woodlands and forests were thoroughly logged. High-quality, water-resistant oak lumber, harvested for centuries for house construction, shipbuilding, and barrel-making (and still widely used in furniture), formed a crucial part of American infrastructure. By the middle of the twentieth century, expansive forests had become fragmented, putting many species at risk. Urban and suburban expansion, climate change, and new diseases still threaten oak populations, and many efforts are underway by our nation's botanical gardens, arboretums, and universities to conserve these magnificent trees and the ecosystems they support. The continued survival of oak woodlands and forests depends as much on soil and climate as on shifting human values.

Today, the oak stands at a crossroads, as conservationists, urban planners, and residents wrestle with questions of heritage, equity, and environmental stewardship. Not only in woodlands but also in cities and towns, these stately trees provide residents with a sense of place, strength, and permanence. Majestic oaks shade parks and line boulevards. They have become integral to the identity of American communities, as reflected in many names—Oakland, Thousand Oaks, Oak Park, Encino, Paso Robles. By planting and protecting oaks, we safeguard a vital part of our enduring natural and historical legacy.

In 2004, the US Congress designated the oak as America's national tree. This is appropriate, since oaks are so entwined with the American story—a reminder of our deep connection to the natural world, but also a resource that is overexploited and in some places threatened. As long as they stand, oaks will teach us where we have been and where we might yet want to go.

Dr. Matt Ritter is an internationally recognized urban forestry expert, decorated professor, and teacher at California Polytechnic State University, San Luis Obispo. He has spent two decades studying trees and has written several award-winning books, as well as many scientific articles.

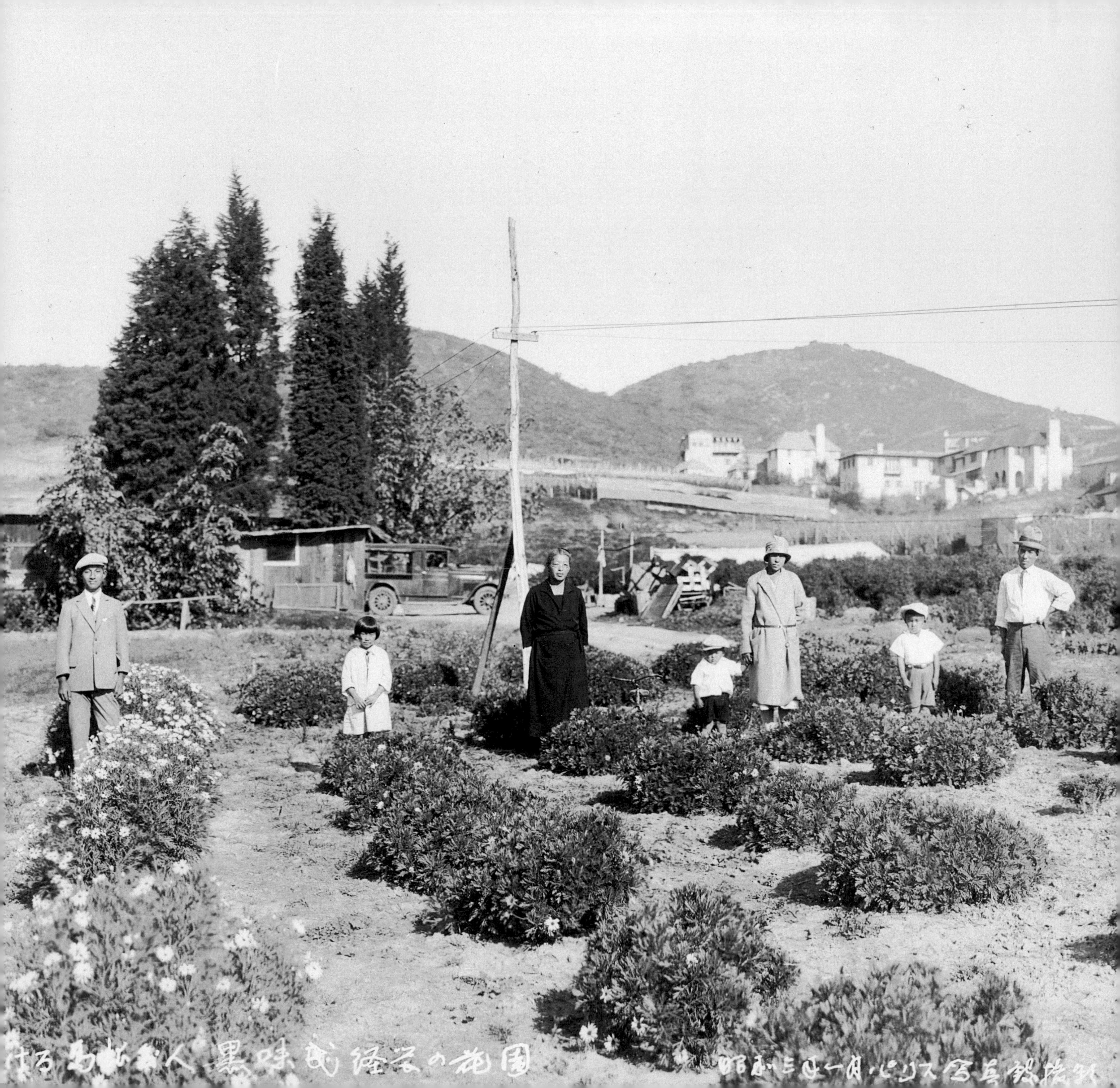

黒味氏経営の花園
昭和三年一月

Uprootings

When a plant is uprooted, it is removed from the earth entirely. It can be relocated to establish a new life or perish in the process. When humans are uprooted, they are displaced from their origins, from their home. Being uprooted is a dynamic event that causes ripples beyond the initial trauma for generations. American history includes countless removals of Indigenous peoples from their homelands. "Uprootings" similarly acknowledges the arrival of new migrants to the land, including the forced migration of millions of enslaved people from Africa to the Americas. The land, much like living organisms, bears the imprint and alteration from these changes.

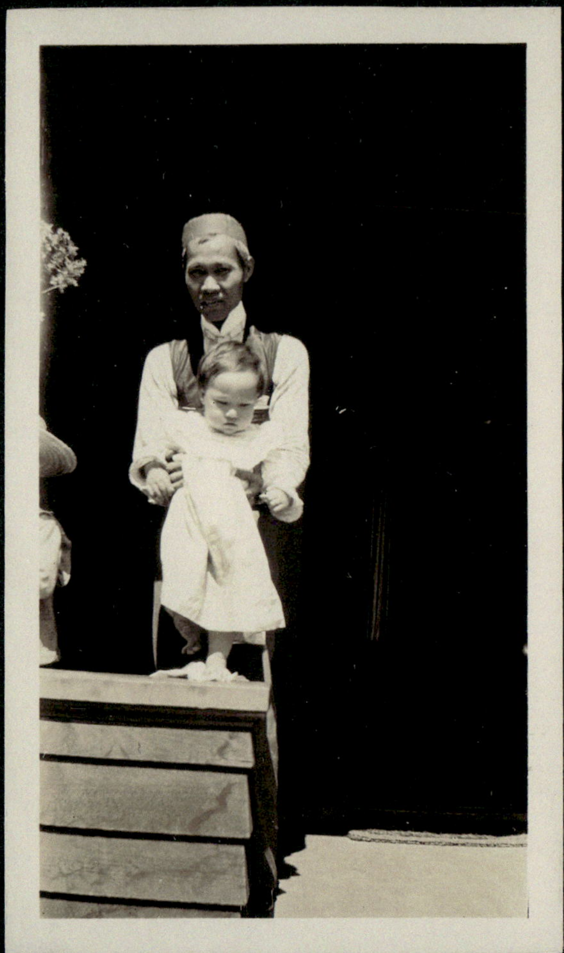

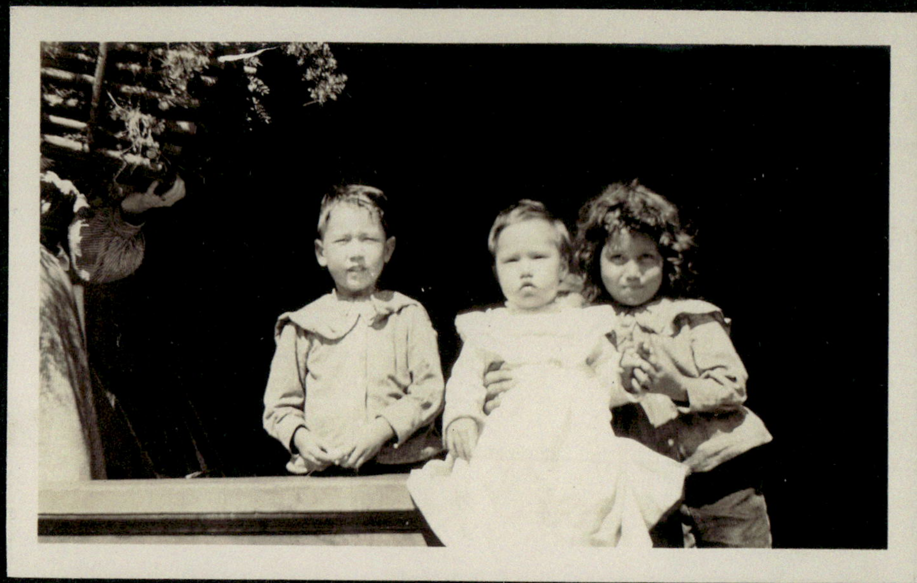

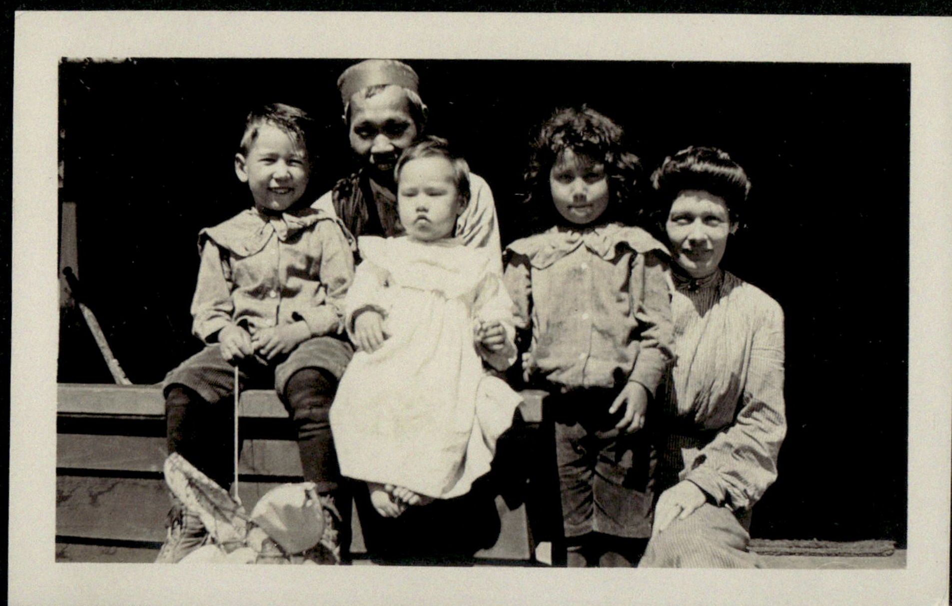

This Land Is . . . Not for My Family

My great-great-grandfather came from China to work on the building of the transcontinental railroad and eventually returned to his home village. His son, my great-grandfather, Fong See, came first to Sacramento, where he did many of the jobs that immigrants do today—washing dishes in restaurants, sweeping up in factories, and working in the fields—but by the early 1890s, he had his first business: making "fancy underwear for fancy ladies." One day, Ticie Pruett, whose family had crossed the country in a Conestoga wagon and homesteaded in Washington, entered the shop and asked for a job. Fong See hired her. One thing led to another, and they decided to get married. I use that term loosely because it was against the law for Chinese down to a quarter to marry a white person in the state of California. Undeterred, Fong See and Ticie Pruett went to a lawyer, who drew up a contract between the two of them as though they were forming a partnership. (My grandparents would go to Mexico to get married, and my parents became one of the first couples in my extended family to marry legally in the state.) The anti-miscegenation law in California was overturned in 1948, but similar laws across the country weren't overturned until 1967 with the *Loving v. Virginia* case.

Discrimination against the Chinese didn't end with who could marry whom. Local laws targeted Chinese laundrymen, fishermen, and other laborers. The Chinese Exclusion Act of 1882 attempted to bar the immigration of *all* Chinese immigrants to these shores. Here in California, the Alien Land Law of 1913 barred the Chinese—"aliens ineligible for citizenship"—from owning property. Later, restrictive covenants would prohibit non-whites and Jews from buying homes in certain neighborhoods. To put it simply, many people, including those of Chinese descent, could work on but not legally stake their claim to American soil.

According to family lore, all my great-grandmother ever wanted was her own home, but Fong See could not buy her one. Instead, he purchased a new car every year, although he never learned to drive. He rented spaces for Chinese antiques shops in Pasadena, Long Beach, Ocean Park, Hollywood, the Mid-Wilshire area, Downtown Los Angeles, and, of course, Chinatown. He was a clever man and even managed to acquire bits of land through bartering. For example, he traded Chinese rugs for a walnut grove in Hacienda Heights. None of these transactions got Ticie any closer to owning her own home, however; Fong See, Ticie, and their children lived above the family store throughout their marriage.

Things began to change with the second generation in the 1920s. The deed for my grandparents' home was held under a friend's name—something that proved quite challenging decades later after my grandmother died. My great-uncle Ray, who could "pass," bought a home in Beverly Hills. "Never tell anyone you're part Chinese," he often warned his daughters. "If you do, we'll lose our house, I'll lose my job, and you'll lose your friends." Even as a child, I understood that the homes my relatives owned marked a triumph over decades of racism and discrimination, but what struck me—and what I loved most—were the gardens. No roses and lawns for my family! Instead, they created cross-cultural, magical spaces lush with Chinese cymbidiums, bamboo, and Bodhi trees and rich with California's bounty of hearty vines and fruit trees. My family had finally made *this* land *their* land.

Lisa See is a New York Times *best-selling author. Her first book,* On Gold Mountain*, tells the story of her Chinese American family's settlement in Los Angeles.*

Figure 1
Page from Grace Nicholson photo album showing Fong See and Ticie Pruett with their three children at the time, Milton (Ming), Ray, and Bennie, ca. 1905. They would have two more children after this, Eddy and Florence (Sissee). Grace Nicholson knew Fong See through her collecting of Asian antiques. Gelatin silver prints. Grace Nicholson Photograph Collection, The Huntington, photCL 56.

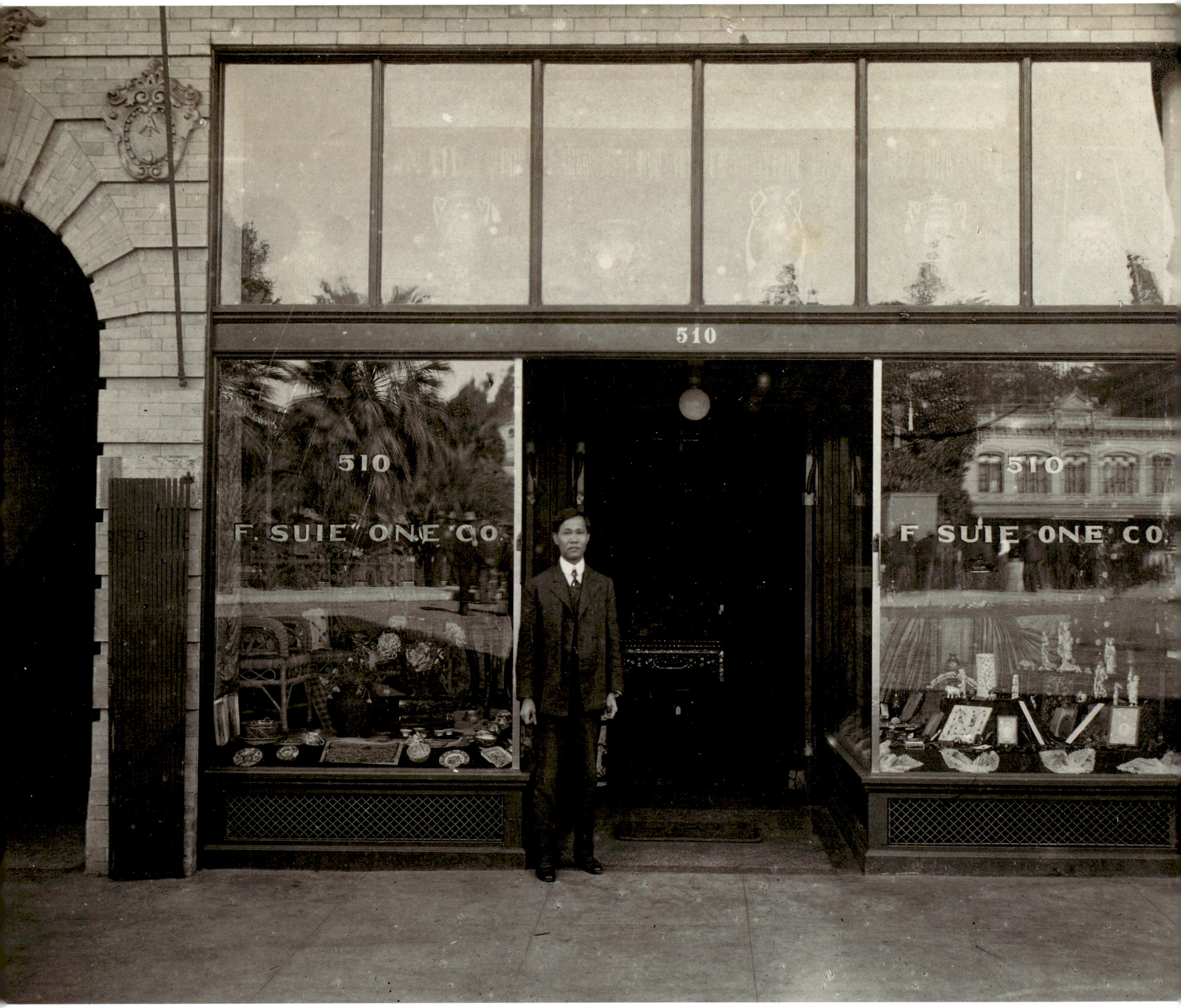
510
510
F. SUIE ONE CO.
510
F. SUIE ONE CO.

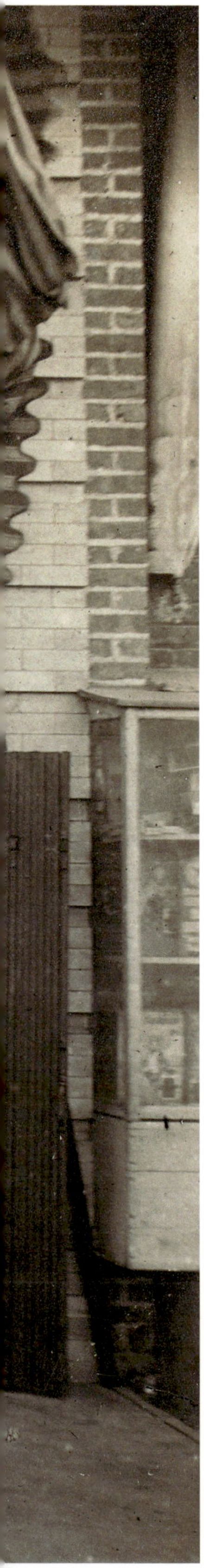

Figure 2
Fong See was born in China and immigrated to the United States at age fourteen. Years later, he and his wife, Ticie Pruett, opened a thriving Asian antiques business in Los Angeles, F. Suie One Co., and became exceedingly prosperous. The oldest continuously operated business of its kind in the country, F. Suie One remains in the family, now on Colorado Boulevard in Pasadena. Fong See in front of F. Suie One Co. storefront, ca. 1906. Gelatin silver print. Gilbert, Florence, and Leslee See Leong Collection, The Huntington.

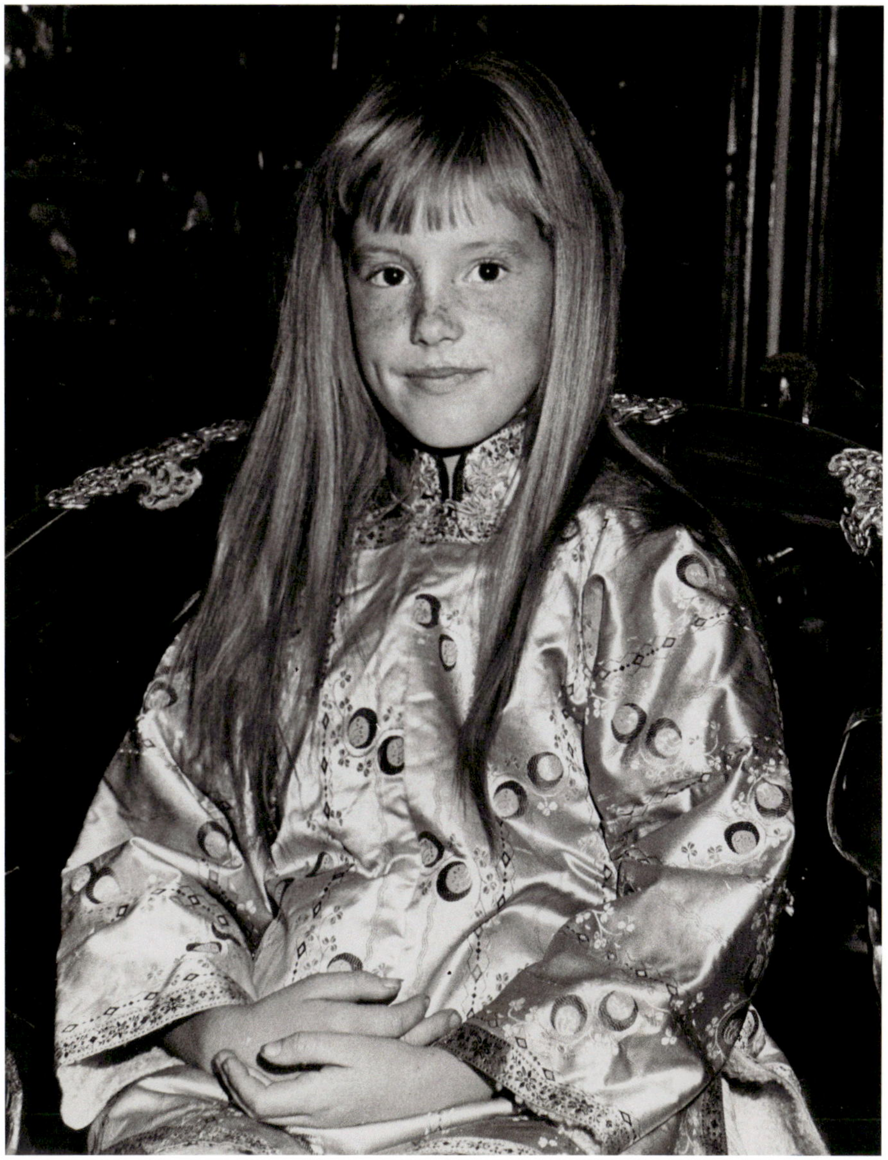

Figure 3
Lisa See in F. Suie One Co. store, 1963, unknown photographer. Gelatin silver print. Courtesy of Lisa See.

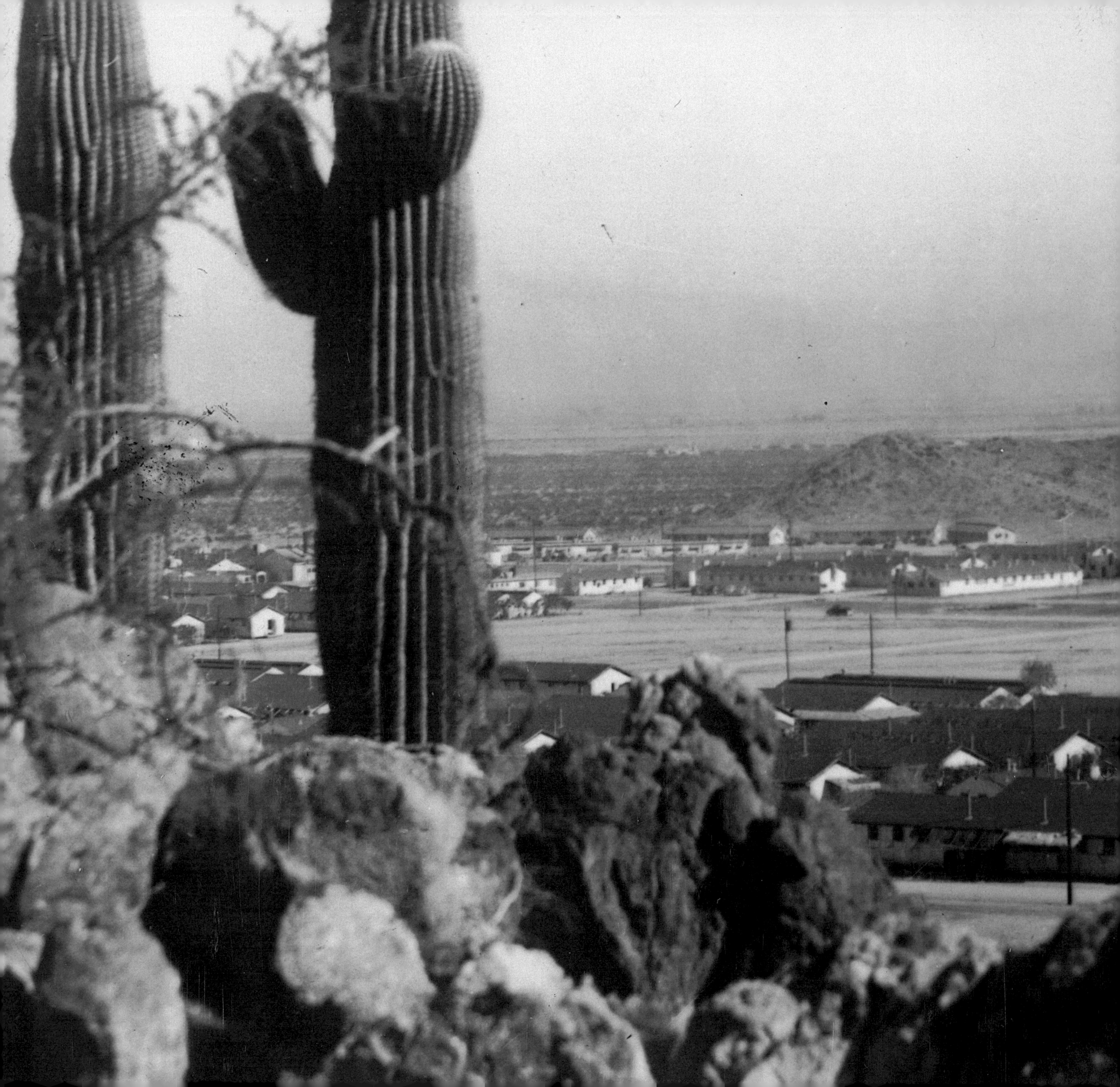

Kiku Hughes and
Julie Fiveash

Seeds

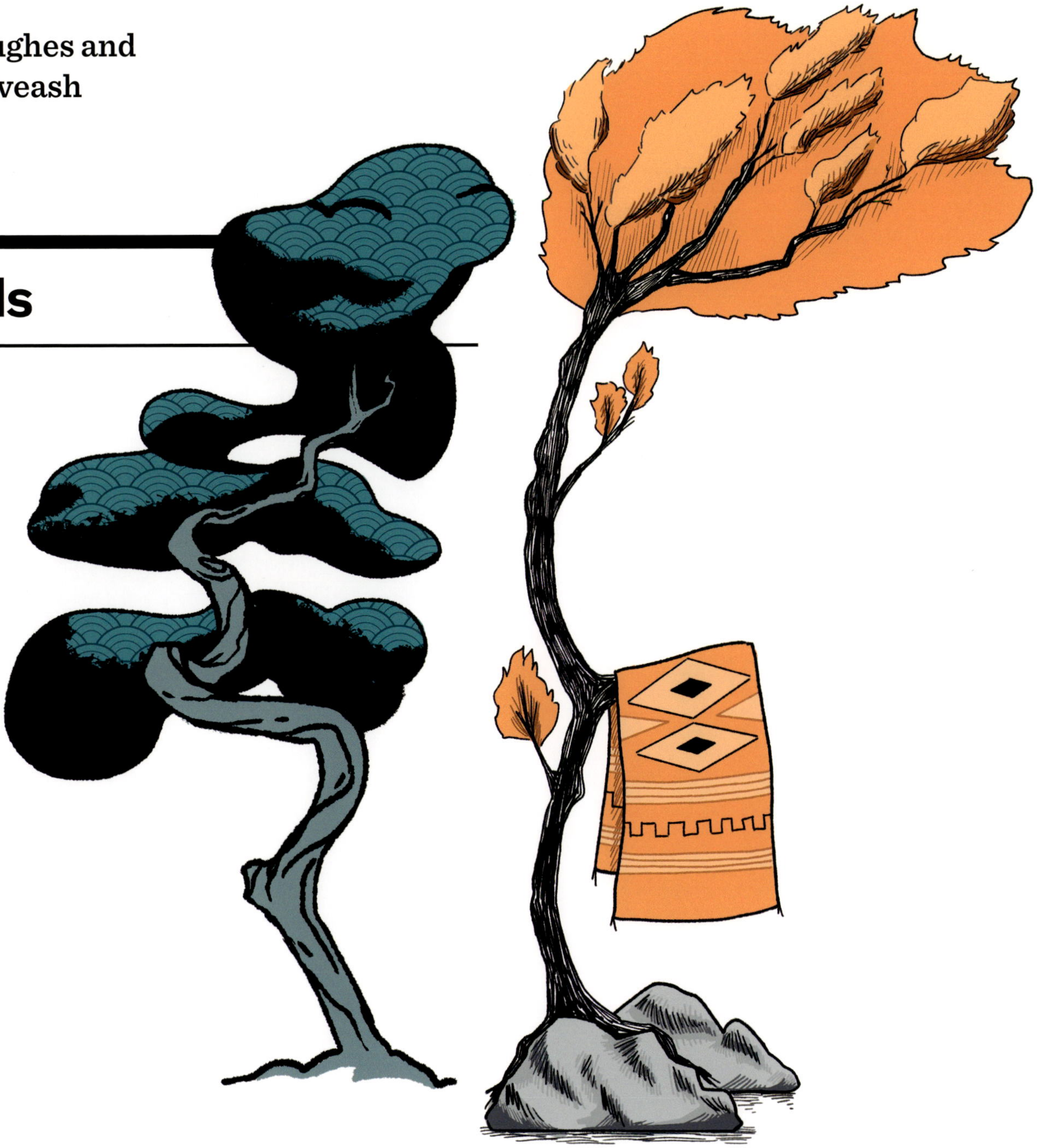

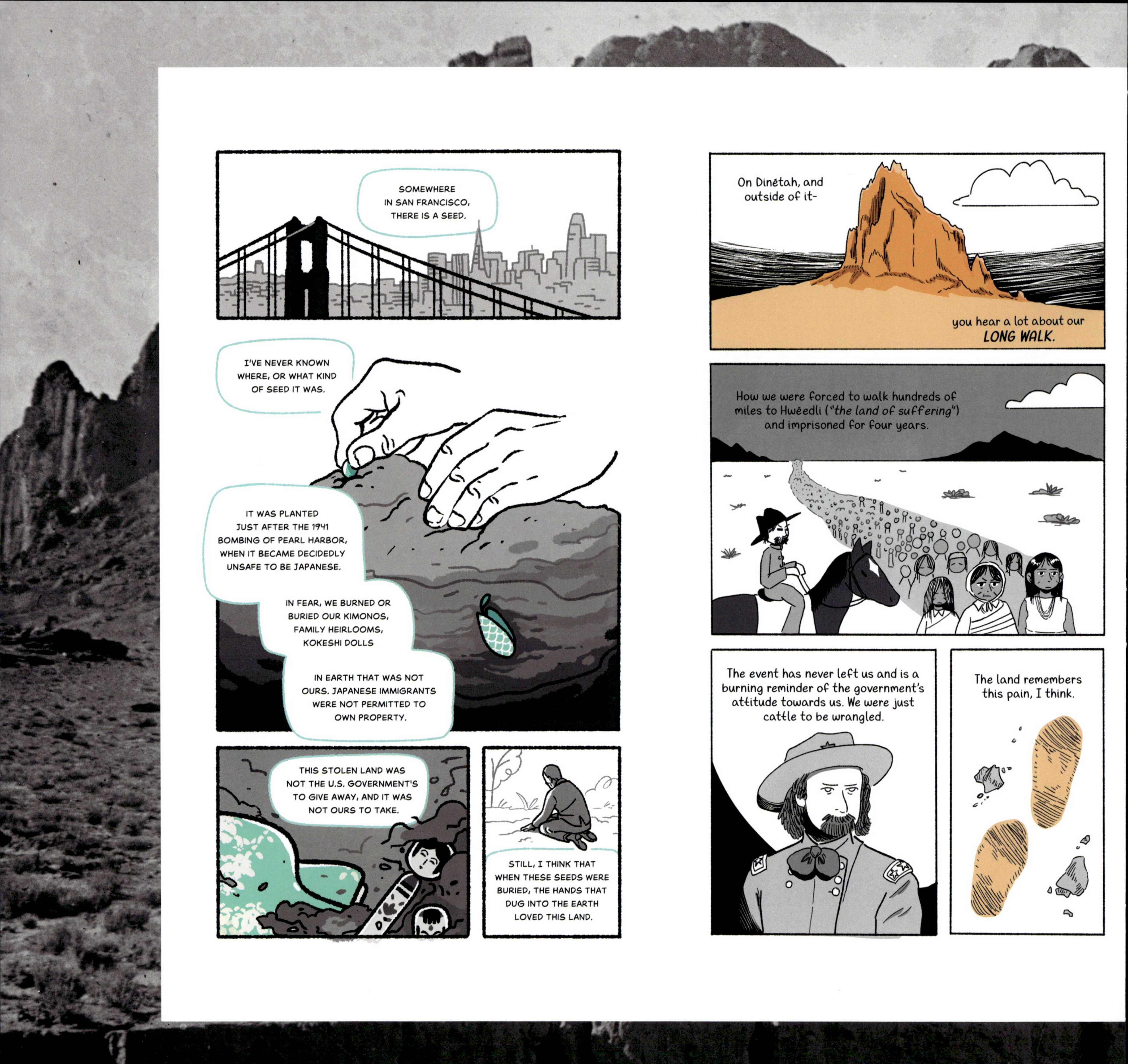

SOMEWHERE IN SAN FRANCISCO, THERE IS A SEED.
I'VE NEVER KNOWN WHERE, OR WHAT KIND OF SEED IT WAS.
IT WAS PLANTED JUST AFTER THE 1941 BOMBING OF PEARL HARBOR, WHEN IT BECAME DECIDEDLY UNSAFE TO BE JAPANESE.
IN FEAR, WE BURNED OR BURIED OUR KIMONOS, FAMILY HEIRLOOMS, KOKESHI DOLLS
IN EARTH THAT WAS NOT OURS. JAPANESE IMMIGRANTS WERE NOT PERMITTED TO OWN PROPERTY.
THIS STOLEN LAND WAS NOT THE U.S. GOVERNMENT'S TO GIVE AWAY, AND IT WAS NOT OURS TO TAKE.
STILL, I THINK THAT WHEN THESE SEEDS WERE BURIED, THE HANDS THAT DUG INTO THE EARTH LOVED THIS LAND.
On Dinétah, and outside of it-
you hear a lot about our LONG WALK.
How we were forced to walk hundreds of miles to Hwéedli ("the land of suffering") and imprisoned for four years.
The event has never left us and is a burning reminder of the government's attitude towards us. We were just cattle to be wrangled.
The land remembers this pain, I think.

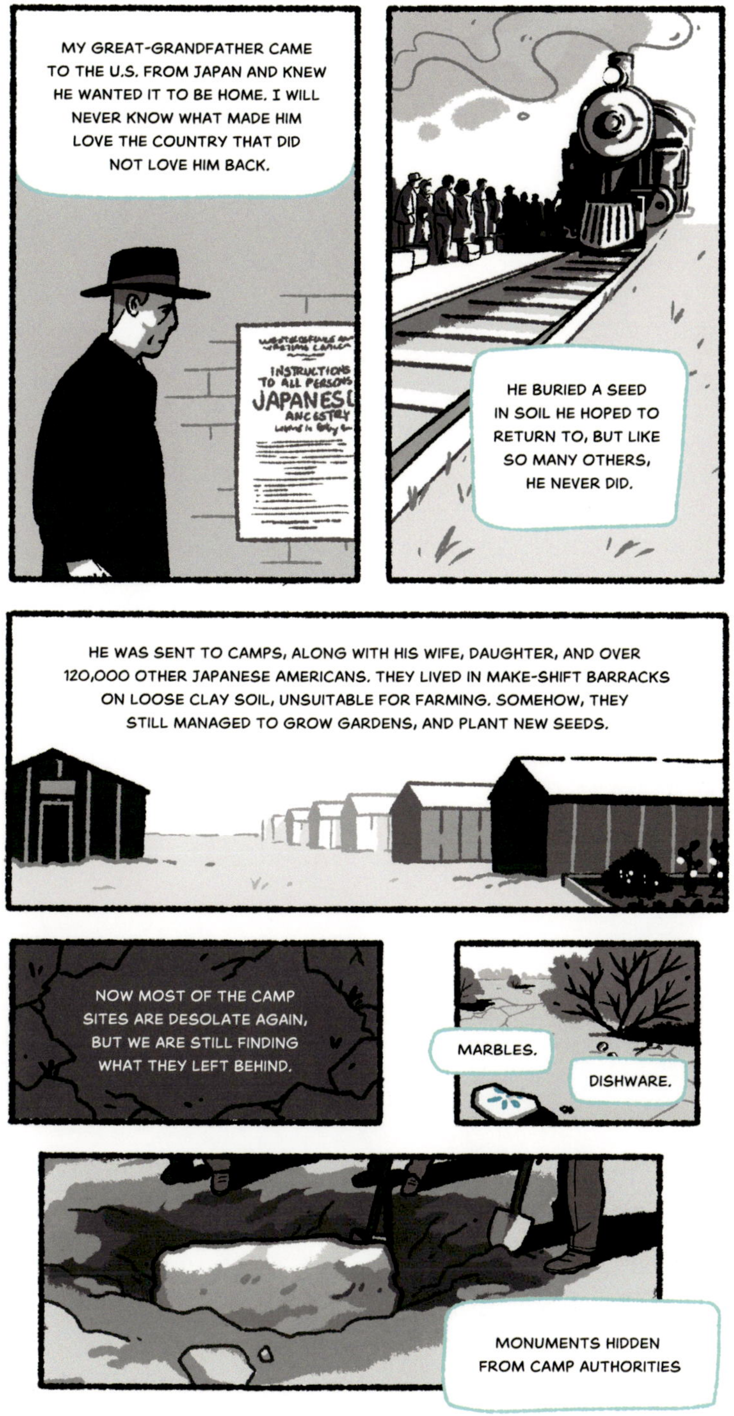
MY GREAT-GRANDFATHER CAME TO THE U.S. FROM JAPAN AND KNEW HE WANTED IT TO BE HOME. I WILL NEVER KNOW WHAT MADE HIM LOVE THE COUNTRY THAT DID NOT LOVE HIM BACK.
HE BURIED A SEED IN SOIL HE HOPED TO RETURN TO, BUT LIKE SO MANY OTHERS, HE NEVER DID.
HE WAS SENT TO CAMPS, ALONG WITH HIS WIFE, DAUGHTER, AND OVER 120,000 OTHER JAPANESE AMERICANS. THEY LIVED IN MAKE-SHIFT BARRACKS ON LOOSE CLAY SOIL, UNSUITABLE FOR FARMING. SOMEHOW, THEY STILL MANAGED TO GROW GARDENS, AND PLANT NEW SEEDS.
NOW MOST OF THE CAMP SITES ARE DESOLATE AGAIN, BUT WE ARE STILL FINDING WHAT THEY LEFT BEHIND.
MARBLES.
DISHWARE.
MONUMENTS HIDDEN FROM CAMP AUTHORITIES

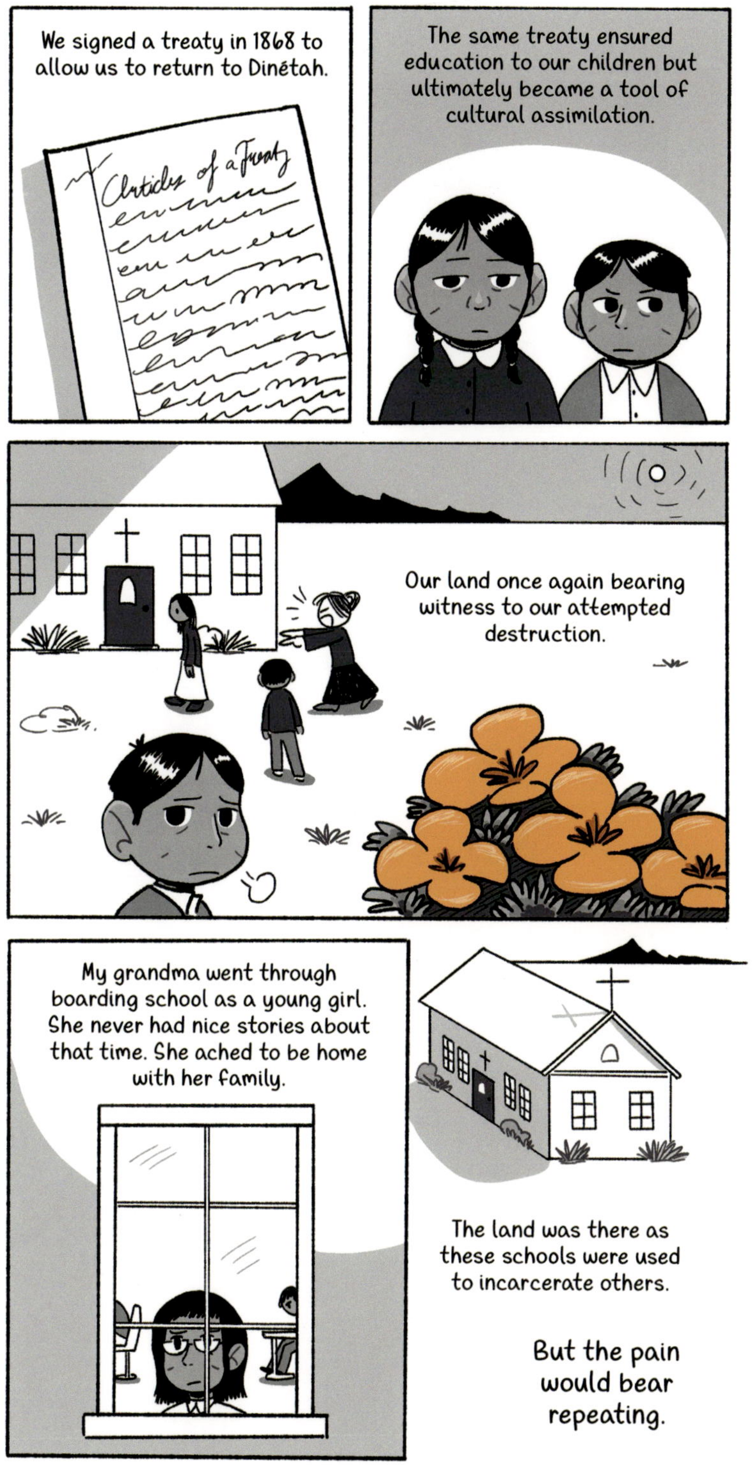
We signed a treaty in 1868 to allow us to return to Dinétah.
The same treaty ensured education to our children but ultimately became a tool of cultural assimilation.
Our land once again bearing witness to our attempted destruction.
My grandma went through boarding school as a young girl. She never had nice stories about that time. She ached to be home with her family.
The land was there as these schools were used to incarcerate others.
But the pain would bear repeating.

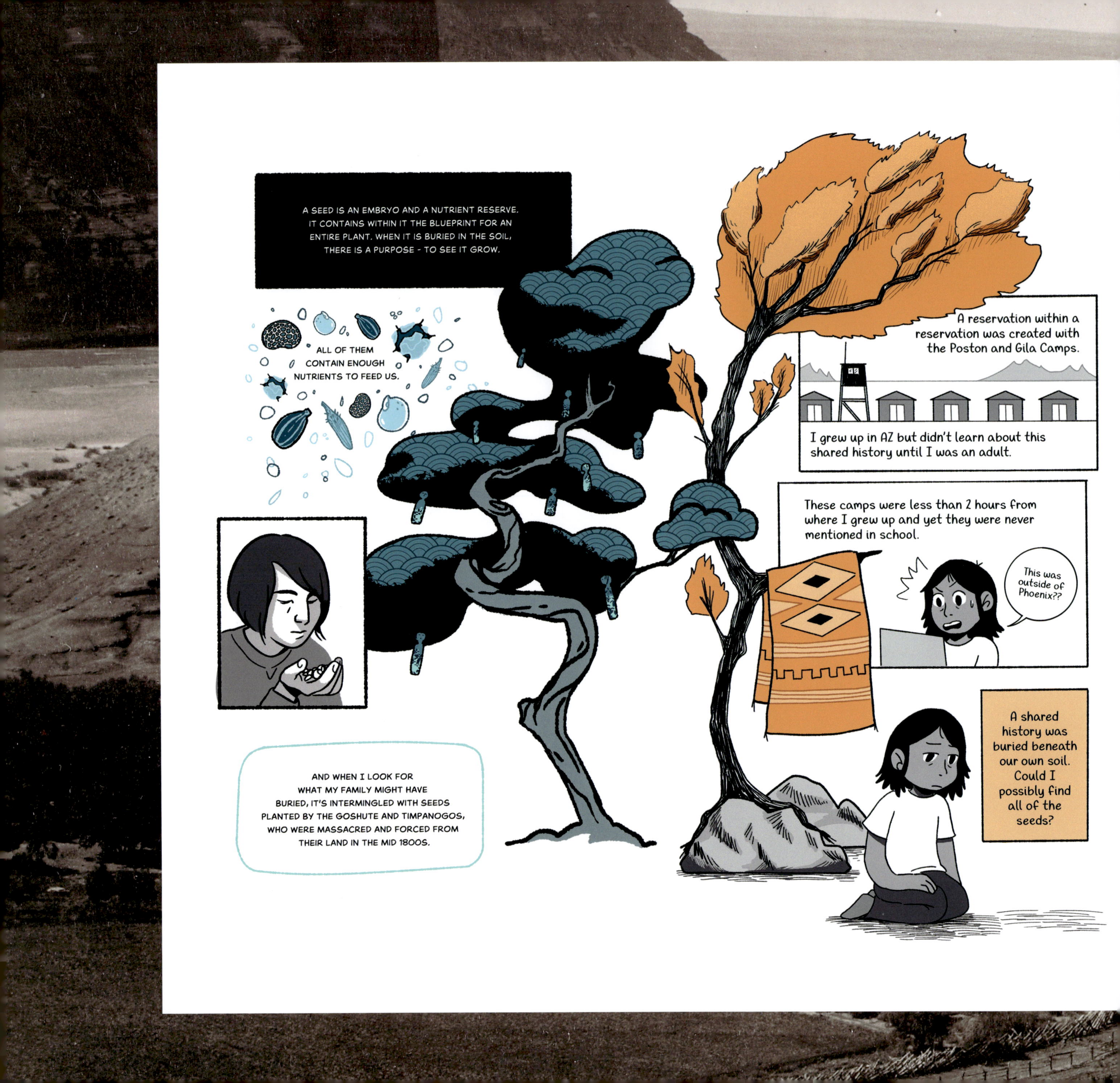

A SEED IS AN EMBRYO AND A NUTRIENT RESERVE. IT CONTAINS WITHIN IT THE BLUEPRINT FOR AN ENTIRE PLANT. WHEN IT IS BURIED IN THE SOIL, THERE IS A PURPOSE - TO SEE IT GROW.
ALL OF THEM CONTAIN ENOUGH NUTRIENTS TO FEED US.
AND WHEN I LOOK FOR WHAT MY FAMILY MIGHT HAVE BURIED, IT'S INTERMINGLED WITH SEEDS PLANTED BY THE GOSHUTE AND TIMPANOGOS, WHO WERE MASSACRED AND FORCED FROM THEIR LAND IN THE MID 1800S.
A reservation within a reservation was created with the Poston and Gila Camps.
I grew up in AZ but didn't learn about this shared history until I was an adult.
These camps were less than 2 hours from where I grew up and yet they were never mentioned in school.
This was outside of Phoenix??
A shared history was buried beneath our own soil. Could I possibly find all of the seeds?

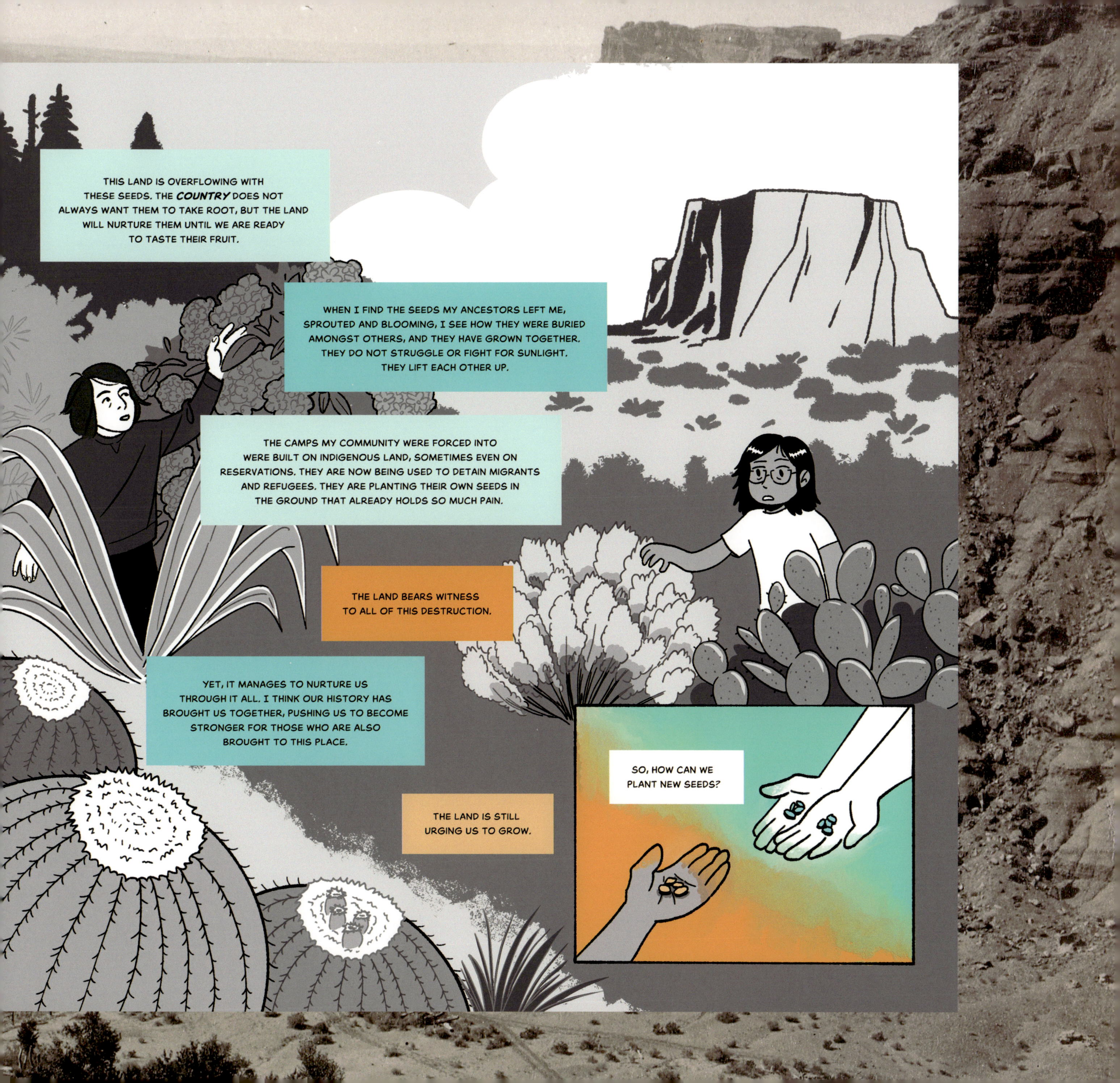
THIS LAND IS OVERFLOWING WITH THESE SEEDS. THE *COUNTRY* DOES NOT ALWAYS WANT THEM TO TAKE ROOT, BUT THE LAND WILL NURTURE THEM UNTIL WE ARE READY TO TASTE THEIR FRUIT.
WHEN I FIND THE SEEDS MY ANCESTORS LEFT ME, SPROUTED AND BLOOMING, I SEE HOW THEY WERE BURIED AMONGST OTHERS, AND THEY HAVE GROWN TOGETHER. THEY DO NOT STRUGGLE OR FIGHT FOR SUNLIGHT. THEY LIFT EACH OTHER UP.
THE CAMPS MY COMMUNITY WERE FORCED INTO WERE BUILT ON INDIGENOUS LAND, SOMETIMES EVEN ON RESERVATIONS. THEY ARE NOW BEING USED TO DETAIN MIGRANTS AND REFUGEES. THEY ARE PLANTING THEIR OWN SEEDS IN THE GROUND THAT ALREADY HOLDS SO MUCH PAIN.
THE LAND BEARS WITNESS TO ALL OF THIS DESTRUCTION.
YET, IT MANAGES TO NURTURE US THROUGH IT ALL. I THINK OUR HISTORY HAS BROUGHT US TOGETHER, PUSHING US TO BECOME STRONGER FOR THOSE WHO ARE ALSO BROUGHT TO THIS PLACE.
THE LAND IS STILL URGING US TO GROW.
SO, HOW CAN WE PLANT NEW SEEDS?

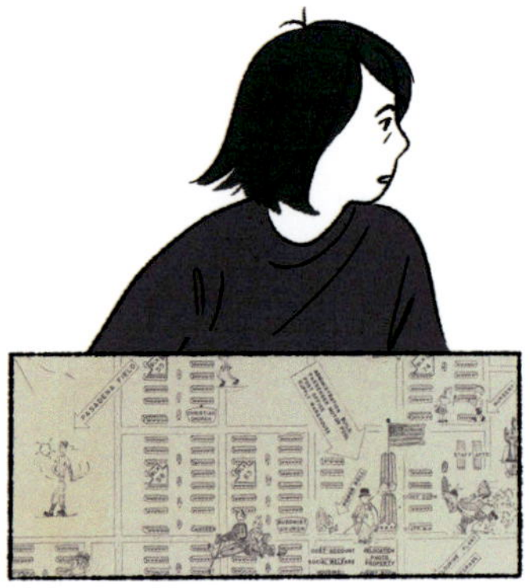

Every time I write about this history, the relatively recent history of Japanese American incarceration and its aftereffects, I'm overwhelmed by all the things I want to share. Stories from the camps are endless, each one providing a unique perspective into the experience and into the systems that fit the camps seamlessly into White America's idea of itself. I want to share everything, but here I'll limit myself to answering a question I get a lot: Why comics?

Comics are not only my preferred storytelling medium, they are also central to camp storytelling. From the beginning, visual arts played a huge role in camp. Cartoonists decorated early camp maps, like this one (opposite page) possibly drawn by Alan Taniguchi, who depicted the geography of Gila River with humor and a personal touch.

Then, in 1946, a young woman named Miné Okubo published *Citizen 13660*, an illustrated diary of her time spent at Topaz, and the first publication about camp written by a Japanese American. This foundation of camp literature was a comic. Okubo's work stands with so many others that demonstrate the power of mixing written words with drawings for a fuller meaning. The fact that *Citizen 13660* was still subject to War Relocation Authority censorship meant that the illustrations must do the work of words Okubo was not allowed to write. Comics are keepers of dangerous history.

Finally, I urge you to look up the Wakasa Memorial Committee and read the story of a "seed." I referenced it briefly as "monuments hidden from camp authorities." The massive stone memorial to James Wakasa, a man murdered by camp guards in 1943, was ordered to be removed by the camp administration and was presumed destroyed until its rediscovery in 2020. We are still finding seeds throughout this country, and if allowed to grow, they will share stories that those in power have tried to keep buried. —KIKU HUGHES

Kiku Hughes is a Japanese American (Yonsei) cartoonist based in the Seattle area. Her first graphic novel, Displacement, *was published by First Second in 2020 and was an APALA Literature Award honor title and an Eisner Award nominee.*

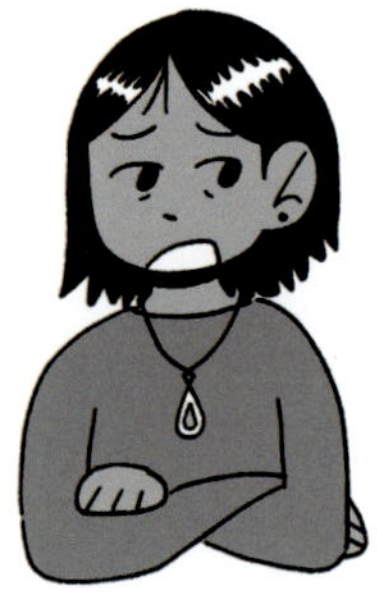

It was funny being pulled into this comic as a co-creator because I was so intrigued by just *how* many connections there were between these two huge events. More and more connections came flooding in as Kiku and I both started talking about how our families were affected by government actions, leading to this shared land history.

Among the things I found out in this project was the dual use of boarding-school sites. The idea that these spaces of forced education would later be used as a space of forced incarceration should not have been surprising for me to find out, and yet it still was. Sadder still was that the land itself was treated as a prison. There's a way that the desert is viewed by others who are not from it. They find it dry and inhospitable, bizarre that any group (or groups) of people could inhabit such a desolate space. But the Diné and so many others have thrived in that land for countless generations. Its beauty can be found by those looking for it, even those who are forced to live in it. I'm gutted that Japanese Americans were not able to find it themselves upon visiting and were rather forced to endure life in a land that should've welcomed them with open arms. The desert and its people deserve better than that.

This project highlighted to me that we need to continue educating Native people and non-Native people about the abuses that happened on this land, at Poston, Gila, and Fort Leupp. We can do so much more together, with our shared history, than we can apart. I hope this comic is another step in that direction and that the desert won't be witness to just pain in the future, but to seeds and regrowth. —JULIE FIVEASH

Julie Fiveash is a Diné and mixed-race cartoonist and librarian originally from Yuma, Arizona. Their work has been featured in two Dirty Diamond comic anthologies, The Baylies *by Laneha House,* Portals of Indigenous Futurisms *by Abalone Mountain Press, and* The Out Side: Trans and Non-Binary Comics *by Andrews-McMeel Publishing. They are currently working on their first graphic novel, to be published through Levine Querido.*

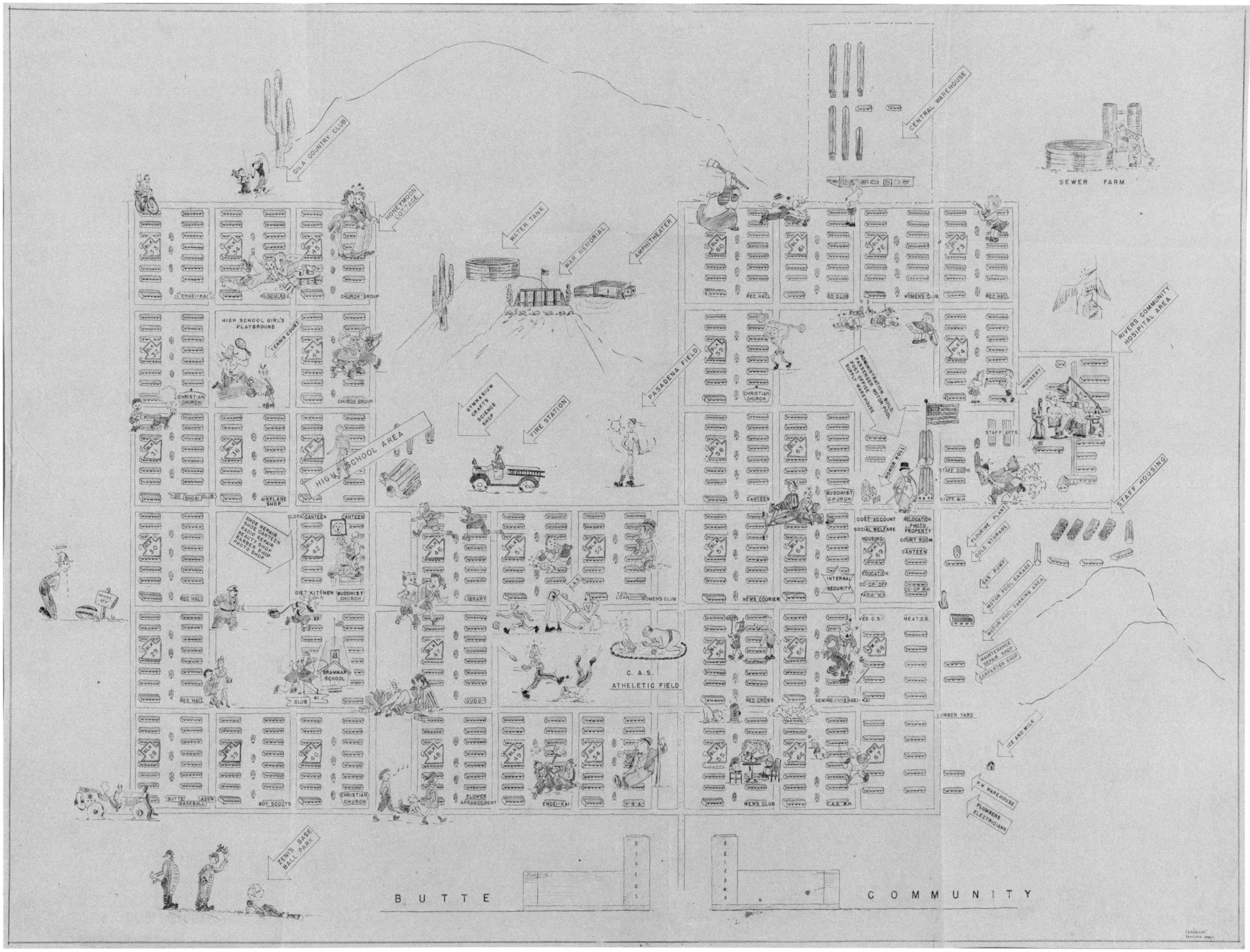

Above: Attributed to Alan Taniguchi, comic map of Butte Community, Gila River Relocation Center, ca. 1942–45 (detail on following spread). Diazotype print, 28¾ × 39 in. Arthur Ito Papers, The Huntington, Gift of James A. Ito and Paul N. Coman.

pp. 62–63: View of the Butte Camp, Gila River Relocation Center (detail), 1945. Gelatin silver print, 8⅛ × 10 in. Arthur Ito Papers, The Huntington, Gift of James A. Ito and Paul N. Coman.

pp. 64–65: Ship Rock, New Mexico (detail), ca. 1910. Lantern slide, 3 × 4 in. Edith Metcalf Collection of Navajo Indian Lantern Slides. The Huntington, Gift of Edith Metcalf, photCL 517.

pp. 66–67: Charles C. Pierce, *Lee's Ferry Junction of Marble and Glen* [*Canyons*] (detail), date unknown. Gelatin silver print, 6 × 8 in. C. C. Pierce Collection of Photographs, The Huntington, photCL Pierce 09688.

p. 68: George P. Thresher, Cave opening in cliff with graffiti (detail), ca. 1898–1910. Photograph from glass negative. The Huntington, photCL 449 (3).

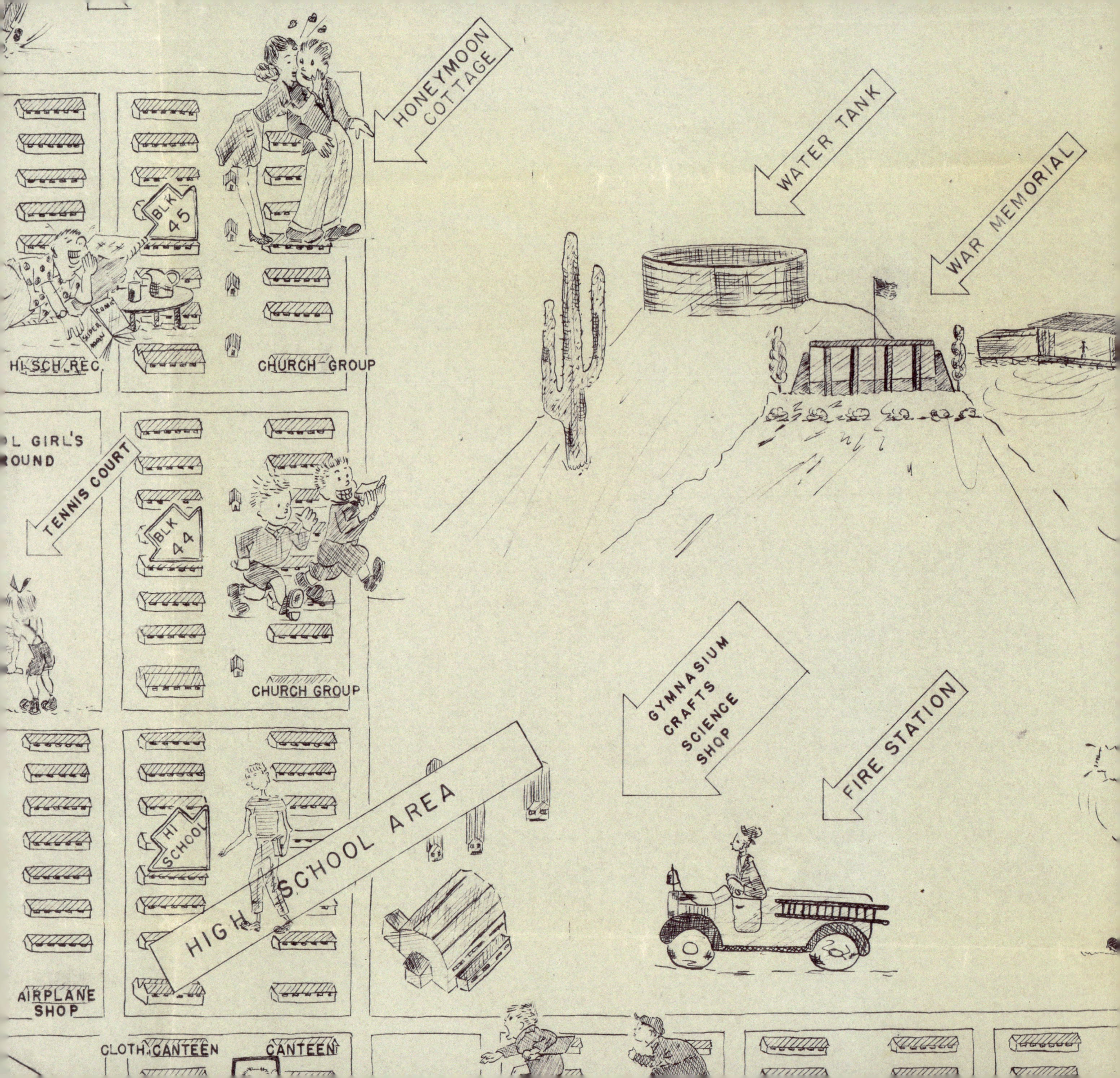

HONEYMOON COTTAGE
WATER TANK
WAR MEMORIAL
BLK 45
HI.SCH.REC.
CHURCH GROUP
L GIRL'S
ROUND
TENNIS COURT
BLK 44
CHURCH GROUP
GYMNASIUM
CRAFTS
SCIENCE
SHOP
FIRE STATION
HI SCHOOL
HIGH SCHOOL AREA
AIRPLANE SHOP
CLOTH. CANTEEN
CANTEEN

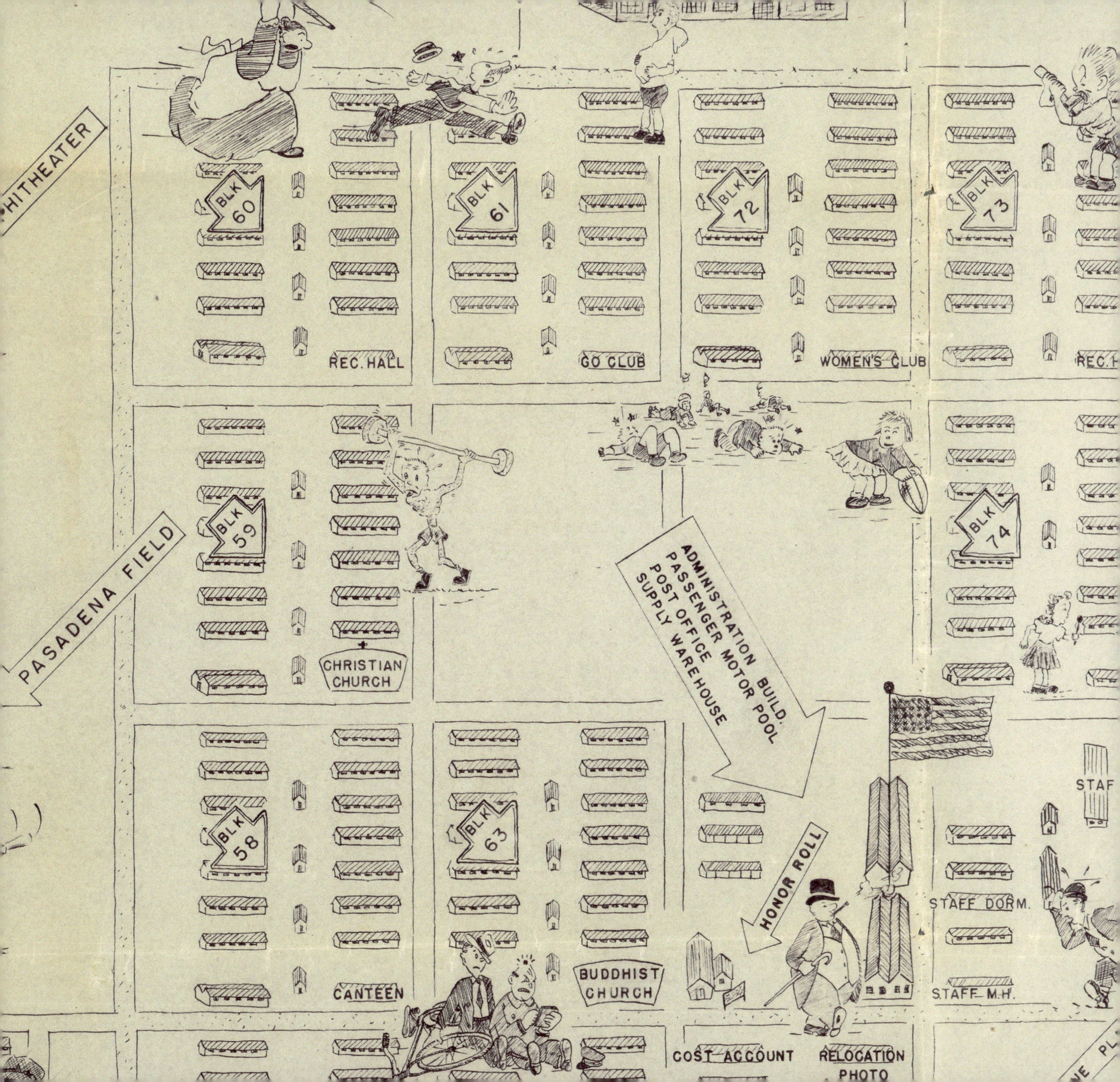

PHITHEATER
BLK 60
BLK 61
BLK 72
BLK 73
REC. HALL
GO CLUB
WOMEN'S CLUB
BLK 59
BLK 74
PASADENA FIELD
ADMINISTRATION BUILD.
PASSENGER MOTOR POOL
POST OFFICE
SUPPLY WAREHOUSE
CHRISTIAN CHURCH
BLK 58
BLK 63
HONOR ROLL
STAFF DORM.
CANTEEN
BUDDHIST CHURCH
STAFF M.H.
COST ACCOUNT
RELOCATION
PHOTO

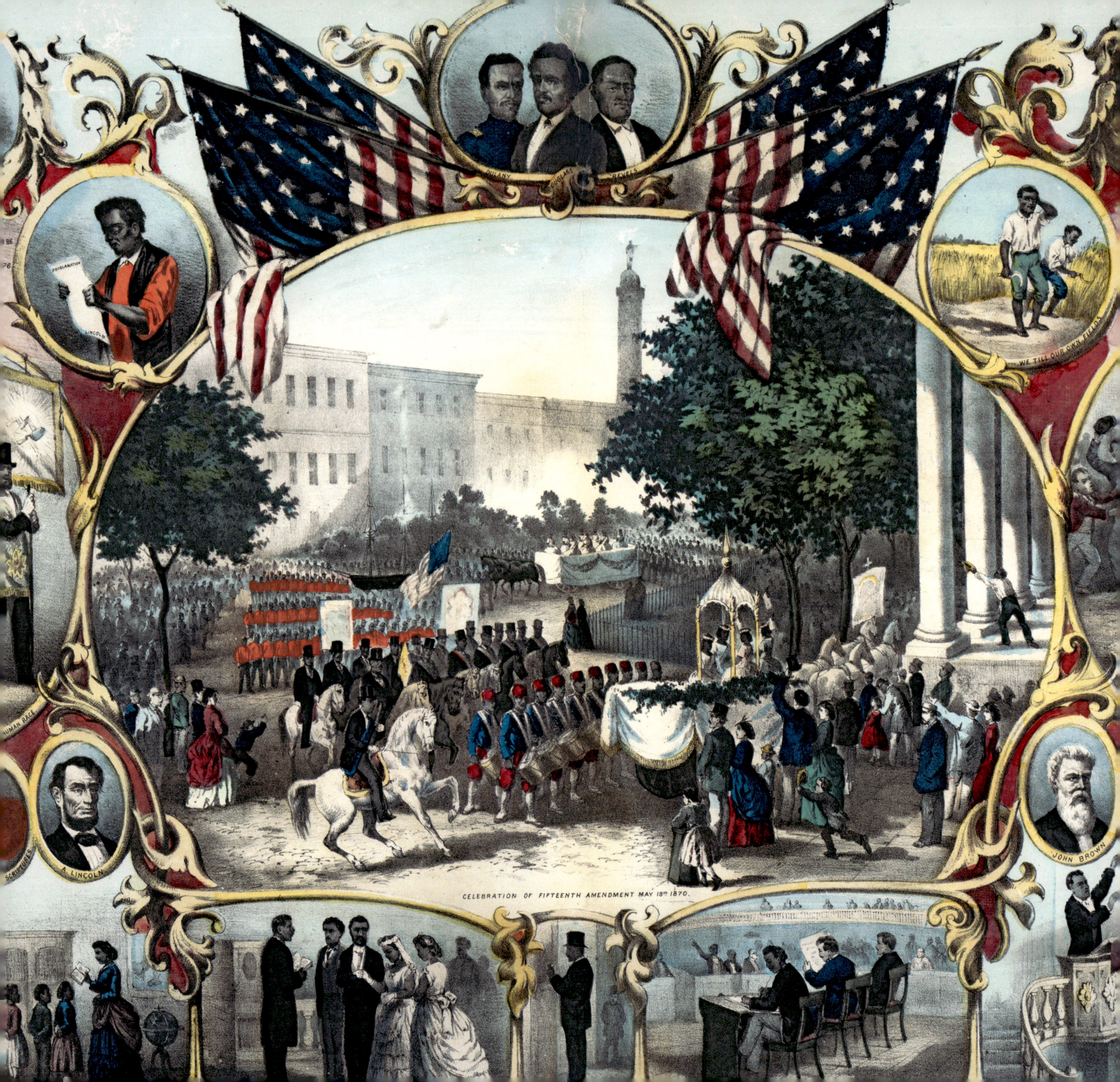
DOUGLASS
REVELS
PROCLAMATION
LINCOLN
WE TILL OUR OWN FIELDS
JOHN BROWN
A. LINCOLN
CELEBRATION OF FIFTEENTH AMENDMENT MAY 19th 1870.

Amendments

In horticulture, an amendment is material added to a soil to improve its physical or chemical properties for plant growth. The goal is to provide a better environment for roots. The United States has similarly amended its governing document—the Constitution—to enhance the societal structure on which it was founded. Authors, lawmakers, and everyday people continually revise other documents and cultural and political practices, written and unwritten. They make amends. This has often led to expanded civil and human rights for historically marginalized groups, improving their lives in an evolving nation. "Amendments" speaks to the dynamic nature of nation-building and history-making.

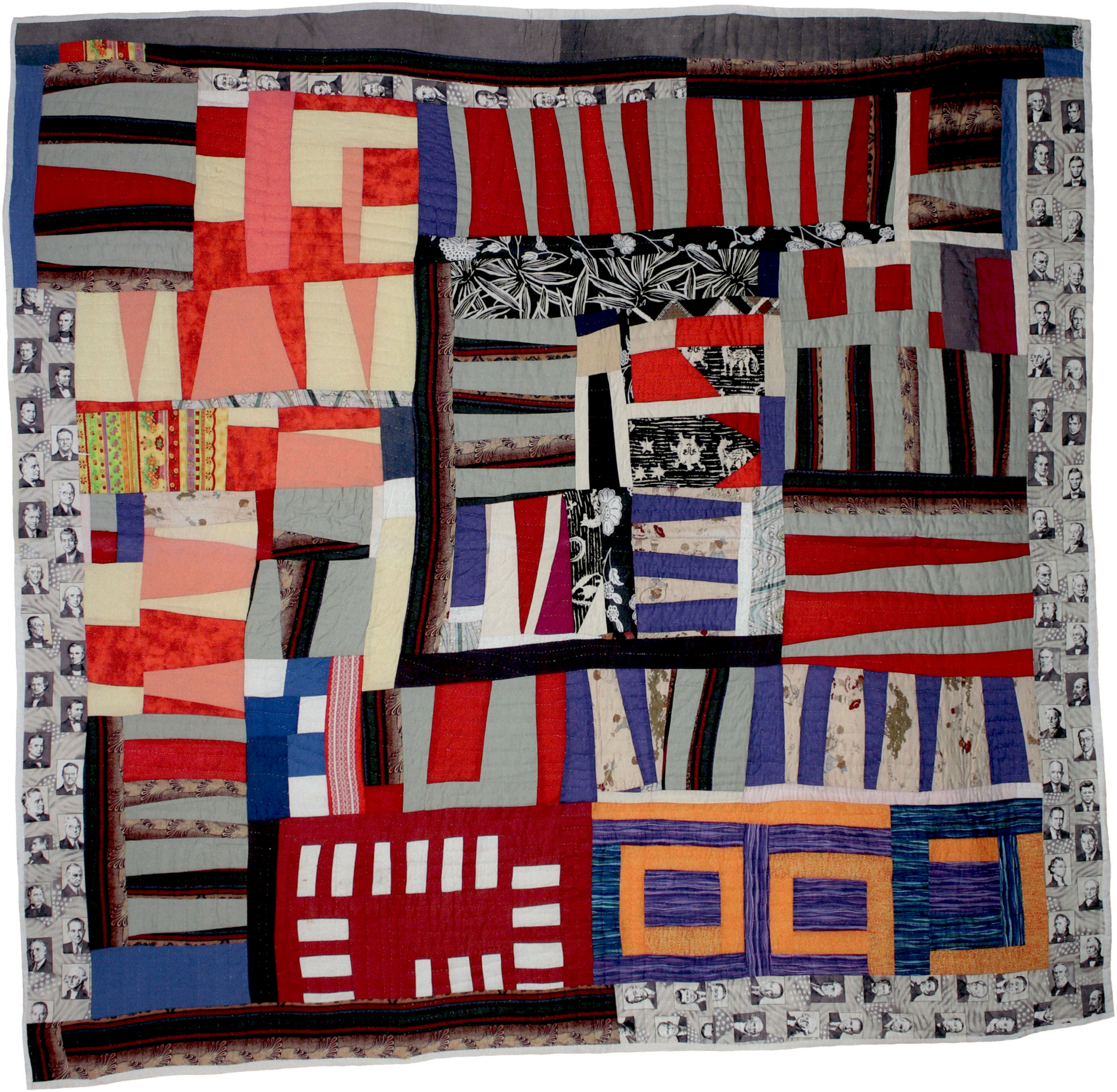

A Handful of Freedom

This quilt was made by Mary Lee Bendolph, one of the artists in the famous collective of African American quilters in Gee's Bend, Alabama. In the 1930s, the descendants of enslaved people and sharecroppers purchased former plantation lands in Gee's Bend through low-interest federal loans. Community members soon established farming and quilting cooperatives and joined the civil rights movement. In 2009, Bendolph intended this quilt, featuring fabric printed with the faces of former American presidents, as an inauguration gift for President Barack Obama and First Lady Michelle Obama. The community of quilters in Gee's Bend made another quilt collectively that was given as a gift to the Obamas, and this quilt remained with Bendolph. Mary Lee Bendolph, *Image of Formal Presidents*, 2009. Cotton, 81 × 73 in. The Huntington, Purchased with funds from the Art Collectors' Council, 2021.3.1.

There is something so powerful and so essential about land: the sustenance that comes from tilling the soil; the spiritual connections that have shaped cultures around the globe; and the marriage of toil, productivity, and character. Yet for African Americans, the land has meant so much more.

In the early 1960s, like so many Black families, we would "go down south" to visit relatives who had not journeyed north during the Great Migration of the early twentieth century. We would travel from New Jersey to visit my maternal grandparents in Woodland, a rural North Carolina town where generations of my family, enslaved and free, were tied to this small agrarian community sharply divided by racial segregation. Three hundred white residents lived on one side of town, and three hundred Black citizens on the other side of the railroad tracks. Johnnie and Flossie Boone—my mother's parents—owned six hundred acres of farmland. Usually, I just reveled in this strange land, where feeding the animals and being surrounded by vast swaths of crops seemed so exotic.

I remember one Easter, my grandfather insisted that I accompany him as he strolled through the fields of corn, peanuts, and cotton. At some point he stopped, reached down to grab a bit of soil, and told me to hold it in my small hand. To me it was just dirt; I could not understand why he wanted me to get my hands dirty. He asked if I knew what this was. I answered, a tad exasperated, that it was just dirt. He told me to squeeze the soil, to revere the land, because I was not holding dirt; I was holding a handful of freedom.

To Johnnie Boone, while the land provided food for his family and enabled him to achieve the middle-class status that was denied to sharecroppers and tenant farmers, more important was the fact that owning his own land was both a symbol of and a means to asserting one's freedom. After all, he was the child of parents who were once enslaved. That notion of the power and importance of owning land as a key factor in obtaining and maintaining Black freedom, while imbued in my family's story, has had a powerful lure and impact on Black America for generations.

A prime example is the significance and influence of land ownership as a key reason for the migration of many African Americans to Los Angeles in the early twentieth century. In 1913, W. E. B. Du Bois concluded his first visit to the region by declaring, a bit too optimistically, "Out here in this matchless Southern California, there would seem to be no limits on your opportunities, your possibilities." Part of his optimism flowed from the fact that the population of Black Angelenos would increase dramatically from 3,000 in 1900 to 7,500 in 1910 to nearly 16,000 in 1920. While some of the appeal of Los Angeles was the escape from so much of the racial violence endemic to the Jim Crow South, a key factor was the ability to acquire land. From 1910 to 1920, Los Angeles had the highest percentage of Black home ownership in the nation, other than all-Black towns such as Mound Bayou, Mississippi, or Boley, Oklahoma.

For African Americans, land was a symbol not just of economic opportunity, identity, or cultural resiliency but of freedom. To this day, the struggle to grasp a handful of freedom is an effective barometer of the progress and the unmet expectations of the African American community.

Lonnie G. Bunch III is the 14th Secretary of the Smithsonian Institution. As Secretary, he oversees twenty-one museums, twenty-one libraries, the National Zoo, numerous research centers, and several education units and centers. Bunch was the founding director of the Smithsonian's National Museum of African American History and Culture.

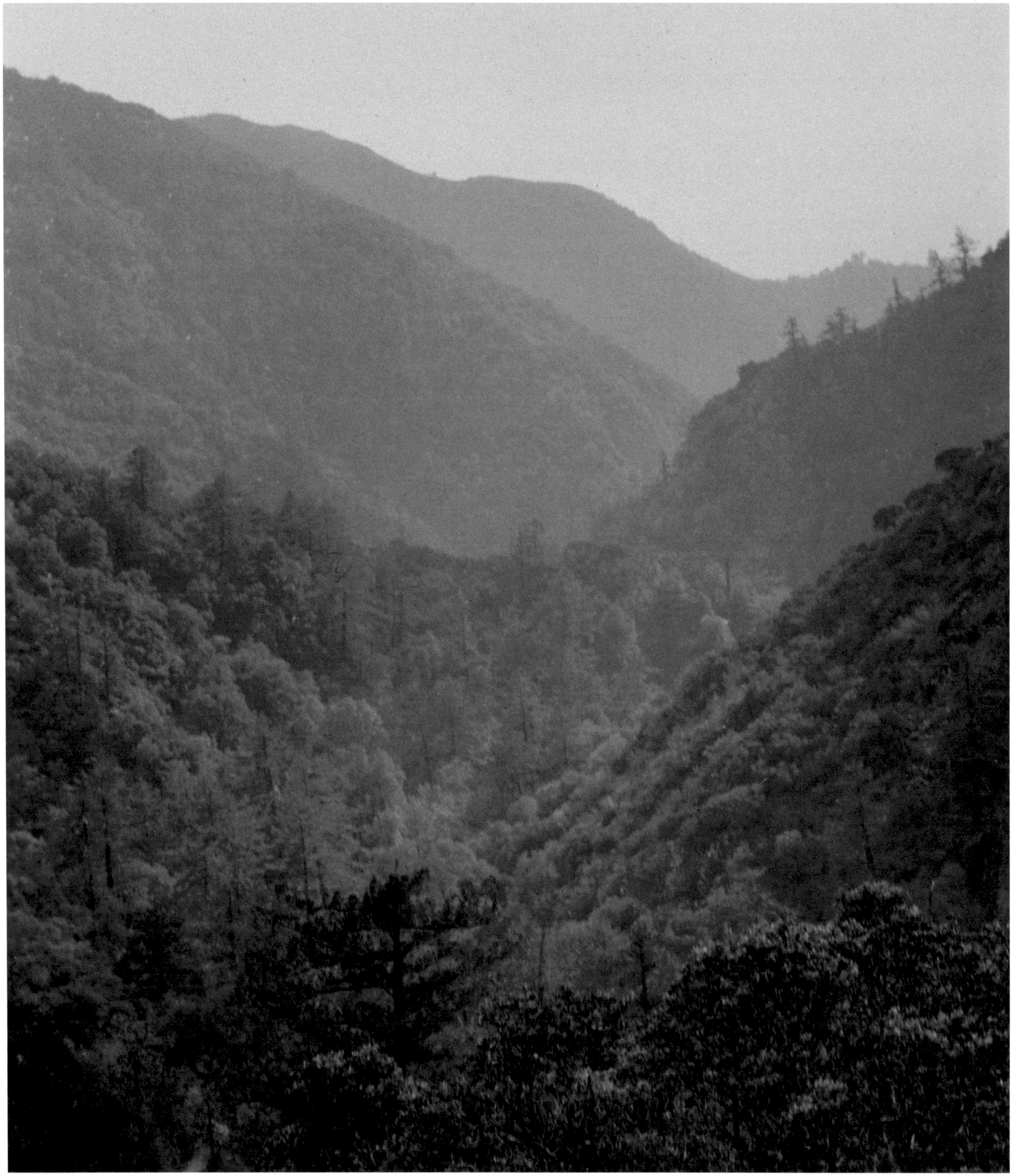

Figures 1–3
The illustrations for this essay come from the unique wood-bound guidebook *Angeles Forest Trails*, sponsored by Los Angeles County and funded by the federal Works Progress Administration during the 1930s. The book sought "to bring to the people of Los Angeles County a better understanding of the wonderful natural resources, recreational and otherwise" in the San Gabriel Mountains, long before it became a national monument. George T. Peabody Scrapbook Reports, 1934–38, The Huntington, Gift of Shelley Fetterman, mssHM 83937–83939.

This Land Is Ours to Protect

The San Gabriel Mountains National Monument

In 2009, when I was first elected to Congress, I was taken on a tour like no other. Passionate volunteers showed me the majesty of the San Gabriel Mountains, but they also revealed families having to crawl on their hands and knees as they hiked to the East Fork River because there was no designated trail. There was the beauty of trees and rivers, but it was marred by trash and graffiti. Some signs were so faded that you could not tell if a trail was 5 miles or .5 miles. This is what led me to advocate for these mountains.

Over eighteen million people live within a ninety-mile radius of the San Gabriels, and many of them, especially those in low-income neighborhoods, lack access to green space in their communities. Los Angeles is one of the most park-poor regions of the country. These mountains are the closest nature accessible to many people, which is why the Angeles National Forest (which contains the bulk of the San Gabriels) receives more than four million visitors per year, more than Yellowstone or Yosemite.

Despite providing Los Angeles County with 70 percent of its open space and one-third of its drinking water, the San Gabriel Mountains lacked the protections and resources they so desperately needed. That was the motivation behind the two-decade movement to preserve them, create infrastructure to support high visitation levels, and expand access to the outdoors. We called on President Barack Obama to use his authority under the Antiquities Act of 1906 to designate these lands as a national monument. In 2014, after years of support from the community and local elected officials, President Obama granted permanent federal protections for the new San Gabriel Mountains National Monument.

Following that 2014 designation, we saw significant progress, including the establishment of a management plan that eliminated harmful amateur mining and the start of the River Rangers program, which engages with visitors to conserve the area's beauty. However, the original declaration did not include the western Angeles Forest. As a result, culturally significant resources, thousands of acres of wilderness, and heavily used trails lacked the protections and resources afforded to the original monument.

That's why, in 2023, Senator Alex Padilla and I called on President Joe Biden to expand the monument to include these lands, which have rich cultural, historical, and geological resources, as well as habitats for endangered species. We told him about our efforts to expand this monument through legislation that passed the House in bipartisan votes multiple times. We also emphasized the mental and physical health benefits associated with recreation and the outdoors, which were often missing from the lives of far too many low-income Angelenos.

On May 2, 2024, President Biden added more than 105,000 acres of federal lands to the existing monument and announced new investments to increase staffing, ensure cleaner water, and improve visitor experience.

As we continue to advocate for the protection of the San Gabriel Mountains, we must recognize that safeguarding these public lands is not only crucial for preserving nature but also for combating climate change and protecting the communities most vulnerable to its escalating impacts. Southern California experienced no significant rainfall for over eight months leading up to January 2025. This drought, intensified by climate change, set the stage for the most catastrophic wildfires in Southern California history. On January 7, 2025, the Eaton Fire—fueled by unprecedented Santa Ana winds reaching up to 100 miles per hour—razed nearly 9,500 structures. Twenty thousand residents were forced to flee, leaving with only the clothes on their backs. They returned to find their homes, businesses, and cherished community institutions destroyed, along with irreplaceable memories. Most tragically, nineteen of our neighbors lost their lives as the fire tore through Altadena and northern Pasadena. As we support our communities in recovering from this unimaginable loss, we must honor the victims' memories by ensuring that survivors receive the resources needed to rebuild their lives, keep their families safe, and protect their homes from the growing threat of climate-driven disasters.

I have been honored to be a part of the movement to protect the San Gabriels, and our work will continue so that more people can responsibly enjoy the San Gabriel Mountains National Monument and secure its good stewardship for generations to come. Together, we will protect the communities that surround the San Gabriels and guarantee that future generations can find solace, healing, and hope in this beautiful landscape, just as so many have done before.

Representative Judy Chu became the first Chinese American woman elected to Congress in 2009. She serves on the House Ways and Means Committee and the House Budget Committee. She represents the 28th Congressional District, which includes Pasadena and the West San Gabriel Valley of Southern California.

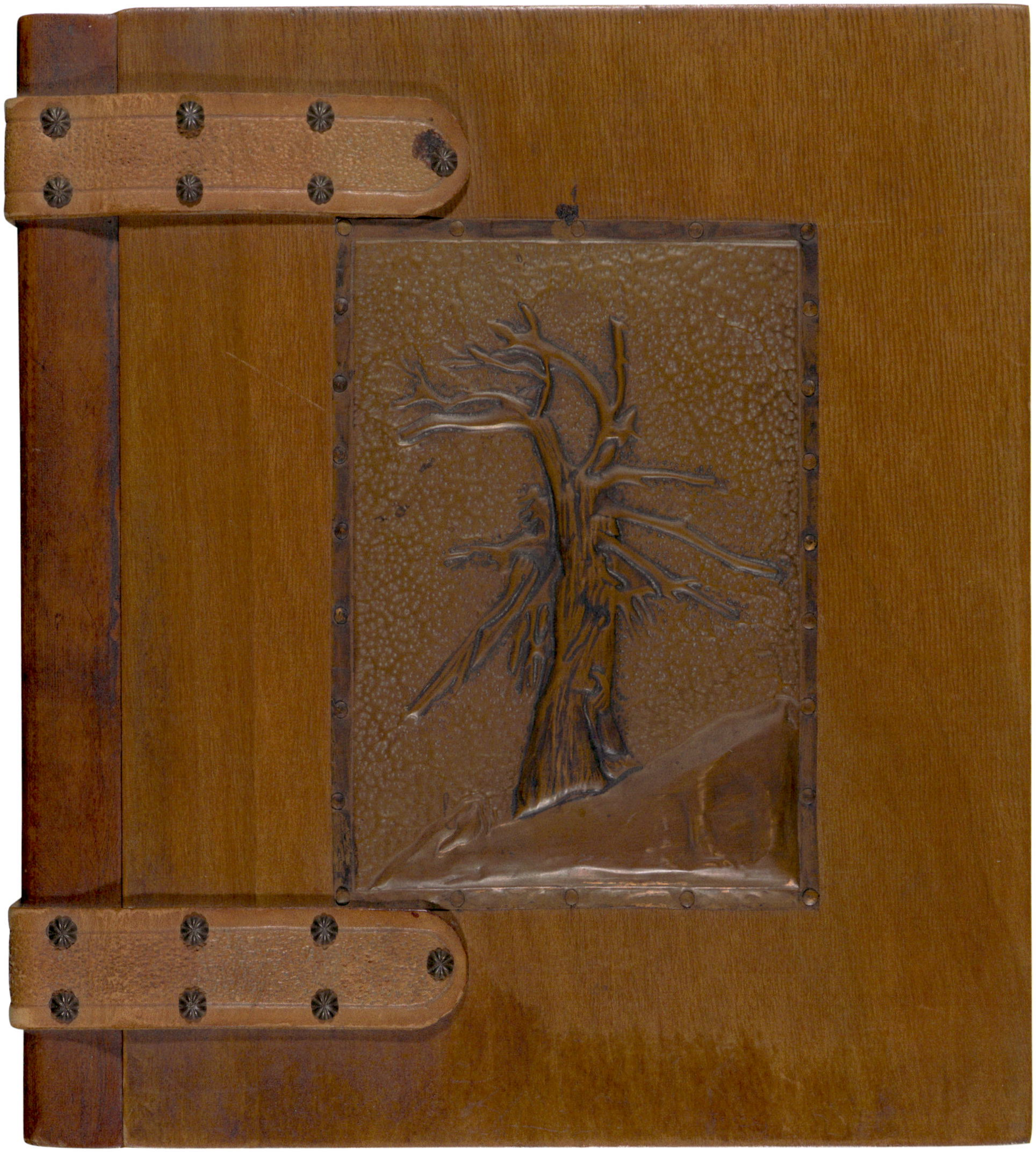

TRAILS OF THE BIG SANTA ANITA CANYON

Compiled by the Division of Hiking, Nature Study and Conservation of W. P. A. Recreation Project Sa-2290, sponsored by the Los Angeles County Department of Recreation Camps and Playgrounds.

Mr. John W. Reel, Supervisor

Big Santa Anita Canyon leads into one of the most beautiful of our forest areas. It is easily reached from all parts of the San Gabriel Valley and the Metropolitan area of Los Angeles.

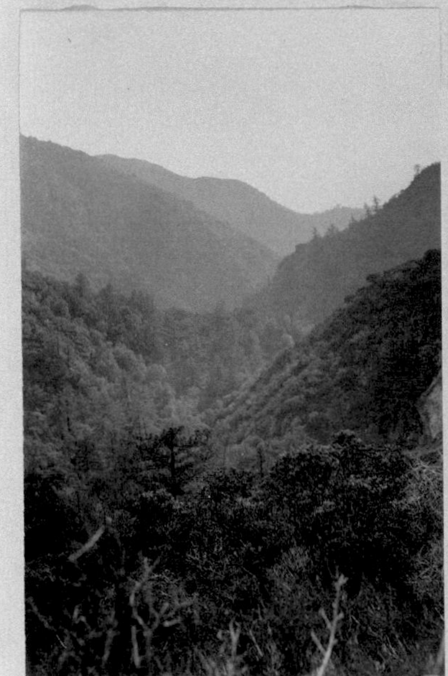

A beautiful view up Winter Creek, a tributary of the Big Santa Anita.

Throughout the canyon area are to be found Public Camps maintained by the United States Forest Service. These camps are open to the public without charge. All camps are equipped with tables, cooking and sanitary accomodations, and, if not located along side of a running stream, have water piped in at convenient places. Here you may picnic for a day, a week or a month in YOUR forest, and, all that the Forest Service asks of you is that you maintain a sanitary camp, take all precautions to prevent forest fires and, generally conduct yourself as thoug you were camped

grey-green on the chaparrel. Clematis climbs everywhere and, with summer, changes its creamy white flowers to fluffy masses of white seed balls which will cause the children to exclaim that,"The Old Man of the Mountain is here again, with his long, white beard". Wild Gooseberries, Thimble Berries, Black berries and Pink Currants add variety not ordinarily found along lowland

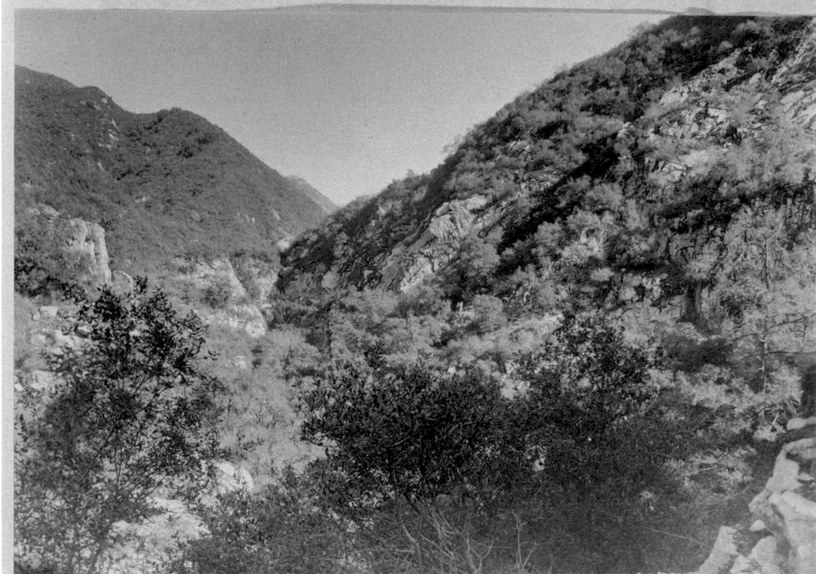

Along the Santa Anita and East Fork

trails and in the Fall, the bright red berries of the Tollen (Toyon) the California Holly are everywhere.

About a mile above Fern Lodge, the trail passes through a dense patch of bracken, and on the far side, a dimly marked trail leads down through the ferns to the stream bed just below "Twin Falls". This is a delightful spot in which to noon if

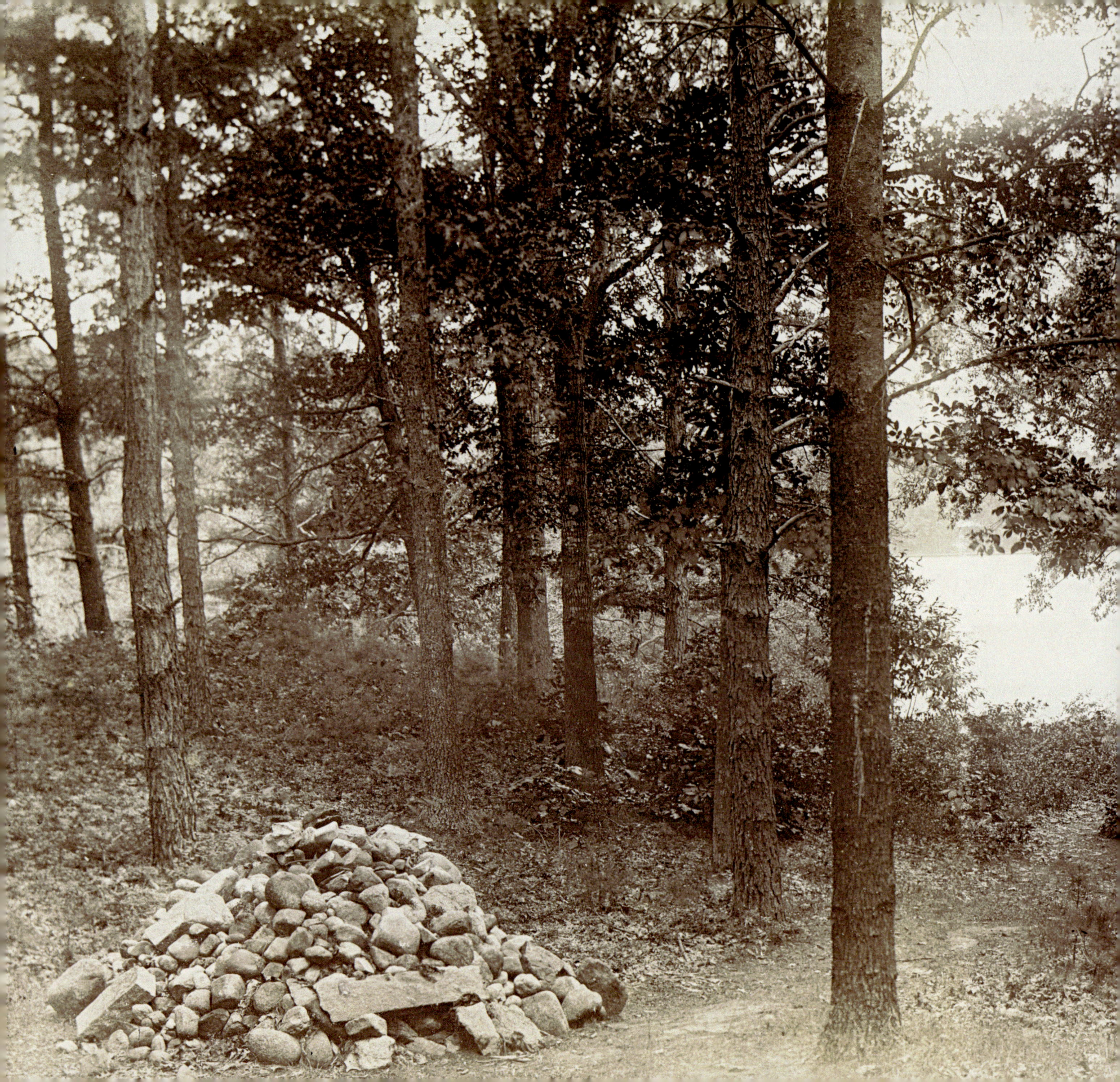

Terry Tempest Williams

Revising Ourselves, Our Democracy

This land is being transformed through fire, floods, and drought.

This land is insisting we change as the climate changes.

This land is speaking to us—Are we listening?

Henry David Thoreau was listening to the land in his cabin in the woods on the threshold of the Civil War. Almost two centuries later, we remain a divided country.

I came to the Huntington Library to confront Thoreau's early drafts of *Walden*, the urgency of his script, his process of revision; and *see if I could not learn what it had to teach, and not, when I came to die, discover. . . .* Thoreau's words have become so intertwined with my own thinking, I don't know where his ideas end and mine begin.

An oversized green leather binder with "WALDEN" embossed in gold was brought from the archives to my table in the library. Each page or "leaf" was protected by an acetate sleeve. A glint met my eyes as I carefully turned each leaf, written on both sides. Familiarizing myself with his handwriting rendered in sepia ink was its own exercise in translation.

In time, the passage I was looking for revealed itself in a slightly different form (fig. 1):

> *I went down to the pond because I wished to live deliberately, to ponder only the essential facts of life, and see if I could not learn what it had to teach, and not when I came to die discover that I had not lived.*

In his second draft, Thoreau made four word changes that survived the eleven drafts of *Walden*. If we merge the two versions of this sentence, striking through the words he deleted and highlighting those he chose instead, we see that changing the language not only altered the tone but transformed the meaning (fig. 3):

> *I went ~~down~~ to the ~~pond~~* ***woods*** *because I wished to live deliberately, to ~~ponder~~* ***front*** *only the essential facts of life, and see if I could not learn what it had to teach, and not, when I came to die discover that I had not lived.*

Deleting "down" quickens his arrival, and Thoreau is now on equal footing with the land. Replacing "pond" with "woods" as his primary place of attention becomes an imperative stance among those with standing; trees become elders rooted in time, whose lifespan exceeds that of humans, as they adapt to changing seasons with grace and dignity.

A pond fluctuates, expands, and contracts depending on the season: In winter, it freezes; in spring, it thaws; in summer, it rises; in drought, it disappears. Thoreau's decision to go "to the woods" instead of "down to the pond" is a shift from observer to participant. His pilgrimage to the woods becomes a commitment to residency; he is not merely a visitor gazing into a reflecting pond (fig. 2).

The change he makes "to front" only the essential facts of life reads with greater urgency and purpose than the passive verb "to ponder." (Perhaps this was a pun on "pond" that pleased Thoreau on his first go-around.) Through his revisions, Thoreau chooses to act rather than be acted upon.

The introduction to the *Digital Thoreau* quotes the scholar John Bryant: "Are we not revising ourselves, always, to find the flow of ourselves, and then too the mixing and revisions of our culture?"

The lines that follow the sentence I was investigating read: *Living is so dear . . . I do not wish to practice resignation, unless it is quite necessary.*

From the vantage point of Thoreau's harrowing and transformative moment to where we find ourselves today,

Detail of Walden Pond (fig. 2).

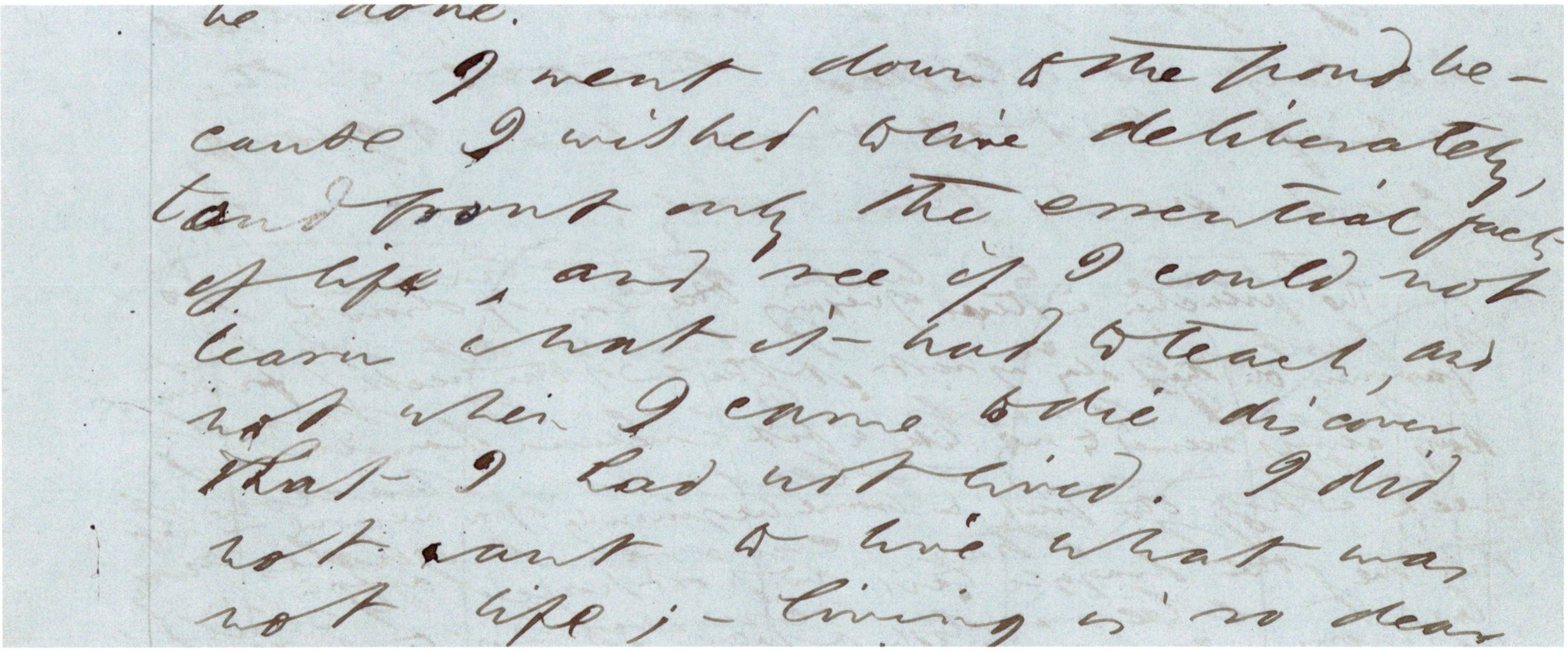
be done.
I went down to the pond be-
cause I wished to live deliberately,
and front only the essential facts
of life, and see if I could not
learn what it had to teach, and
not when I came to die discover
that I had not lived. I did
not want to live what was
not life; - living is so dear

Figure 1
Detail of Henry David Thoreau, *Walden; or, Life in the Woods*, 1846–47. Draft A. The Huntington, Purchased by Henry E. Huntington, HM 924, vol. 1.

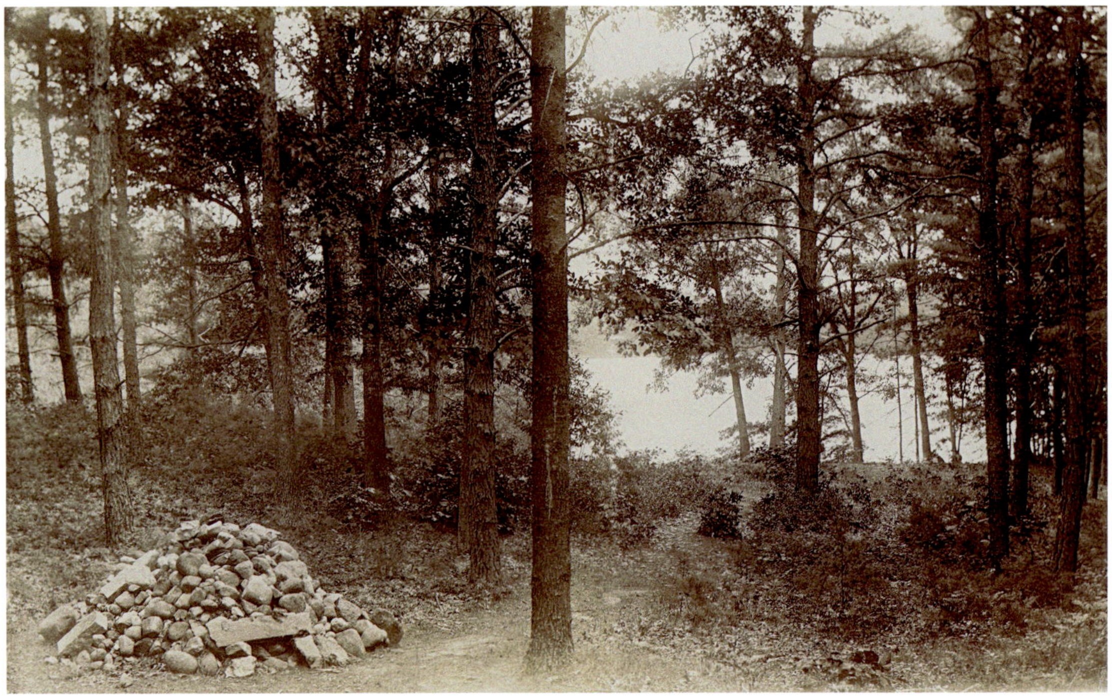

Figure 2
The site of Thoreau's cabin, Walden Pond, ca. 1895. Albumen print, 4½ × 7½ in. The Huntington, Correspondence of Prudence Ward and Anne J. Ward, 1839–1906.

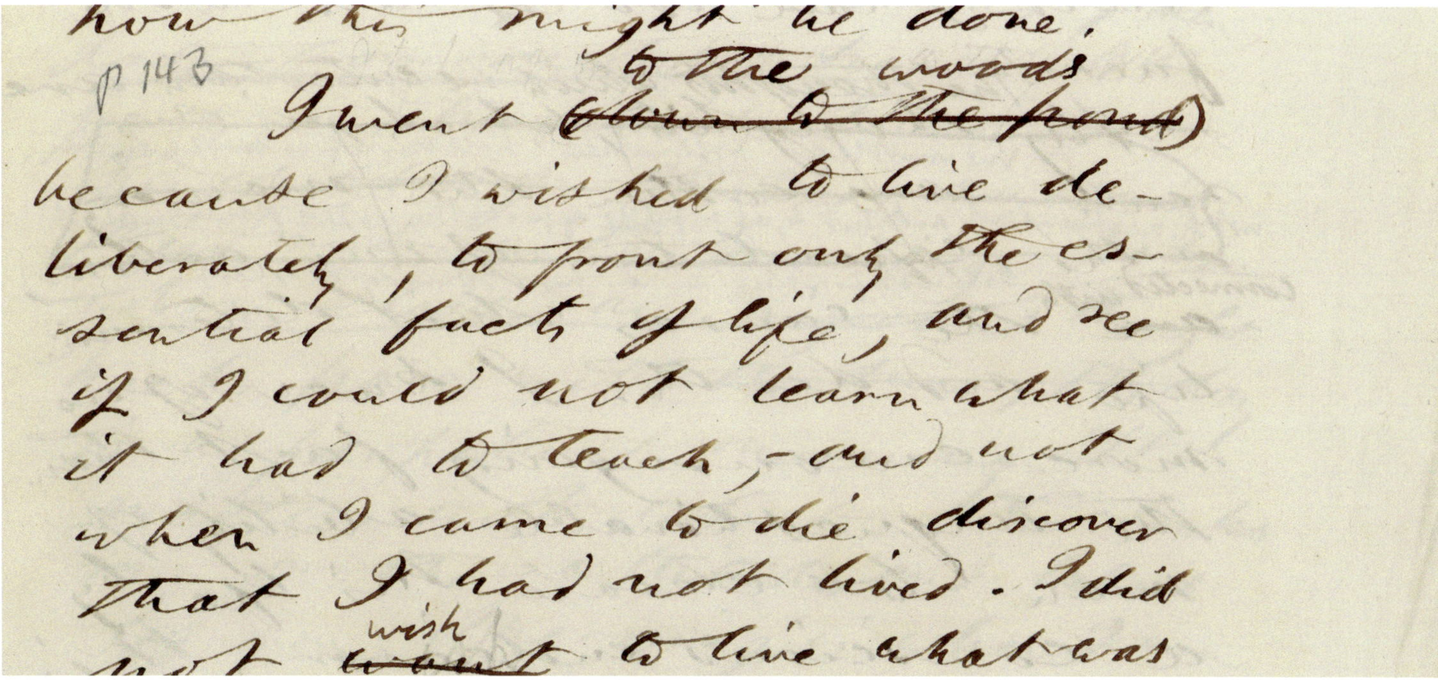

how this might be done.
p 143
I went ~~down to the pond~~ to the woods
because I wished to live de-
liberately, to front only the es-
sential facts of life, and see
if I could not learn what
it had to teach, - and not
when I came to die discover
that I had not lived. I did
not ~~want~~ wish to live what was

Figure 3
Detail of Thoreau, *Walden*, 1848–49. Draft B-C. The Huntington, Purchased by Henry E. Huntington, HM 924, vol. 2.

resignation is not necessary, but revision is. Revision is essential to any creative process. Democracy is a creative process. We the People are in process. And the land is in process, too.

How shall we live? To practice revision within private and public life is to make amends for the harm we have caused on this planet by our hunger for more, when we can do with so much less. *Simplify. Simplify.* In reimagining America, ~~greed~~ and ~~wreckage~~ are two words worth deleting. **Revision** and **restoration** are two words that can bring forth an Earth-facing consciousness.

"Only that day dawns to which we are awake," writes Thoreau in the last paragraph of *Walden*.

This land is inviting us to awaken to another way of being.

This land is revealing what has been hidden, so that we might see what is here.

This land is speaking to us—if we listen, we will know what to do.

Terry Tempest Williams is the Provostial Scholar at Dartmouth College. Her writing has appeared in the New Yorker, *the* New York Times, Orion Magazine, *and numerous anthologies worldwide as a crucial voice for ecological consciousness and social change. In 2015, she and her husband, Brooke Williams, purchased BLM oil and gas leases in Utah as conservation buyers. They divide their time between Castle Valley, Utah, and Jackson Hole, Wyoming.*

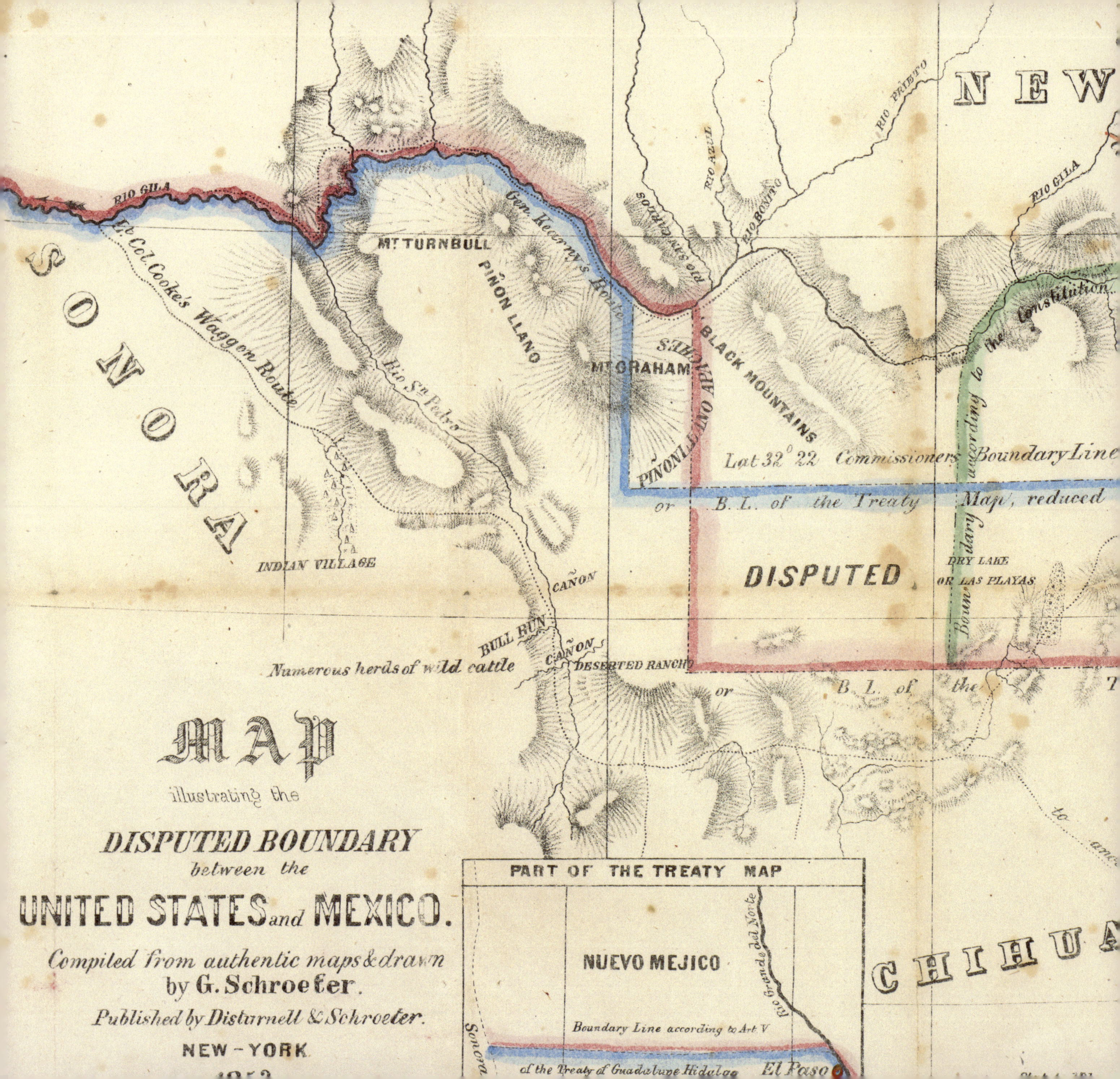

NEW
RIO PRIETO
RIO AZUL
RIO BONITO
RIO GILA
RIO GILA
SONORA
Lt. Col. Cooke's Waggon Route
MT TURNBULL
Gen. Kearny's Route
PIÑON LLANO
MT GRAHAM
BLACK MOUNTAINS
Rio Sn Pedro
Boundary according to the Constitution
Lat 32° 22 Commissioners Boundary Line
or B. L. of the Treaty Map, reduced
DISPUTED
DRY LAKE OR LAS PLAYAS
INDIAN VILLAGE
CAÑON
BULL RUN
CAÑON
Numerous herds of wild cattle
DESERTED RANCHO
or B. L. of the
CHIHUA
MAP
illustrating the
DISPUTED BOUNDARY
between the
UNITED STATES and MEXICO.
Compiled from authentic maps & drawn
by G. Schroeter.
Published by Disturnell & Schroeter.
NEW-YORK
PART OF THE TREATY MAP
NUEVO MEJICO
Rio Grande del Norte
Sonora
Boundary Line according to Art V
of the Treaty of Guadalupe Hidalgo
El Paso

Edge Effects

Edge effects describe the changes that occur at the boundary between two or more ecological zones. This natural process allows for greater biodiversity in these habitats. Humans have also altered locations through urbanization and the demarcation of geopolitical borders. Imperial expansion has long required the surveying and mapping of land for international commerce and war. In this sense, "Edge Effects" encapsulates the ecological, political, cartographic, and militarized nature of these blurred edges and contours of land. These borderlands can be generative, destructive, or a lesson in coexistence.

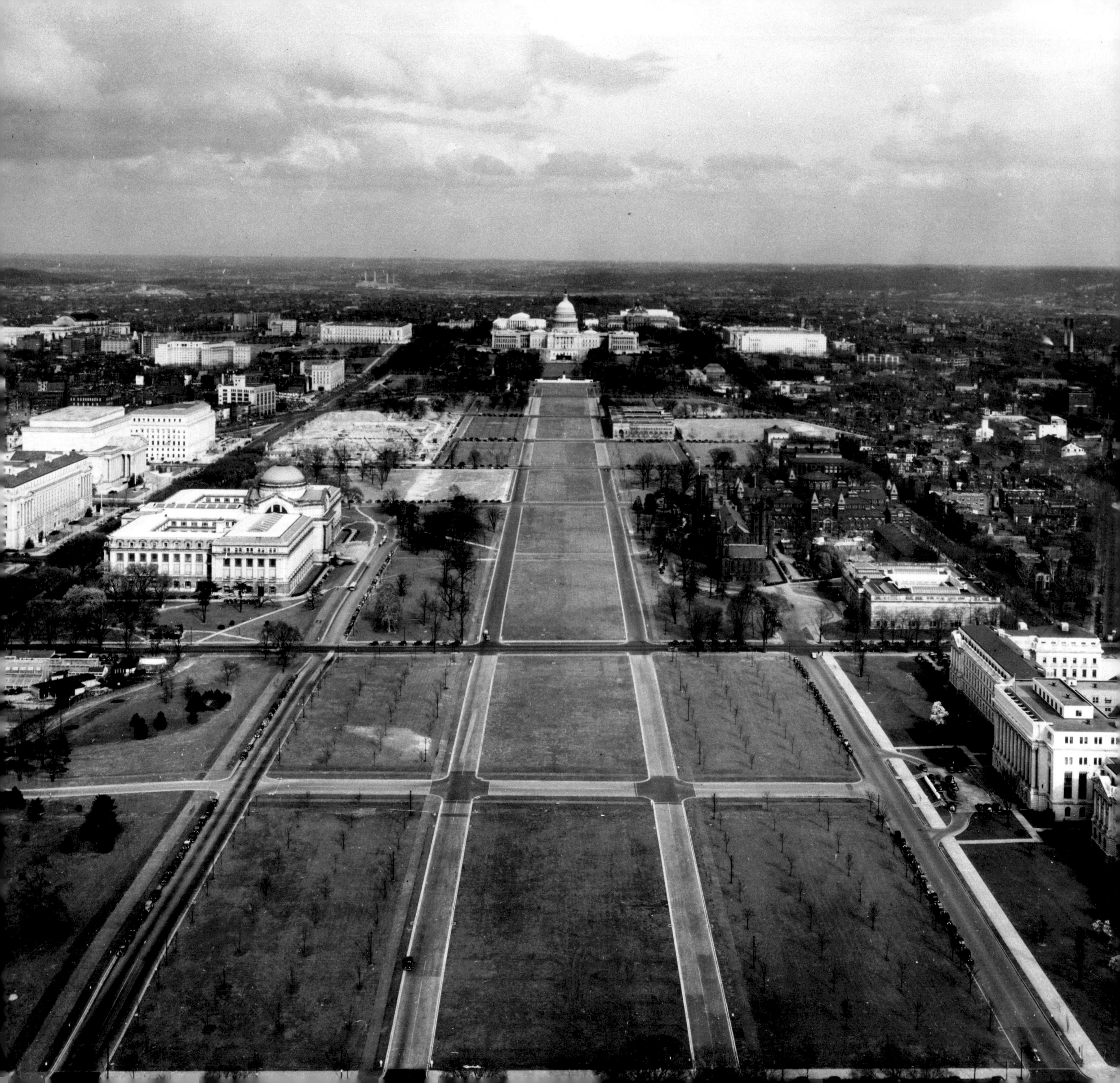

Living Connections

Within a narrow strip of land between the Smithsonian National Museum of Natural History and a bustling thoroughfare in Washington, DC, hummingbirds, butterflies, beetles, and bees dart to and from a native persimmon tree (*Diospyros virginiana*), spotted bee balm (*Monarda punctata*), and calamint (*Calamintha nepeta* var. *nepeta*). The delicate edges between the garden's woodland border and meadow ecosystem teem with life (fig. 2).

The Pollinator Garden is one of many Smithsonian gardens woven throughout the National Mall. Nestled among government buildings, monuments, and museums, they share stories of cultural heritage and urban ecology. Smithsonian Gardens, an accredited museum, stewards these landscapes and living collections.

The idea for the National Mall as a broad promenade, lined with trees and bordered by gardens, comes from the 1791 L'Enfant Plan, commissioned by George Washington and designed by Pierre Charles L'Enfant. Andrew Jackson Downing's 1851 plan for the Mall included curvilinear carriage drives and zones with distinct characteristics. The Smithsonian Pleasure Grounds were designed in the picturesque style, favoring intricacy, variety, and irregular massings to complement the Smithsonian Castle's mid-nineteenth-century Romantic architecture (fig. 3). Decades later, the 1902 McMillan Plan reimagined the Mall as an immense greensward, framing views of the US Capitol, the Washington Monument, and the Lincoln Memorial (fig. 1).[1] Smithsonian Gardens exists within this context, engaging with the monumental landscape while embracing Downing's vision of a naturalistic setting.

Today, each garden reflects how communities have relied on and nurtured plants. Outside the National Museum of the American Indian, traditional cropland features Cherokee White Eagle dent corn (*Zea mays*), rattlesnake pole beans (*Phaseolus vulgaris*), and Seminole pumpkin (*Cucurbita moschata*), bordered by an upland hardwood forest and grassland meadow (fig. 5). Native Americans have long used these plants for food, medicine, fiber, dyes, and ceremonial and building materials.

Across the Mall, the Southern live oak trees (*Quercus virginiana*) at the National Museum of African American History and Culture honor African American communities of the Southeastern coast (fig. 4). This keystone species has symbolized safety and strength, providing gathering places for centuries. During the American Civil War, Virginia's "Emancipation Oak" shaded one of the first Southern readings of the Emancipation Proclamation. Later, it became the site of open-air classes for newly freed African Americans and the foundation of Hampton University.

Framed by the dense urban landscape of buildings, roadways, and the Mall, the gardens are dynamic ecosystems. As they evolve, through natural changes and horticulturists' interventions, visitors learn about the systems that sustain life. Using data from the gardens and information from repositories like the Archives of American Gardens, researchers reveal the environmental consequences of our actions as we adapt to life on a changing planet.

Smithsonian Gardens enhances the well-being of all who interact with its grounds. Like public gardens everywhere, they inspire exploration, stewardship, and balance at the edge of the built and natural worlds. As cultural landscapes, they teach and transport us, extending the Smithsonian experience beyond gallery walls. At their heart is the symbiotic relationship between people and plants.

Figure 1
Historic image of the National Mall showing the transition away from the Downing Plan to the more orderly McMillan Plan, 1936. NARA RC 66. Records of the Commission of Fine Arts, 2A.SG.3.

Joy Columbus is a public garden leader and advocate dedicated to creating a greener, plant-rich world. She serves as Director of Smithsonian Gardens.

1. Smithsonian Institution, South Mall Campus Cultural Landscape Report, 2015.

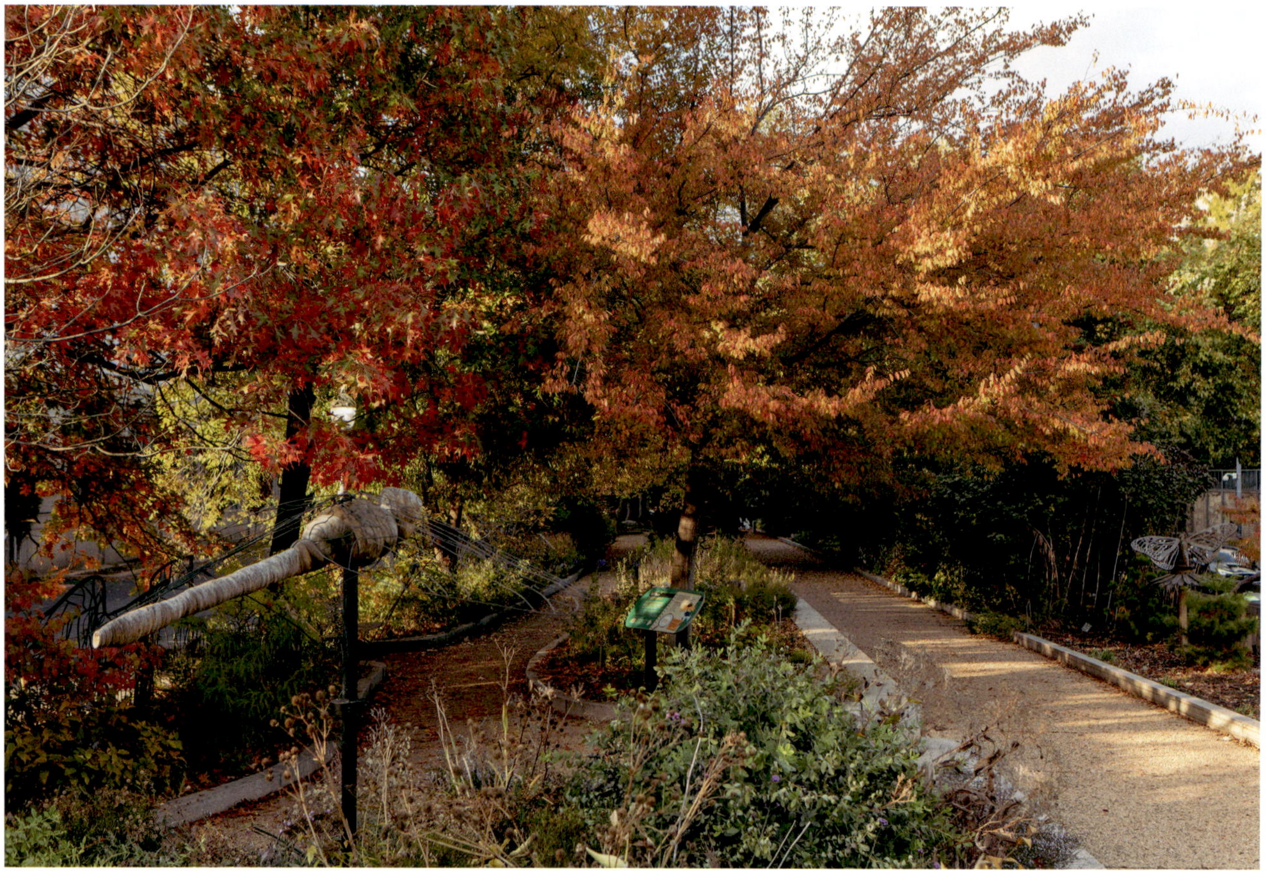

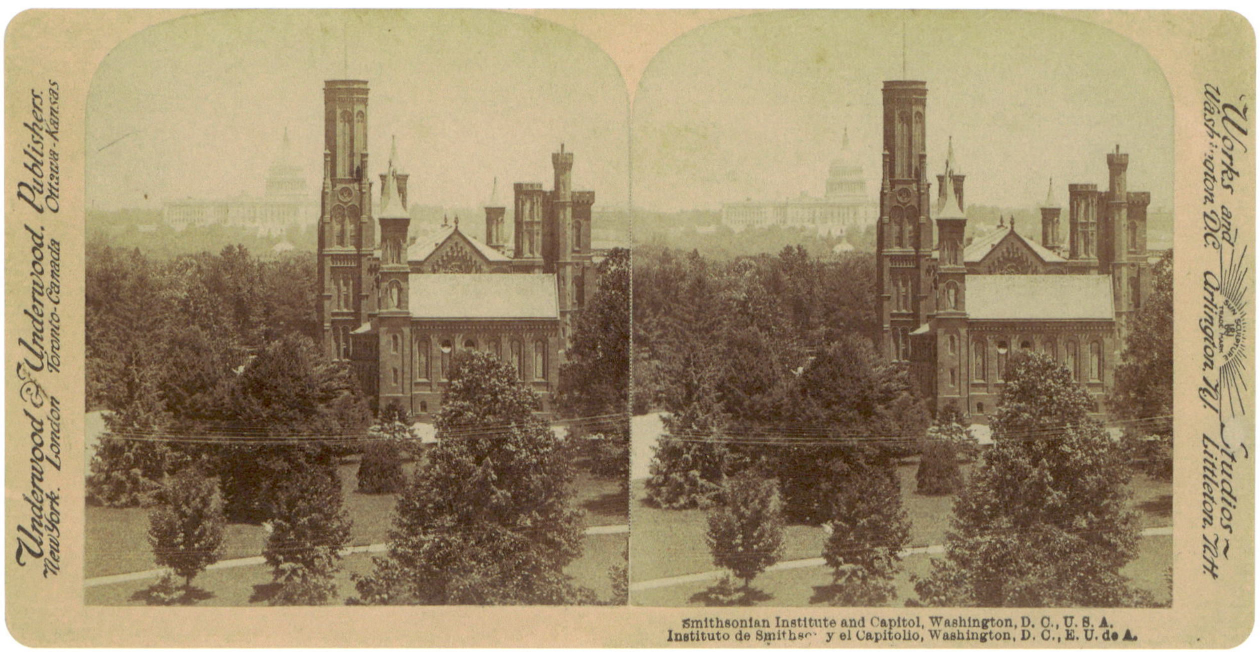

Figure 2
Pollinator Garden at the National Museum of Natural History, Smithsonian Gardens, 1A.SG.3.

Figure 3
National Mall, ca. 1870–1900. Stereograph, 3½ × 7 in. Smithsonian Gardens, Archives of American Gardens, Historic Stereograph Collection, 2A.SG.1.

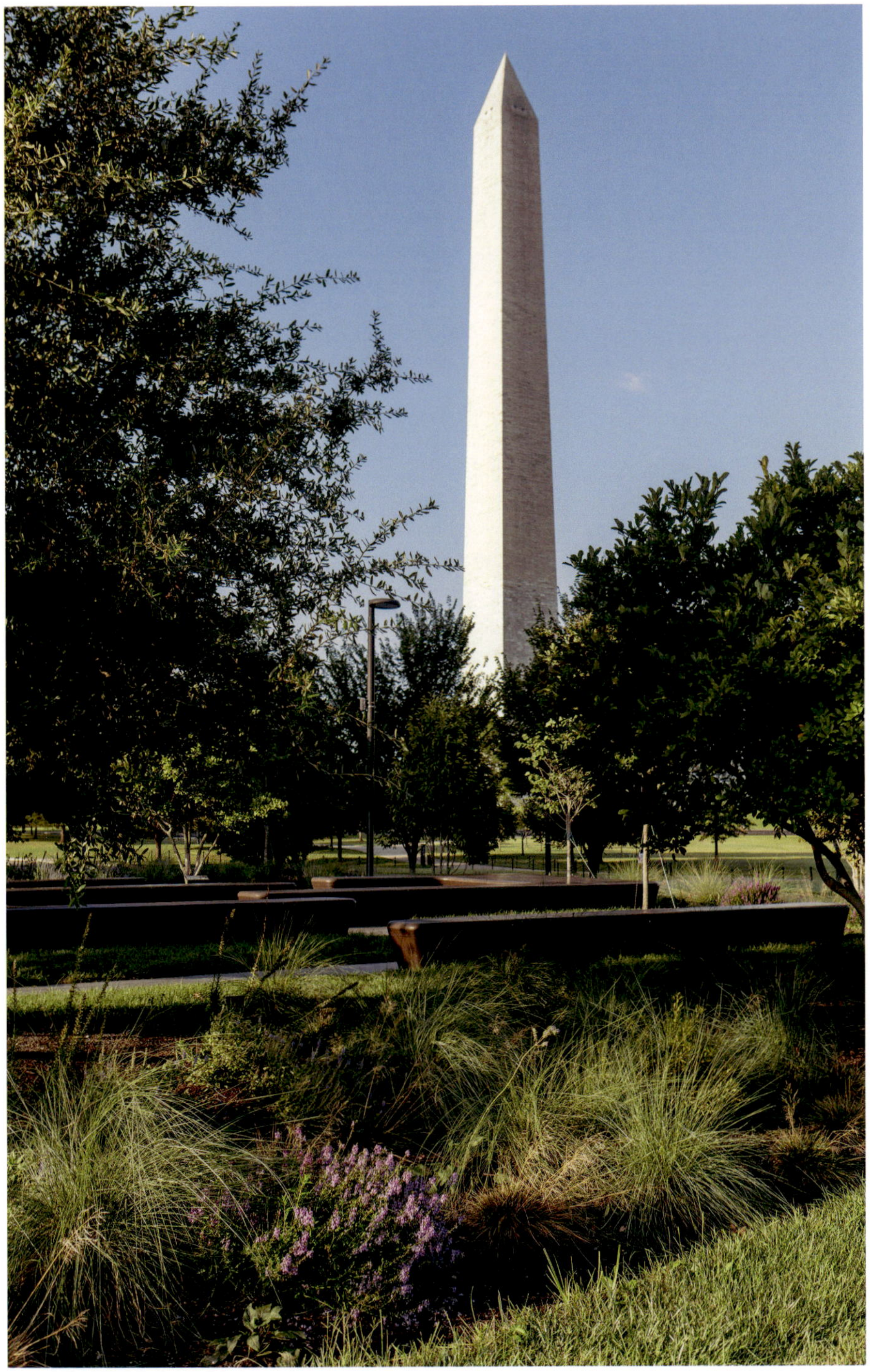

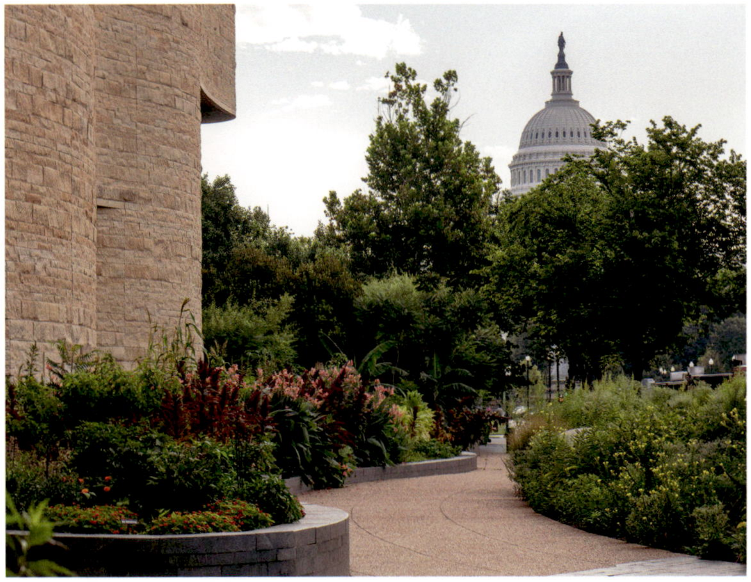

Figure 4
Landscape at the National Museum of African American History and Culture. Smithsonian Gardens, 1A.SG.1.

Figure 5
Landscape at the National Museum of the American Indian, Smithsonian Gardens, 1A.SG.2.

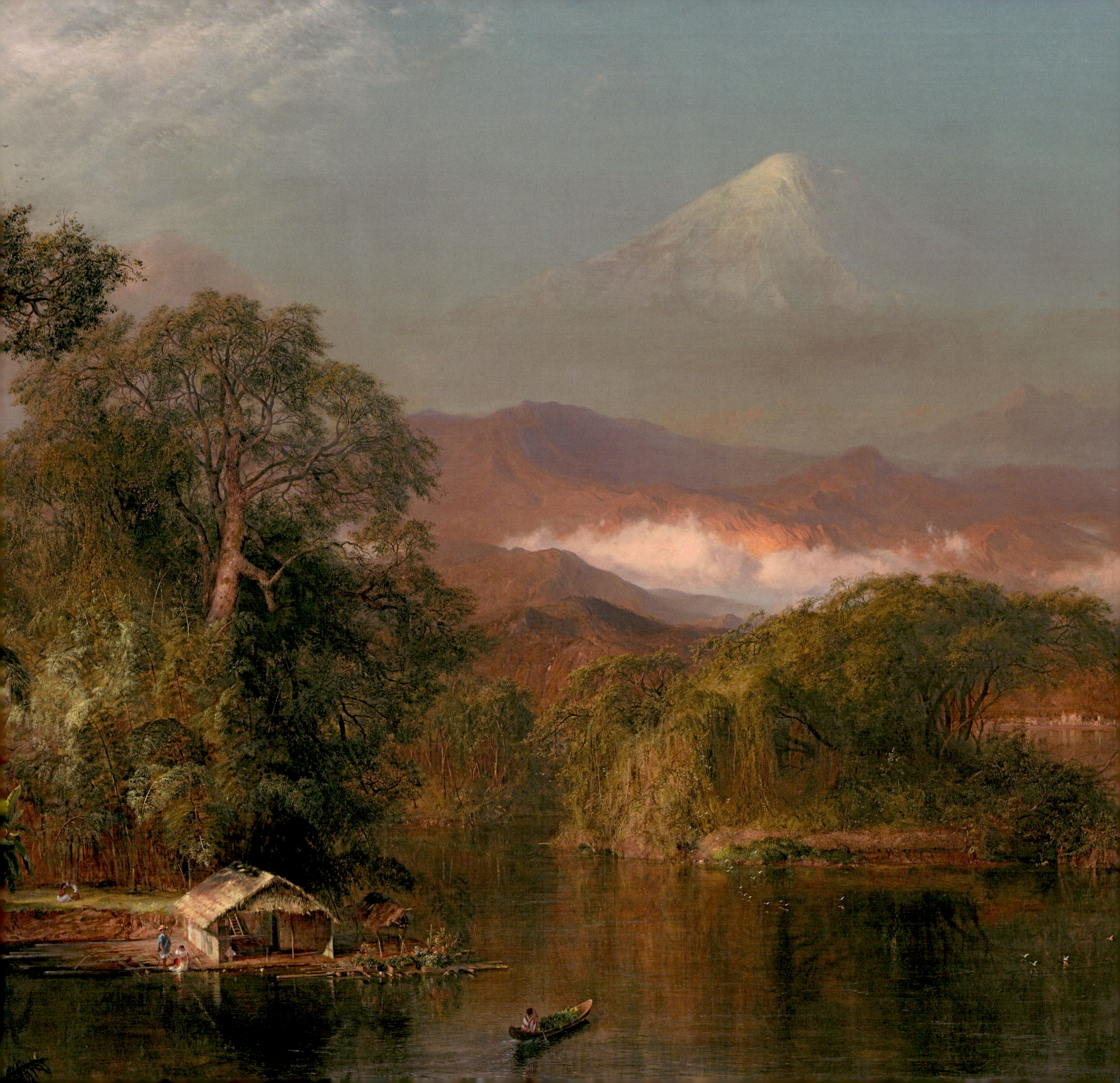

Borderlands

In 1895, the American painter Winslow Homer traveled north from his home in Prouts Neck, Maine, to Innu territory in Quebec. Led by Indigenous and French Canadian guides, he explored the region from the Saguenay River to the shores of Lake Saint-Jean, primarily on fishing and hunting expeditions. Near the town of Roberval (Mashteuiatsh) on the western shores of the lake, he created a series of watercolors of Innu camps showing women making birchbark canoes (fig. 1). Homer, who had been employed as a newspaper illustrator during the Civil War, brought a journalistic approach to images like these, which were painted quickly in the field. He documented various stages of preparing and bending the bark, which, like his aqueous watercolor medium, was worked wet, to make it pliable around a wooden frame. By the time Homer visited the region, French Canadian settlers had begun to occupy the land, a border region that had a rich Indigenous history, primarily associated with the Pekuakamiulnuatsh First Nation, also known as the Ilnuatsh of the Pekuakami. His images suggest the convergence of cultures in this borderlands region, but also recenter the geographies of American art through Homer's peripatetic artistic lens.

Placing Indigenous French Canada at the center, rather than the periphery, of his artistic production and showing Indigenous women makers on an equal footing with a well-known, Anglo-American artist suggests the fluidity of American art as a category and the diversity of cultural and creative expression. More broadly, the concept of borderlands highlights stories of place, histories of migration, and representations of the landscape, and the close relationship between art, land, and ecology. This helps us think hemispherically and globally, as artists, then as now, traveled widely, crossing borders in search of inspiration and sometimes opportunity, and to connect with other cultures and artistic traditions.

Borderlands, as a creative and scholarly approach, grows out of the Spanish and Mexican *frontera*. As scholars David J. Weber and Gloria Anzaldúa have argued, the history of the United States—and thus our art history—has been defined by a series of cultural encounters along a constantly shifting and highly contested border.[1] From the earliest period of European settlement in the late fifteenth and sixteenth centuries, to the Westward Expansion movements of the nineteenth century to today, the borderlands of the Americas were zones of cultural contact and exchange. They have been places where cultures met, and where the objects created or interchanged reflected the complex multiracial, multiethnic, multilingual, and multicultural contexts in which they were made. The Huntington, located on Gabrielino-Tongva homelands in greater Los Angeles, is well positioned to bring this tradition into the broader field of historically Anglo- and East Coast–centered national art narratives. Since 2021, we have been reorienting the American Art galleries under the theme "Borderlands" to think about our own place and to connect to audiences from Southern California and far beyond.[2]

Contemporary artists illuminate this place-based history. Cuban-born Los Angeles–based artist Enrique Martínez Celaya, with his dramatic installation *There-bound* (2021) in the American Art galleries, explored borders in very personal terms, showing how histories of migration profoundly shape individuals. Talented, high school–aged students working with Ghetto Film School have created many short films inspired by The Huntington's American art collection and botanical gardens that teach us to see how stories about families and communities can tell both micro and macro histories of the city in our time. They show us what indeed the historical record tells us—that our story is not fixed, but ever evolving, and the result of movement and change. Bringing these Southern California lenses to artists

Detail of Frederic Edwin Church, *Chimborazo* (fig. 6).

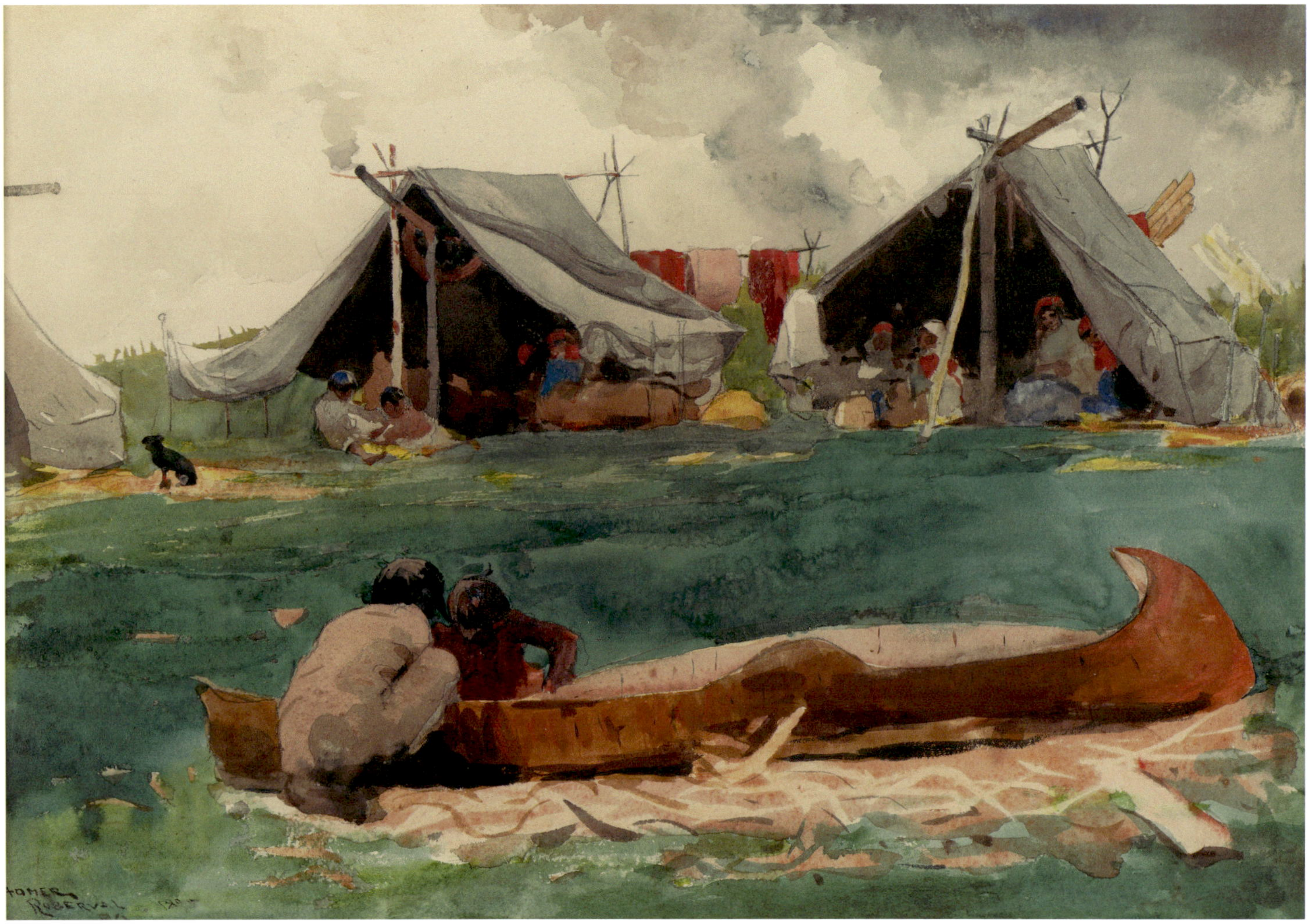

Figure 1
Winslow Homer, *Indians Making Canoes (Montagnais Indians)*, 1895. Watercolor on paper, 14 × 20 in. The Huntington, Gift of the Virginia Steele Scott Foundation, 83.8.24.

like Winslow Homer and the Innu women making canoes—and many others—can inspire reflection as the United States marks its 250th anniversary.

Homelands

Before we cross a border, we all have a place we call home. A starting place. A place of origins, of family and memory. Native peoples have inhabited the place we know as California for millennia. Despite attempted genocide, containment, and assimilation, Indigenous peoples have persisted and carried forward their ways of representing and relating to the world, maintaining their artistic traditions while also innovating new forms of creative expression.

Born in Los Angeles, contemporary Chemehuevi photographer Cara Romero creates images that seek to recognize and celebrate Indigenous presence in the region. Her photographs explore themes of identity, survivance, and the power of place from a California Indigenous perspective.[3] Her photograph *Hermosa* (2021) is a dramatic portrait of her daughter Crickett Tiger dressed in the regalia of the coastal peoples of California as she emerges from the waters of Hermosa Beach (fig. 2). Romero evokes the Chemehuevi mythos of Great Ocean Woman (Hutsipamamow) and the oral histories of Los Angeles and the California coast as a place of creation—and as a sacred site. The photograph resulted from a series of images that appeared on billboards across Los Angeles in the summer and fall of 2021, which Romero created in collaboration with intertribal California First Peoples, Tongva artists, and cultural leaders, boldly proclaiming Indigenous presence throughout the city. The images pay homage to Los Angeles, which is today home to the largest population of Indigenous peoples in the nation, and to the original caretakers of this land, known traditionally as *Tovaangar*, a place of origins.

In the work *YOU ARE HERE—Tovaangar / El Pueblo de Nuestra Señora la Reina de los Ángeles de Porciúncula / Los Angeles* (2021), artist Sandy Rodriguez created an eight-foot-square watercolor map of the city (fig. 3; see her essay in this volume). Rather than feature the familiar

Figure 2
Cara Romero, *Hermosa*, 2021. Archival pigment print, 50 × 40 in. The Huntington, Purchased with funds from The Philip and Muriel Berman Foundation, 2021.12.1.

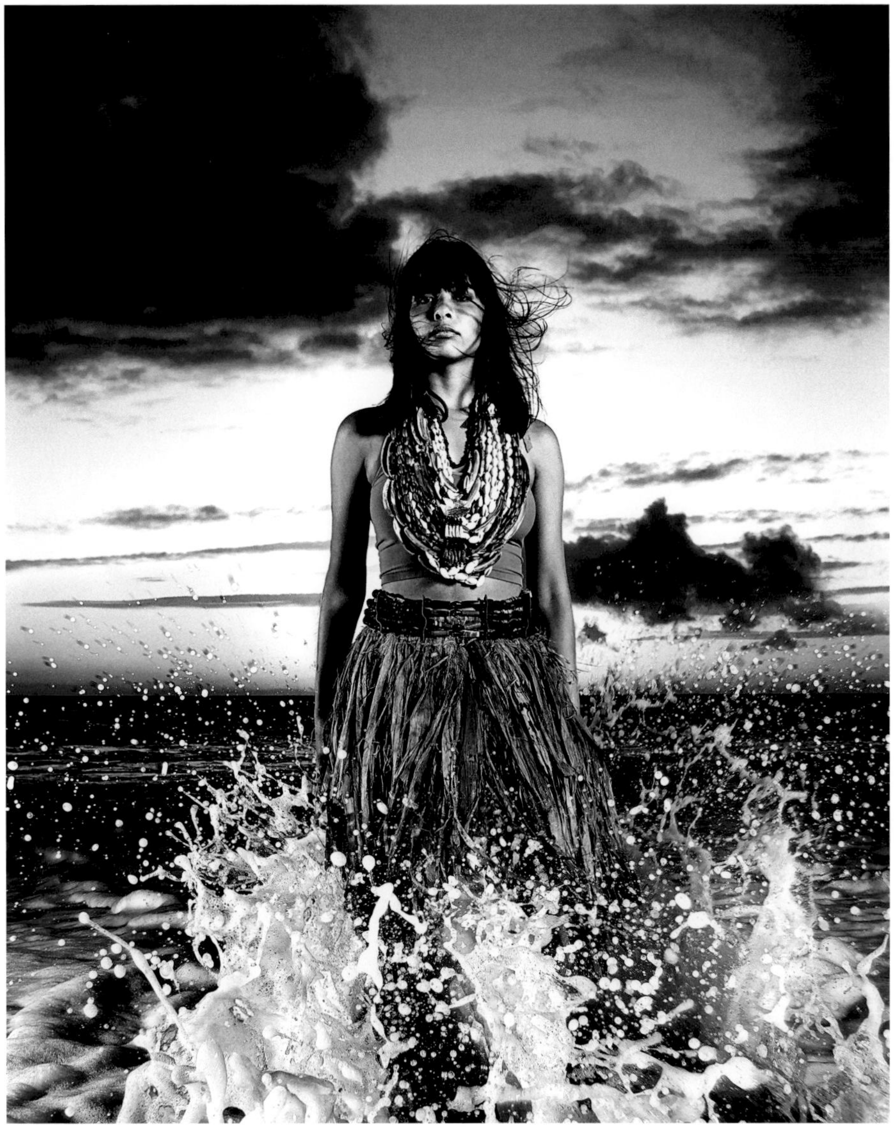

network of freeways that usually characterizes the cartography of LA, the work highlights the psychic, historic, and natural place markers of the region. Locations are identified by their English, Spanish, and Tongva names, revealing a layered, multilingual history of the city five hundred years after the Spanish invasion and conquest of Mexico (1519–21). Images of native plants and animals populate the land, rendered in a style drawn from early colonial painted manuscripts from New Spain. Rodriguez also used locally sourced pigments and colorants, derived from mineral and organic sources, and 23-karat gold leaf applied to amate paper, a hand-beaten, native fig-bark paper traditionally used in Mexico. Rodriguez's work is firmly rooted in research on historical maps and other primary documents, as well as intergenerational relationships with scholars and culture bearers, including the late Tongva elder Julia Bogany.

Tongva photographer Mercedes Dorame creates striking images of the land that explore, reimagine, and connect to her culture and bring visibility to contemporary Indigenous experience. Her photograph *Well of Moon and Sky—Kotuumot Kehaay* (2013) centers on an ancient grinding bowl (metate) carved into a boulder at a sacred Tongva site in a canyon in Los Angeles once used for grinding food, like acorns, or preparing pigments (fig. 4; see her essay in this volume). Upon the boulder she has placed a metate that belonged to her grandmother and leaves from an oak tree, poetic echoes that evoke presence and absence—the well is filled with water that reflects an image of the sky. Dorame's photographs become a visualization that these places, now developed and privatized, remain sacred and deeply meaningful to First Peoples. They also suggest how fragile this culture can be, like the leaves of the oak tree or the scattered powder on the rock that can blow away in an instant. Juxtaposed with the solidity of the ancient boulder signifying the longevity of Indigenous presence in

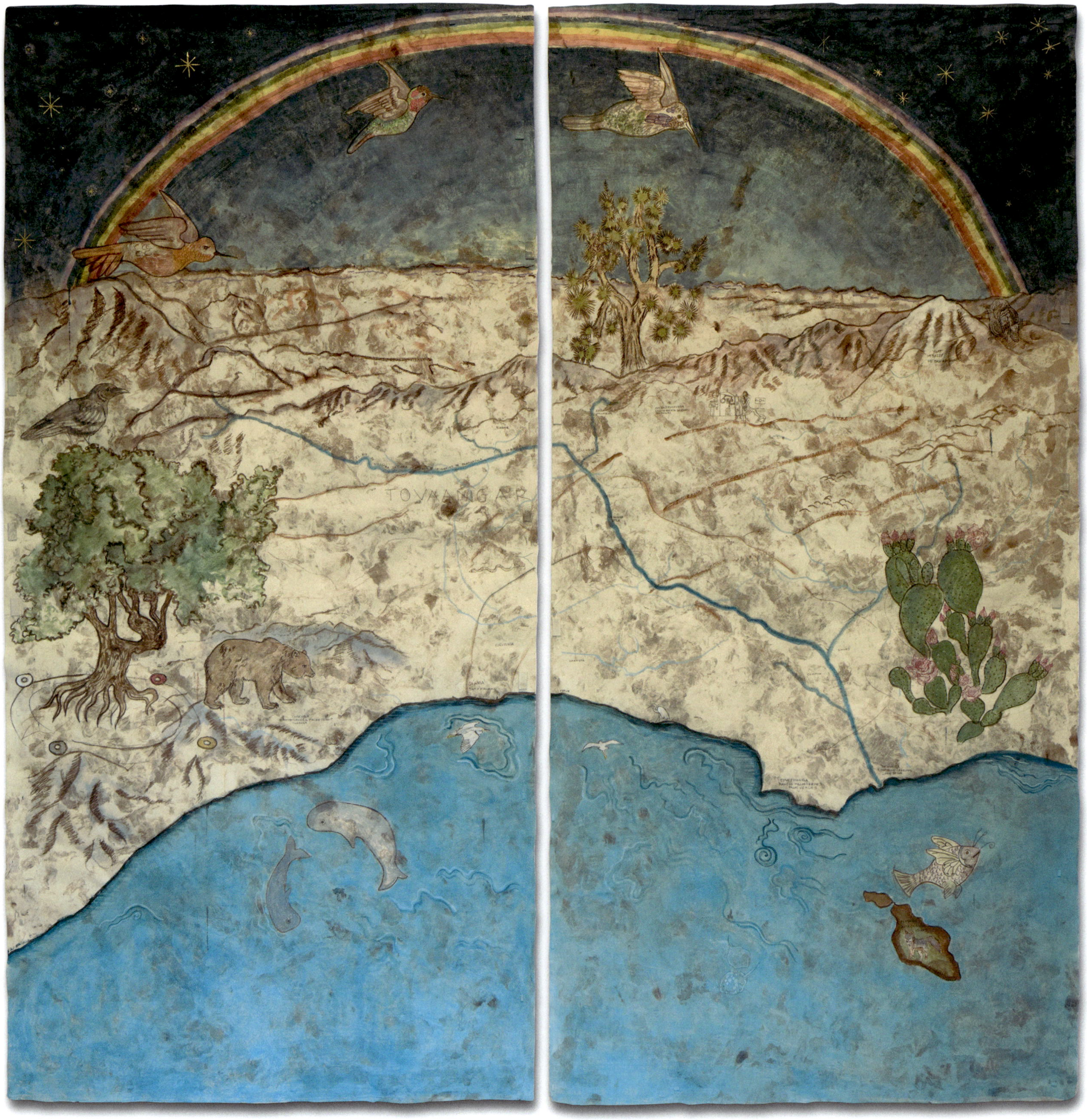
TOVAANGAR

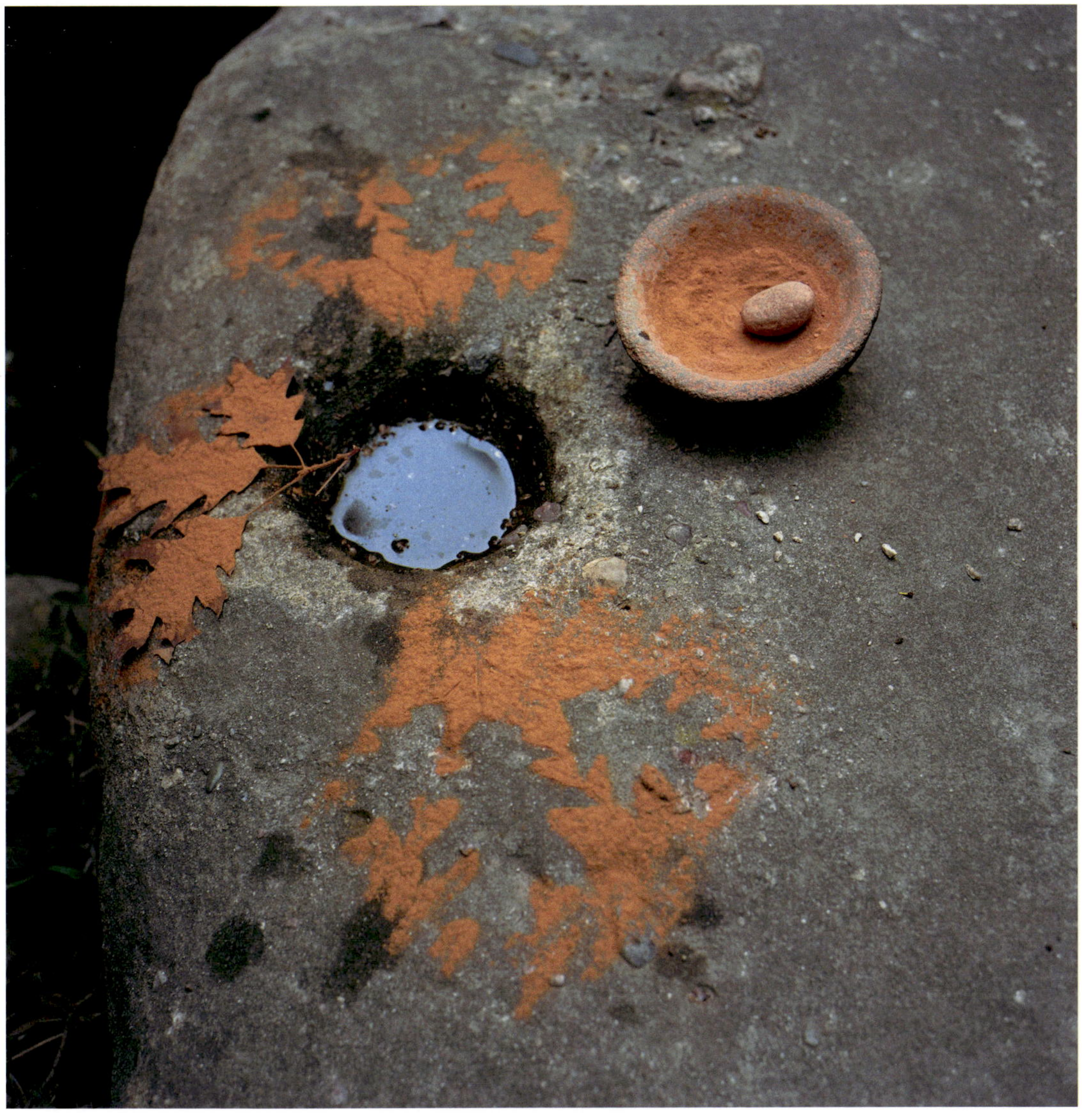

Figure 4
Mercedes Dorame, *Well of Moon and Sky—Kotuumot Kehaay*, 2013. Archival pigment print, 30 × 30 in. The Huntington, Purchased with funds from The Philip and Muriel Berman Foundation, 2021.14.2.

this region, these elements propose that the culture needs to be carefully tended and, like her grandmother's metate, passed down from generation to generation.

Crossing Borders

Artists also crossed borders. American artists traveled widely in the nineteenth century, many venturing abroad to connect with not only Europe's history but also its flourishing art scene. Others stayed closer to home, exploring the farthest reaches of the hemisphere—North, Central, and South America. The nineteenth century ushered in a wave of travel through the extension of railroads, economic development, and land speculation that permitted and encouraged this travel. Some of these artists were sponsored by governmental expeditions or private investors, while others followed their own wanderlust, capturing and selling landscapes for an eager public. Their pictures, whether romantic views of distant lands or documentary scenes resulting from close observation, often showed the landscape as if devoid of human occupation, ripe for economic development. This colonialist view had a dramatic effect on Americans' perceptions of the landscape and the politics of land use for generations, after a period of nationalistic revolutions and independence movements had swept across the hemisphere in the late eighteenth and nineteenth centuries. These pictures embodied an environmentally centered view of nationhood—comforting, albeit deceptive—at a time when land was being profoundly altered by development and industrialization. This new internationalism also prompted curiosity and anxiety around what exactly it meant to be "American." Art expressed this soul-searching and its multifaceted answers.

The American West was a draw for many East Coast artists. One such artist was the New York painter Thomas Moran, who traveled extensively in the Western territories, initially on governmental expeditions. In 1873, Moran accompanied Major John Wesley Powell's geological survey team to explore areas of the American Southwest, including Utah and the Grand Canyon. Using sketches that he had made in Utah during that journey, Moran created his painting *Rock Towers of the Rio Virgin* (fig. 5) in 1908. The work depicts the north fork of the Virgin River in what is now Zion National Park. Part of the Colorado River watershed flowing down to the Gulf of California, this region had been part of Mexico just two decades before. It was also home to the Southern Paiute and historically ancestral Puebloan cultures, as well as recently arrived Mormon immigrants, who settled in this borderland region. Merging a detailed, realistic foreground with a romantic, ethereal background, this painting becomes less a literal record of what the artist saw than a personal, spiritual vision inspired by nature.

Figure 3
Sandy Rodriguez, *YOU ARE HERE—Tovaangar / El Pueblo de Nuestra Señora la Reina de los Ángeles de Porciúncula / Los Angeles*, 2021. Hand-processed walnut ink and 23-karat gold on amate paper, each panel: 94½ × 47 in. The Huntington, Purchased with funds from the Diversity, Equity, and Inclusion Committee and the estate of George and Nancy Parsons, 2023.3.

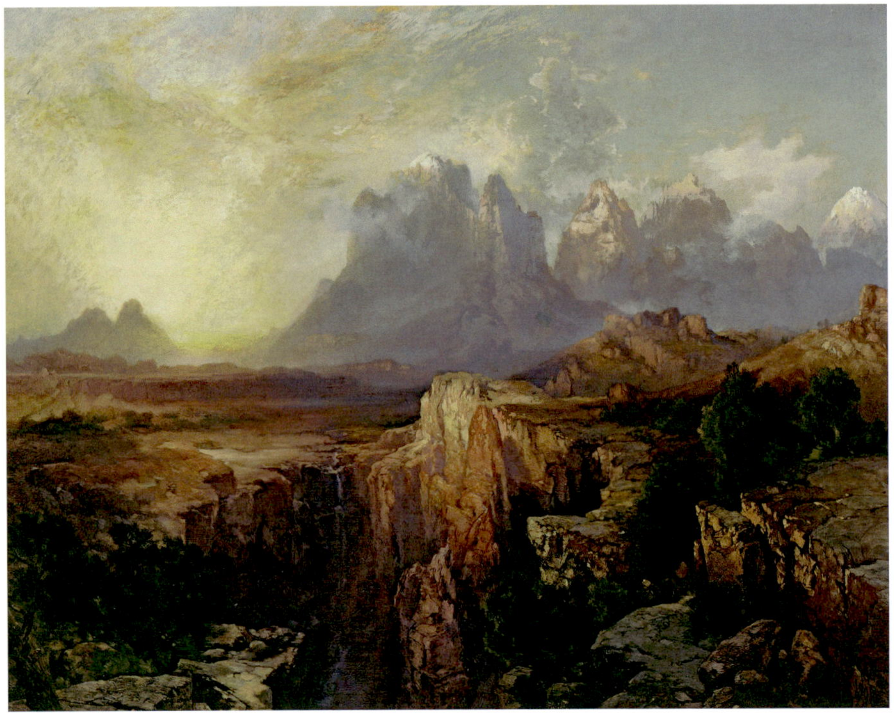

Figure 5
Thomas Moran, *Rock Towers of the Rio Virgin*, 1908. Oil on canvas, 23 × 30 in. The Huntington, Gift of the Virginia Steele Scott Foundation, 83.8.34.

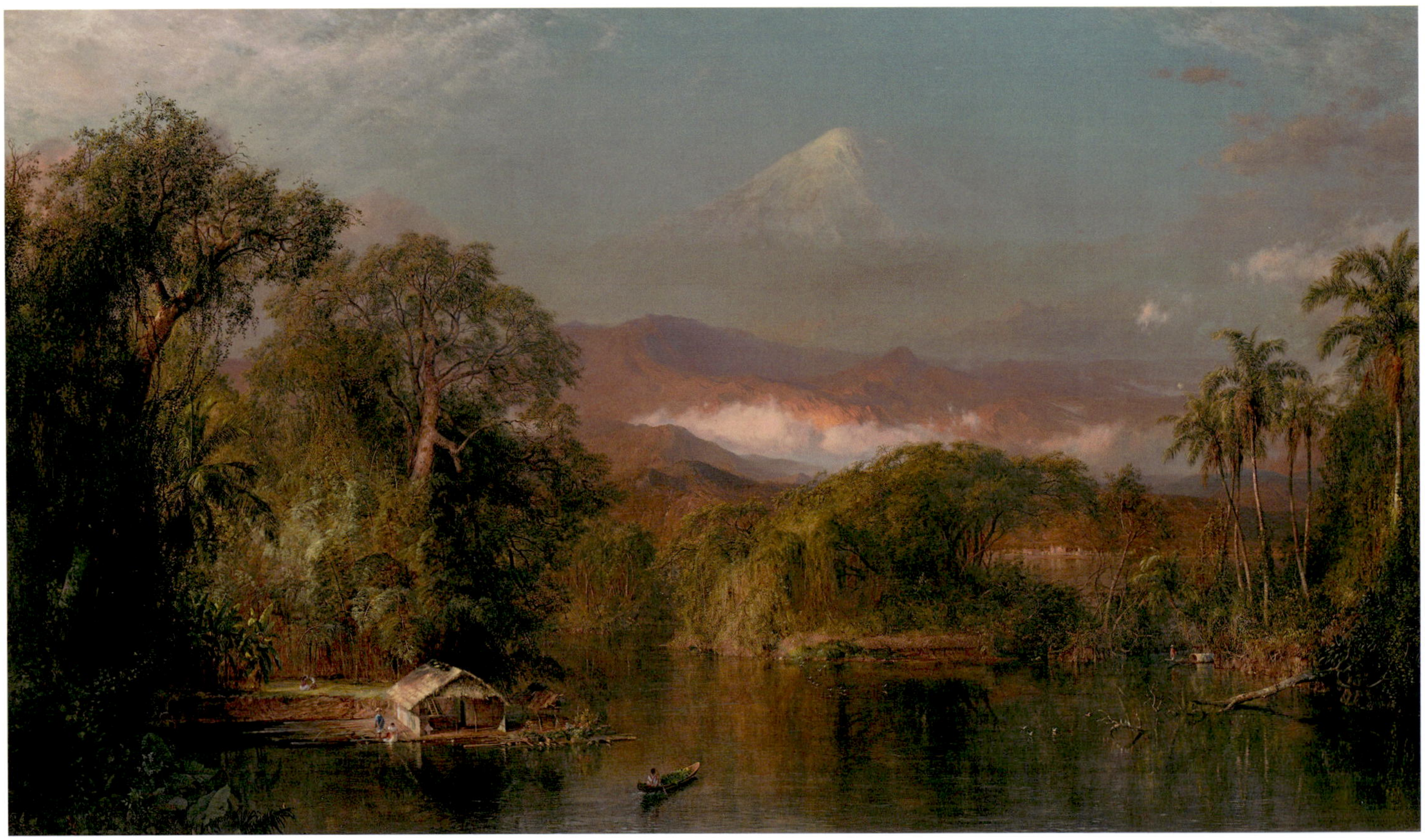

Figure 6
Frederic Edwin Church, *Chimborazo*, 1864. Oil on canvas, 48 × 84 in. The Huntington, Gift of the Virginia Steele Scott Foundation, 89.1.

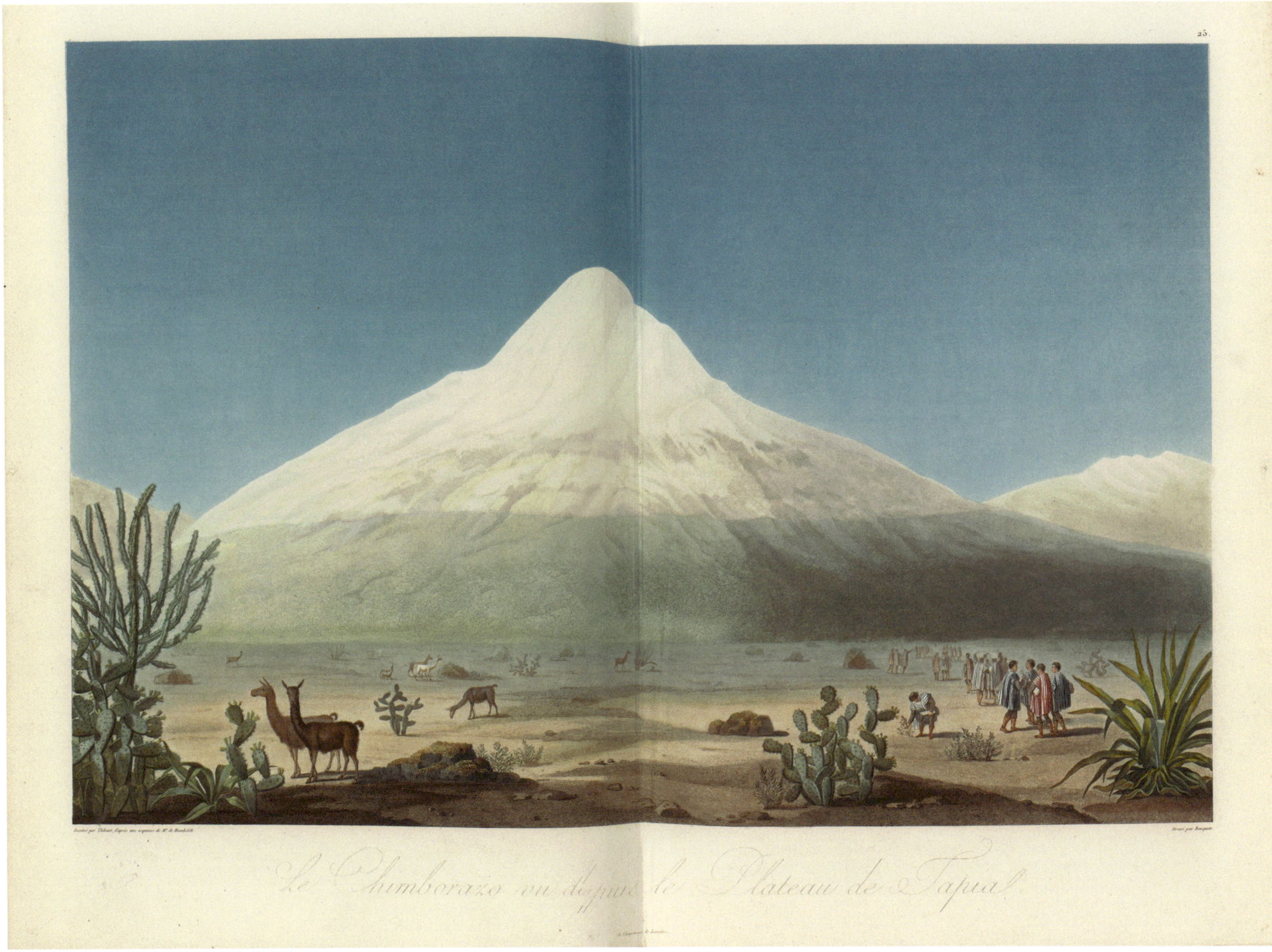

Figure 7
"Chimborazo," frontispiece to Alexander von Humboldt, *Vues des Cordillères, et monumens des peuples indigènes de l'Amérique* (F. Schoell, ca. 1810). The Huntington, 88919.

Two years prior to Powell's survey, Moran had accompanied another federally sponsored team exploring the Upper Yellowstone, led by geologist Ferdinand Vandeveer Hayden. On that trip Moran befriended the photographer William Henry Jackson, and together their photographs and paintings helped persuade the US Congress to designate the Yellowstone region the first National Park.

Fellow American artist Frederic Edwin Church also traveled widely throughout the hemisphere, venturing to the Arctic to record images of icebergs and to the tropical climes of South America. In 1853 and 1857, Church journeyed to Ecuador, following in the footsteps of the Prussian/German explorer Alexander von Humboldt, the leading naturalist of the generation before Charles Darwin. The resulting paintings, including *Chimborazo* (fig. 6), painted in 1864, and his famed *Heart of the Andes* (1859), embody Humboldt's theory of the interdependence of natural systems. Church takes the viewer on a virtual voyage from the torrid, tropical Ecuadorian rainforest in the foreground of the painting to the temperate grasslands in the center to the frigid, ice-clad peak of Mount Chimborazo, which hovers over the scene. Although committed to scientific accuracy, Church presents a composite view of Chimborazo based on his own extensive field studies and illustrations from Humboldt's publications, such as *Vues des Cordillères* (ca. 1810) (fig. 7). Rather than simply transcribing nature, Church wished to convey the whole experience of Ecuador to the viewer. Even so, Church has imbued the painting with specific details, including the area around the village of Bobahoyo in western Ecuador, which is visible in the clearing through the trees at right. In the foreground along the riverbank is a small hut and a canoe transporting flowers to market. Because the artist sketched from life in Ecuador, botanists can compare his images with species that are known to grow there. The tall palms at the right of the painting appear to be *Syagrus sancona*. Along the riverbank to the left, a crop of bananas or gingers (*Musa* sp. or *Heliconia* sp.) is shaded by another palm, likely *Phytelephas aequatorialis*, which was often used among Indigenous communities for this purpose. The bamboo growing behind the hut is *Guadua angustifolia*, a widely cultivated plant, and in the left foreground are the giant leaves of the aroid *Xanthosoma*.[4]

Still other American artists, such as Lockwood de Forest, traveled farther afield to Europe and the Middle East, Africa, and South Asia. The son of an elite New York family in the shipping industry, De Forest was one of the first American artists to travel to Egypt after fellow landscape painter Frederic Edwin Church, his great-uncle through marriage. De Forest's painting *Bank of the Nile Opposite Cairo, Egypt* (1879/86) (fig. 8) evokes a still, sun-drenched afternoon experienced during his travels through Egypt in 1875 and 1878. This painting is a composite of multiple views he sketched of the area. Beginning in 1881, De Forest lived for two years in British-occupied India, where he founded the Ahmedabad Wood Carving Company that sourced traditional woodwork from master craftsmen in India, and then imported it into the United States for designers such as Louis Comfort Tiffany. The original, elaborately carved teakwood frame on this rare studio painting by De Forest speaks to the complex relationship between art, design, and the global economy at the end of the nineteenth century. It also signals the growing imperialism of the United States, as the country went from being a continental empire to a global empire with the taking of Hawai'i, the Philippines, Puerto Rico, Cuba, and other territories. Like Thomas Moran, in the last two decades of his life, De Forest began to winter each year in California. He eventually retired full-time to Santa Barbara, where he continued to sketch and paint, creating hundreds of images of the California coast and the inland mountains and valleys of the state. Yet, De Forest's views are still inflected with the internationalism that characterized his earlier career, during which he became adept at selling these exotic visions to an eager American public.

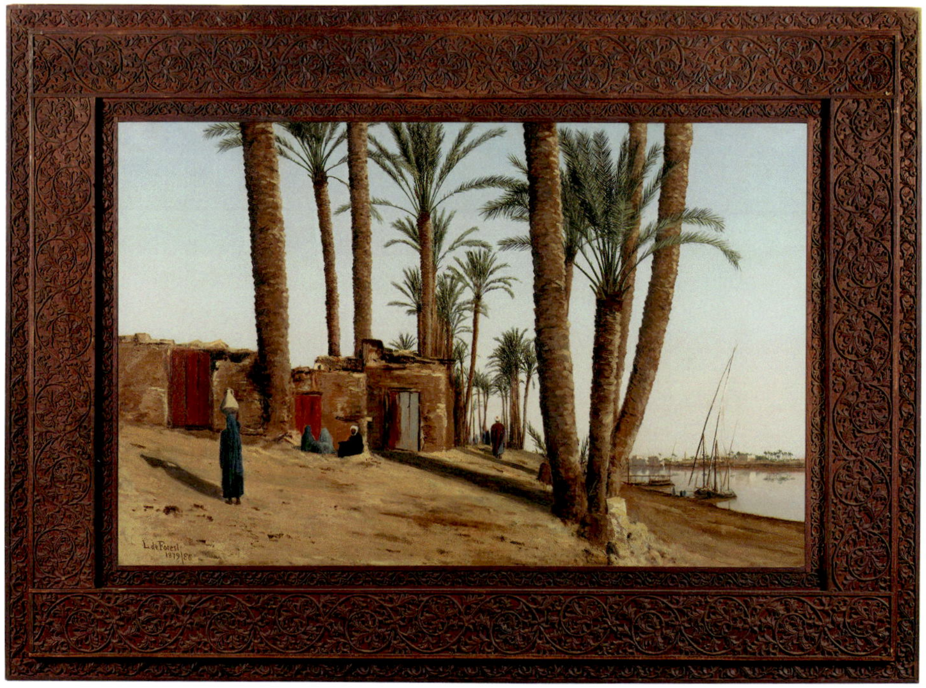

Figure 8
Lockwood de Forest, *Bank of the Nile Opposite Cairo, Egypt*, 1879/86. Oil on canvas, frame: 45⅜ × 63⅜ in. The Huntington, Purchased with funds from the Art Collectors' Council, Connie Perkins Endowment, Schweppe Art Acquisitions Fund, the Virginia Steele Scott Foundation Acquisition Fund for American Art, Ida Crotty Print and Graphic Arts Endowment, Robert R. Wark Acquisition Fund, and the Kelvin Davis Endowment, 2021.4.

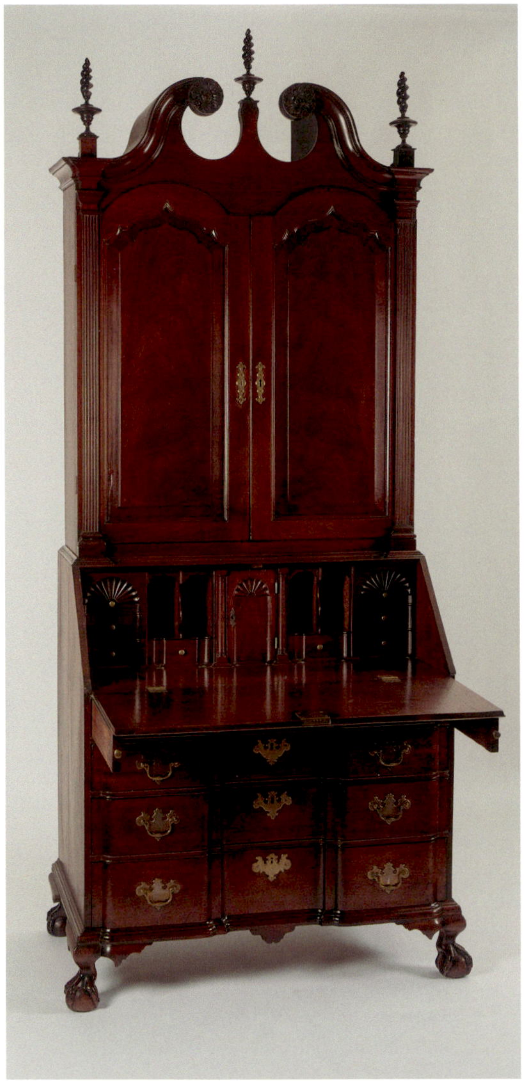

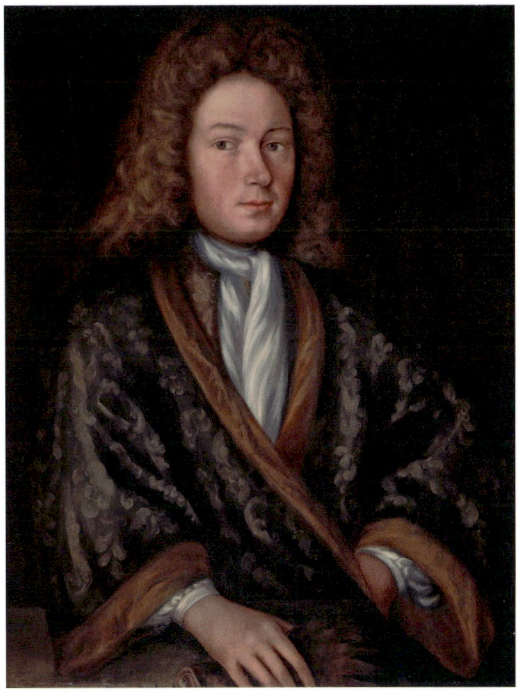

Figure 9
Desk and bookcase, ca. 1775. Mahogany, Eastern white pine, and brass, 100 × 40 × 23½ in. Gail-Oxford Collection, The Huntington, 2021.4.

Figure 10
Attributed to Gerrit Duyckinck, *Portrait of a Man*, ca. 1690. Oil on panel, 30 × 24 in. The Huntington, Gift of Mr. and Mrs. Bradford M. Mishler, 2001.18.1.

Global Objects

Globalism is not a new phenomenon. From the late fifteenth century onward, the world was connected through trade and communication as never before. This period marked the first time that the four parts of the world—the European conception of the "four continents," namely Europe, Africa, Asia, and the Americas—were interconnected through robust transoceanic trade networks. The colonial Americas were at the center of these networks, linked via the transatlantic and transpacific trade. This trade brought in precious luxury items from across the world and fostered waves of immigration, which have continued to shape the history and culture of these regions. Whether within the Spanish, Portuguese, Dutch, British, German, or French colonial settlements in the Americas, or the Indigenous lands of Native populations, these areas were part of a complex hemispheric borderland where people, goods, languages, and cultures intermixed.

Artworks and objects made during this period are also products of an economy of extraction that brought raw materials to market. These global trade networks carried goods and materials from around the world, such as timber, silver, and other valuable commodities, that were transformed into finished products in colonial workshops in the Americas. Such objects expressed their worldliness both through their cosmopolitan styles and through the ability of the producers and consumers to control long-distance trade networks over land and water. They are also products of gaping inequalities of a mercantile economy and forced labor that fueled colonial expansion across the hemisphere. Objects made of mahogany (fig. 9)—which was imported either from the Caribbean, *Swietenia mahagoni*, or mainland Central America, *Swietenia macrophylla*—or silver, the raw material for which most likely came from the prodigious mines of Mexico and South America, reflected these long-distance trade networks as well as the many hands involved in the extraction, shipping, and processing of the materials. Likewise, expensive objects meant to hold commodities, such as sugar, tea, coffee, or spices, were costly both in terms of price but also the toll taken in human terms, given the brutality of the silver mines, the exploitation of Indigenous peoples, and the inhumanity of the slave trade.

Portraits of the period often include objects or attributes that signify global markets or long-distance trade. Dutch émigré painter Gerrit Duyckinck's portrait of a man from the late seventeenth century shows these connections to the larger world of trade (fig. 10). Although the identity of the sitter is unknown, he wears a fashionable, silky, loose-fitting robe called a *Japonse rok*, which was associated with the style of Dutch merchants. Modeled on the Japanese Edo-period *kosode*, *Japonse rokken* signaled the early trade connections between the Dutch Republic and Japan. Given that the painter was a Dutch artist working in New York City and upstate New York, the sitter was likely a successful merchant engaged in the newly expanding global markets in New York, which then, as today, drew traders and businesspeople from around the world. The portrait dates to after the transfer of power from Dutch to British rule in 1664, when the name of the colony formally changed from "New Netherland" to "New York," and the area became regulated under the British Board of Trade rather than the Dutch East India Company.

In his striking portrait of the Indigenous leader *Moanahonga (Great Walker), An Ioway Chief* (ca. 1824), the painter Charles Bird King portrays markers of the sitter's leadership and power: his extraordinary gunstock war club with pierced decoration on the iron blade, his tufted deerskin headdress (called a "roach"), red-tipped feathers, silver and shell jewelry, and his body paint in red and black, all of which refer to his tribal status and skill as a warrior (fig. 11). These attributes center on Moanahonga's (Mah-ne-hah-nak) careful choices in what he wore to the sitting, and the borderlands region in which he acquired his regalia. With the exception of the fur wrapped around his body, the deerskin roach, and feathers, which would have been available locally, many of the other elements were goods and materials obtained through long-distance trade. The iron blade and brass nails decorating the war club were typically imported from manufacturers on the East Coast or Europe, and the silver jewelry would have been brought in via minted coins or silver objects, which themselves

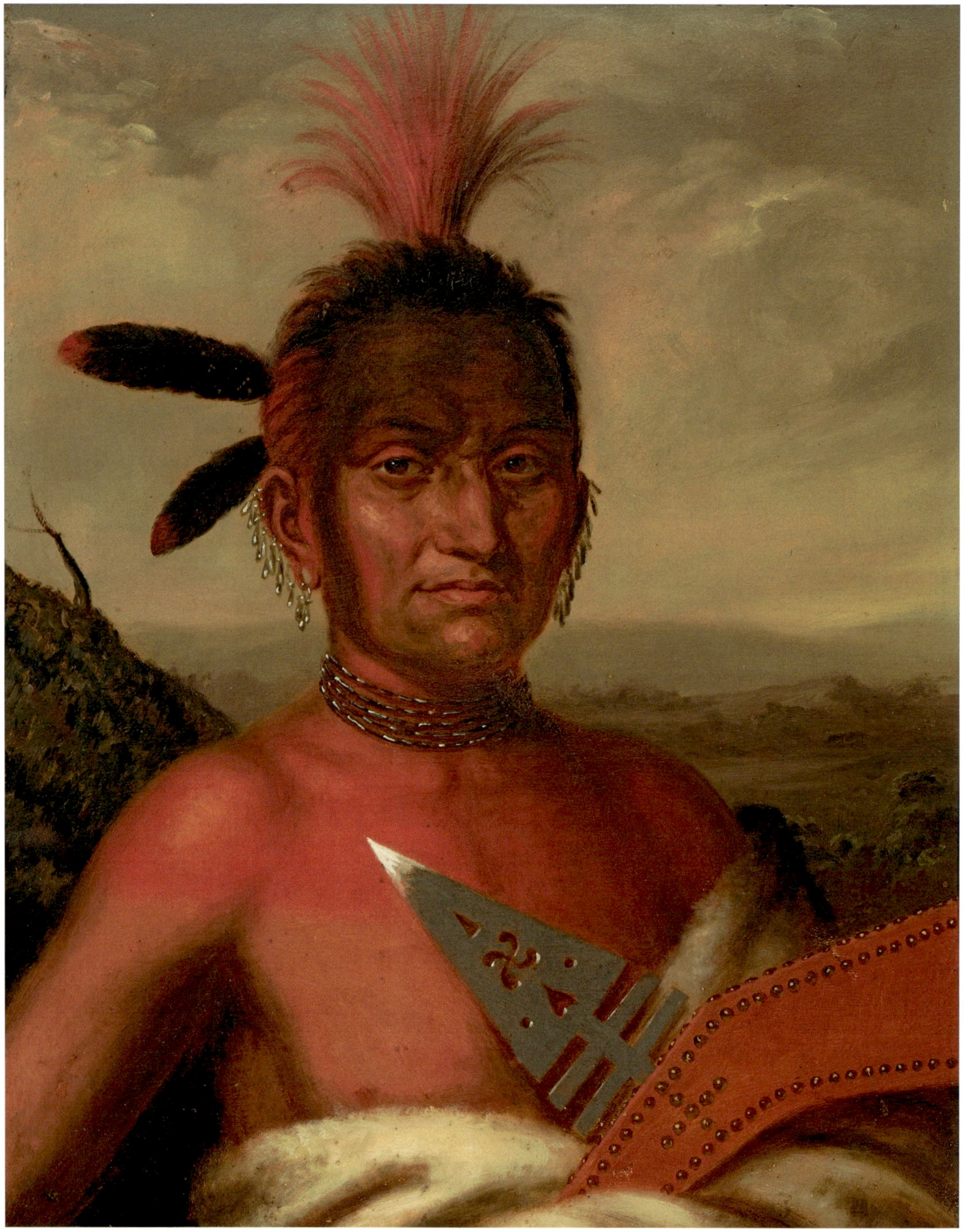

Figure 11
Charles Bird King, *Moanahonga (Great Walker), An Ioway Chief*, ca. 1824. Oil on panel, 17½ × 13¾ in. The Huntington, Purchased with funds from the Virginia Steele Scott Foundation Acquisition Fund for American Art and the Art Collectors' Council, the Lynn K. Altman Family Trust, Janis and Rudy Mercado Art Acquisitions Fund, the Angeles Attic Museum Fund for Art Acquisitions, in memory of Jackie McMahan and Eleanor Pitts La Vove, 2021.2.

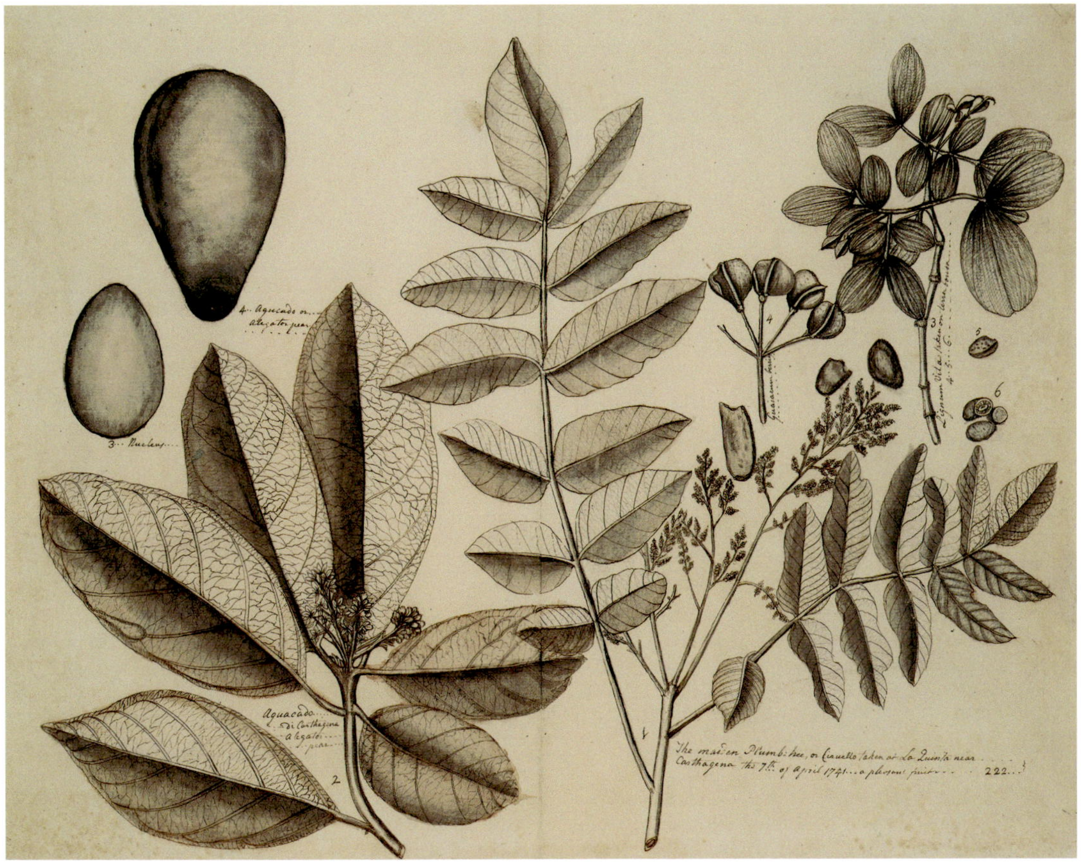

Figure 12
Thomas Malie, *Botanical Study (Plumb Tree and Avocado)*, 1741. Ink and wash on laid paper, 12½ × 15¾ in. The Huntington, Purchased with funds from the Virginia Steele Scott Foundation, 89.21.10.

probably originated through the Spanish trade from Mexico or Peru. Even the red paint decorating his body and the tips of the feathers, which could have been made from locally available red ocher, was, by this date, more likely imported vermilion, an expensive pigment that came from Europe, often traded for furs by tribes in the Great Lakes region and the Midwest. The detailed clothing, jewelry, and weaponry in the portrait are in stark contrast with the soft, atmospheric landscape in the background, a rare inclusion given that the picture was created in the painter's studio in Washington, DC.

Commissioned by the US government, King produced over a hundred such studio portraits of Native American leaders who had traveled to Washington during the 1820s to the 1840s to negotiate treaty settlements. The diplomatic visits were part of a decades-long strategy orchestrated by the US government to displace Native peoples and force them from their homelands under the guise of diplomacy. The visit in 1824 by Moanahonga and seventeen Ioway (Iowa) leaders resulted in the dispossession of their land in the northern half of Missouri and the group's removal westward to what is now the Kansas-Nebraska border. "Moanahonga, also known as Big Neck or No Fear, was an Ioway warrior patriot," writes Ioway tribal member and scholar Lance Foster. "He died defending his people and his homelands. During the War of 1812, he fought against US expansion west of the Mississippi River. Misled into signing the 1824 treaty that ceded lands in Missouri, he refused to leave. He continued to fight the United States, including a battle in 1829. He remained in his Missouri and Iowa homeland until a final battle in 1831, during which he and an enemy Sioux chief killed each other in hand-to-hand combat. Finding their two great leaders where they had fallen, the Sioux and the Ioway made peace, and from that time on the two nations lived in friendship."[5] While Moanahonga died less than a decade after the portrait was made, having fought to protect his people and their homelands, the portrait survives as visual evidence of his political and economic status within the shifting borderlands of the United States.

The extractive economy of the colonial Americas and the land grab that displaced Indigenous populations also brought naturalists in search of botanical specimens and ecological knowledge. This contributed significantly to general scientific understanding, while at the same time supporting the British Crown's colonialist efforts. In 1741, the British naturalist Thomas Malie traveled to the Spanish-held territories of Cuba and New Granada, now modern-day Colombia, as part of a British military expedition. His sketches provide a rare portrait of an ecosystem in the Caribbean through a lens of extraction and commodification. On April 7, 1741, he recorded the leaves and flowers of the "Plumb-tree" or "Ciruello," commonly known as the jocote (*Spondias purpura*), collected in La Quinta near Cartagena, Colombia (fig. 12). Described in the drawing as a "pleasant fruit," the jocote tree grows widely in the tropical regions of Latin America and was exported to the Philippines by the Spanish. Also in his drawing are images of the fruit, seed, and leaves of the avocado tree—referred to in his sketch as an "alegator [alligator] pear," an apt name that apparently didn't stick—a species Henry Huntington cultivated on his ranch in Southern California. At the top right of the sketch are images of the wood, leaves, and berries of the *Lignum vitae* tree, also known as *Guaiacum*, an unusually hard and dense wood native to the Caribbean and the northern coast of South America. *Lignum vitae* became a major export product used in shipbuilding and occasionally as ornamental wood on furniture. Extremely durable, it was even used as a substitute for metal parts in pendulum clocks. Malie's expeditions into the Spanish territories, unusual for a British subject at the time, were made possible when the British invaded and briefly occupied Cartagena and an area near Santiago de Cuba in 1741 during the ill-fated War of Jenkins' Ear, as the British tried to expand their colonial territories in the Americas.

The Caribbean became a highly contested region during the colonial period, as islands and coastal cities were taken over, switched allegiances, and became vassal states of warring European powers. It was also fertile ground for the development of cash crops, such as sugarcane and tobacco, supported by the influx of enslaved peoples from Africa. The transatlantic slave trade, largely eschewed by the Spanish, was heavily promoted by the British, French, and Portuguese, as millions of enslaved peoples were brought to the Americas from the sixteenth through the nineteenth centuries. Islands frequently changed hands, especially during the aftermath of the Seven Years' War, including the island of Dominica, which had been French since the seventeenth century. The island attracted artists, such as Agostino Brunias, who painted images for the emergent colonial elites who controlled the labor and agricultural economies under the colonial governments. Born and trained in Rome, Brunias began his career as a Grand Tour painter before moving to England, where he worked under the famed architect and interior designer Robert Adam. In 1764, he sailed to the British West Indies, eventually taking up residence in Dominica, one of the Windward Islands of the Caribbean that had recently come under British rule following the Treaty of Paris in 1763. He traveled widely in the region, and his portrayal of local society provides a record of Indigenous, Afro-Caribbean, and Creole culture, specifically the role of both free and enslaved people of color within colonial society. A set of six paintings, dating to the 1770s, depicts groups of figures in the landscape (fig. 13). As a type of portraiture practiced in the Americas in the eighteenth century, they are akin to Mexican *castas* (caste paintings) or *costumbristas* (paintings of local customs), which capture not only scenes of daily life but also social and racial stratifications in colonial society.

This period continues to be a source of interest to artists who are interrogating aspects of American history. African American, Jamaican-born artist Nari Ward is renowned for his deeply moving and thought-provoking installations and assemblage works of art made of objects found in his neighborhood in Harlem. His work *Anchoring Escapement: Baule* (2018) consists of a modified eighteenth-century tall-case clock that relates to the history of slavery (fig. 14). Placed inside the body of the clock, a West African wooden figure peers out through the window. The artist has replaced the clock face with a diamond-shaped Kongolese cosmogram, which he first encountered in the First Baptist

Figure 13
Clockwise from top left: Agostino Brunias, *Free Women of Dominica Bathing in a Stream; Free Women of Dominica; A Young Couple and Child Promenading, Dominica; A Native Family of Saint Vincent; Free Women of Dominica with a Child;* and *Flower Girls of Dominica*, 1770s. Oil on canvas, 11¾ × 9⅛ in. each. The Huntington, Purchased with funds from the Art Collectors' Council, with additional support from the Schweppe Art Acquisitions Fund, the Connie Perkins Endowment and the estate of George and Nancy Parsons, 2023.3.1–6.

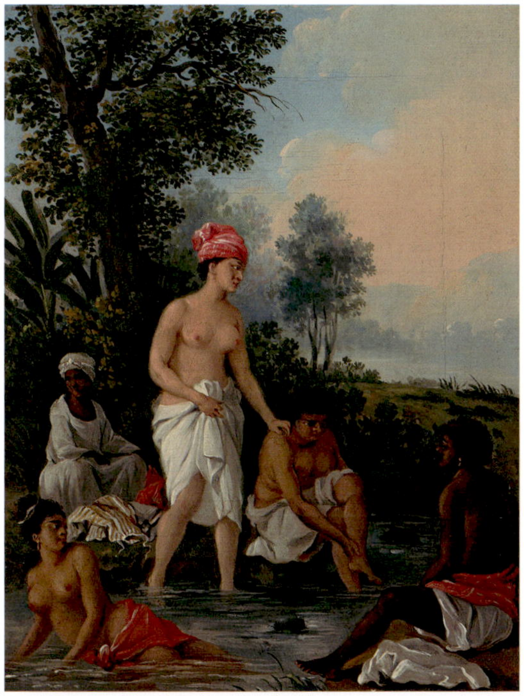
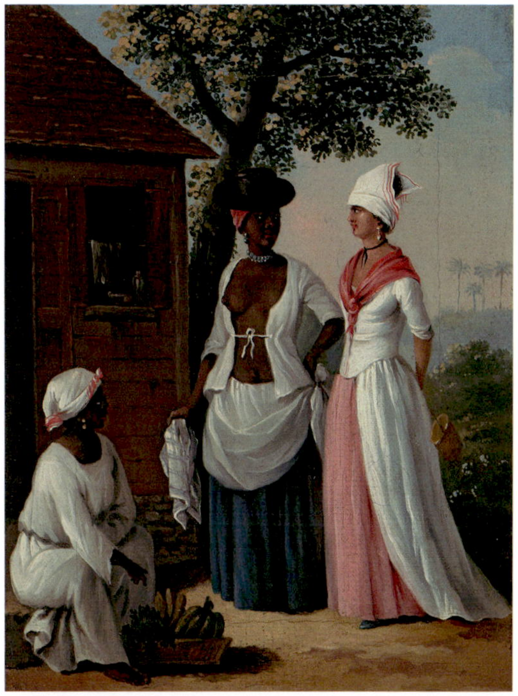
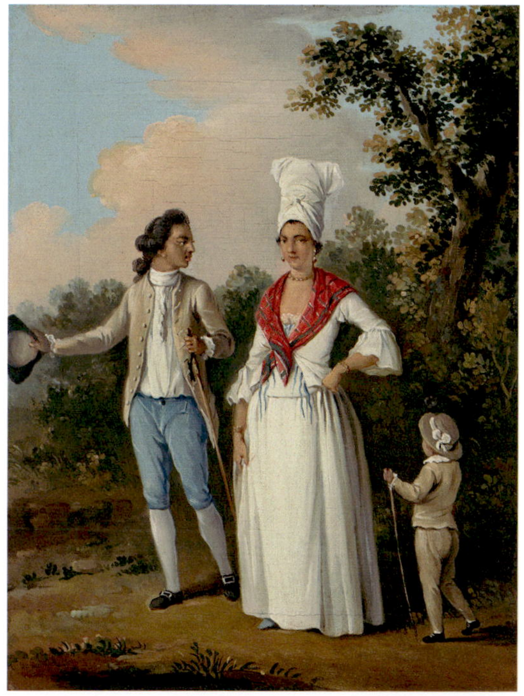
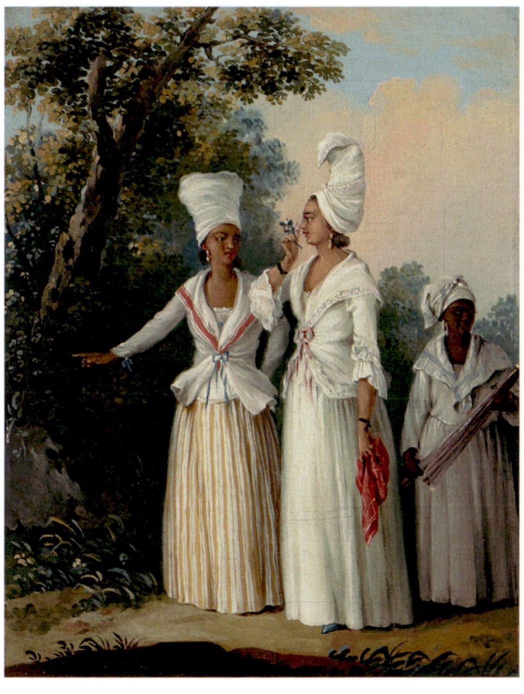
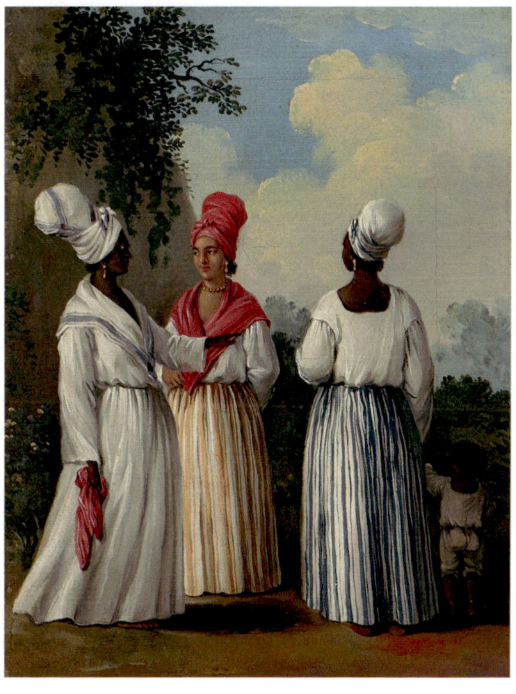
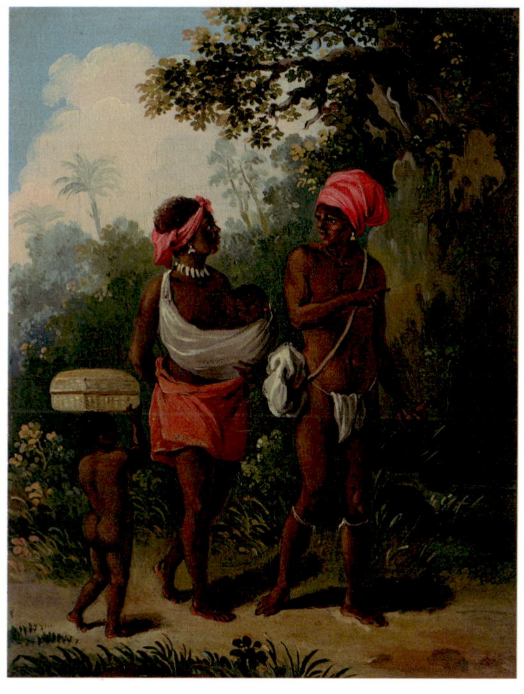

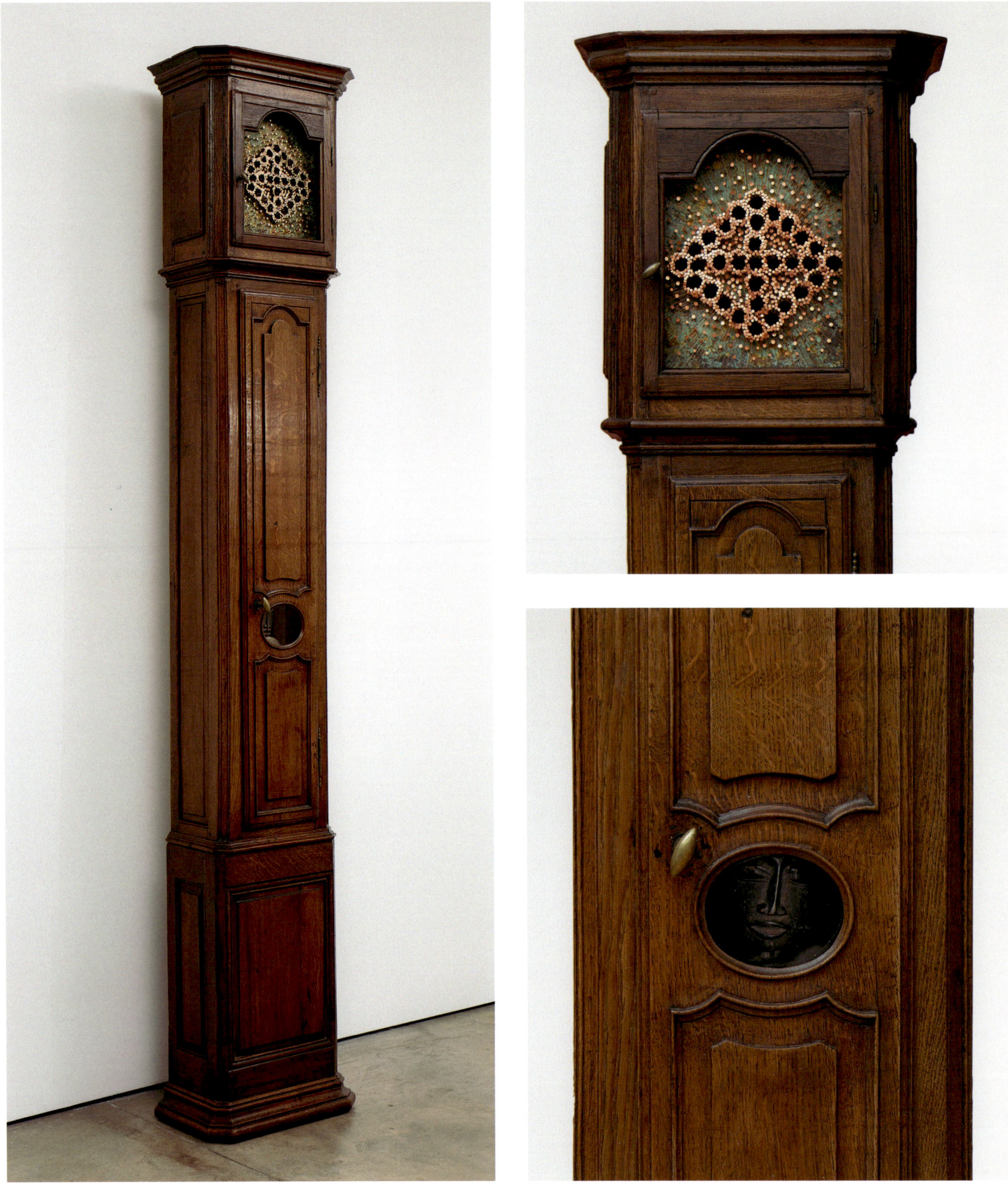

Figure 14
Nari Ward, *Anchoring Escapement: Baule* with two details, 2018. Grandfather clock case, copper sheet with patina, copper nails, and African statue, 99 × 17 × 12 in. The Huntington, Purchased with funds from the estate of George and Nancy Parsons, 2023.5.

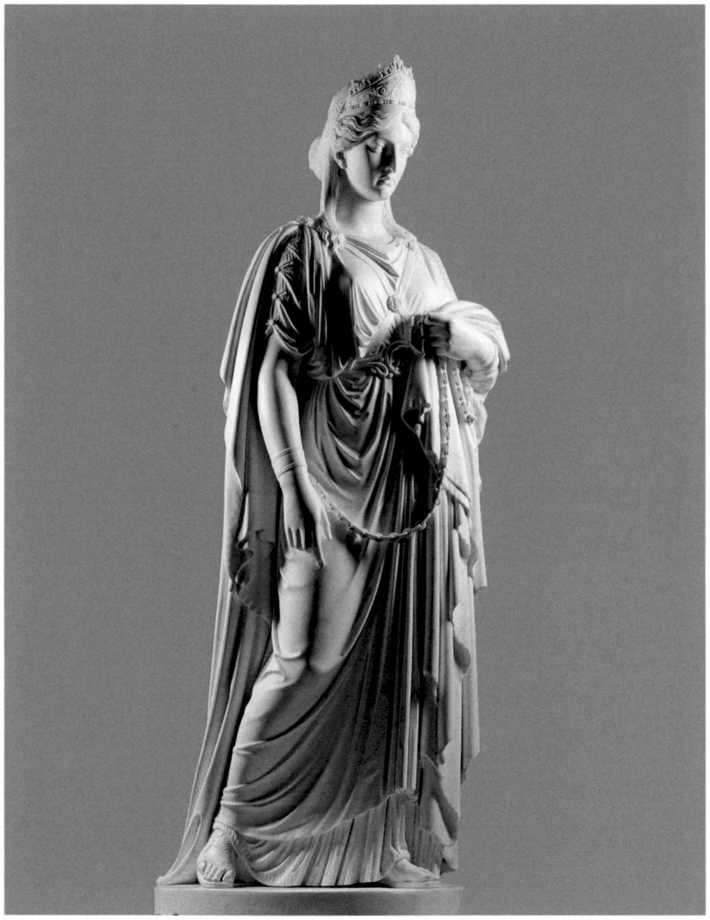

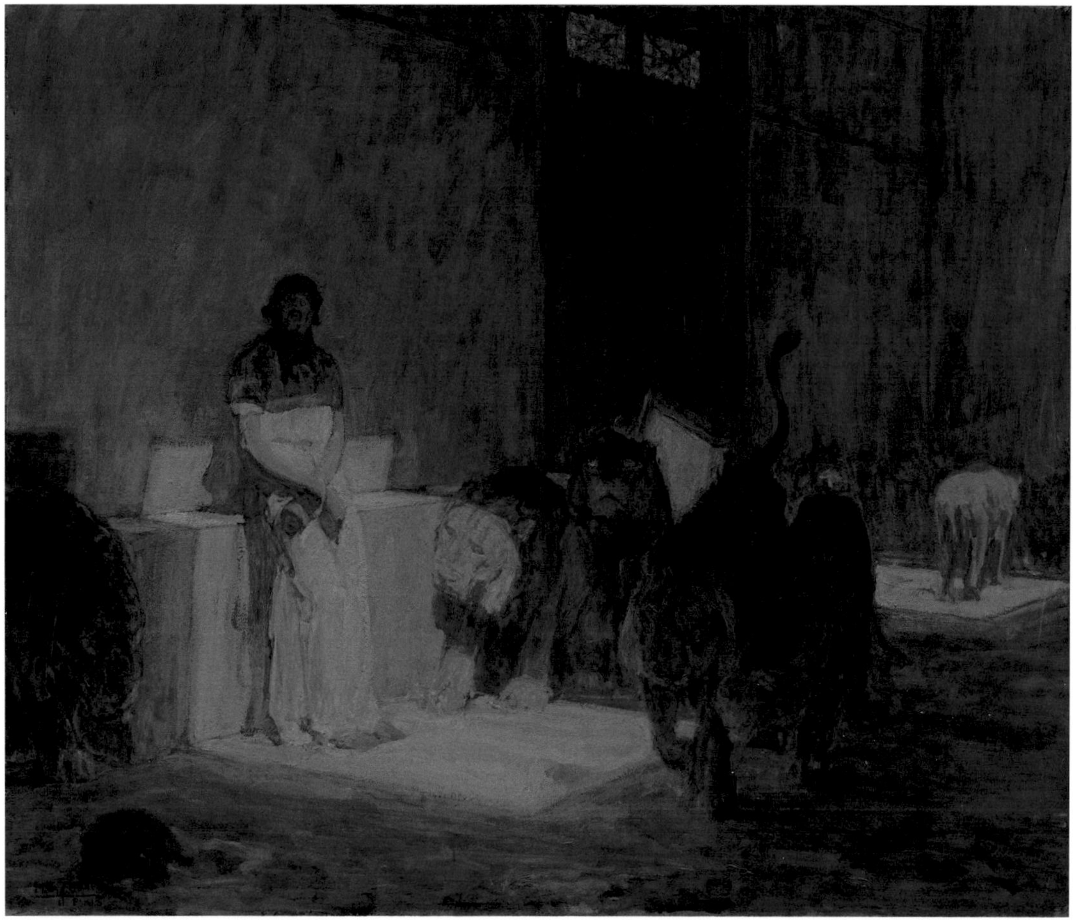

Figure 15
Harriet Goodhue Hosmer, *Zenobia in Chains*, 1859. Marble, 82 × 27 × 33 in. The Huntington, Purchased with the Virginia Steele Scott Acquisition fund for American Art, 2007.26.

Figure 16
Henry Ossawa Tanner, *Daniel in the Lions' Den*, 1907–18. Oil on paper mounted on canvas, 41⅛ × 50 in. Los Angeles County Museum of Art, Mr. and Mrs. William Preston Harrison Collection, 22.6.3.

Church in Savannah, Georgia, one of the earliest African American churches in the United States and a site on the Underground Railroad. Drilled into the floorboards of the church, this symbol allowed persons escaping slavery who were hiding under the floorboards to breathe. Created with hammered copper nails, this emblem in Ward's work also relates to the tradition of West African power figures with nailed surfaces—each nail signifying a misdeed within the community that is ritually hammered into the sculpture. Ward's work is a profound critique of colonialism and how the eighteenth-century Enlightenment, represented by the tall-case clock, was underpinned by the transatlantic slave trade. The title, referring to the act of escaping, also refers to the "anchor escapement" of an eighteenth-century clock, the part of the mechanism hidden behind the dial that keeps time. Ward offers a powerful commentary on the period, one that created great wealth and intellectual and technological advancements, but also immense imbalance and inequality.

Breaking Barriers

The Huntington's galleries also present artworks that explore personal and societal boundaries, highlighting artists who broke barriers in their own time. These works are epitomized by Harriet Goodhue Hosmer's *Zenobia in Chains* (1859), one of the most significant American sculptures of the mid-nineteenth century (fig. 15). It represents the third-century queen of Palmyra (in present-day Syria) who was captured and imprisoned after leading a rebellion against the occupying Roman Empire. According to legend, when Emperor Aurelian saw Zenobia's dignity and beauty while shackled, he freed her. Hosmer's life, like that of the ancient queen, was defined by rebellion. At age twenty-two, Hosmer moved to Rome to become a professional sculptor, finding support within a circle of creative expatriate women that included Edmonia Lewis, a sculptor of mixed Black and Native American (Mississauga Ojibwe) heritage, and the actor Charlotte Cushman. These women transcended nineteenth-century social expectations by living alone, pursuing artistic careers, and, in the case of Hosmer, being open about her queer identity. When *Zenobia* was exhibited in London's International Exhibition of 1862,

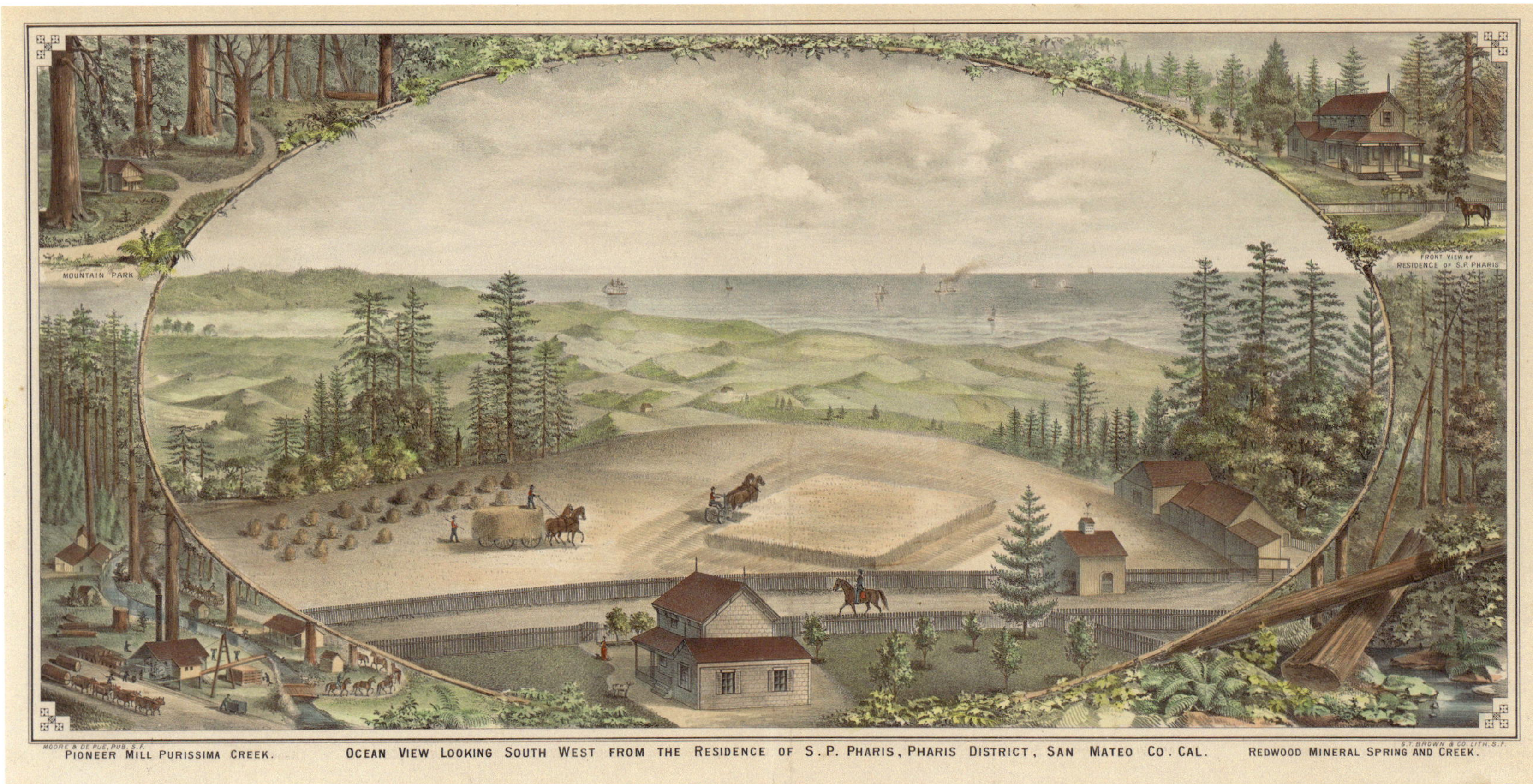

Figure 17
Grafton Tyler Brown, *Ocean View Looking South West from the Residence of S. P. Pharis. Pharis District, San Mateo Co. Cal.*, ca. 1870. Color-printed lithograph, $13\frac{5}{8} \times 29\frac{3}{4}$ in. Jay T. Last Collection of Views Prints and Ephemera, The Huntington, priJLC_VIEW_000635.

disparaging male critics wrote that a woman could not have had the skill or strength to execute such a monumental work. Thought to be lost for nearly 150 years, the sculpture appeared at a London auction in 2007 and is now recognized as one of the artist's masterworks.

Some African American artists left the United States in the nineteenth century, finding greater freedom from the strictures of race, sexuality, gender, and class than they experienced at home. One such artist is Henry Ossawa Tanner, who in 1891 moved to France, where he spent most of his professional life in self-exile. In his painting *Daniel in the Lions' Den* (1907–18), the biblical figure Daniel, a trusted Hebrew advisor to the Babylonian king, awaits death as punishment for praying to his god instead of the ruler (fig. 16). A beam of moonlight shines down on Daniel, who, despite the horror of his situation, appears still and contemplative. Tanner was born in Pittsburgh, where his father was an African Methodist Episcopal bishop and where, years earlier, his mother had gained freedom from enslavement through the Underground Railroad. After studying art in Pennsylvania and Paris, Tanner garnered international acclaim for his religious paintings. Tanner's choice of Daniel—a man unjustly condemned to death—was poignant at a time of systemic persecution and violence against Black Americans. Yet Tanner's symbolism is a hopeful one: With God's aid, Daniel survives the night.

Other Black artists of the nineteenth century forged careers in landscape painting, such as Robert Scott Duncanson, Edward Mitchell Bannister, and Grafton Tyler Brown. Duncanson was born a freeman in New York State and spent most of his career in Cincinnati, Ohio, where

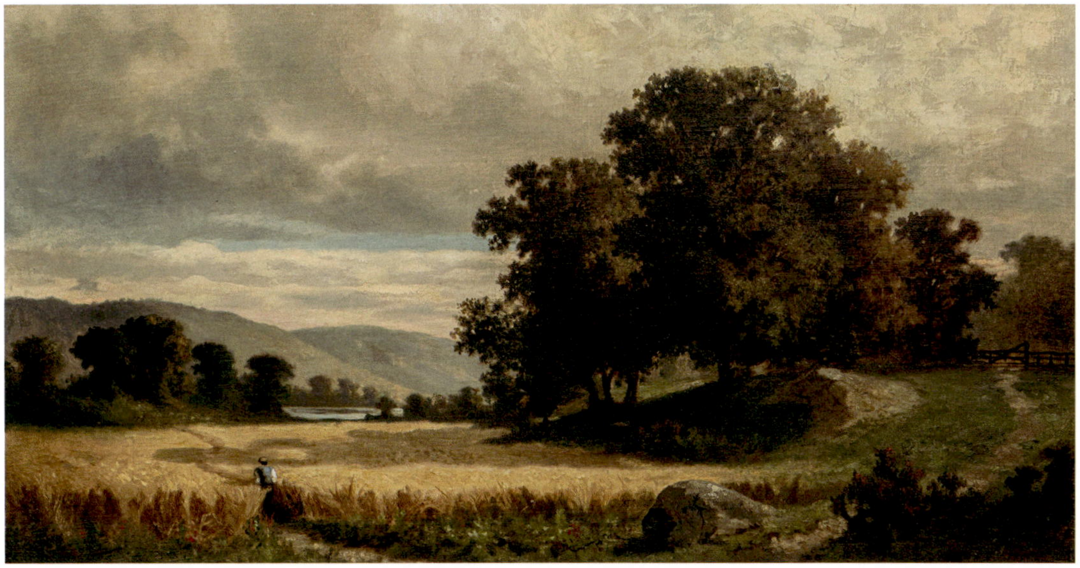

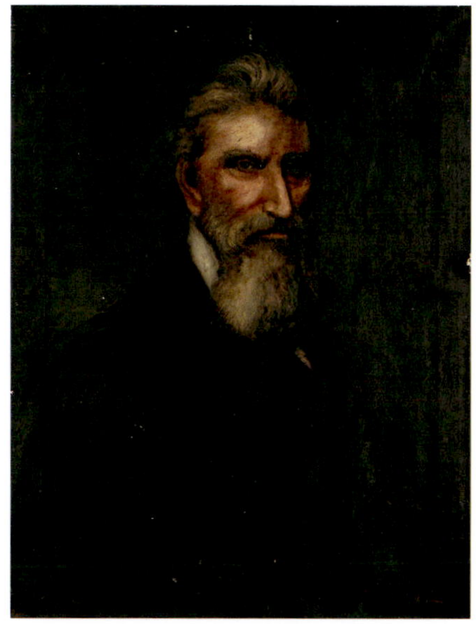

Figure 18
Edward Mitchell Bannister, *Untitled (Walking Through a Field)*, ca. 1870–80. Oil on canvas, 22 × 42¼ in. The Huntington, Purchased with funds from the Art Collectors' Council with additional support from the Douglas and Eunice Erb Goodan Endowment Fund, 2023.13.

Figure 19
Cloyd Lee Boykin, *John Brown*, ca. 1913. Oil on canvas, 28¼ × 22⅛ in. The Huntington, 14.66.

slavery was illegal. Like Tanner, he traveled to Europe for training and inspiration. His *Landscape with Ruin* (1853) reflects his interest in the compositions and color palette of Dutch old master paintings, as well as the use of idealized and allegorical imagery. Duncanson left the United States during the Civil War, moving to Canada, where he helped launch the country's landscape movement.

Grafton Tyler Brown immigrated to California in 1858 as part of the Great Migration, settling in the Bay Area, where he found success as a lithographer and topographic artist in San Francisco. His firm, GT Brown and Co., produced skillful lithographs, some showing burgeoning development in areas such as San Mateo County, California (fig. 17). After 1881, he became a full-time painter, producing scenes of popular Western landscapes for eager tourists, such as *Grand Canyon of the Yellowstone from Lookout Point* (1887) in The Huntington's collection.

Born in Canada to a Barbadian father and a mother of Scottish ancestry, Bannister moved to Massachusetts, a free state, and later to Rhode Island, where he lived with his wife, businesswoman, hairdresser, and abolitionist Christina Carteaux. Bannister often painted landscapes in and around the state of Rhode Island and the Providence Plantations, which, during the colonial period, had supported a system of enslaved labor on an unprecedented scale compared to other areas of New England. A staunch abolitionist, Bannister was concerned about the plight of formerly enslaved Black citizens during the Reconstruction period after the Civil War. His paintings offer sanguine views of agriculture and laborers, including his untitled landscape from the 1870s (fig. 18). Imbued with soft light radiating from a pastel-infused sky, the composition reveals both how Bannister emulated Hudson River School painters like Thomas Cole and John Frederick Kensett, but also how he embraced the more international style of the Barbizon School of artists, such as Jules Breton, Gustave Courbet, and Jean-François Millet.

Bannister became a respected and award-winning painter of landscapes, portraits, and seascapes. He achieved critical acclaim in 1876 when his work *Under the Oaks* received a first prize in painting at the Philadelphia Centennial Exposition. When he was denied entry into the exposition to accept the award because of his race, his fellow artists rallied to his defense. Bannister was especially influential in the growing art scene in Providence, where he served as one of the original board members of the Rhode Island School of Design in 1878 and two years later co-founded the Providence Art Club, an important organization of artists, amateurs, and art collectors created to stimulate the growth of art within the city.

The successful careers of these Black artists paved the way for future generations of American artists. Cloyd Lee Boykin, who was part of New York's Harlem Renaissance, revived themes from the nineteenth century, including depicting historical figures instrumental in fighting for Black rights. Trained in Boston and Paris, he founded Boykin's School of Art, the first school for Black artists in the United States, with centers in Boston and New York's Harlem and Greenwich Village neighborhoods. His portrait of John Brown, acquired by Henry and Arabella Huntington in 1914, is a rare painting of the radical abolitionist by a Black artist (fig. 19). It may have come to The Huntington through Arabella's philanthropic support for Hampton Institute and Tuskegee Institute, both historically Black colleges. There was also a close familial connection to Pasadena, as John Brown's sons Owen and Jason and daughter Ruth moved to Pasadena and nearby Altadena in the 1880s as part of a community of abolitionists. This area of Southern California later became a haven for Black artists, including the influential artist Charles White, who taught at Otis Art Institute (now Otis College of Art and Design) and inspired generations of students and fellow artists, as well as the sculptor Richmond Barthé, who lived in Pasadena during the last decade of his life. Artist Betye Saar, who grew up partly in Pasadena, and ceramist Doyle Lane, who lived and worked in nearby El Sereno, were also part of the vibrant Black community in the area. The 2025 fires in Los Angeles, which destroyed large sections of Altadena, have raised awareness of the important history of the Black community there, as well as serving as a sobering example of the losses and injustices that many have endured.

A final border, or barrier, that artists cross is the threshold of mainstream galleries and museums. In some cases, previously unrecognized works have gained new visibility decades or even centuries after their makers'

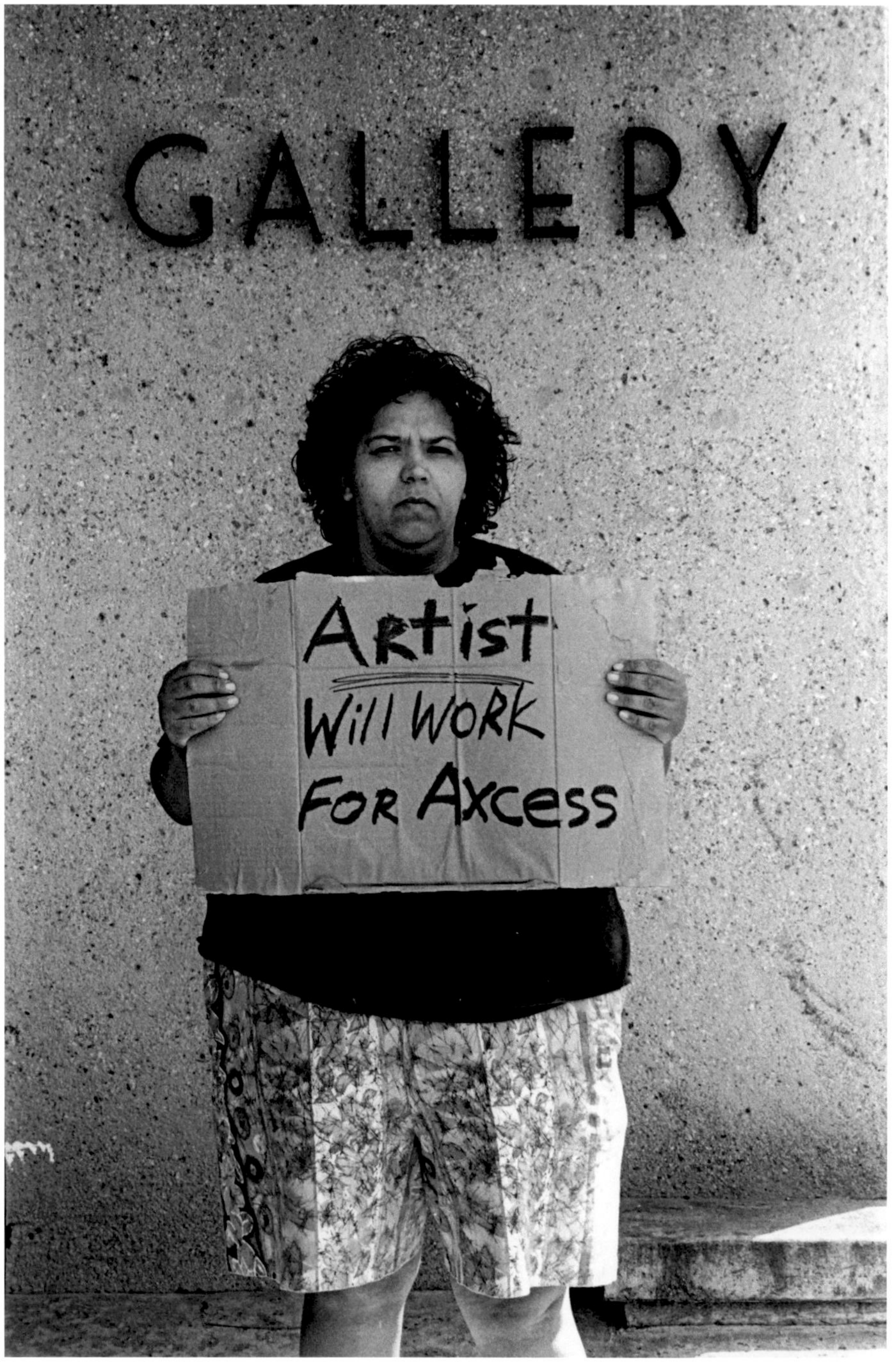

deaths. Artists have long struggled for recognition and access. A Chicana photographer raised in East Los Angeles, Laura Aguilar used her camera to document marginalized communities in the city and to critique the inaccessibility of the mainstream art world. Her nude self-portraits within the Southern California landscape (see p. 20) seek to place themselves within what was at the time the largely male-dominated world of traditional landscape photography. In one of her images, she stands outside of the original Vincent Price Art Museum building at East Los Angeles College holding a sign that reads "Artist Will Work For Axcess" (fig. 20). The word "access" is misspelled, a possible reference to Aguilar's dyslexia, but also symbolic of the alienation she experienced. The photograph highlights multiple definitions of the word "access," including not only the right to enter but also a sudden surge of anger. She long fought for representation for herself and her fellow artists. Aguilar's photographs are imbued with a deep desire to belong and to find her place. To cross a border is to be searching. Like many of the artworks in this essay, Aguilar's images provide us with a new way of looking at the land and seeing borderlands as not only physical but also psychological, emotional, and disruptive spaces.

Dennis Carr is the Virginia Steele Scott Chief Curator of American Art at The Huntington.

1. See Gloria Anzaldúa, *Borderlands/La Frontera: The New Mestiza* (Aunt Lute Books, 1987). For further understanding of the Spanish Borderlands from a historical perspective, see Herbert Eugene Bolton, *Spanish Borderlands* (Yale University Press, 1921), and more recent works by David J. Weber, such as *The Spanish Frontier in North America* (Yale University Press, 1992) and David J. Weber and Jane M. Rausch, eds., *Where Cultures Meet: Frontiers in Latin American History* (Rowman & Littlefield, 1997).

2. With gratitude, I acknowledge the many curatorial colleagues in the American Art department who have added to this ongoing project, including Yinshi Lerman-Tan, Lauren Cross, Angélica Becerra, Lily Allen, Cambra Sklarz, Sophia Quach McCabe, and Kikesa Kimbwala.

3. For examples of survivance across cultural production and disciplines, see Gerald Vizenor, ed., *Survivance: Narratives of Native Presence* (University of Nebraska Press, 2008).

4. Thanks to Sean Lahmeyer, Associate Director, Botanical Collections and Research at The Huntington, for the assistance in identifying plants in the painting.

5. The author is grateful to the late Lance Foster for providing this commentary on the portrait. Correspondence with the author, September 14, 2021.

Figure 20
Laura Aguilar, *Will Work For #4*, 1993. Gelatin silver print, 9 × 7 in. The Huntington, Gift of the Laura Aguilar Trust of 2016, 2024.6.2.

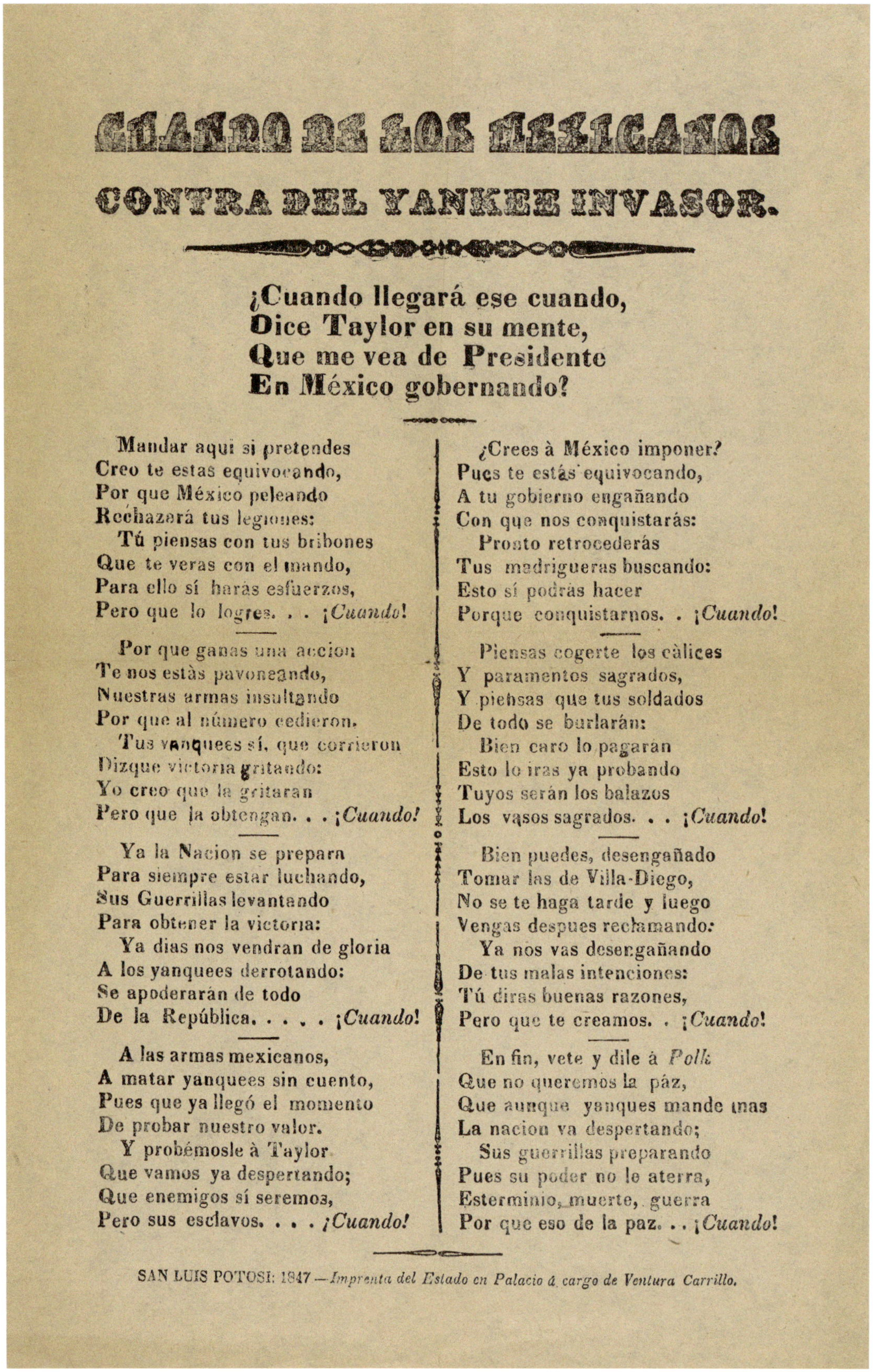

CUANDO DE LOS MEXICANOS
CONTRA DEL YANKEE INVASOR.

¿Cuando llegará ese cuando,
Dice Taylor en su mente,
Que me vea de Presidente
En México gobernando?

Mandar aquí si pretendes
Creo te estas equivocando,
Por que México peleando
Rechazará tus legiones:
Tú piensas con tus bribones
Que te veras con el mando,
Para ello sí harás esfuerzos,
Pero que lo logres. . . ¡*Cuando*!

Por que ganas una accion
Te nos estàs pavoneando,
Nuestras armas insultando
Por que al número cedieron.
Tus yanquees sí, que corrieron
Dizque victoria gritando:
Yo creo que la gritaran
Pero que la obtengan. . . ¡*Cuando*!

Ya la Nacion se prepara
Para siempre estar luchando,
Sus Guerrillas levantando
Para obtener la victoria:
Ya dias nos vendran de gloria
A los yanquees derrotando:
Se apoderarán de todo
De la República. . . . . ¡*Cuando*!

A las armas mexicanos,
A matar yanquees sin cuento,
Pues que ya llegó el momento
De probar nuestro valor.
Y probémosle à Taylor
Que vamos ya despertando;
Que enemigos sí seremos,
Pero sus esclavos. . . . ¡*Cuando*!

¿Crees à México imponer?
Pues te estás equivocando,
A tu gobierno engañando
Con que nos conquistarás:
Pronto retrocederás
Tus madrigueras buscando:
Esto sí podràs hacer
Porque conquistarnos. . ¡*Cuando*!

Piensas cogerte los càlices
Y paramentos sagrados,
Y piensas que tus soldados
De todo se burlarán:
Bien caro lo pagarán
Esto lo iras ya probando
Tuyos serán los balazos
Los vasos sagrados. . . ¡*Cuando*!

Bien puedes, desengañado
Tomar las de Villa-Diego,
No se te haga tarde y luego
Vengas despues reclamando:
Ya nos vas desengañando
De tus malas intenciones:
Tú diras buenas razones,
Pero que te creamos. . ¡*Cuando*!

En fin, vete y dile à *Polk*
Que no queremos la páz,
Que aunque yanques mande mas
La nacion va despertando;
Sus guerrillas preparando
Pues su poder no le aterra,
Esterminio, muerte, guerra
Por que eso de la paz. . . ¡*Cuando*!

SAN LUIS POTOSI: 1847.—*Imprenta del Estado en Palacio á cargo de Ventura Carrillo.*

Figure 1
"Cuando de los Mexicanos contra del Yankee invasor" (When the Mexicans fought against the Yankee invader) (Imprenta del Estado en Palacio á Cargo de Ventura Carrillo, 1847). 12¼ × 8¼ in. The Huntington, Library Purchase, 2023, 642171.

Fight Song

Anti-American songs are a small but hilarious sub-subgenre of Mexican music. "Corrido a Pancho Villa" by Los Hermanos Zaizar mocks President Woodrow Wilson with accordion giggles and old-timey biplane sounds for sending six thousand soldiers on an unsuccessful mission to nab the "Centaur of the North." "El Muro" (The Border Wall) by rock dinosaurs El Tri takes the perspective of an immigrant about to cross the US-Mexico *frontera* without papers, who vows to, um, use the obstacle before him as toilet paper (sounds so much cruder and funnier in the original Mexican Spanish).

Superstars from Juan Gabriel to Vicente Fernández to El Piporro have all taken their anti-gringo shots with glee. But "Cuando de los Mexicanos contra del Yankee invasor"? It's a whole other level of haterade.

The song is a promise to Army Major General Zachary Taylor—charged by President Polk to lead the United States into the Mexican-American War—that his incursion is "awakening [Mexicans] / We will become your enemies." It's almost laughably proud—although we do not know exactly when in 1847 this broadsheet was printed, by that spring American forces had already conquered what is now the American Southwest, occupying Veracruz and marching toward Mexico City. So the unnamed author's vow, "No matter the more Yankees you [Polk] send / The nation is waking up," reads like something that the Black Knight would say in *Monty Python and the Holy Grail*.

And yet, I *get* why someone would write something like this in such a dire moment. And it takes me back to Woody Guthrie's "This Land Is Your Land." When he wrote it in 1940, the United States was in a world where nations were fighting back against tyrants hell-bent on dominion. Jingoism was the religion of our land, much to Guthrie's chagrin, since his love of country was predicated more on the eternal freedom manifest in the idea of brotherhood rather than the exclusionary freedom of exceptionalism. His famous refrain—"This land was made for you and me"—was an invitation to those who thought like him and a subtle rejection of people who didn't.

"Cuando de los Mexicanos contra del Yankee invasor" doesn't sing about the beauty of its author's homeland, à la Guthrie's masterpiece. Yet the ballad is still a paean to the love of one's country. "The nation is preparing / to always be struggling / its guerrillas rising / to obtain victory," the stanzas sing, letting Americans know to expect a hell of a fight even if Mexicans realize they're most likely going to lose. "To the Mexican forces / time to kill countless Yankees / Now that the moment has come / to prove our valor" is as great a rallying cry as "This Machine Kills Fascists" (see p. 13).

One hundred and seventy years later—to paraphrase Led Zeppelin—the song remains the same. The United States has tried to govern Mexico again and again, yet Mexico remains standing. The strident patriotism Guthrie criticized is ascendant once more—but the spirit of resistance he embodied is ready to fight until the end. Both songs offer this revolutionary challenge: Freedom is made for *yo* and you.

Gustavo Arellano is a columnist for the Los Angeles Times *and co-author of* A People's Guide to Orange County. *He has spent his entire life in Southern California and has listened to ballads and corridos for just as long.*

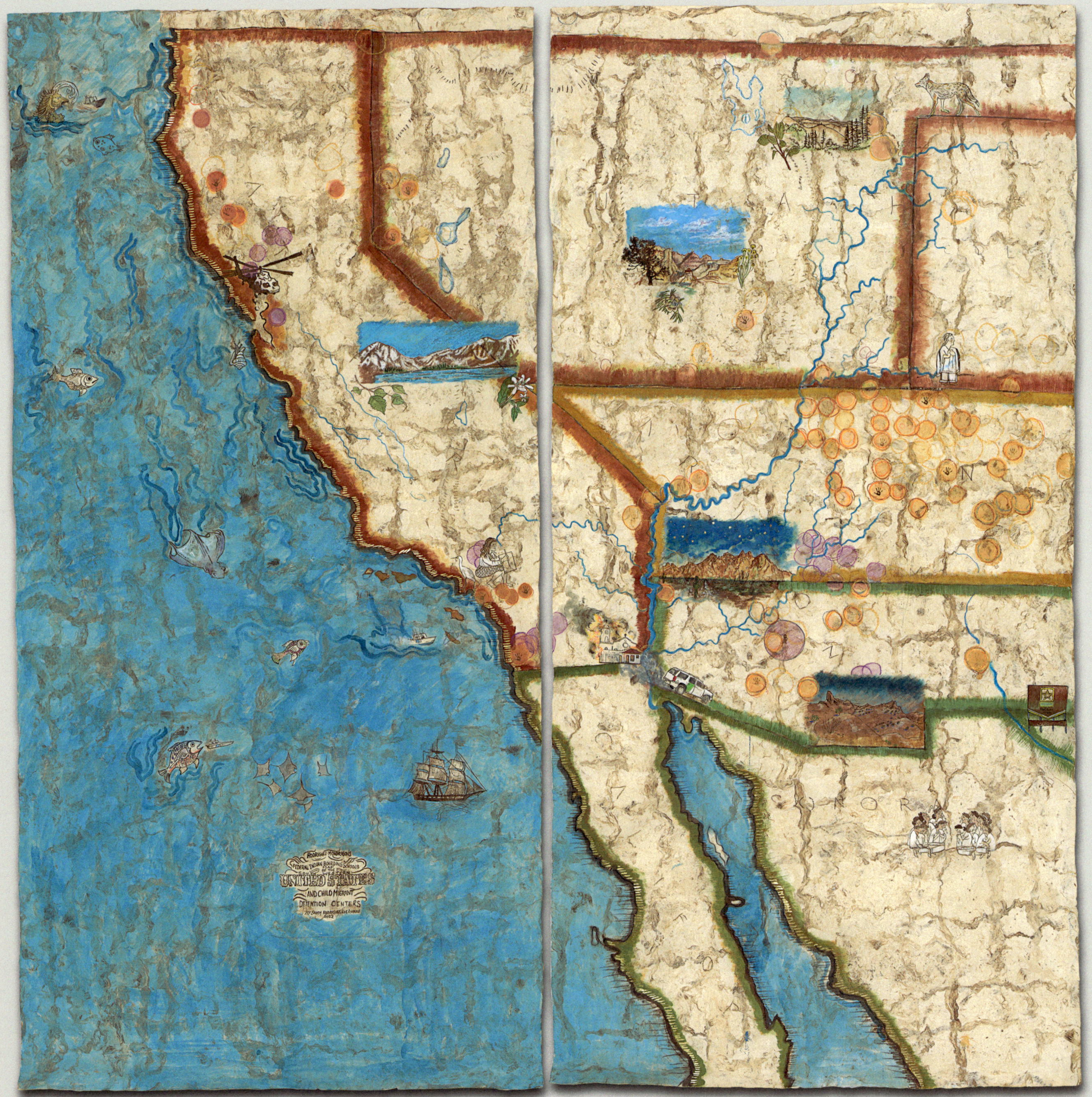
RODRIGUEZ MONDRAGON'S
FEDERAL INDIAN BOARDING SCHOOLS
MAP OF THE
SOUTH WESTERN
UNITED STATES
AND CHILD MIGRANT
DETENTION CENTERS
BY SANDY RODRIGUEZ, LOS ANGELES
2022

Mapping Borderlands

As a research-based artist, I engage with historical materials to envision and work toward a more just future. In my ongoing series *Codex Rodriguez-Mondragón*, the borderlands are a site of contention. I draw upon personal field sketches, historical maps, federal reports, and recent news stories to highlight the resistance to enduring cycles of colonial aggression across the United States and Mexico.

For 150 years, the US government forcibly separated tens of thousands of Indigenous children from their families, cultures, and communities, sending them to federal Indian boarding schools. Between 1860 and 1978, 114 boarding schools operated in the Southwestern United States out of a total of 408 across the nation. Family separation and child detention gained national attention in 2018 under the "zero-tolerance policy," when thousands of children were forcibly removed from their families at the US border. We continue to witness large-scale immigration raids across the country, particularly in the borderlands.

The map I've reconstructed juxtaposes the locations of historical federal Indian boarding schools with the present-day facilities run by Southwest Key (figs. 1, 2).[1] Southwest Key is a federally subsidized private company that has faced public scrutiny over reports of sexual assault and abuse of children at its detention centers. Because these crimes are happening at the border, I draw upon the *Report on the United States and Mexican Boundary Survey*, published in two volumes between 1857 and 1859.[2] The survey includes chapters on landscapes, botanical specimens, and ethnographic illustrations created shortly after the 1848 Treaty of Guadalupe Hidalgo, which granted more than half of Mexico's land to the United States following the Mexican-American War.

My map also references the boundary lines drawn from the 1862 *Colton's Rail-Road and Military Map of the United States, Mexico, the West Indies, &c.*[3] Branded symbols within orange and violet circles plot both historical and present-day sites of atrocities, compressing linear time to highlight the slow violence imposed upon the region (fig. 3). It is painted with earth pigments collected during field study trips to the borderlands of California, Arizona, New Mexico, and Texas and prepared according to colonial Mexican recipes.

Once I travel to a site via plane, train, or automobile, I walk, survey, observe, and draw at various locations and elevations—preferably in remote areas. I paint small postcards in the field that serve as visual references for continued ethnobotanical research on each site. These studies are integrated as details into the maps back in my Los Angeles studio (figs. 5–8). My plant portraits incorporate Native medicinal, utilitarian, and ceremonial uses and are labeled in Latin, English, Spanish, and Indigenous

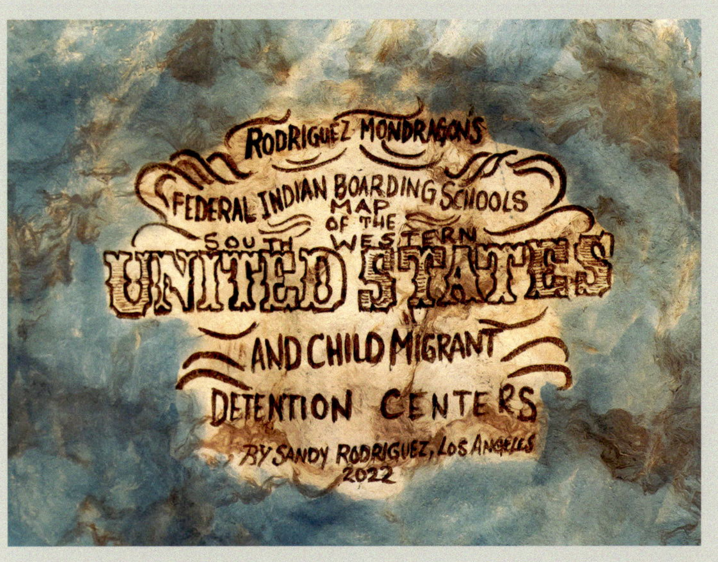

Figure 1
Sandy Rodriguez, *Rodriguez-Mondragón's Federal Indian Boarding Schools Map of the United States and Child Migrant Detention Centers* (detail), 2022–26. Hand-processed walnut ink and 23-karat gold on amate paper, five panels, each approx. 97 × 48 in. Collection of the artist.

Figure 2
Rodriguez-Mondragón's Federal Indian Boarding Schools Map of the United States and Child Migrant Detention Centers (detail).

languages, highlighting accumulated knowledge in a region over time. Near Nogales, Arizona, I painted watercolor postcards of the same landscapes and plants recorded in the historical *United States and Mexican Boundary Survey* (fig. 4). Among these are desert landscapes featuring a pair of saguaro cacti near Dome Mountain and the Sonoran Desert ocotillo—an indicator plant that reflects the condition of its ecosystem. The striking familiarity of the borderlands in the historical images and reports reminds me of how the land has been marked, recorded, and scarred—yet has persisted—over generations.

Sandy Rodriguez is a Los Angeles–based Chicana artist and researcher who was The Huntington's 2025–26 Hannah and Russel Kully Distinguished Fellow in American Art. Her ongoing series Codex Rodriguez-Mondragón *comprises a collection of maps and paintings that explore the intersections of history, social memory, contemporary politics, and cultural production.*

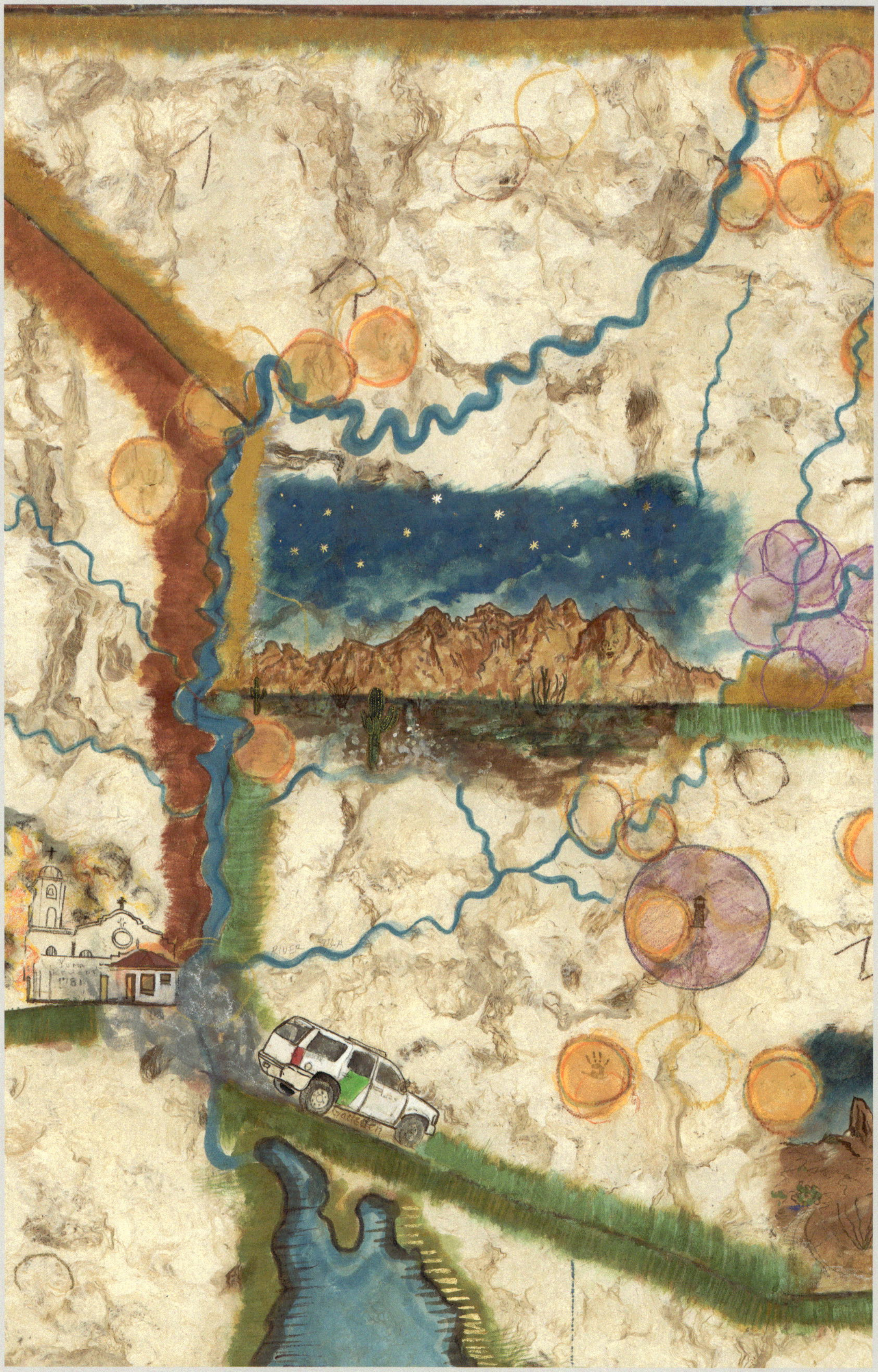

1. The locations of the Indian boarding schools were published online in a Department of the Interior report in May 2022.

2. William H. Emory, *Report on the United States and Mexican Boundary Survey: Made Under the Direction of the Secretary of the Interior*, 2 vols. (Washington, DC, 1857–59).

3. *Colton's Rail-Road and Military Map of the United States, Mexico, the West Indies, &c.* (J. H. Colton, 1862), https://www.loc.gov/item/gm71000834.

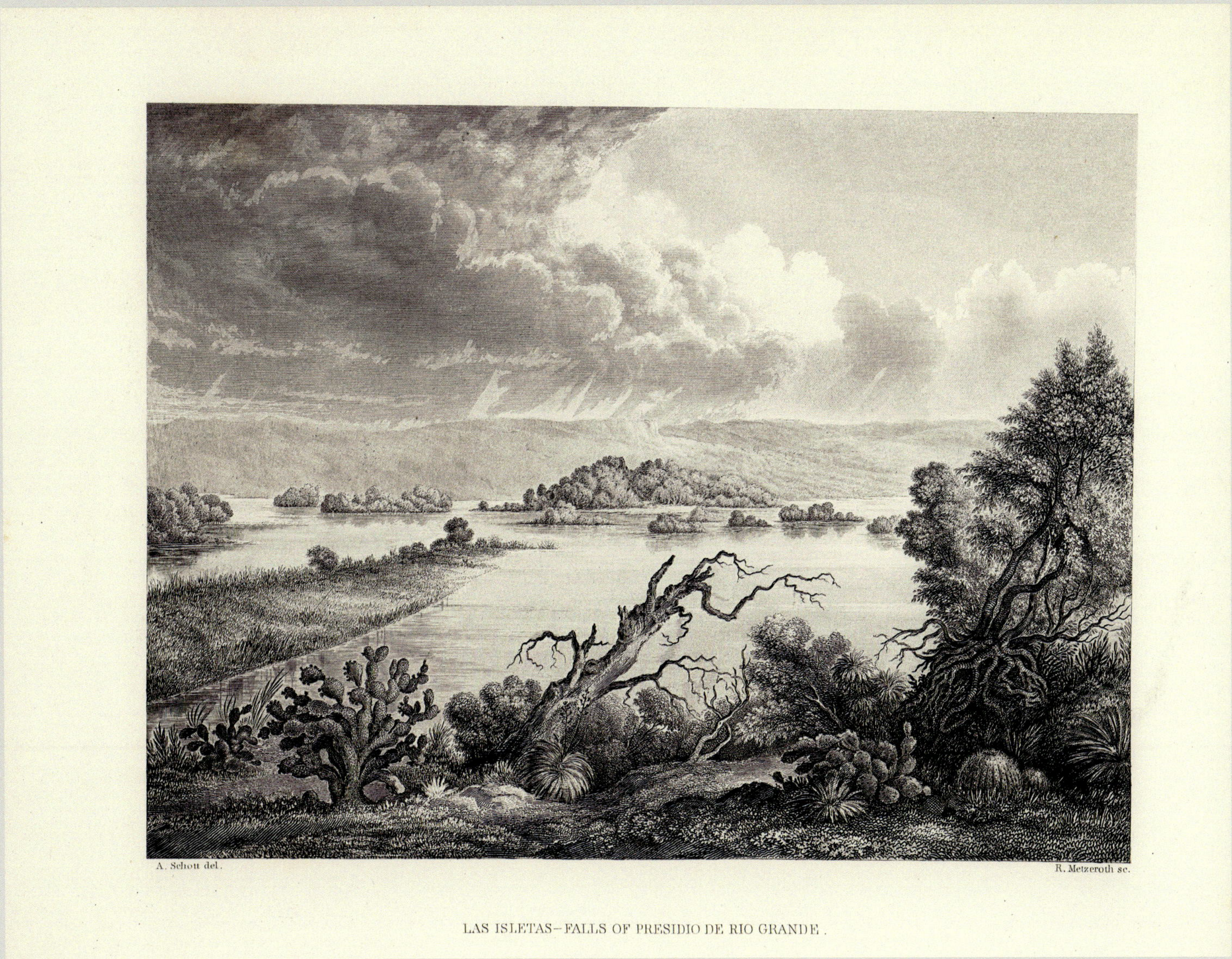

Figure 3
Rodriguez-Mondragón's Federal Indian Boarding Schools Map of the United States and Child Migrant Detention Centers (detail).

Figure 4
R. Metzeroth after A. Schott, "Las Isletas—Falls of Presidio de Rio Grande," in *Report on the United States and Mexican Boundary Survey* (US Department of the Interior, 1857–59), 9 × 11¾ in. The Huntington, Purchased by Henry E. Huntington, 1922, 56504, vol. 1, facing p. 68.

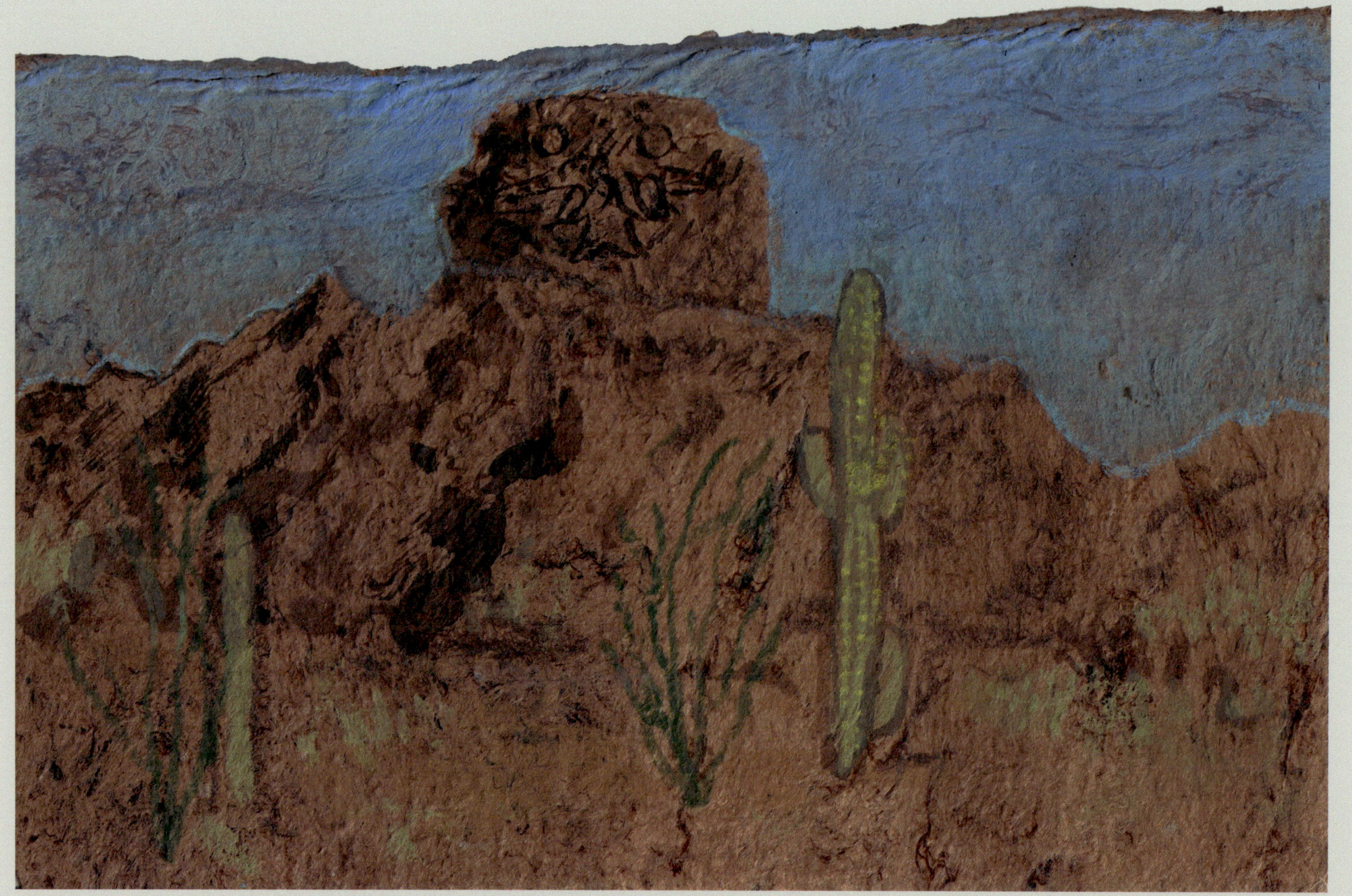

Figure 5
Sandy Rodriguez, *Border Field Sketch from the Codex Rodriguez-Mondragón, near Castle Dome Mountain, Arizona*, 2019. Hand-processed walnut ink and pastel on amate paper, 4 × 6 in. Collection of the artist.

Week 1—Field Study Winter 2019 Arizona

Final trip of the year to Kofa National Wildlife Refuge. It is so damn cold, I lost feeling in my hands yesterday while drawing in Palm Canyon. Last night, we moved to a spot near Castle Dome Mountains. The road was impossible to find, and sleep was elusive but the stars made up for it. I woke up to this stunning view of Coatlicue watching over us. The ocotillo and saguaro framing my view of this rhyolite porphyry volcanic range. I need to research pre-1860s history.

Yuma, Arizona—December 30, 2019

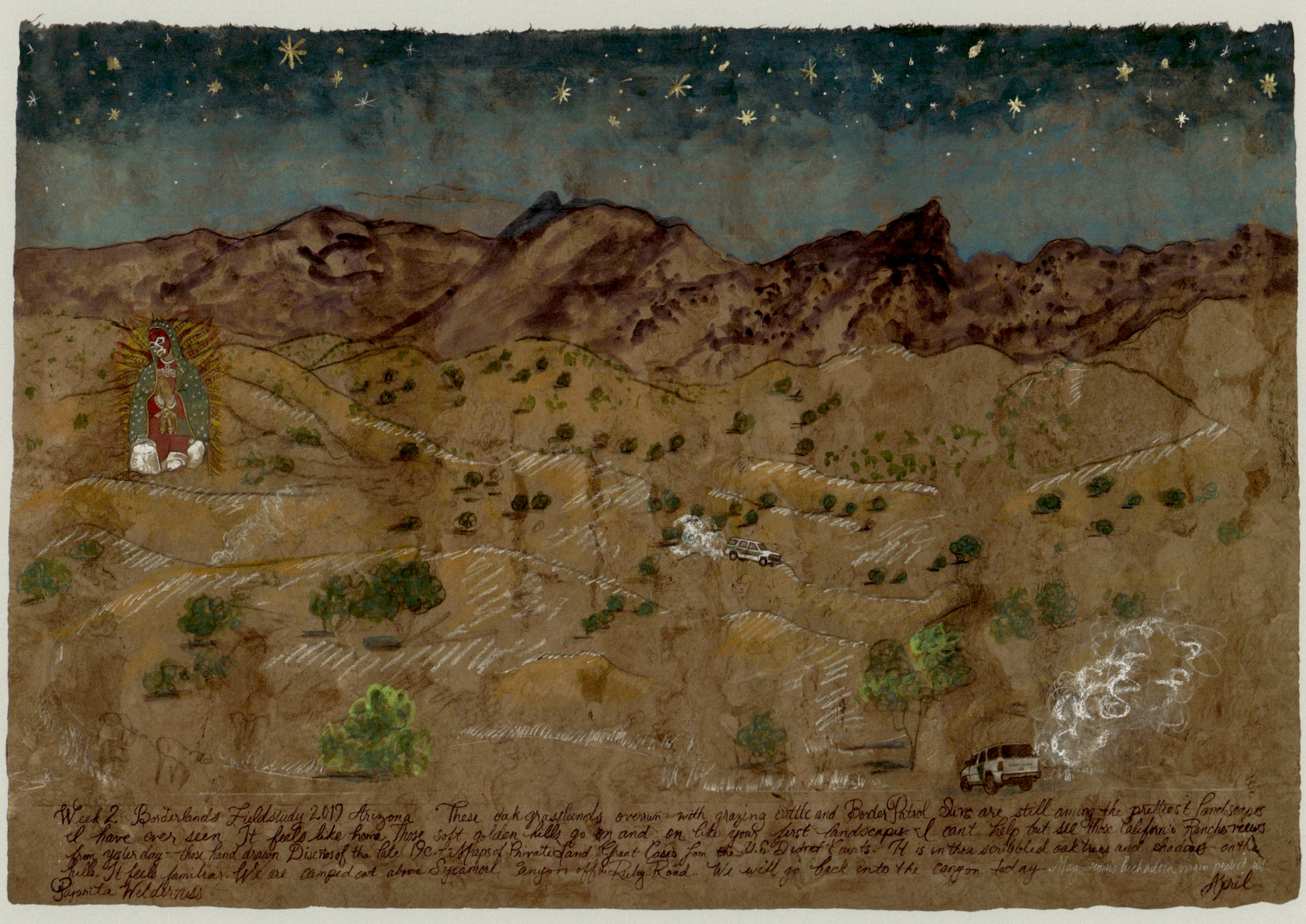

Figure 6
Sandy Rodriguez, *Borderlands No. 1: Off the Ruby Road, Arizona (near Sycamore Canyon)*, 2019. Hand-processed walnut ink on amate paper, 31 × 47 in. Private collection.

Week 2—Borderlands Field Study 2019 Arizona

These oak grasslands, overrun with grazing cattle and Border Patrol SUVs, are still among the prettiest landscapes I have ever seen. It feels like home. Those soft golden hills go on and on like your first landscapes. I can't help but see the California Rancho views from yesterday—those hand-drawn Diseños of the late 19c. Maps of Private Land Grant Cases from the US District Courts. It is in those scribbled oak trees and shadows on the hills. It feels familiar. We are camped out above Sycamore Canyon off the Ruby Road. We will go back to the canyon today. May mom's Luchadora Virgen protect us.

Pajarita Wilderness—April 22, 8:45 a.m.

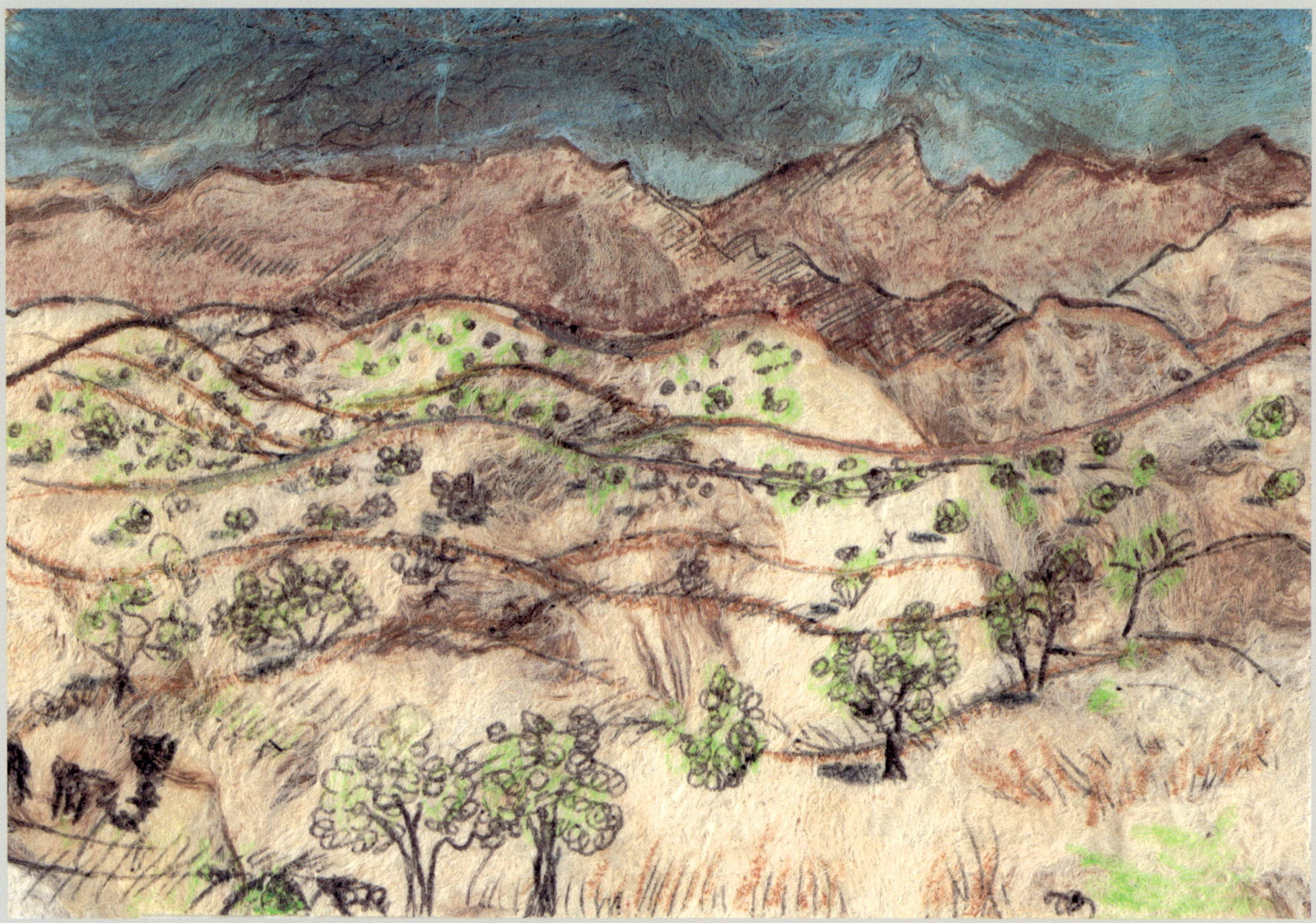

Figure 7
Sandy Rodriguez, *Field sketch post-card for Borderlands No. 1: Off the Ruby Road, Arizona (near Sycamore Canyon)*, April 22, 2019, 8:45 a.m. Hand-processed walnut ink and pen on amate paper, 4 × 6 in. Collection of the artist.

Week 2—Field Study 2019 Arizona

Woke up to this view today, cow pies all around these oak tree-dotted rolling hills. We camped on a hill off the graded dirt road. Today was the first day we attempted to reach the border via Sycamore Canyon. The hike along the waterway was made under the shadow of a flash flood, a circumstance rendered more unsettling by Customs and Border enforcement activity and hostile retired military we met along the way. I spent a few hours drawing in a cave after my boots would no longer grip the rocks, and we went our separate ways. The light began to fade in the slot canyons as the storm began to move in, and the sounds of the native canyon treefrog grew louder, trickling water, gold light turned to blue, then cobalt as the sun set. My companion and I agreed to meet at the car before sundown to head back to our camp, and were questioned by CBP officers as we were changing out of our poison oak-covered clothing. We will try again tomorrow.

Off the Ruby Road 8:45 a.m. April 22, 2019

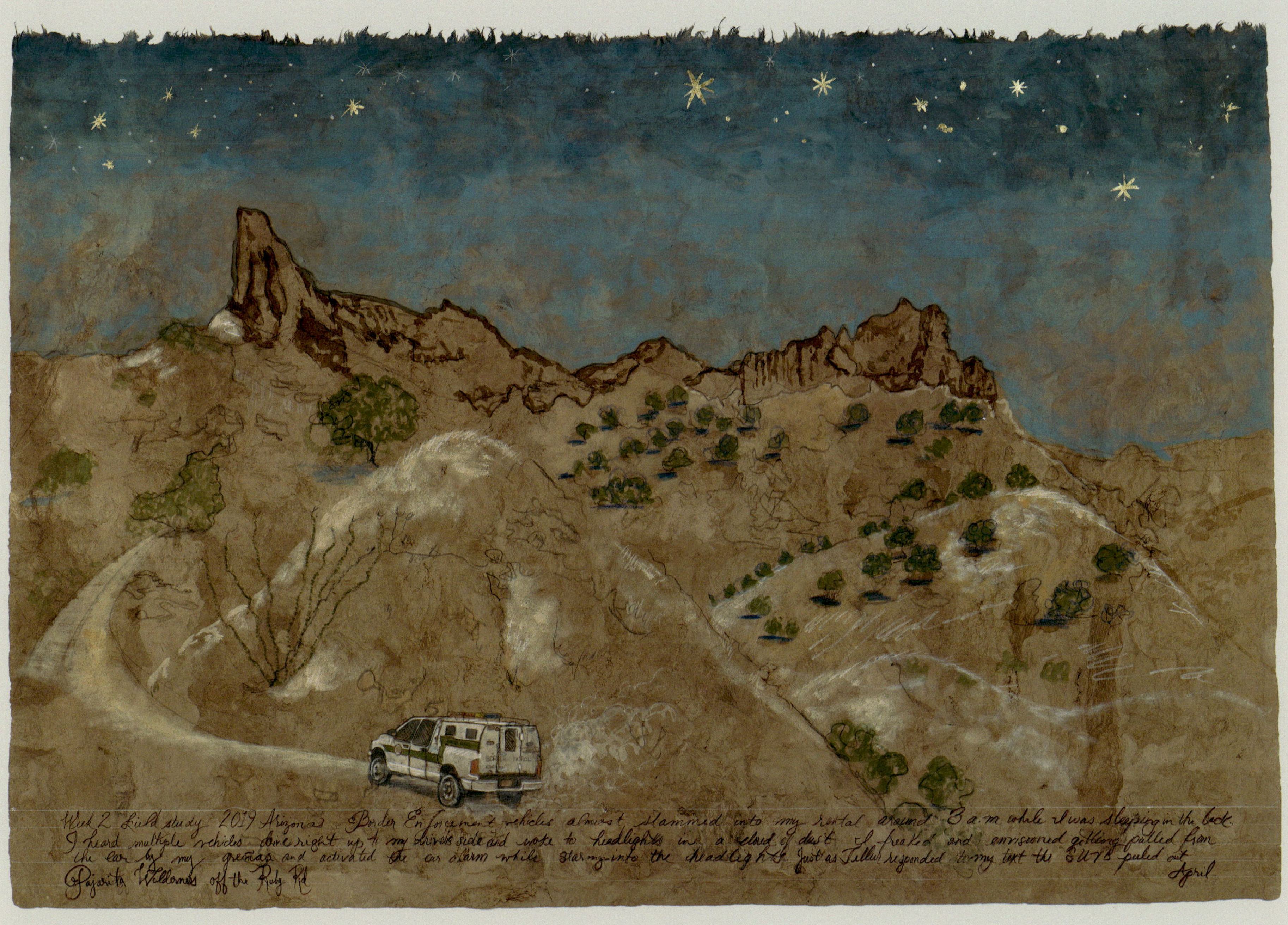

Figure 8
Sandy Rodriguez, *They Almost Got Me—Pajarita Wilderness*, 2019. Hand-processed walnut ink and pastel on amate paper, 31½ × 47 in. Collection of Beth Rudin DeWoody.

Week 2—Field Study 2019 Arizona

Border Enforcement vehicles almost slammed into my rental around 3 a.m. while I was sleeping in the back. I heard multiple vehicles drive right up to my driver's and woke to headlights in a cloud of dust. I freaked and envisioned getting pulled from the car by my *greñas* and activated the car alarm while staring into the headlights. Just as Tellur responded to my text the SUVs pulled out.

Pajarita Wilderness off the Ruby Road—April 2019

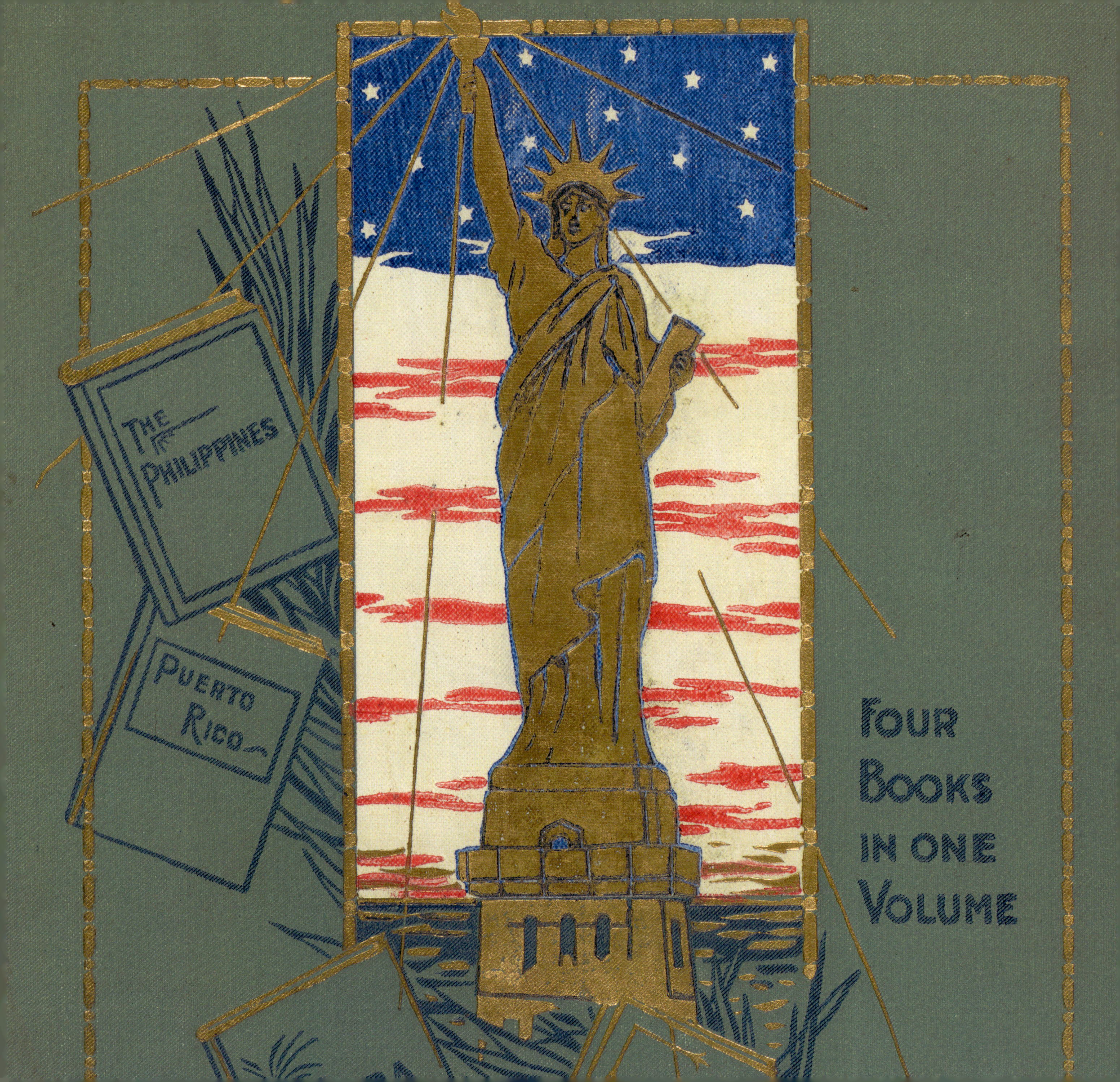
THE PHILIPPINES
PUERTO RICO
FOUR BOOKS IN ONE VOLUME

An ecological disturbance is a force that disrupts environmental conditions and changes a biological community. Such events can be human-caused or naturally occurring but are often deadly. Animal and plant species in much of the Western United States have adapted to the forces of fires, both intentional and natural. One might consider periodic wars and massacres in this country as disturbances of their own. Their cyclical nature seems to follow the patterns set by environmental disruptions. Revolutionary movements in the Americas often used destabilizing violence to advance human rights, while imperial wars were fought over land. Such change makes room for moments of reconsideration and rebirth.

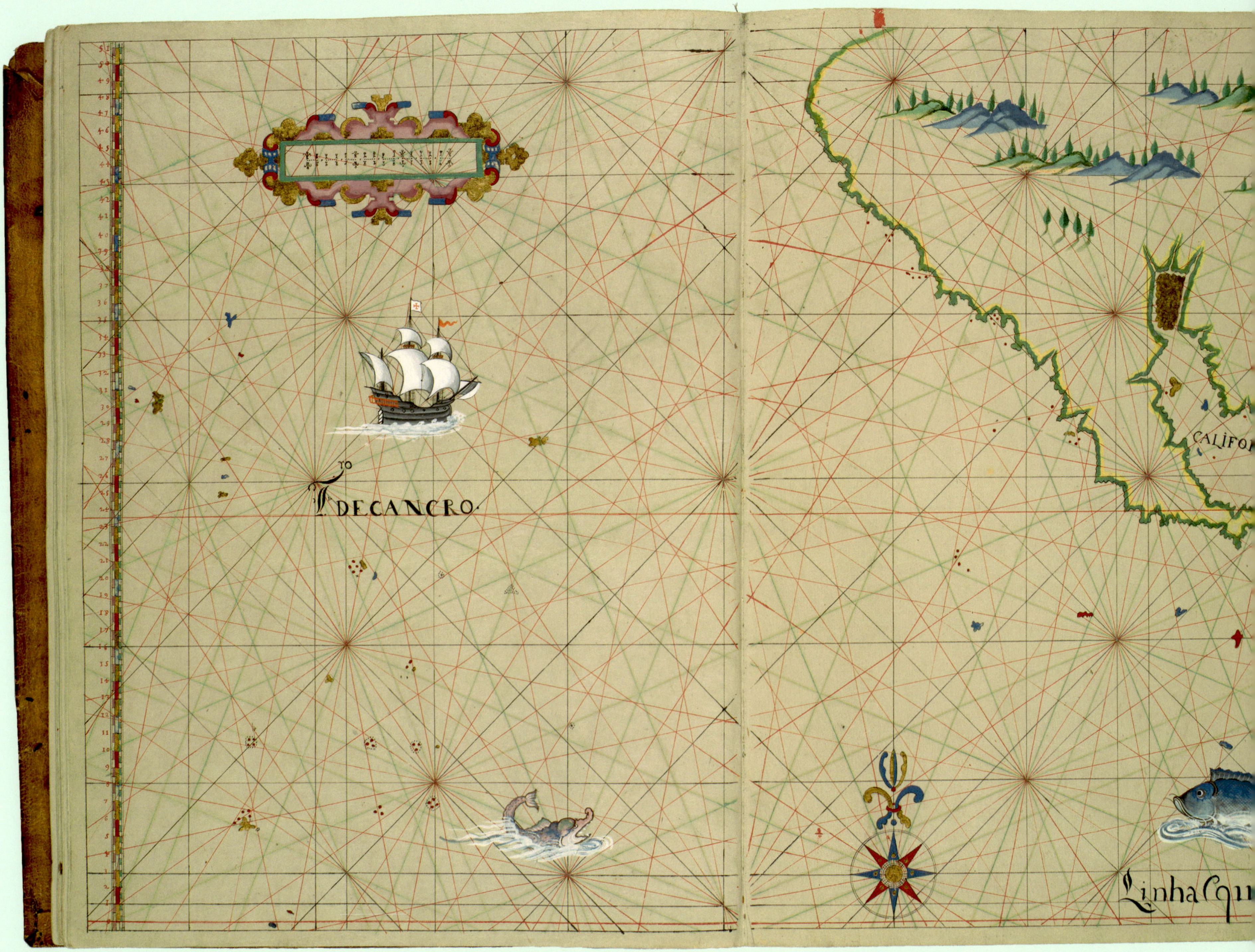

Figure 1
This page, from the type of atlas known as a portolan chart, depicts a global navigator's way of seeing the world around 1630. The crisscrossing lines, running in thirty-two directions, are rhumb lines, providing direction across the sea. This page depicts the west coast of North America, including Baja and Alta California. The text is in Portuguese, in the renderings of the Tropic of Cancer at left and the equinox line or equator at the bottom. This atlas may have been made in Macau. Its detailed notation of coastlines and mostly imaginary depiction of inland areas suggests an incomplete knowledge of the world. Western coast of United States and Mexico, Portolan atlas, Portuguese, ca. 1630. 10½ × 14 in. The Huntington, Purchased by Henry E. Huntington, HM 39.

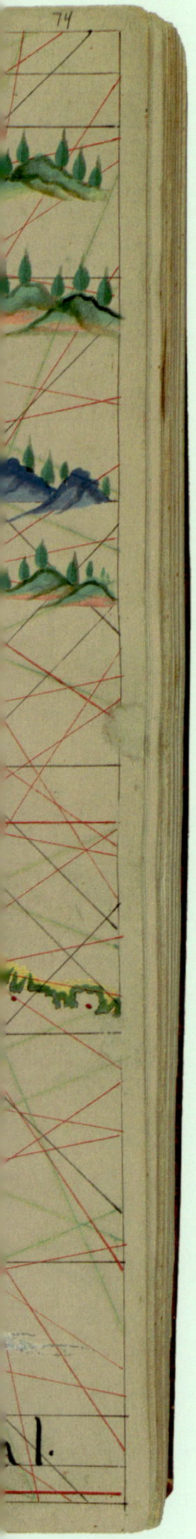

The Land

We say "the Land" as a way of making the Earth manageable to us, as a way of domesticating the Earth, as a way of familiarizing ourselves and also diminishing the reality that the Earth, the third planet from the Sun, is vast and complex and is held in its place by forces we can give a name to but cannot see, though we can explain those forces to ourselves in varying and various compositions. But the Earth seems indifferent to whatever we say or make of it when we make the tales or accounts of our invention of ourselves. There are tales and scientific facts of the human appearance on the Land, there are tales of our origins and traces in the Periodic Table (Lithium, Oh Lithium!), and the traces of those elements have become essential to our daily life (the cell phone).

We see the sunken footprints of ourselves in the ashes deposited on the Land as we walked away from an unrecorded catastrophe that took place in what we now call Africa. We see evidence of ourselves, our footprints again, in what is now known as White Sands, New Mexico, having presumably crossed the Bering Strait, an area now submerged under a body of water. We see lines converging on a horizon and insist that one day, something, someone, will emerge from it and change our very being, and if that does not occur, we will venture out to see why. That is the Land.

The Earth is indifferent to us, as it seems to have been to all the other occupants of its surface, be they animal, vegetable, or any other classification. Do the other occupants of the Earth, which we have divided into Kingdoms, have something to tell us? Do we want to know? Do we care? The Earth is not ours, but there is something in us that cannot accept this. We seem unable to make sense of our human selves, our stories or narratives of ourselves, without an appropriation of the Earth, reducing it to the Land. The Land!

The Land is our way of making sense of the Earth, of making it not just the third planet in the solar system, but of making it the destiny of our desires, subjugated to our needs, reduced to the familiar and commonplace, something we eventually call "Homeland." And then we make ourselves into something we imagine the Land is: rugged, untamable, beautiful, honest, and we make a legend of the Land (our Gods came from it and even now still live in it), and so the Land makes its imprint on us, or so we tell ourselves. But the Land, which is the Earth, will go on its way!

Jamaica Kincaid is an award-winning writer, novelist, and professor who has published several acclaimed novels and works of nonfiction, most recently Encyclopedia of Gardening for Colored Children *and* Among Flowers. *She is Professor Emerita of African and African American Studies at Harvard University.*

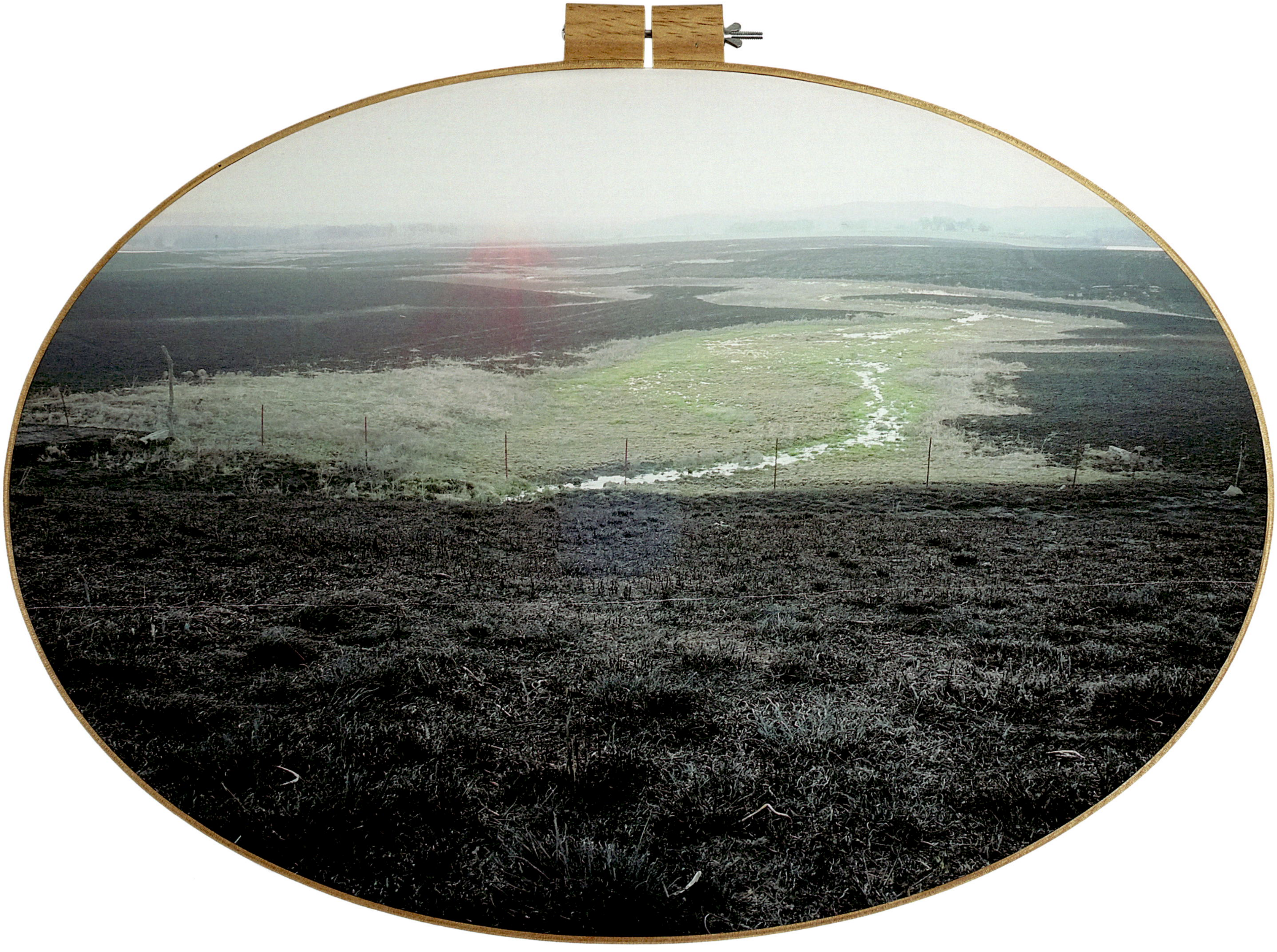

Land of the Free, Home of the Brave

A Conversation

In the eighteenth and nineteenth centuries, silhouettes—or shadow portraits—of everyday individuals were critical forms of preserving a people's history of the United States. Made using scissors, black paper, and fabric, silhouettes were a very affordable, democratizing medium. Early silhouette makers were often Europeans who had emigrated from France and Britain. Itinerant artists like William Bache, Auguste Edouart, and Samuel Metford moved along the East Coast of the United States, capturing portraits of middle-class Americans.

Contemporary artist Letitia Huckaby has built an expansive practice by bringing silhouette portraiture together with landscape photography (fig. 1). Using both traditions, her work features families and communities of the twenty-first century whose histories and stories often go under the radar.

Lauren Cross (LC): Letitia, you grew up in Oklahoma, went to school in Boston. You have roots in Louisiana and Mississippi. And now you live in Texas. All these places have their own unique histories. How has your relationship with where you have lived played a role in how you see landscapes, places, and people?

Letitia Huckaby (LH): Oklahoma was my dad's last duty station. It is the place where I went to high school. But we lived all over the place, since he was in the military. We even lived in Texas for a little bit when I was young. We lived in Indiana, and he did two tours in Germany. My parents were from Louisiana and Mississippi, but we only went there for vacations, so it had this special kind of romantic thing for me because it was so different from every other landscape that we lived in. Each one has its own personality, but I have always felt that Mississippi and Louisiana have this richness to them. You can smell the richness of the earth. The diversity of plants, which felt tropical in ways. It was so different than the other landscapes I had lived in, the forested mountains of Germany or the flat plains of Oklahoma.

And I don't know if it was just the difference in the way the land looked and felt, or me knowing that I have a special connection to that land that my ancestors were on for generations, back to slavery. And so that had some weight. I think that as African Americans we are always looking for a connection to our past. And so, Louisiana and Mississippi have that for me. I did not really appreciate Oklahoma until after I had left there and gone back. And the interesting thing about Oklahoma is that's where I started photographing the landscape.

And so, when I went back, after my father passed, we would put flowers on his grave. Then I would go back to some of the places I used to frequent. And they had a different meaning to me then.

LC: You began your career as a documentary photographer and then later used photography to create silhouette portraits and print them on fabric. When and why did that transition from documentary photography to silhouette portraits happen?

LH: So, the switch happened in graduate school not long after I lost my father. He was from Greenwood, Mississippi, a small town, but it was the fourth-largest producer of cotton in the country. That was one of the places that I never really thought about the history of. And by history, I mean the kind of devastation and conditions that African Americans were living in, and I noticed after he passed that my grandmother's neighborhood was surrounded by cotton fields on three sides.

And the way the town looked on one side of the river was completely different than the way it looked on the other

Figure 1
Letitia Huckaby, *Black Nature*, 2020. Pigment print on cotton fabric with embroidery hoop, 19½ × 27¾ in. Courtesy of the artist.

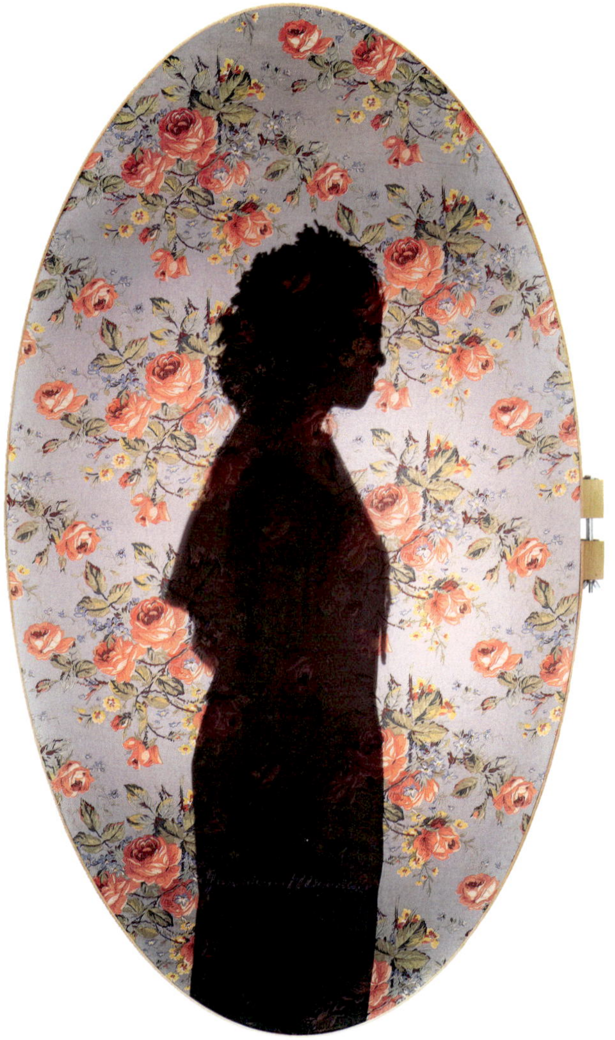

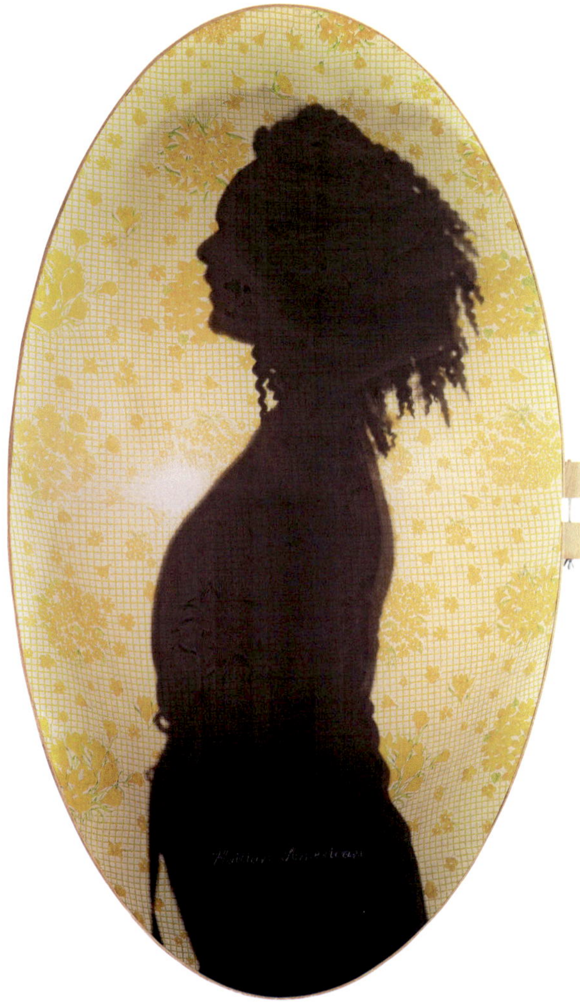

Figure 2
Letitia Huckaby, *And Thy Neighb(our) (Shwanda)*, 2020. Pigment print on fabric with embroidery, 70 × 40 × 2 in. The Huntington, Purchased with funds from the Art Collectors' Council, with additional support from Nancy M. Berman and Alan J. Bloch, and The Philip and Muriel Berman Foundation, The Hannah and Russel Kully Family, Margaret F. Leong and Michael P. Checca, Allen Shay and Kristen Hansen and the estate of George and Nancy Parsons, 2023.11.1.

Figure 3
Letitia Huckaby, *And Thy Neighb(our) (Chaulinne)*, 2020. Pigment print on fabric with embroidery, 70 × 40 × 2 in. The Huntington, Purchased with funds from the Art Collectors' Council, with additional support from Nancy M. Berman and Alan J. Bloch, and The Philip and Muriel Berman Foundation, The Hannah and Russel Kully Family, Margaret F. Leong and Michael P. Checca, Allen Shay and Kristen Hansen and the estate of George and Nancy Parsons, 2023.11.2.

side. It was a complete separation of race, but also a stark difference in economy and quality of life.

So, I wanted to start making work that talked about that, and I used cotton as the first step into that. I started photographing cotton as if it were a rose. Then I started printing on cotton. And then I started photographing people behind cotton sheets.

When I first started, I would take a cotton sheet out into the landscape and use the sunlight to cast the shadow. So there were images of the sheet hanging in some dense trees. And all you could see was my family that I was photographing, my husband and our son, their silhouettes, the landscape [fig. 4].

The idea of cotton was grounding for me in my heritage and ancestry. And then the fact that you could only see these figures because of the light had a connection to my faith. Now all I print on is cotton fabric.

LC: I know cotton is a huge connection in your work, and yet for some in the Black community, cotton can be difficult to look at because of the history that some of our ancestors had with the material.

LH: I can relate to that, because initially I did see it as a negative: a reminder of the horrific treatment of our ancestors, our elders. But now I see it as a way to take back the narrative from what is honestly a beautiful plant.

There are flowers on cotton in the spring, and cotton comes in more colors than just white naturally. In southern Louisiana, cotton is brown and is called Acadian cotton. I have some of the seeds; they're like a rust color that reminds me of the color of clay in Louisiana, which is beautiful.

I like to think about what my ancestors did so that I could be here and do this. I visited the Hayes Plantation in North Carolina right after the state had acquired it as a

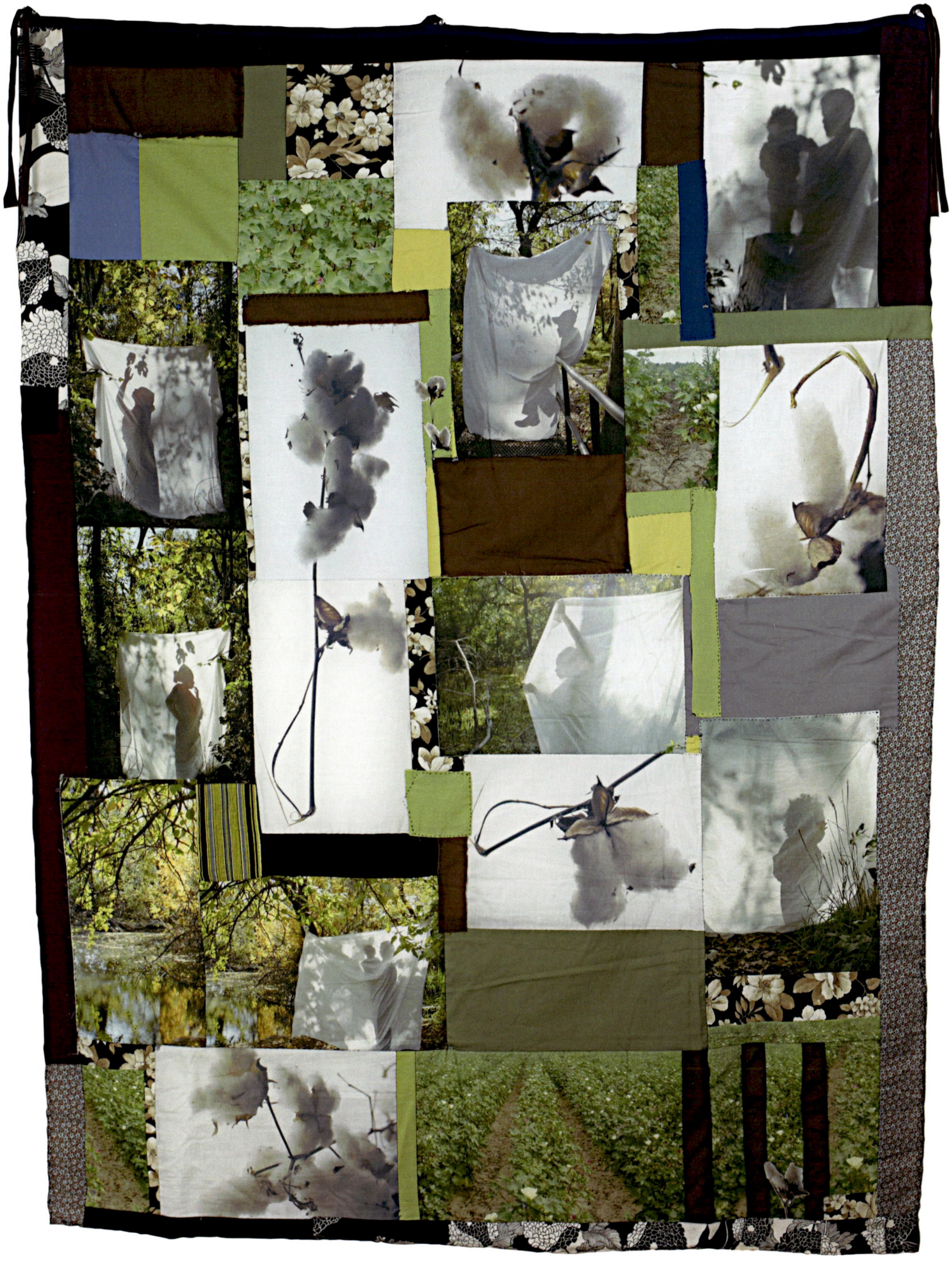

Figure 4
Letitia Huckaby, *Quilt #2*, 2006. Pigment prints on fabric sewn into a patchwork quilt, 81 × 61 in. Courtesy of the artist.

historical site. When we went through the main house, there were three kitchens. There were five stagecoaches that were still in the carriage house. There was furniture from different historical periods.

And I was staying at a nearby house of one of the relatives of the plantation owner. Her ancestor brought over slaves on ships, but she was practicing what she calls "restorative hospitality."

And she asked me, "How did it feel to be in that space?" And I said I felt like I did not belong there. I felt like I was trespassing, basically, because it was seen as the other's house, right? And that the only way I could have been there is if I were cleaning or cooking or something like that.

Michelle Lanier, who directs the historical sites in North Carolina, is a Black woman, and she told me, "Well, when you go in those spaces, I want you to look at the wood and when you look at the wood, think about your skin color. Because it was somebody who looked like you that cut that wood, that shaped that wood, that cleaned that wood, that maintained that wood. And so, you have as much right as anybody else to be in those spaces." And so, that expresses why I began to see the representation of cotton in my work both physically and materially as a way of taking back that power and reimagining it in a new way. My ancestors were forced to pick the cotton, and, yes, it was in brutal conditions. But because they did, I am here. So, I want to take back that power and tell those stories, not from a place of subjugation, but from a place of strength.

LC: That is powerful. It is like so many traditions that our ancestors did, from working in the fields to making pottery, quilts, or garments while enslaved. In some ways, it is easier to see a pot or quilt as beautiful, but cotton is something that brings up certain emotions, images, movies, and stories from our ancestors.

LH: And it is not the plant's fault.

LC: Right. Our ancestors were not enslaved by plants; people enslaved them. And yet, I am sure that they learned so much about the land because of those experiences.

In the creation of early American silhouette portraits, I think of formerly enslaved silhouette artist Moses Williams and even Martha Anne Honeywell, who was born without fully formed arms and legs, yet made silhouettes with her mouth. These artists used the figure in a democratizing way, representing anybody you know. In terms of other contemporary artists, Kara Walker represented the history of the American South through more stylized silhouettes, often depicting the horrifying landscape of slavery.

And so, I just wonder how you see your work in the context of these silhouette traditions?

LH: I love Kara Walker's work. I do not know if I could tackle the same subject matter that she does, but there's poetry in her work.

Silhouettes have this built-in history. So, when you see one, it automatically catapults you back in time. I love that, and it is the same thing I enjoy with certain fabrics; they have this kind of history. Or with patterns; some of the patterns that I use on my silhouette come from vintage bedsheets—people connect to that. They will say, "Oh, my grandmother had this sheet, or my mom had this sheet."

Also, I like the tension between using a style that is historical but with a contemporary figure. They are wearing today's hairstyles with today's clothing or speak to the body image of today.

LC: This is what really strikes me: where you are creating a living history, suggesting that people today are also worthy of representation.

LH: Just like with cotton. It is not a rose. It is not a plant that gets glamorized. It is a plant that connects to every day, right?

And the people that I represent are working, everyday people that hopefully I am immortalizing and elevating.

LC: Often in your work, you are addressing Black communities in the South and historically Black freedmen's towns. Louisiana, which I know you come back to repeatedly. How do you go about deciding that a particular community or landscape is something you want to historicize?

LH: I see the development of my practice in four stages, really. First, I started with my own family, and I think that's where Louisiana comes in. Because I have a large family there, and there was a great deal of information for me to pull from, a substantial amount of history about, maybe, where the land was that my family worked as slaves, or who were the people that owned our ancestors, and that kind of thing. So, I started first looking at the difference between the land where we worked and the land where we live now, thinking about Black landscape and the lack of Black land wealth.

And after I finished that project, then I thought, "OK, well, I do not want to just spend all the time focused on my own roots." There are a lot of other stories out there, and then I became really interested in other freedmen's towns.

For the project on the Black freedmen's towns, I had an opportunity to create a piece for the centennial of the Tulsa Race Massacre that was pretty much a landscape project, but it was looking at a specific block in Tulsa and one in Greenwood, Mississippi, which is where my father came from. A lot of the people who started the Greenwood community in Oklahoma had migrated from Greenwood, Mississippi, to build a new community that would allow them to build a better life.

So, it was a kind of love letter to the two Greenwoods in Tulsa, Oklahoma, and in Mississippi. In Tulsa, there was a block where there were no houses, just stairs that led to nowhere, like there was a potential for something, but there was nothing there. I photographed absent houses and juxtaposed those images against the block where my father grew up in Greenwood, Mississippi [fig. 5]. That opened the door to focusing on one community at a time.

Bitter Waters Sweet was that project. This body of work explores the legacy of Africatown, a historic community near Mobile, Alabama, that was founded by a group of West African people who were trafficked as slaves to the United States. When I first approached the Africatown project, I was originally planning to do a landscape project, and it was going to be about the water and the last slave ship, the *Clotilda*, but it became more than that when I started talking with people. Then it was important to incorporate the descendants into the project, so the silhouettes brought their stories to life, and the landscapes showed the spaces that still exist within the community today. I also followed the trail of the *Clotilda* as it came into the bay and where it was sunk.

LC: I think what I really love about your Africatown project is how you marry your two loves by bringing the landscape imagery in conversation with the silhouettes of the people and descendants within the region. But in this case, it is the evidence of illegal enslavement through the last slave ship to America and the oral histories left behind that helped recover the sunken ship. [Huckaby's *Bitter Waters Sweet* series documents descendants of the *Clotilda*, an illegal slave ship sunk in Mobile Bay, Alabama, in 1860, more than half a century after the United States forbade participation in the transatlantic slave trade. Many of them live in the nearby community of Africatown.]

LH: For me, the portraits and the landscape—they are both about history.

These individuals are the living DNA of their ancestors who came over on the *Clotilda*, and the landscape is the keeper of the stories in the community [figs. 6, 7]. While I was in Africatown, I explored the back of a cemetery where the tombstones are illegible. You cannot read the names or decipher any information anymore. A grove of huge mulberry trees surrounds the graves. I mentioned the trees to one of the elders I was photographing, who was in his eighties, and he shared that the mulberries were planted in the cemetery before he was born. And I just thought, you know, that is a story within itself; somebody decided that this site where their mulberry trees grew would be where our ancestors were laid to rest. There is history in those trees.

This is an example of why, for me, the landscape is a church. I have always felt like this spiritual connection to the earth. In ways that I cannot explain.

LC: You also incorporate needlework such as embroidery in your silhouettes as a way of identifying and interweaving hidden narratives. When and why did that become a crucial element in your work?

LH: I started adding embroidery during my residency at Artpace in San Antonio, and I continued applying them into the portraits from Africatown. It is really a space for the voice of the sitter. For *And Thy Neighb(our)*, I was looking specifically at immigrants and refugees of African descent. And I just thought that it would be powerful for the viewer to see how they describe themselves, because I think sometimes, we can put a blanket title on a group of people even though they are not just this one thing. People might see all Black people or all African Americans as the same when you are walking down the street, but that is not the case. They may look like they are Black, but they may also be Haitian.

This project was about confronting that reality. We can treat people a certain way and never really get to know them as individuals. And that is why the title *And Thy Neighb(our)* references scripture in the Bible about loving the Lord your God with all your heart and "thy neighbor as thyself" [Luke 10:27]. The inscriptions of text describe their ethnic heritage and are in a thread that was a similar color to the silhouette. At first glance, you can't really see them. You have to get close. You have to get to know somebody. You have to engage, and the more you engage that individual, the more you learn about them.

In the Africatown project, I asked the individuals I photographed what they wanted for their embroidery, and how they wanted me to designate their ancestor. I told them I was going to put "seed of." Some of them chose their ancestor's common name, and some of them chose their ancestor's African name. So, it allowed them to have some agency.

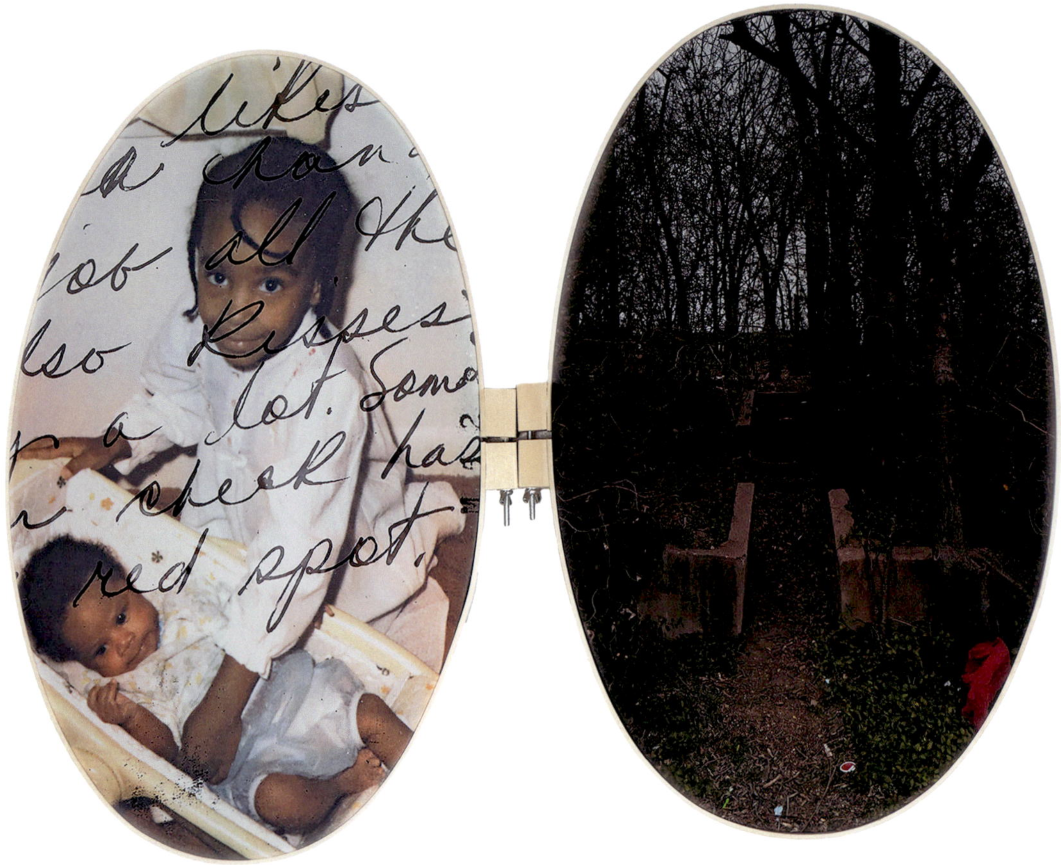

Figure 5
Letitia Huckaby, *A Little Red Spot/ Haskell Place*, 2021. Pigment print on cotton fabric with embroidery hoop, 27¾ × 34¾ in. Courtesy of the artist.

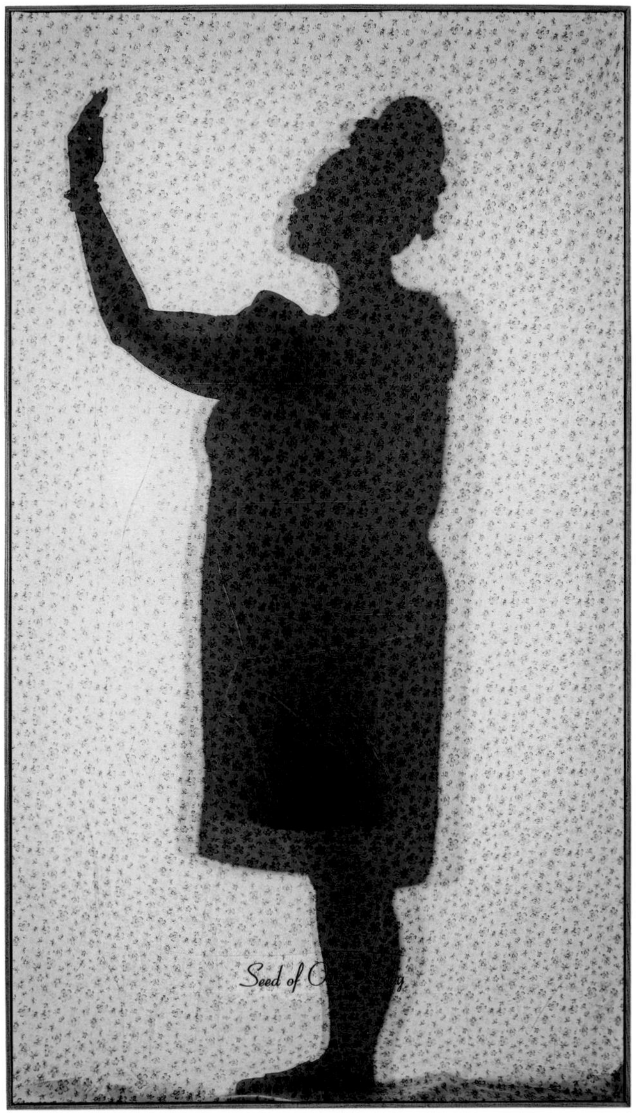

Figure 6
Letitia Huckaby, *Ms. Claudia (Seed of Ossa Kooby)*, 2022. Pigment print on fabric, 71 × 41 in. Courtesy of the artist.

LH: I recently went to a talk that Imani Perry gave at the Dallas Museum of Art. And you know how at the beginning of a talk, they will acknowledge the Indigenous communities who lived on the land before it was stolen by colonizers? In this case, they acknowledged that the place where the museum was built on was a freedmen's town.

LC: Wow.

LH: That is the first time I heard someone use a freedmen's town and not mention the Indigenous community that originally owned the land. So that was really shocking for me to hear that.

You could feel in the room, which was a mostly Black American audience, that there was a sense of pride. The audible gasps about sharing that side of history. Everyone is hungry for anything they can find out about their history, ancestry—anything.

LC: That is interesting, because I understand that this was a moment when they were reclaiming the history of a Black freedmen's town, settlements established for formerly enslaved communities after emancipation. In other discussions, I have heard both the historic Black spaces referenced while also acknowledging the Indigenous communities that previously existed on the land.

LH: That makes me think about all those freedmen towns in Oklahoma and Kansas. Because Oklahoma was where most of the Indigenous people were forced to move. Black communities were invited to come. They were sent flyers saying, "Come, move to Kansas."

So, for all these communities in Kansas, like Nicodemus, you will find examples of the flyers that were sent out. Due to the lack of trees in the Plains, the Black people

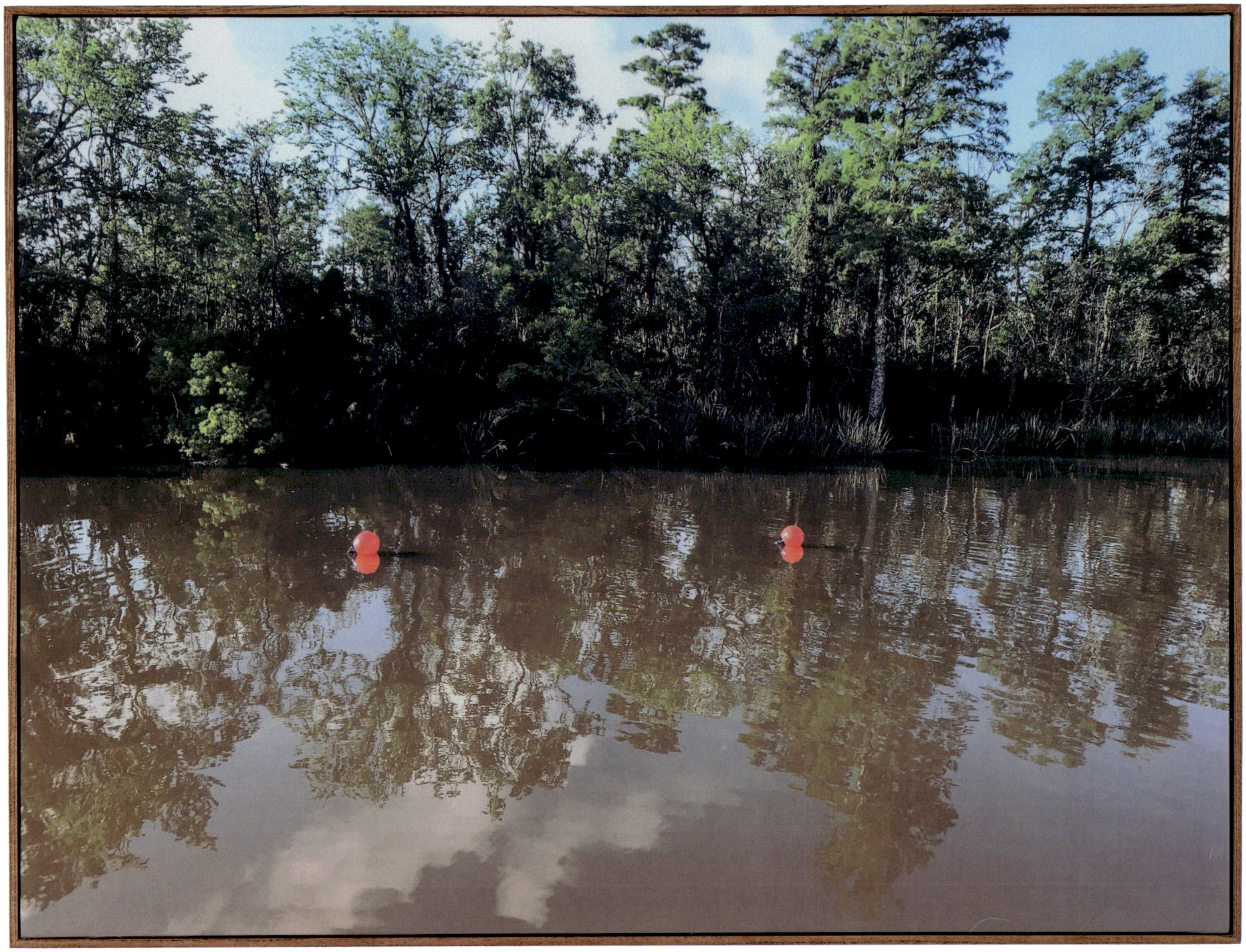

Figure 7
Letitia Huckaby, *The Clotilda*, 2022.
Pigment print on fabric, 33 × 45 in.
Courtesy of the artist.

would end up digging holes in the ground to create living spaces. I have a photograph of one dugout shelter in my *Beautiful Blackness* series. I captured one, which was halfway between Nicodemus and a sundown town. They built this one because they couldn't stay in the White town when they were shopping after dark, but it was too far of a distance to go back at night, so they would spend the night at this place in the ground and would go the rest of the way home the next day. That was how these families lived when they first got there until they could get enough wood to build structures. Those were the areas Indigenous people were forced to leave during the Trail of Tears.

LC: This is an important interconnection within the story of Black landscapes and Indigenous landscapes across the American South. Why are these stories particularly important to tell?

LH: They carry the legacies of slavery in the South and what it did to the landscape.

For contemporary communities, you can see it because there is a residual effect. There is still heavy control over Black bodies in the South. Not that there are not in other areas of the country. The South is maybe dearer to my heart because of my family.

The first time my husband went to visit my grandmother in Mississippi, he was appalled by the conditions. Like, "we need to call somebody!" Seeing it through his eyes was a little bit of a shock because I was just used to seeing the land and spaces that way. I really had a sort of awakening after my father passed away. It was like a veil dropped off my eyes, and what had become normal seemed unnormal to me in this place that I had seen as beautiful. And so that has been my obsession ever since, to tell the story of the effects of slavery on Black communities and how it is still playing out today.

LC: What do you observe most in the landscape today? What is the land telling you now about where we are?

LH: The land is telling me how much was taken away. I am seeing lost hopes and dreams. Towns that were once flourishing—there is nothing left. There is this tendency for the government to run highways through the middle of these Black towns or allow big industry to build near them, and you have these higher levels of cancer and other illnesses because of the manufacturing plants that were allowed alongside these freedmen's towns. And so, I am seeing generations of families having to sell off their land for little to nothing, for the sake of their health. It is not a beautiful picture.

I do not know if that will change as I continue to explore more, but I have not come across one situation yet that feels completely like a realization of the dream.

Letitia Huckaby is an artist and photographer who has exhibited internationally and whose works are featured in the collections of institutions such as the Library of Congress, the McNay Art Museum, the Smithsonian National Museum of American History, and many more. She is the co-founder of Kinfolk House, a collaborative project space where community and art converge in a predominantly Black and Latina/e/o neighborhood in Fort Worth, Texas.

Lauren Cross is the Gail-Oxford Associate Curator of American Decorative Arts at The Huntington. She curated the installation By and By: Telling Stories Through Silhouettes *(2025–26) at The Huntington.*

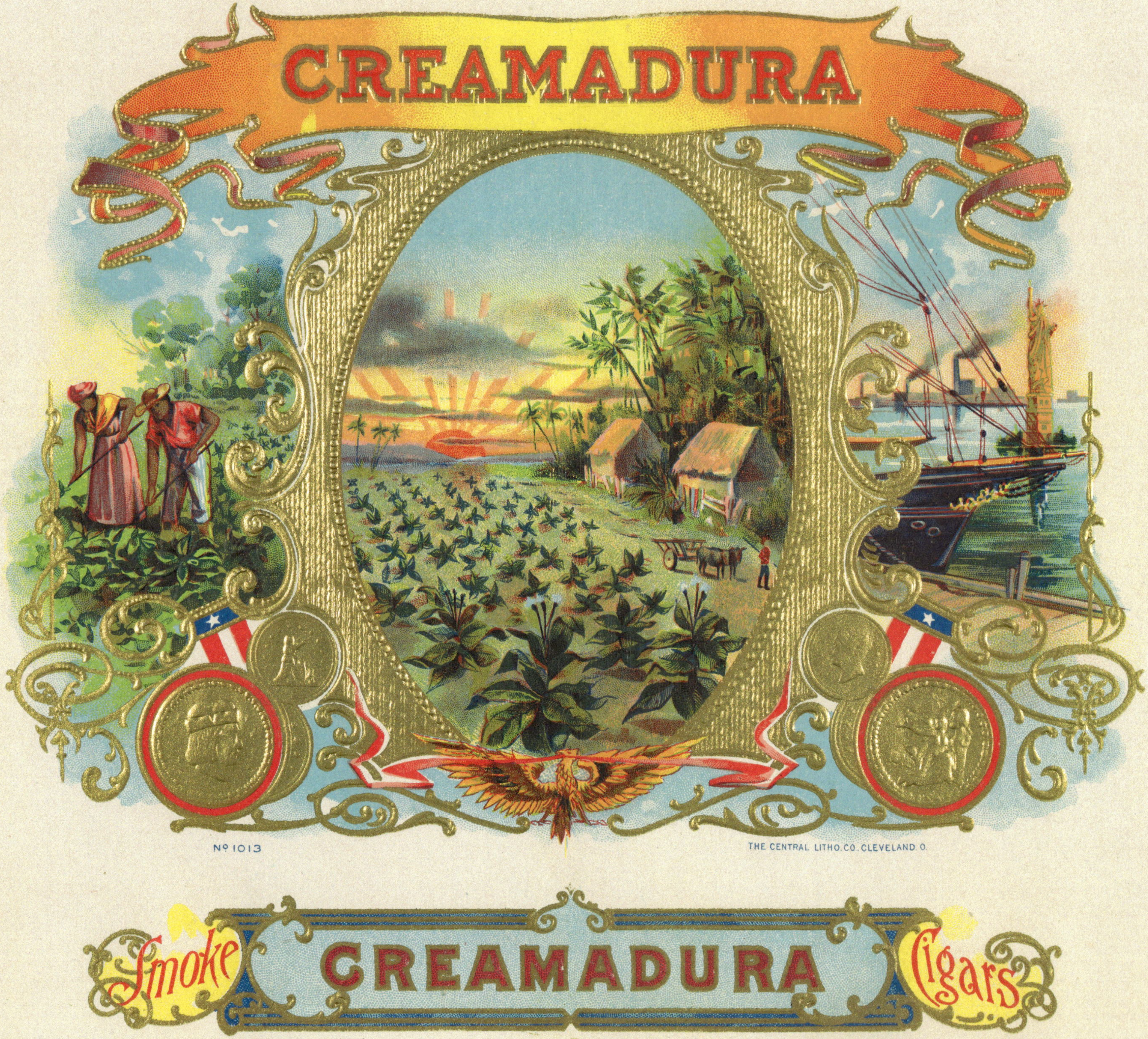
CREAMADURA
Nº 1013
THE CENTRAL LITHO. CO. CLEVELAND. O.
Smoke
CREAMADURA
Cigars

Smoke and Soil

Land, Labor, and the Marketing of Tobacco

Created at the turn of the twentieth century, this nine-color lithograph used to advertise tobacco opens a portal into American land history. It evokes the deep histories of forced labor and agricultural economies while foreshadowing the dawn of modern consumerism. Among a sea of open-lid boxes in stores, "Creamadura" sold the polished, vibrant tranquility of a sunset over a tobacco plantation. Dark-skinned laborers and a lustrous Statue of Liberty frame the landscape to create a compelling story enveloping the Caribbean within a US-dominated marketplace.

Produced in Cleveland, the advertising label cunningly embeds American flag imagery, a patriotic eagle, and aggrandized seals into the gold leaf. Among the seals is a silhouette of Christopher Columbus, evoking the origins of European exploitation of this "New World" plant. Columbus first encountered tobacco in the Caribbean islands in 1492, witnessing the Taíno peoples using it for medicinal and spiritual purposes. The cigar brand's name, "Creamadura," contains the Spanish gendered suffix "dura" attached to the English "Cream" to create a bastardized word suggesting a smooth smoking experience. These promotional techniques attempt to associate the product with Cuba's premium tobacco, casting the Caribbean landscape and Spanish-inflected brand name as symbols of authentic Cuban origin.

Although the label depicts an idyllic landscape, tobacco products were extremely destructive because they required a sustained, exploited labor source. A century after Columbus, North American colonists began cultivating the West Indian tobacco variety, *Nicotiana tabacum*, for trade with London, catering to European tastes. In 1612, English colonist John Rolfe introduced the systemic cultivation of tobacco in Virginia. From the Caribbean to the American colonies, enslaved labor formed the foundation of tobacco plantations, which enabled their outsized economic prosperity for over two centuries.

By the time the "Creamadura" label was produced, the United States (1865) and Cuba (1886) had abolished slavery, but exploited labor still allowed the industry to flourish. The US victory in the Spanish-American War (1898) transferred Cuba from a Spanish colony to an American protectorate. Thus, "Creamadura" becomes representative of the tobacco crop's intertwined labor and imperial histories. While modern labor practices have since improved, tobacco's popularity today in the form of cigarettes obscures the fraught economic origins of tobacco plantations in the Spanish and American Empires.

American desires for Cuban tobacco and its ties to plantations across the Western Hemisphere reached a turning point in 1962, when President John F. Kennedy signed the Cuban Embargo Act that halted all trade with Cuba. This effectively ended the centuries-long consumption of Cuban tobacco in the United States. Yet nostalgic marketing tactics for companies like American Spirit and Marlboro cigarettes remain powerful tools to recall a past that has been "great" for some and traumatic for others. Tobacco's story unites the temporal and spatial distances between Columbus's contact, the American colonies, and Cuba. And, as the "Creamadura" label shows, these convoluted histories remain visible in packaging labels we encounter in markets and convenience stores every day.

Armando Pulido is the Assistant Curator for Library Special Projects at The Huntington.

Figure 1
"Creamadura" cigar-box label, ca. 1900. Color lithographed and gold embossed by the Central Litho Co., Cleveland. Jay T. Last Collection, The Huntington.

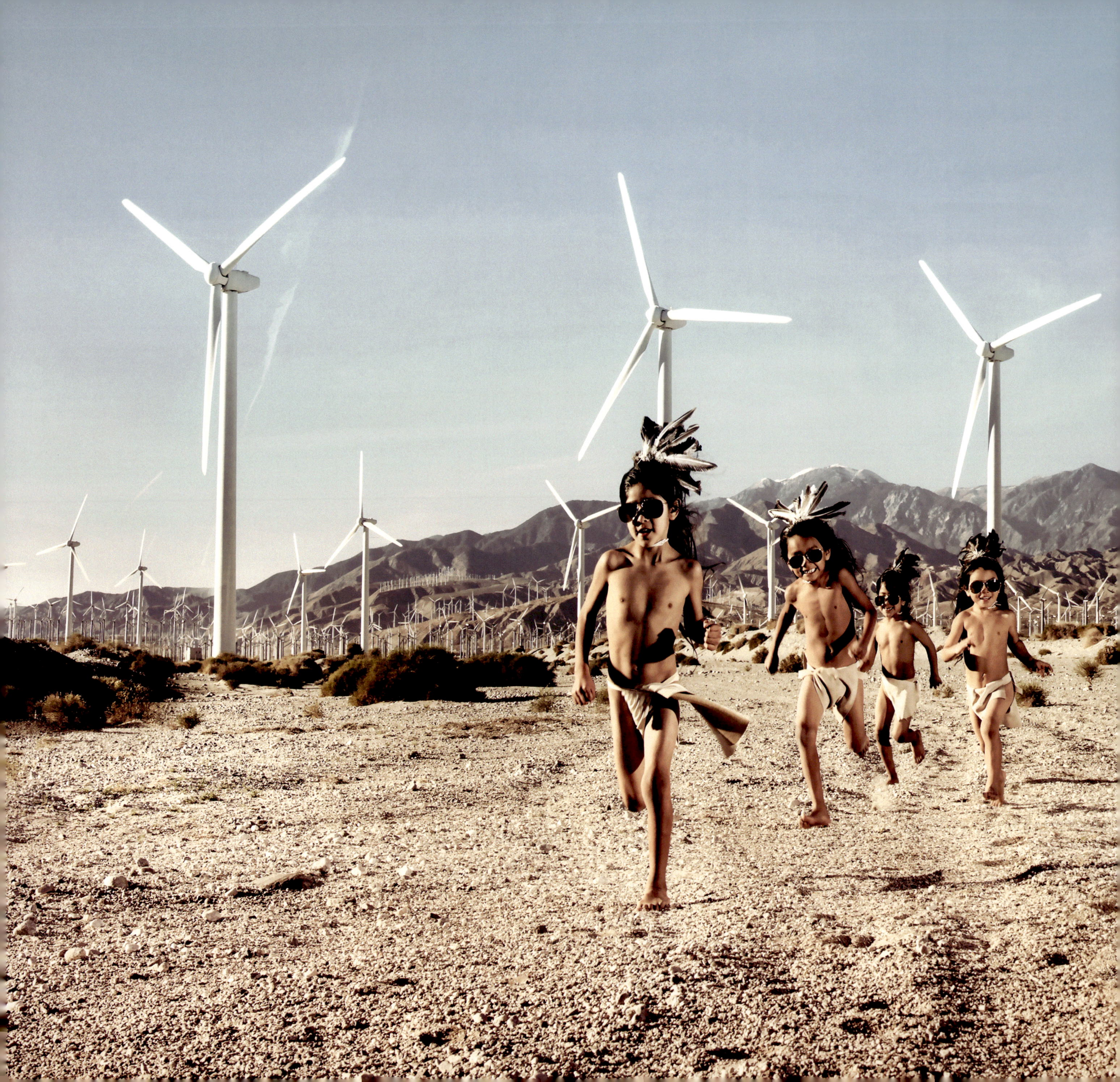

Regenerations

Regenerative processes replace or restore damaged or missing elements of an ecosystem. Plants transform solar energy and nutrients (often from dead or decaying organisms) into plant biomass. This allows ecosystems to flourish after destructive events. Many farmers and gardeners seek to learn from regeneration to form reciprocal rather than extractive relationships with the land. Kinship, spiritual connections, and ancestral ties to the land can also encourage such processes of renewal and repair. Artists and writers offer vivid observations of landscapes to imagine new ways of living, including Indigenous reclamation of ancestral lands.

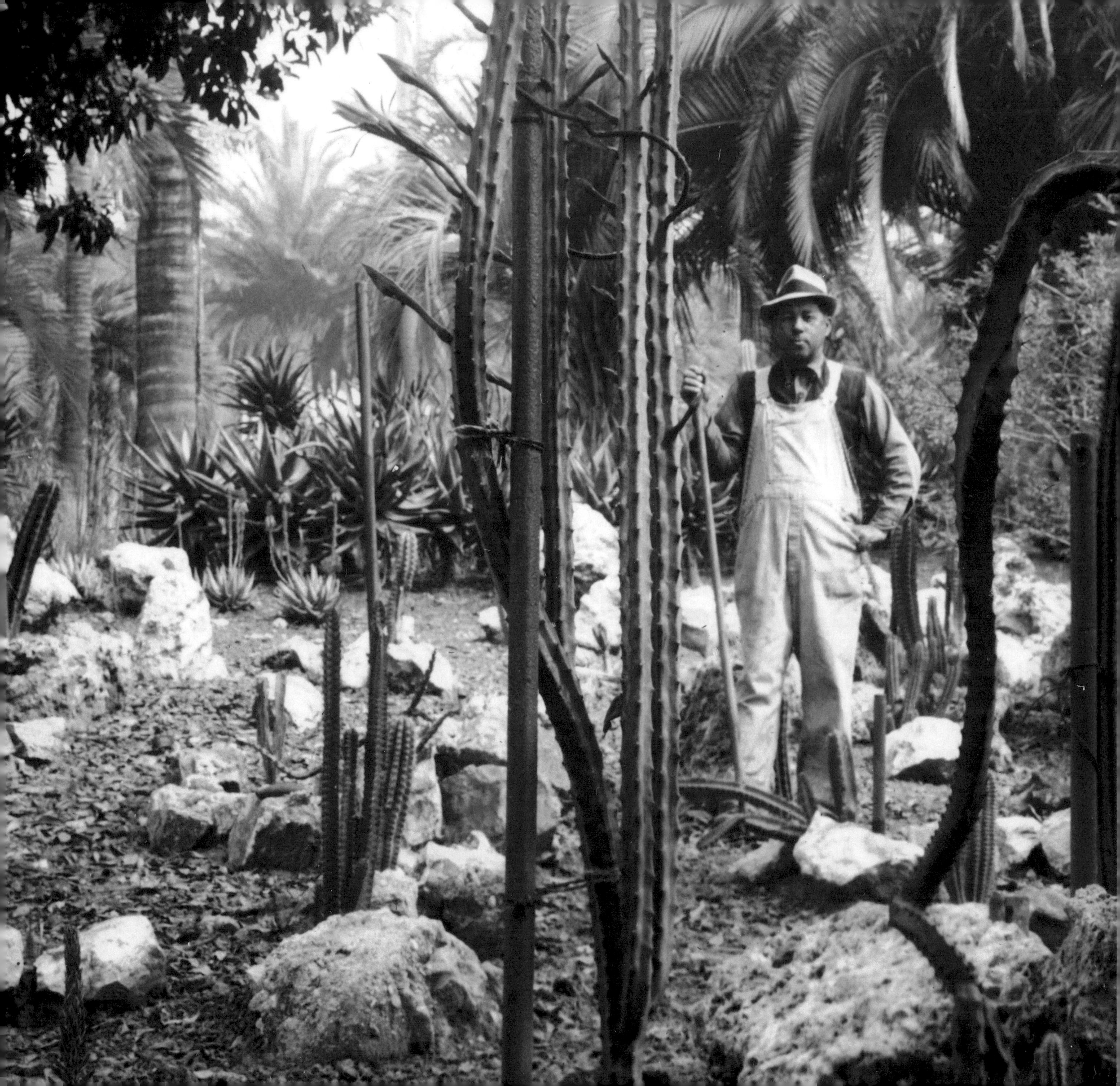

We Built This

I first came to The Huntington years ago, as a graduate student researching my dissertation. I was daunted. For all my eagerness to embark on my research, the place overwhelmed me. The dark wood paneling, the fancy library lamps, and the hush of the reading room created an atmosphere that felt far removed from my upbringing in the Echo Park neighborhood of Los Angeles. I was one of only a handful of scholars of color, and often the only Latino in the room.

One day I invited my dad, a Mexican immigrant with an elementary school education, to see the place for himself. He was floored—the rolling green lawns, the towering trees, the vastness of the grounds, with the original Huntington mansion now turned into an art museum, and the sheer scale of it all. At lunch he told me how impressed he was and how proud he felt that I had made it here. I hesitated, then admitted the truth: "Yeah, but I sometimes feel intimidated."

"Why?!" he asked.

"It's isolating, being the only one. I sometimes feel so out of place."

He leaned across the table. "*Hijita*, why? We built this."

He was referring to a story we both knew, of the many Mexican workers who immigrated to the United States in the early twentieth century, many fleeing the Mexican Revolution. Many found jobs in agriculture, railroads, and construction, including at The Huntington. The Huntington's story and mine were already connected.

I've returned to The Huntington many times over the years, as a professor, researcher, presenter, and board member. When I was asked to consult for The Huntington's one-hundredth anniversary, I finally found a concrete way into the story my father had invited me to reclaim. The curators came upon an old payroll book whose entries were bare: mostly men and a handful of women, listed by first initial and last name (M. Martinez). This is one of the only surviving records of the Mexican workers who built this place, highlighting a striking absence in a vast historical collection.

Detail of Huntington Cactus Garden album (fig. 1).

William Hertrich, The Huntington's first ranch superintendent—Huntington's right-hand man and a German immigrant himself—seldom allowed these workers to be photographed, though he took dozens of photos of the gardens. The workers, it seems, detracted from the myth.

Still, in rare instances, they appear. In one photo, a Mexican worker stands proudly, boldly looking into the camera—one arm akimbo, the other holding his gardening tool. The label accompanying this photo in the album reads "*Monvillea anisitsii*, IA-59," reinforcing that the plant is the intended subject. The worker appears only in a supporting role, likely for scale (figs. 1, 2).

Yet he stands with pride at the center of the frame, meeting the camera's gaze head-on. Perhaps he knew he would be asked to pose that day—his white overalls and hat are more suited for a Sunday picnic or church than for laboring in a garden. Through his expression, his stance, his clothing, he signals to us: *I am here. Look at me. I alone define my place.*

The Huntington is usually presented as a vision brought to life by one man's imagination and ambition. Fruit orchards, oak trees, ponds, succulents, roses, and botanical gardens seem to have sprung miraculously from the soil through the sheer force of his will.

But those trees were planted, those tracks were laid, and those gardens were tended by hundreds of human hands—hands that remain largely invisible in the institution's official history. These workers brought not only their labor but also their knowledge, botanical skills, and cultural practices that deeply shaped the landscape.

Even today, traces of their labor remain. The Huntington's marmalade, a top seller in its gift shop, comes from

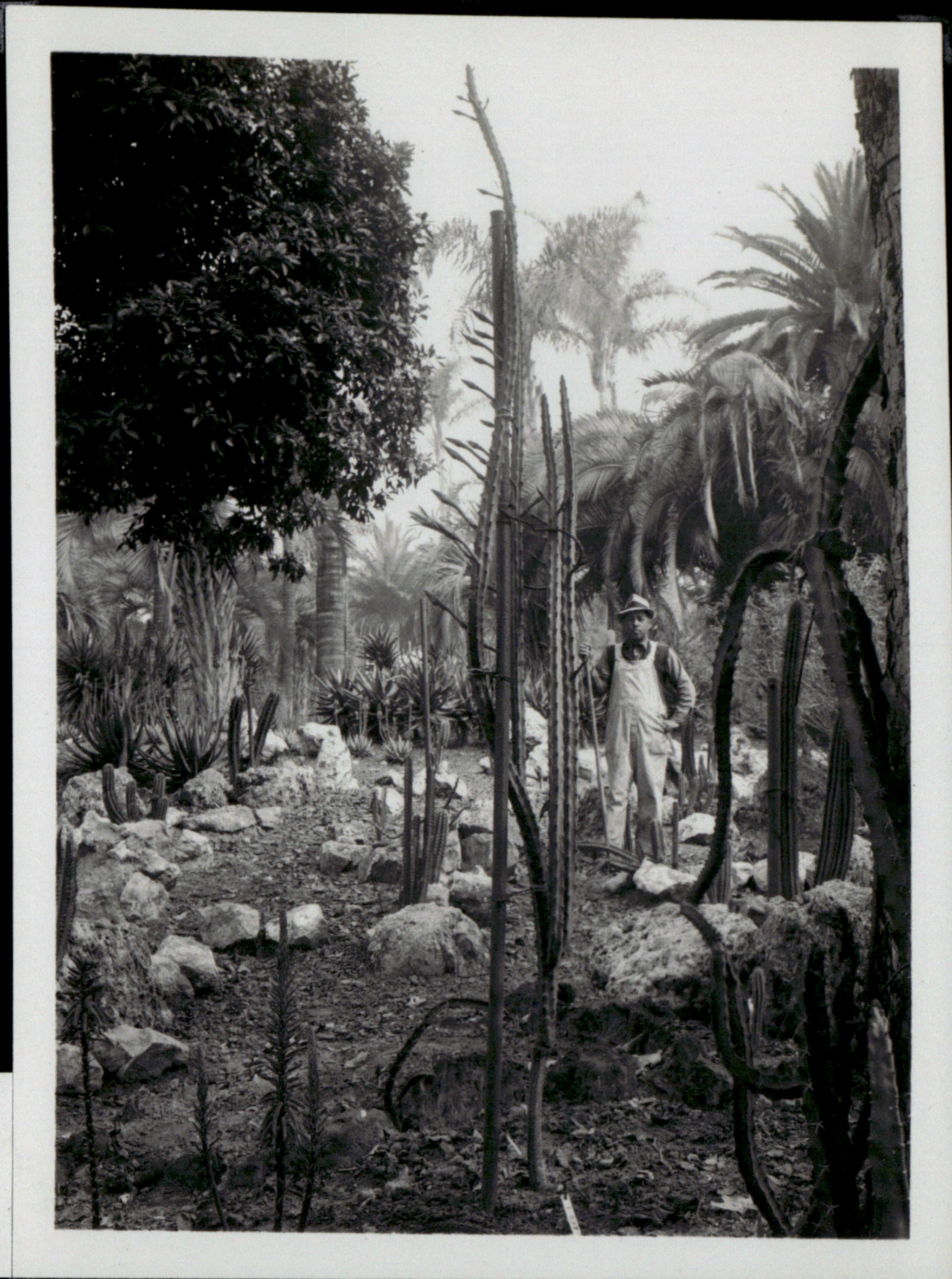

MONVILLEA ANISITSII

IA-59

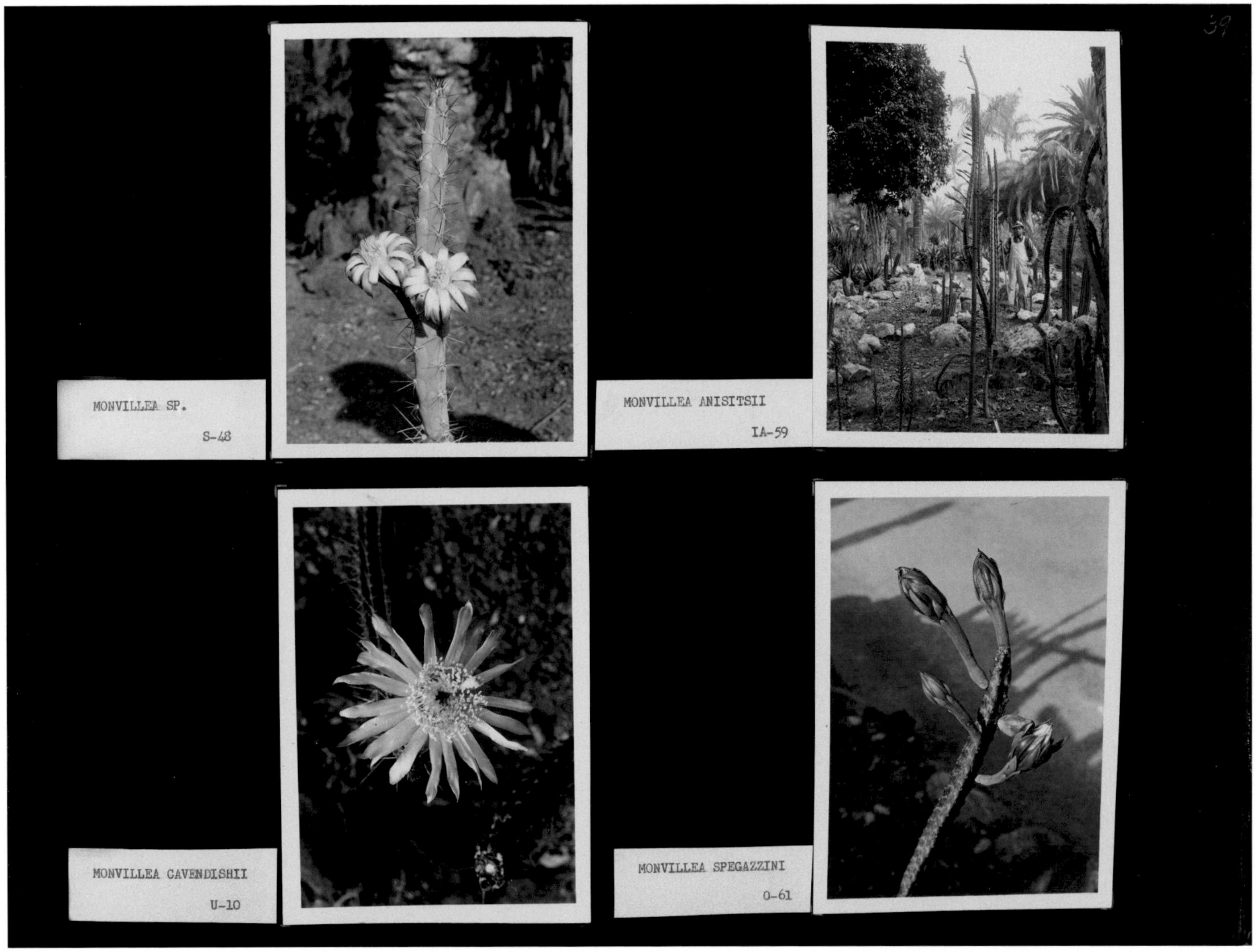

Figure 1
Unidentified worker in what is today the Desert Garden at The Huntington. *Monvillea anisitsii IA*-59, May 15, 1938. Gelatin silver print. From Cactus Garden album, vol. 2. Henry E. Huntington Estate Photograph Collection, The Huntington, photCL 107.

Figure 2
Cactus Garden album, vol. 2, ca. 1954. Henry E. Huntington Estate Photograph Collection, The Huntington, photCL 107.

the same orange trees that those long-ago workers planted, fumigated, pruned, and harvested. Those workers' names don't appear on the label or on the website or on plaques, but their legacy is here, woven into the landscape.

This isn't just Henry Huntington's story.

This is an immigrant story.

This is a California story.

We built this.

Natalia Molina is Distinguished Professor and Dean's Professor of American Studies and Ethnicity at the University of Southern California. Her research explores the interconnected histories of race, place, gender, culture, and citizenship.

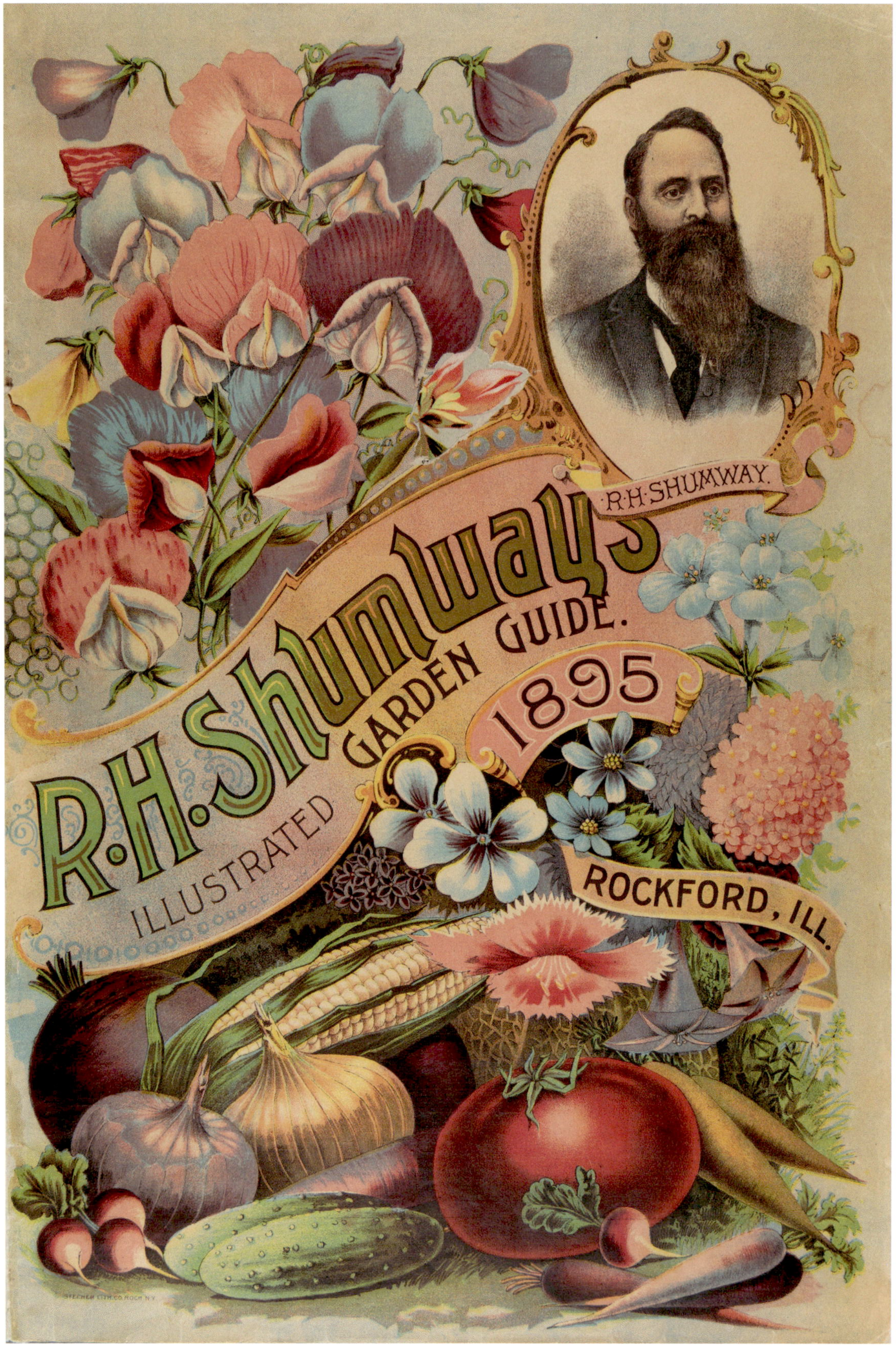
R·H·SHUMWAY.
R·H·Shumway's
ILLUSTRATED GARDEN GUIDE.
1895
ROCKFORD, ILL.

A Short Garden History

All gardens grow at the intersections of culture and nature. They represent the ever-changing and diverse relationships between human and nonhuman nature. In some cases, gardens provide tangible sustenance—food that nourishes us, medicines that heal us, fibers that clothe us (fig. 1). But gardens also sustain us in more abstract yet equally powerful ways. They offer a spiritual connection with the natural world, a sense of place and belonging. They represent an idealized realm that is both wild and safe. Our connection to nature has been at times harmonious and at other times exploitative. These attitudes are reflected in how we create landscapes, and whether they tell tales of conquest and domination, or respect and reciprocity.

Humans have played an important role in shaping the landscape since the appearance of our hunter-gatherer ancestors. Indeed, our ability to modify the environment to suit our needs and desires is a distinctly human characteristic. Tens of thousands of years before humans began developing agriculture in the Middle East and North Africa, groups in what is now northern Malawi used fire to make advantageous changes to their environment. According to environmental and archaeological evidence, they burned forested areas to favor open-woodland hunting or encourage the growth of certain plants as sources of food or textiles.[1] Humans' increasing command of technology amplified our effect on nature and has become more intense in the modern era. With gardens, we generate our own interpretation of the natural environment.

Figure 1
R. H. Shumway's Illustrated Garden Guide, 1895. Printed by Stecher Lithographic Co. Jay T. Last Collection of Horticulture Prints and Ephemera, The Huntington, priJLC_HORT_002472.

Tangled Roots of American Gardens

The origins of gardens and horticulture in America are long and complex, interwoven from the knowledge and traditions of many peoples, some native to this continent, some who came here in search of a new home, and some who had no choice in the matter.

The history of gardens in the United States looks different at The Huntington, which displays the influence of cultures from around the world on its grounds. It features plants from six continents and incorporates varied garden principles and traditions, especially those from Europe, Asia, and North America. The Huntington is an American garden of sorts, yet it emerges out of a history that connects to Latin America and across the Pacific—as well as being rooted in California's complicated landscape—in a way that tells a distinct story about plants and people.

For thousands of years, Indigenous peoples throughout the Americas have cultivated gardens according to both functional and aesthetic principles. Over generations, they selectively bred plants such as corn, tomato, peppers, potato, agave, pineapple, and avocado, as well as managing "wild" landscapes (fig. 2).

As Spanish, Dutch, French, and English colonists arrived at different sites in the Americas, they marveled at the landscape that Indigenous peoples had created through both forest agriculture and cropland horticulture—yet Native expertise and labor were invisible to them. Even as Europeans exported some of the world's most important food plants developed by Indigenous peoples (such as corn, potatoes, tomatoes, and cacao), they described the land as undeveloped and tended by "primitives." Gonzalo Fernández de Oviedo y Valdés, who explored the Americas in the early sixteenth century, attributed the quality of the avocados offered by the Indigenous people he encountered to the divine. He wrote in his 1526 report to King Charles V of Spain, "Those who have these fruits [avocado] guard them and esteem them highly and the trees are wild as are the others which I have mentioned, for the chief gardener is God, and the Indians apply no work whatever to them."[2]

The European colonists who settled in North America brought with them myriad plants and horticultural practices that they considered essential. These contributions took root and adapted to their new environment. The first public garden space in the English colonies was a portion of the Boston Common, established in 1634. The townspeople there voted to tax each household six shillings for the purchase of William Blackstone's farm to be used as a community space that served a variety of military, agricultural, and recreational purposes.[3]

At the founding of the United States a century and a half later, the primary influences on gardening among elite colonists in the first thirteen states came from Europe. The seventeenth and eighteenth centuries saw the rise of elaborate pleasure gardens as expressions of growing wealth and power. From kitchen gardens that provided food, medicine, textiles, and ornamental plants arose such ostentatious landscapes as the gardens of Versailles. Created by landscape architect André Le Nôtre under the direction of King Louis XIV, the gardens took about forty years to complete. They featured carefully manicured plants, lavish water features, and an orangerie that made it possible to grow Louis's beloved citrus—which originated in tropical and subtropical Asia—outdoors during the warm months and indoors in winter. Versailles attests to the determination to bend nature to human will.

Plants were also on the minds of the United States founders. As Andrea Wulf documents in her book *Founding Gardeners*, the first four presidents of the fledgling republic were devoted horticulturalists.[4] George Washington's wartime correspondence reveals an intense yearning to return to his gardens. Thomas Jefferson and John Adams, during treaty negotiations in Britain, availed themselves of some of Europe's most renowned gardens. Washington, who was interested in native North American plants, emphasized

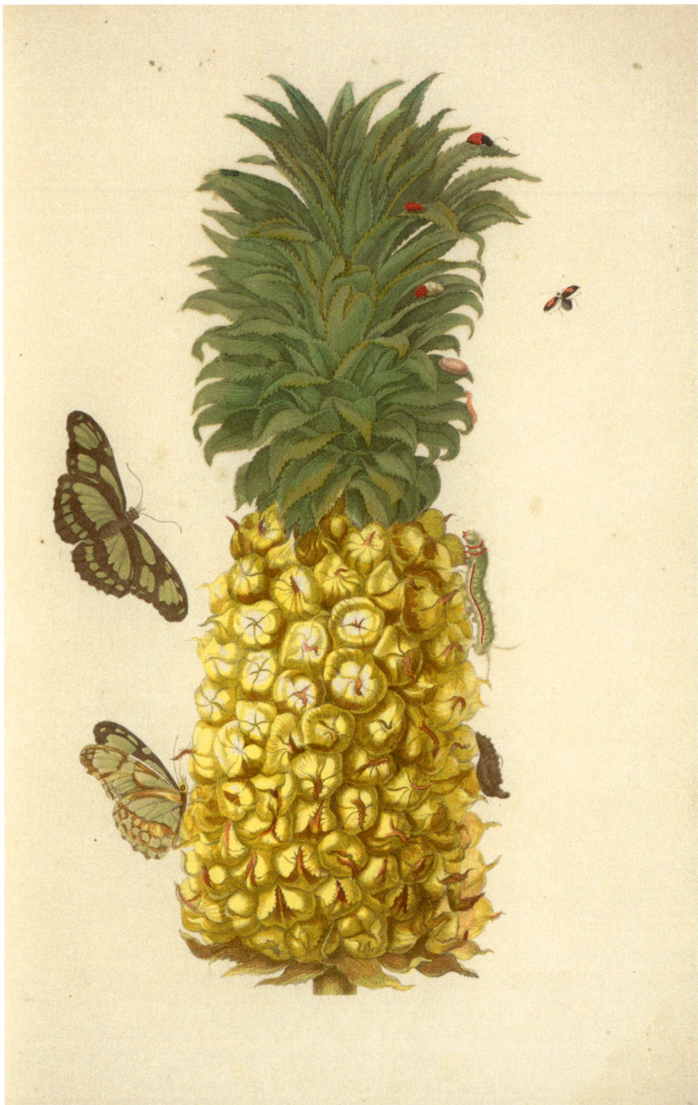

Figure 2
The pineapple (*Ananas comosus*) is native to a region between southern Brazil and Paraguay. Cultivated by Indigenous groups, particularly the Tupi-Guarani and Carib peoples, it spread throughout South and Central America, the Caribbean, and Mexico. Maria Sibylla Merian, *Metamorphosis insectorum Surinamensium* (Amsterdam, 1730). The Huntington, 145365.

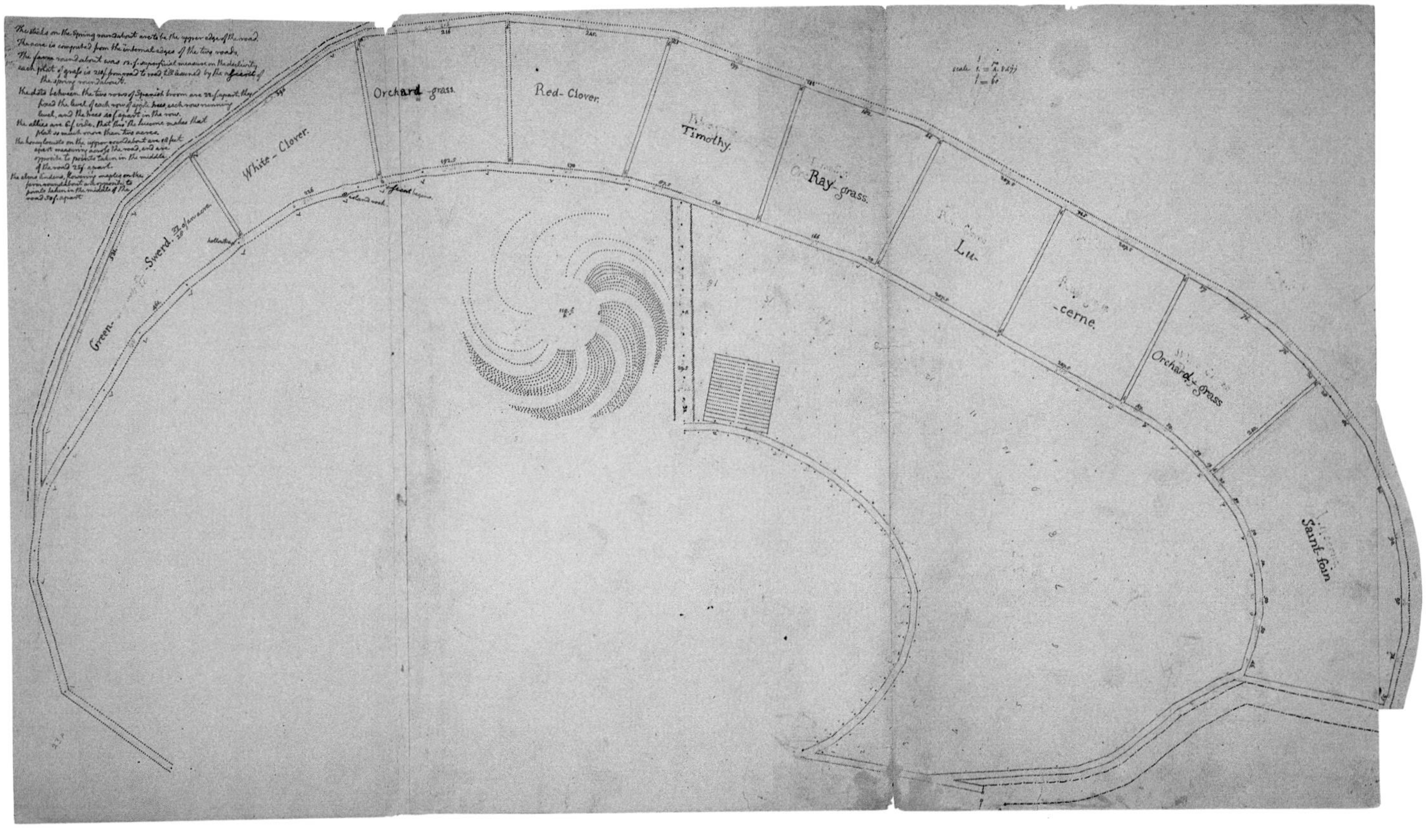

Figure 3 and detail

This garden plan includes instructions for how and where specific plants were to be added to the landscape at Thomas Jefferson's Monticello. Thomas Jefferson, "Plan of Spring Roundabout, Monticello," before 1794. Pen and ink on autograph manuscript, 15 × 26⅘ in. Thomas Jefferson Collection, The Huntington, Purchased by Henry E. Huntington, 1916, HM 9396.

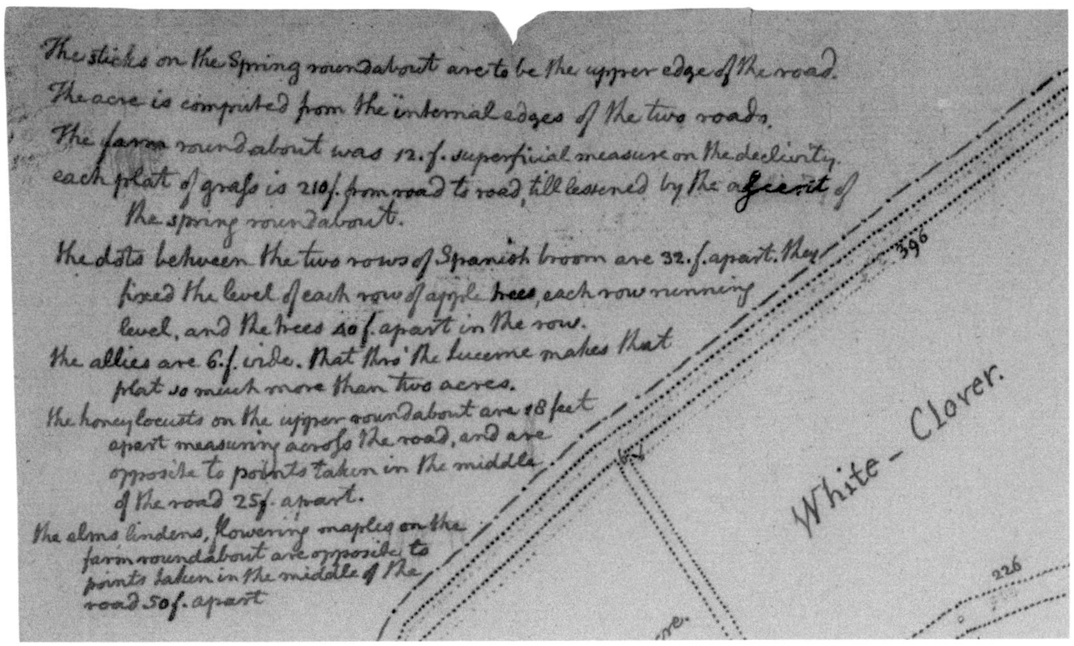

planting only natives in his Mount Vernon landscaping as a political statement. This embodied a complex relationship between admiration for the beauty and diversity of native plants and an adherence to the horticultural practices of the Old World.

At the same time, the monoculture of commodity crops such as tobacco, cotton, and sugarcane dominated American commercial agriculture, and the labor of enslaved Africans generated national wealth, including at Mount Vernon, Jefferson's Monticello (fig. 3), and James Madison's Montpelier. Additionally, African horticultural experience with rice and indigo cultivation made these crops economically significant. Africans also brought broader botanical knowledge, as well as the seeds of plants that many continued to grow in subsistence gardens they tended when they could, often at night or on Sundays.[5] Plants that originated in Africa—among them rice, sorghum, millet, collard greens, okra, black-eyed peas, and watermelon—provided familiar foods for uprooted people. They went on to become enmeshed in American food and garden culture.

Harriet Tubman, now celebrated for her role in guiding enslaved people to freedom, was also a skilled herbalist and healer. During her journeys on the Underground Railroad, Tubman drew on knowledge passed down from her grandmother to use wild plants as medicine—treating

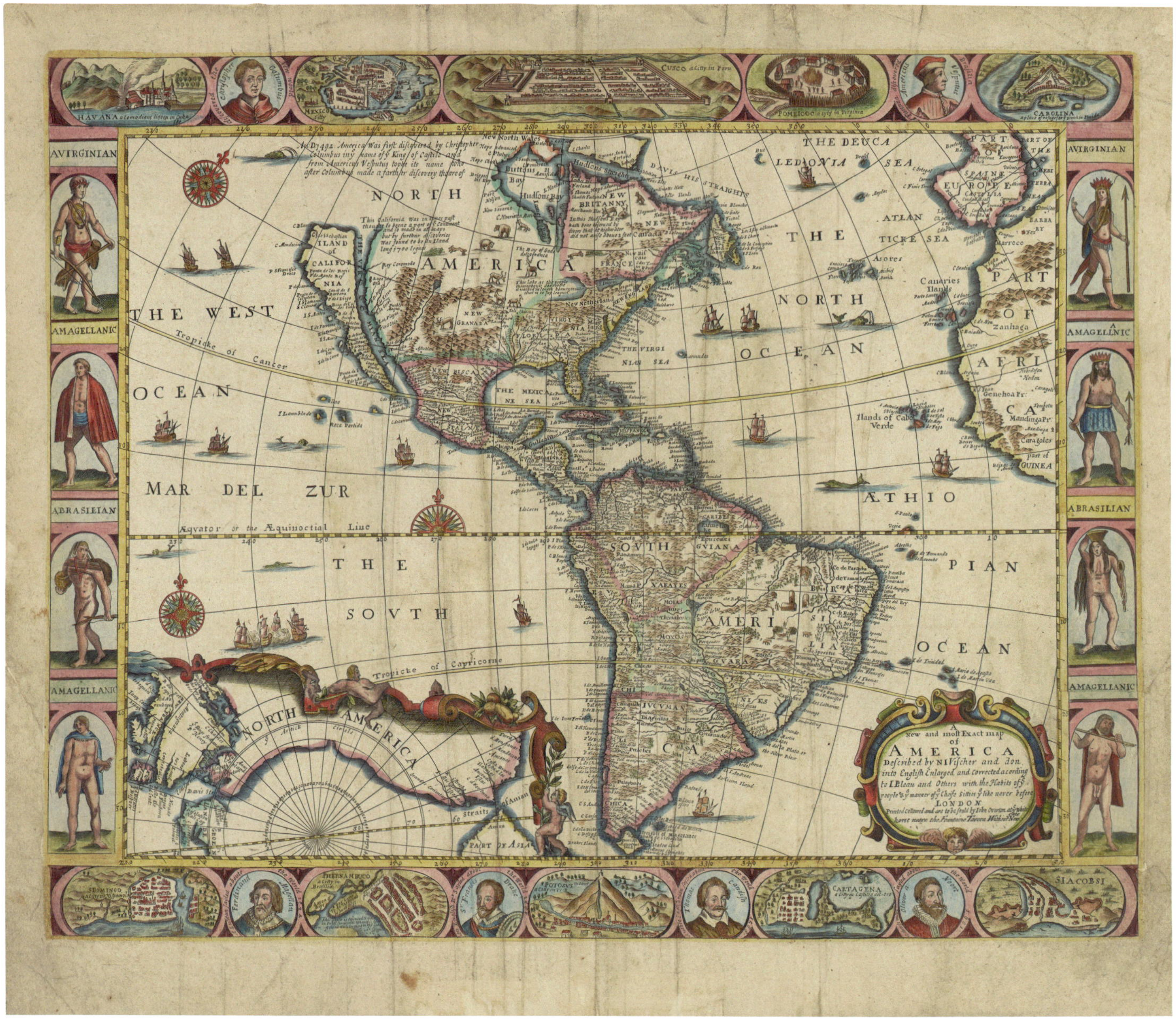

Figure 4
John Overton, *A New and Most Exact Map of America*, 1671. Hand-colored map, 19¾ × 22⅘ in. The Huntington, 311147.

illness, tending to wounds, and even soothing crying babies to avoid detection.

Born into slavery in 1864, on the eve of Emancipation, George Washington Carver later worked as an agronomist and innovator who championed the power of farming to improve community life. As a teacher at Tuskegee Institute, he taught poor farmers how to restore soil health by employing regenerative practices, such as composting and crop rotation. He encouraged planting alternative crops to cotton, such as peanuts, soybeans, and sweet potatoes. In addition to teaching, he distributed free bulletins that included recipes and farming tips to promote self-sufficiency.

The California Context

In California, hundreds of Indigenous nations understood how to coax the land to produce what they needed. For example, they have long known that fire is a crucial tool in managing various landscapes. Desirable plants that are "fire followers" were encouraged with cultural burns (prescribed burns intended to sustain the land). The people of inland desert regions used fire to increase seed production in fan palms (*Washingtonia filifera* and *W. robusta*), whose tiny fruits are a reliable food source. In forested areas, others used fire to promote the growth of oaks over pines and prevent the buildup of brush. Reducing the dominance of large, densely forested areas allowed for more open meadow and scrub areas with a wider range of plant species. Like others around the world, Indigenous people in the "New World" understood how to channel water to irrigate and manage it in accordance with the natural rain cycles in California and throughout the hemisphere.

Early European maps that depicted California as an island may have been cartographically incorrect, but they captured the evolutionary process that makes the state's flora distinctive and rare (fig. 4). Major mountain ranges and deserts to the east resulted in geographic isolation and rates of endemism (species that occur nowhere else in the world) that are on par with island ecosystems. In short, California is a biodiversity hotspot. Indeed, within the United States, only Hawai'i, a chain of islands isolated in the Pacific, is home to a greater number of endemic plants and animals. Such dense and specific ecosystems, however, are fragile and susceptible to pressure from human activity.

When Spanish missionaries and settlers introduced cattle ranching and Mediterranean agriculture in the late 1700s—simultaneously with the American Revolution on the other side of the continent—they began to revolutionize the long-standing landscape Indigenous peoples had tended. But as colonial populations grew, the Spanish and later Mexican populations contended with the seasonal scarcity of water in the province.

After the United States conquered California in the Mexican-American War, the influx of Americans began to change the landscape even more dramatically. By the twentieth century, intensive irrigation transformed the state. Supplemental water rerouted from Northern California and the Colorado River made it possible for a wide range of plants from around the world to add a lush tropical ambience to ornamental gardens. Farmers also developed parts of Southern California and the Central Valley—once a region of biodiverse ecosystems, from savannas to vernal pools, seasonal wetlands, and riparian habitats—into an immense agricultural system. Today, California produces nearly half of the country's vegetables and more than three-quarters of its fruits and nuts.[6]

The Lawn

Ornamental gardens in both Europe and the United States were historically ensconced in estates and manors, reserved for the private enjoyment of the wealthy. Lawns were a signature feature of these pleasure gardens. Requiring armies of caretakers to manually trim and maintain them with scythes and clippers, the verdant swaths of turf were both places for the affluent to mingle and a symbol of status. Turf grass was a prominent feature at Mount Vernon and Monticello, carefully tended by enslaved gardeners. When Jefferson founded the University of Virginia in 1819, a central part of the university was the main green that served as a literal common ground between residences and academic buildings housing faculty from different disciplines. It was a reinvention of the estate as a community space where people—usually excluding the enslaved and free laborers who tended the gardens—could meet and exchange ideas.

In the twentieth century, particularly the post–World War II era, lawns in America linked the common and the private, representing not only "the people" but also the

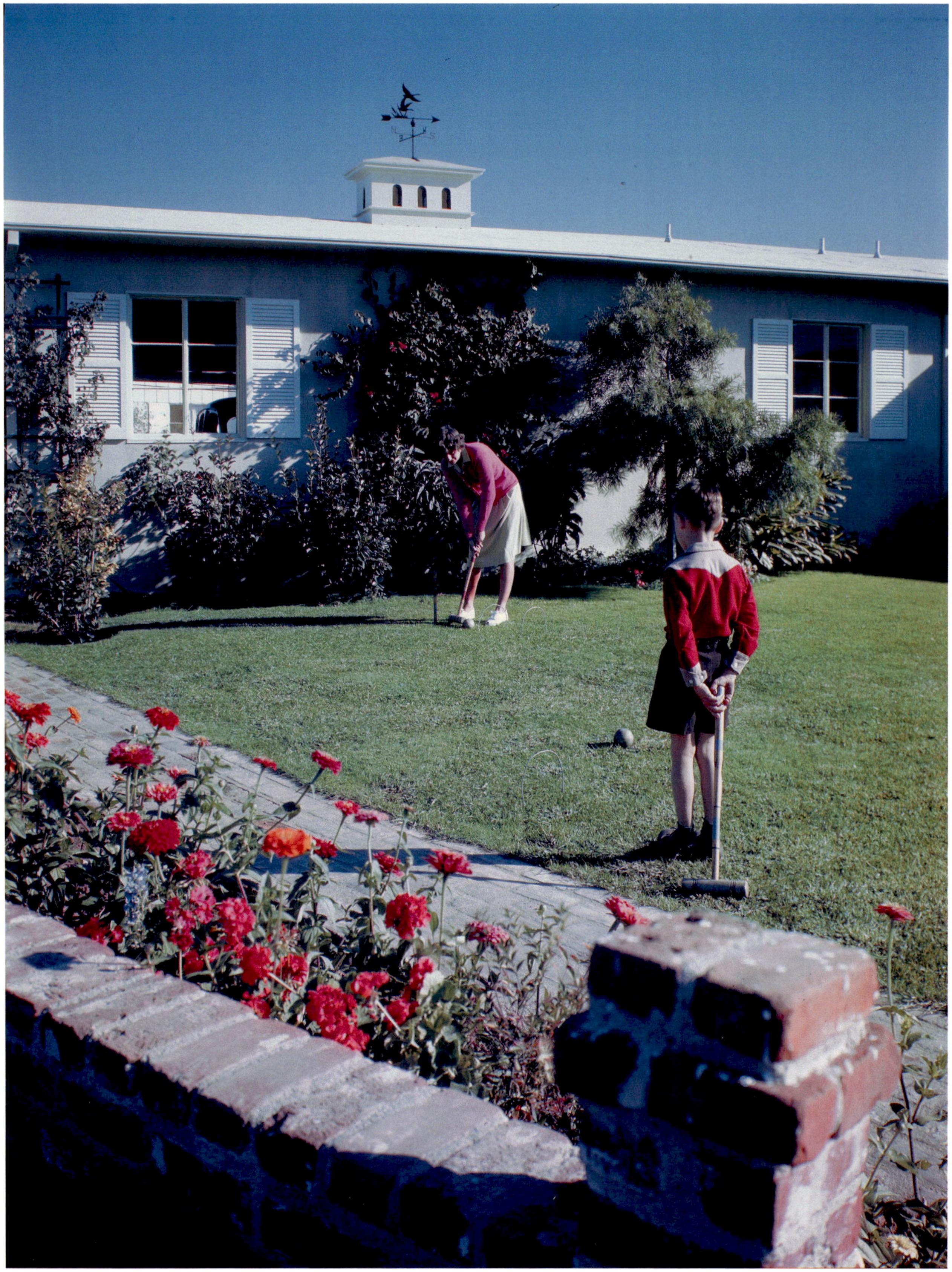

Figure 5
Maynard L. Parker, *Suburban Development Model Shoot, Southern California*, 1945–46. Color transparency, 5 × 4 in. The Huntington, Gift of Ann Carawan, Elizabeth Buxton, and Diane Parker Carawan, 1995, photCL MLP 2222.

distinctly American suburban communities they had created (fig. 5). As Michael Pollan observes in his book *Second Nature*:

> *The front lawn symbolized the collective face of suburbia, the backyard its private aspect. In the back, you could do pretty much whatever you wanted, but out front you had to take account of the community's wishes and its self-image. . . . The conventional design of a suburban street is meant to forge the multitude of equal individual parcels of land into a single vista—a democratic landscape. To maintain your portion of this landscape was part of your civic duty. You voted each November, joined the PTA, and mowed the lawn every Saturday.*[7]

Lawns are essentially domesticated meadows. Simplified, uniform, and predictable, they are the setting for social gatherings, from picnics, barbecues, and birthday parties to weddings and sporting events. Although issues of sustainability and biodiversity have caused many to criticize the lawn, it nevertheless continues to play a vital role, providing a sense of continuity and a symbol of democratic culture, as seen in Walt Whitman's masterpiece, *Leaves of Grass* (see p. 21).

A World of Landscapes

Turf grasses—most of which are not native to the Americas, despite names like "Kentucky Bluegrass" and "Bermuda Grass"—were not the only plants that were reinvented on American soil. Many plants that have come to be considered quintessentially American were introduced from distant places. The idiom "as American as apple pie" relies on fruit from a tree (*Malus sieversii*) that originated in Kazakhstan. The flour in most American breads and pastries comes from wheat, which was brought to the Americas by the Spanish but developed from grasses native to the region known as the Fertile Crescent in Western Asia and North Africa. The palms, citrus, and eucalyptus that are California icons come from Asia, Africa, the Caribbean, and Australia. The tea roses that are emblems of Pasadena originated in Central Asia and China and are the result of millennia of selective breeding by horticulturists around the world.

The Huntington's gardens reflect this wide range of traditions. The many historical threads of rose horticulture are entwined in the Rose Garden's collection of cultivated varieties, many of which are named to honor American celebrities: Barbra Streisand, Julia Child, Neil Diamond, Marilyn Monroe, and even Richard Nixon. The Desert Garden links Baja California and Alta California cacti and succulents with similarly adapted plants from arid habitats in Africa and South America. A century-old grapevine is believed to be a cutting from one that was cultivated by Franciscan priests and Indigenous laborers at the nearby Mission San Gabriel.

The Huntington's Chinese Garden—known as Liu Fang Yuan, the Garden of Flowing Fragrance—takes inspiration from the famous scholars' gardens of Suzhou, China. During the mid- to late Ming dynasty (fifteenth to seventeenth century), economic and social factors led to a period of increased garden-making. These scholars' gardens incorporated five elements: rocks, water, plants, architecture, and connections to literature and culture. By contrast, The Huntington's Japanese Garden, created in 1912, combines the traditions of Japanese stroll gardens, dry landscape gardens, and tea gardens. Its iconic structures—a traditional house, bell tower, and moon bridge—were built or rebuilt by master carpenter Toichiro Kawai, who had emigrated from Japan in 1902.[8] The recently added Japanese Heritage Shōya House highlights agricultural traditions of

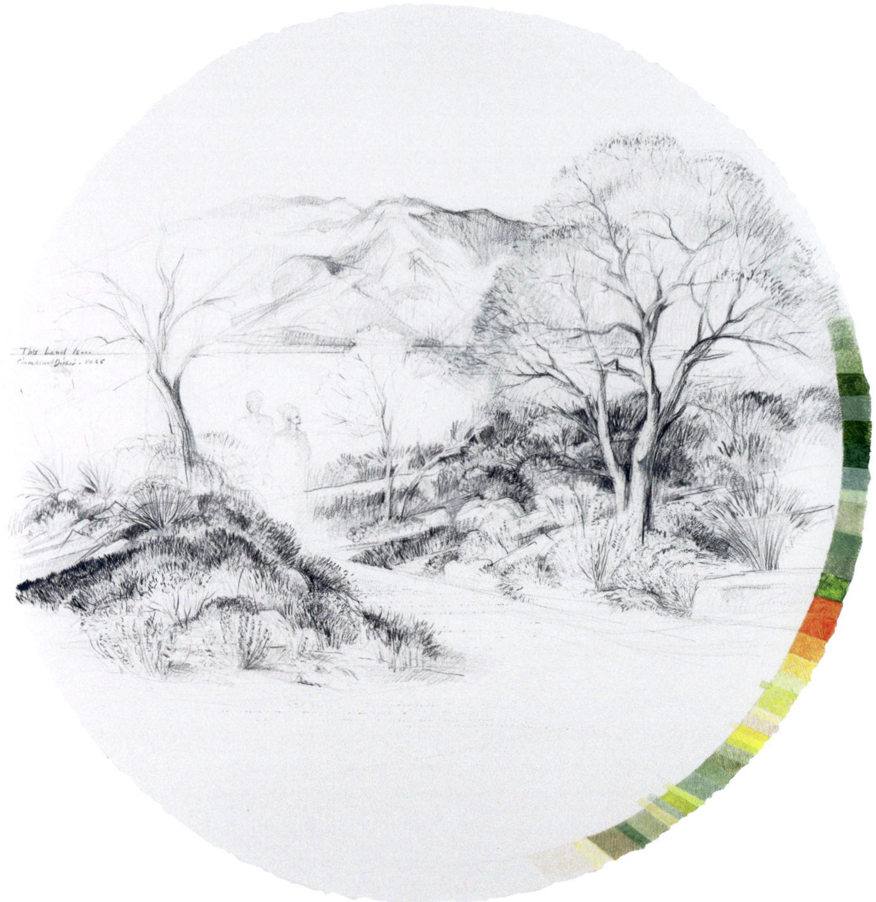

Figure 6
Rendering of the Oak Meadow, with the San Gabriel Mountains in the distance, 2025. Illustration by Emmanuel Didier.

sustainability, but even this practical element evolves into a reflection on beauty and spirituality.

Both Chinese and Japanese garden design include the principle of “borrowed landscape” or “borrowed scenery” (Ch. *jiejing*; J. *shakkei*). A distant view, such as a faraway mountain, is borrowed or incorporated into the garden composition. American gardens, including The Huntington’s, have not only drawn from their immediate surroundings but have also adopted techniques, plants, and knowledge from the farthest corners of the world to form a kaleidoscopic and sometimes contradictory whole.

A Huntington Commons Renewed

In considering the entire Huntington as a type of American garden, with its influences from both North America and around the world, the new Oak Meadow represents a renewed space within that garden.[9] Construction of this commons coincides with the US semiquincentennial, and it will follow a phased approach, acknowledging that no garden is ever truly finished. It is a landscape that will continue to evolve over time. The Oak Meadow highlights North American flora, including distinctive California native plants, a group that has not historically been strongly emphasized, and the ways in which gardens might regenerate the land in response to limited water and a changing climate.

The Oak Meadow, which links the Virginia Steele Scott Galleries of American Art, the MaryLou and George Boone Gallery, and the Rose Hills Foundation Conservatory for Botanical Science, comprises multiple adjoining zones: a woodland promenade, a floriferous meadow, and a gathering lawn spreading out into the commons. Standing at the main entrance of either exhibition gallery, the view of the San Gabriel Mountains to the north is stunning. A future section of locally sourced chaparral plants and stones will bring this vista into immediate focus, an adaptation of the “borrowed landscape” (fig. 6).

The nearby woodland promenade serves to increase shade and acts as a transitional space to the adjacent garden areas. This promenade takes advantage of existing as well as newly planted trees, especially oaks, which are iconic North American trees and a genus that connects America coast to coast with some ninety species. Native species include the coast live oak (*Quercus agrifolia*) and Pasadena oak (*Q. engelmannii*). Highly adaptable, these large trees support a tremendous amount of biodiversity. As urban trees, they also provide shade, beauty, stabilization, and cultural meaning (see p. 55).

In addition to oaks, one of the few large trees native to Southern California is the western sycamore (*Platanus racemosa*). Among the new trees in the woodland promenade is

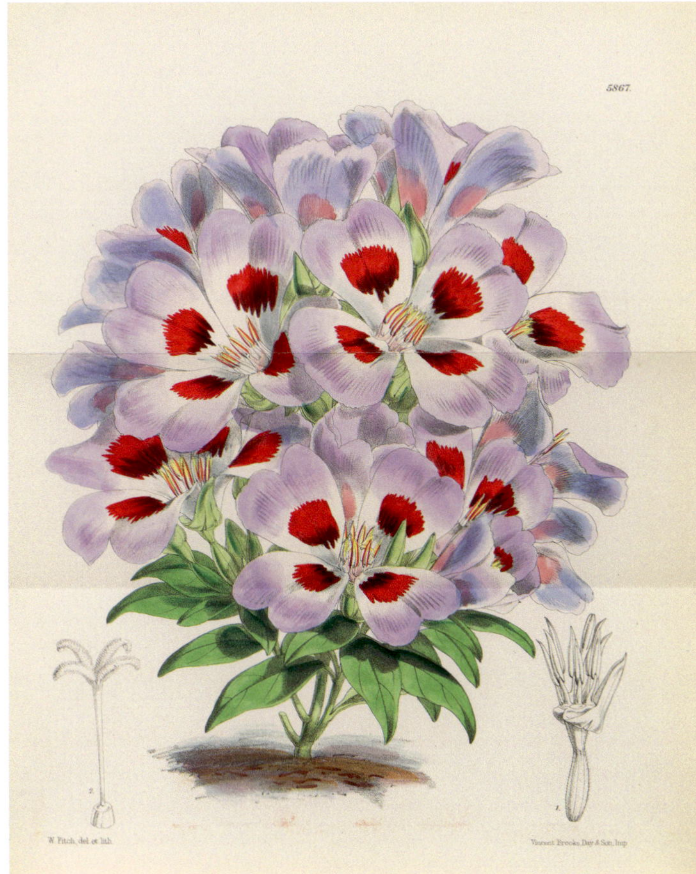

Figure 7
Oenothera whitneyi (now *Clarkia amoena*), commonly known as Farewell to Spring, is a wildflower endemic to California. Hand-colored copperplate engraving by Walter Hood Fitch for *Curtis's Botanical Magazine* (1870). The Huntington, 321581.

a clone of an iconic individual sycamore known as the Eagle Tree, named for the raptors that nested in its branches periodically over more than three centuries, beginning well before Spanish colonization of the region. The Eagle Tree stood in what is now the city of Compton in South Los Angeles. In 2022, the tree fell, possibly the result of a lightning strike the year before. Thanks to a collaborative effort by Donald R. Hodel, environmental horticulturist for the University of California Cooperative Extension, Los Angeles County, staff from the California Botanic Garden, the Theodore Payne Foundation, and The Huntington, cuttings were collected and clones made for future use.

Other trees and shrubs of great ecological and cultural importance in California join a variety of oaks and sycamores in the promenade: toyon (*Heteromeles arbutifolia*), blue elderberry (*Sambucus cerulea*), and California black walnut (*Juglans californica*). Acorns have always been a cultural and dietary staple for Indigenous peoples in California, and elderberry and black walnut have provided both food and dyes. The riparian woodland portion of the Oak Meadow features a swale that includes grasses and shrubs Native Californians use in creating textiles and art, echoing the art installations on display just inside the Scott galleries by Los Angeles–based artists Sandy Rodriguez and Mercedes Dorame (Tongva) (see pp. 113, 155).

Extending out from the riparian and woodland zones, broad swaths of floriferous meadow evoke prairies—the grassland biome. Although primarily associated with the Great Plains and the Midwest, grasslands also appear throughout California in a wide range of landscapes. Grasslands and meadows add texture to the landscape amid forested mountains, oak woodland, arid deserts, and coastal environments across the state. They stabilize and improve the soil, and can serve as buffers to wildfire, in addition to their beauty.[10]

The Huntington's new planting is also a nod to the iconic American prairie, an ecosystem that generally consists of over 70 percent grasses, many of which are long-lived and provide the same ecological infrastructure as trees in forest biomes. Strong, fibrous root systems can reach depths of ten feet or more, maintaining soil integrity. Grasslands have been described as inverted rainforests because of the huge quantity of carbon sequestered in their root systems and for the bounty of life they support.

This floriferous meadow includes a greater ratio of forbs (flowering plants) to grasses. (Both are distinct from woody plants, such as shrubs and trees.) The mixture of annuals and perennials supports pollinators, which are essential parts of a functioning savanna ecosystem. This adaptable feature of the garden will change over time as it matures and the oaks grow. The meadow abuts the gathering lawn, an element of the colonial legacy that has survived and adapted to become a stalwart component of the American landscape. The lawn will host events and offer a setting where visitors can rest and immerse themselves in the surrounding landscape.

A Regenerative Garden

In recent years, The Huntington has sought to integrate regenerative practices into the gardens' ever-evolving landscapes. Regenerative agriculture and gardening refer to ways of tending the land that build the soil and seek a reciprocal and harmonious—rather than extractive—relationship to the earth. They often adopt aspects of Indigenous and other traditional approaches to horticulture. In her book *Braiding Sweetgrass*, botanist Robin Wall Kimmerer (Citizen Potawatomi) recommends that the best first action people can take to begin restoring the relationship between land and people is to plant a garden: "It's good for the health of the earth and it's good for the health of the people. A garden is a nursery for nurturing connection, the soil for cultivation of practical reverence. And its power goes far beyond the garden gate—once you develop a relationship with a little patch of earth, it becomes a seed itself."[11]

The Oak Meadow seeks to follow this regenerative path. Conventional garden wisdom in the United States has long been based on the temperate regions of the Northeast, where water is a more plentiful resource, and seasonal changes play out in a specific pattern. In areas like the Northeast and the Midwest, where precipitation occurs throughout the year, spring is the prime planting season. California, by contrast, is one of five mediterranean zones in the world (along with the Mediterranean Basin, central Chile, South Africa, and Australia) that feature long, dry summers and cool, rainy winters. In these regions, fall is the best time to put in native plants, because the ensuing winter rains help them become established before the dry summer heat sets in.

California, like the other mediterranean regions, has witnessed its rich ecosystems threatened by habitat loss and climate change. Along with concerns over water conservation and wider awareness of Indigenous ecological knowledge, the current moment has brought an increased interest in the native plants that have evolved here. The North American plants selected for the new garden, most though not all California natives, were chosen to complement the climate of the San Gabriel Valley.

Part of the planning process for this garden was a detailed study of how water moves through this part of the property, allowing as much water as possible to be absorbed back into the landscape. Meadow plants are exceptionally effective at absorbing water and retaining it for long periods of time. A prominent swale is a key garden feature that models best practices for stormwater management and addresses our largest regional sustainability challenge: the conservation of resources such as water, soil, and wildlife biodiversity.

Chaparral plants are also water-thrifty and adaptable, supporting wildlife, notably pollinators. The plants selected tolerate winter rainfall and are less dependent on summer water, though in this controlled environment, they will receive some supplemental water. Lawns have become the center of often heated debates about their value as compared with the water needed to maintain them. However, through careful selection of turfgrass and mindful watering practices, even lawns can become more resilient and less water-intensive while serving important social and aesthetic functions.

The woodland promenade also sustains wildlife—from the mycorrhizal fungi that live in a mutualistic connection with the roots of trees and other plants to the insects that serve as pollinators and the birds that make their homes in this habitat. In the many ecosystems where they are found, oaks are keystone species, supporting hundreds of organisms, from tiny wasps that lay their eggs in the trees' tissues and caterpillars that rely on them as their sole food source,

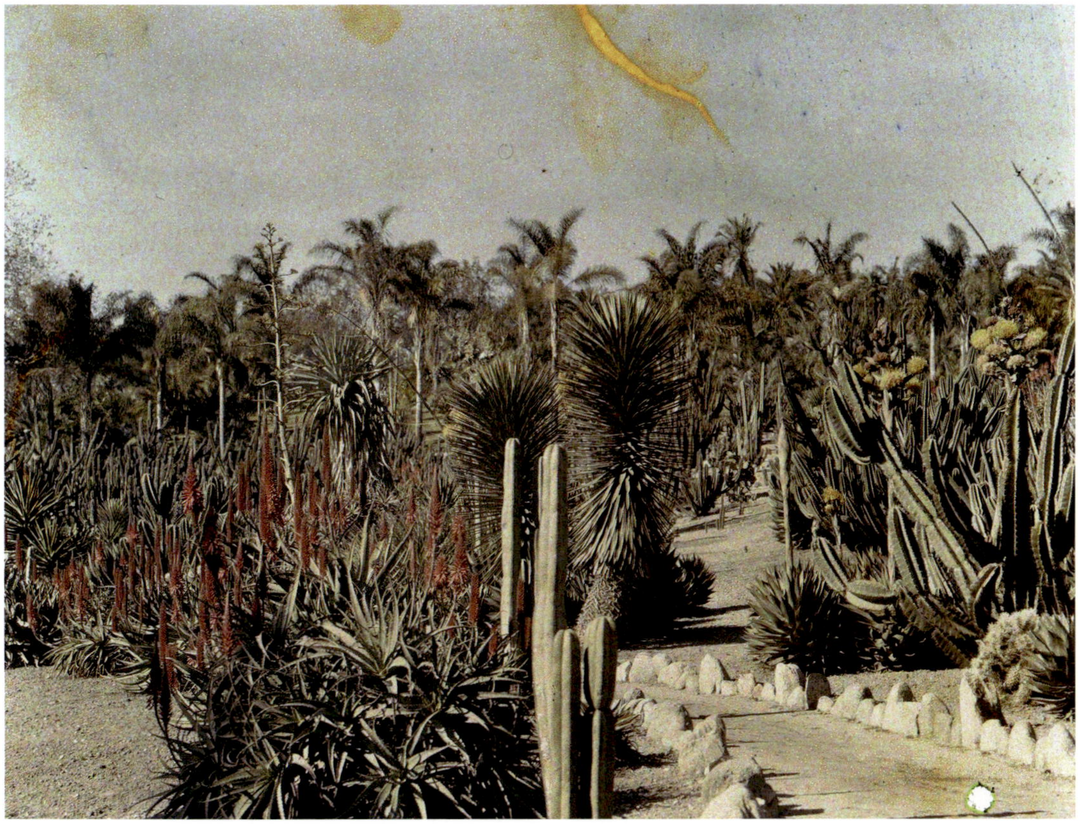

Figure 8
Attributed to William Hertrich, Huntington Desert Garden, general view, ca. 1924. Autochrome. Henry E. Huntington Estate Photograph Collection, The Huntington, photCL 107.

to birds and mammals for whom acorns are reliable sustenance and lichens and mosses that grow on limbs and bark.

In a botanical garden, regeneration also characterizes the effect that engaging with plants and the environment has on visitors. Many people in the twenty-first century are suffering from what writer Richard Louv has called "nature-deficit disorder," a disconnection that results in depression and anxiety, a diminished use of the senses, and reduced creativity. Smelling, touching, and seeing plants can counteract this deficit and significantly benefit our health.[12] Rather than an escape from culture, enjoying green spaces is a return to nature, a way of balancing our experience in the world.

Historically, gardens have been valued as places of beauty where we can indulge our senses, but they can also inspire a more active, reciprocal approach to the environment in our broader lives. As we continue to address the challenges of climate change and expanding human development, public gardens will become increasingly important as places for people to rest, recharge, and regenerate their relationship with the land.

Nicole Cavender is the Telleen/Jorgensen Director of the Botanical Gardens at The Huntington.

Sandy Masuo is the Botanical Content Specialist at The Huntington.

1. Jessica C. Thompson et al., "Early Human Impacts and Ecosystem Reorganization in Southern-Central Africa," *Science Advances* 7, no. 19 (2021), doi: 10.1126/sciadv.abf9776; Mike Cummings, "Study Offers Earliest Evidence of Humans Changing Ecosystems with Fire," *YaleNews* blog post, May 5, 2021, https://news.yale.edu/2021/05/05/study-offers-earliest-evidence-humans-changing-ecosystems-fire.

2. Gonzalo Fernández de Oviedo y Valdés, *Sumario de la natural historia de las Indias* (Toledo, Spain, 1526; reprint, Fondo de Cultura Económica, 1996); Wilson Popenoe and G. A. Zentmyer, "Early History of the Avocado," *Avocado Society Yearbook* 81 (1997): 163–71.

3. "Boston Common," National Park Service, https://www.nps.gov/places/boston-common-ma.htm.

4. Andrea Wulf, *Founding Gardeners: The Revolutionary Generation, Nature, and the Shaping of the American Nation* (Vintage, 2012).

5. "Honoring Black Botanists and Horticulturists," Fort Worth Botanic Garden, February 26, 2025, https://fwbg.org/2025/02/26/honoring-black-botanists-and-horticulturists.

6. "California's Top 10 Agricultural Commodities," California Agricultural Production Statistics, California Department of Food and Agriculture, https://cdfa.ca.gov/statistics.

7. Michael Pollan, *Second Nature: A Gardener's Education* (Delta, 1991), 24.

8. Toichiro Kawai died at the Gila River War Relocation Center in 1943 during the Japanese American incarceration. See Naomi Hirahara, "From Japan to America: The Garden and the Japanese Community," in *One Hundred Years in the Huntington's Japanese Garden: Harmony with Nature*, ed. T. June Li (Huntington Library, Art Collections, and Botanical Gardens, 2013), 94–99.

9. Thanks to Didier Design Studio and the Urban Water Group for garden design concept and plant selection, and to Huntington botanical garden staff.

10. "Bay Area Working Rangelands: Grasslands," University of California Agriculture and Natural Resources, https://ucanr.edu/site/bay-area-working-rangelands/grasslands.

11. Robin Wall Kimmerer, *Braiding Sweetgrass: Indigenous Wisdom, Scientific Knowledge, and the Teachings of Plants* (Milkweed Editions, 2013), 126.

12. Richard Louv, *Last Child in the Woods: Saving Our Children from Nature-Deficit Disorder* (Algonquin Books, 2005); Kathy Willis, *Good Nature: Why Seeing, Smelling, Hearing and Touching Plants Is Good for Our Health* (Bloomsbury, 2024).

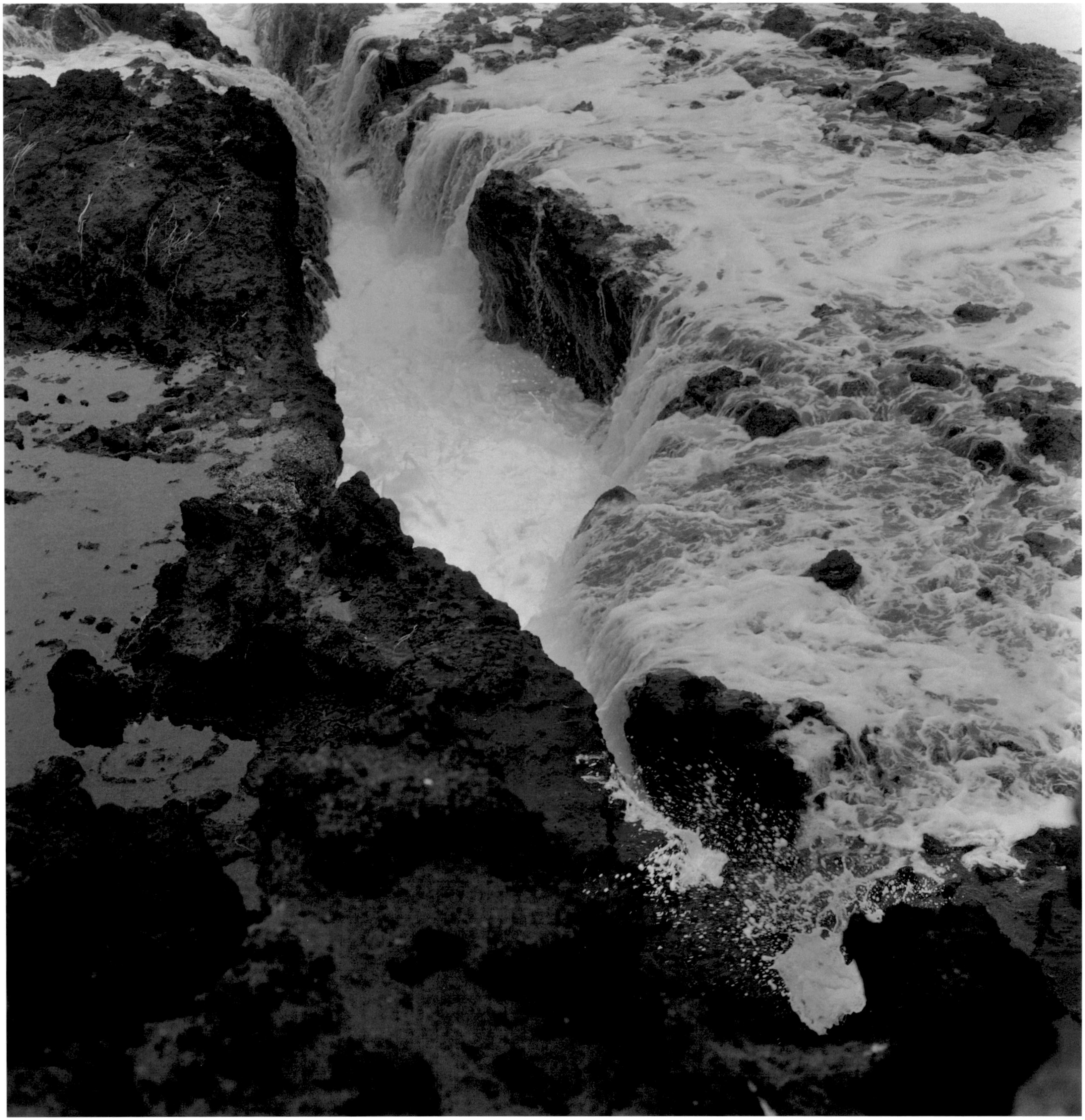

Deliquescence

Sites of Transformation

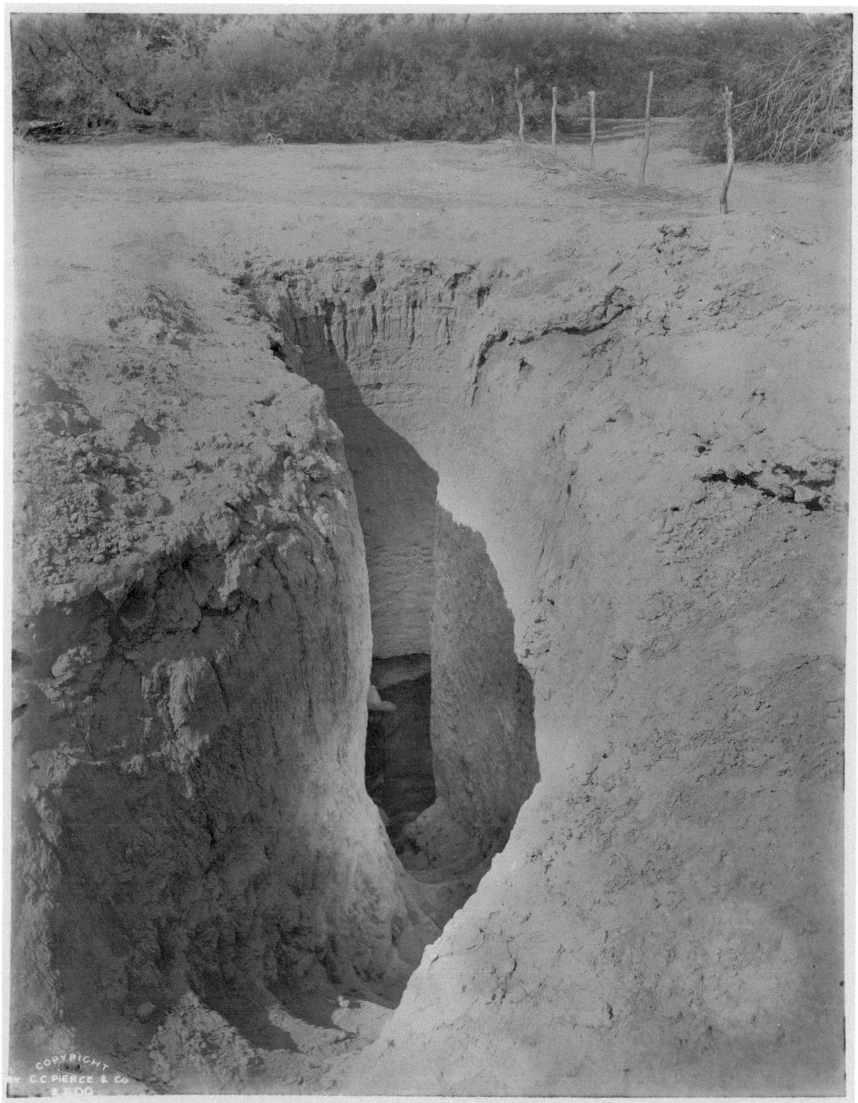

Water holds the power to transform and be transformed, to dissolve or melt away. Sometimes a substance absorbs moisture from the atmosphere until it dissolves in the absorbed water, transforming itself into a new physical state of being; this process is called deliquescence.

The water that remains belowground before emerging from a spring and the early photographs of Southern California stored in the archive run on parallel timelines. The historical images also prompt a closer look at how the land has been, and is continually, approached by image makers.

Figure 1
Mercedes Dorame, *To Hold Water—Shyeenaxre*, 2023. Inkjet print. Collection of the artist.

Figure 2
Charles C. Pierce, *Coahuilla Indian Well at Torres, dug about 20 feet and 50 feet below that to water,* ca. 1900–10. Gelatin silver print, 9¾ × 7¾ in. C. C. Pierce Collection of Photographs, The Huntington, photCL Pierce 01781.

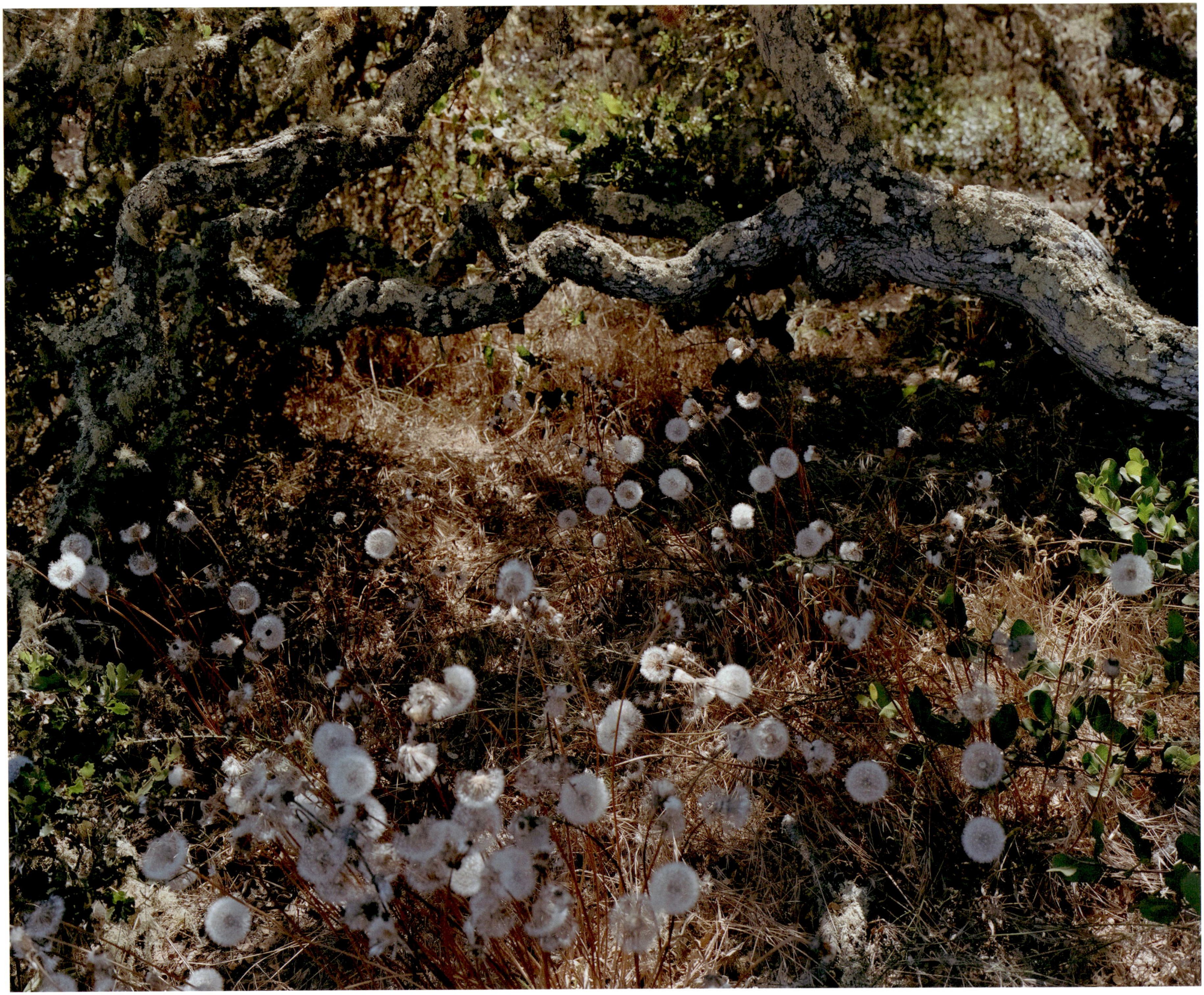

Exploring the flow between dormancy and emergence, materials such as water and the archive rejoin our consciousness through new exposures to time and place after periods of inactivity.

Light has the ability to erase and illuminate, while darkness functions to obscure and preserve. In these interchangeable roles in photography, I propose a more complicated and nuanced role of light and darkness.

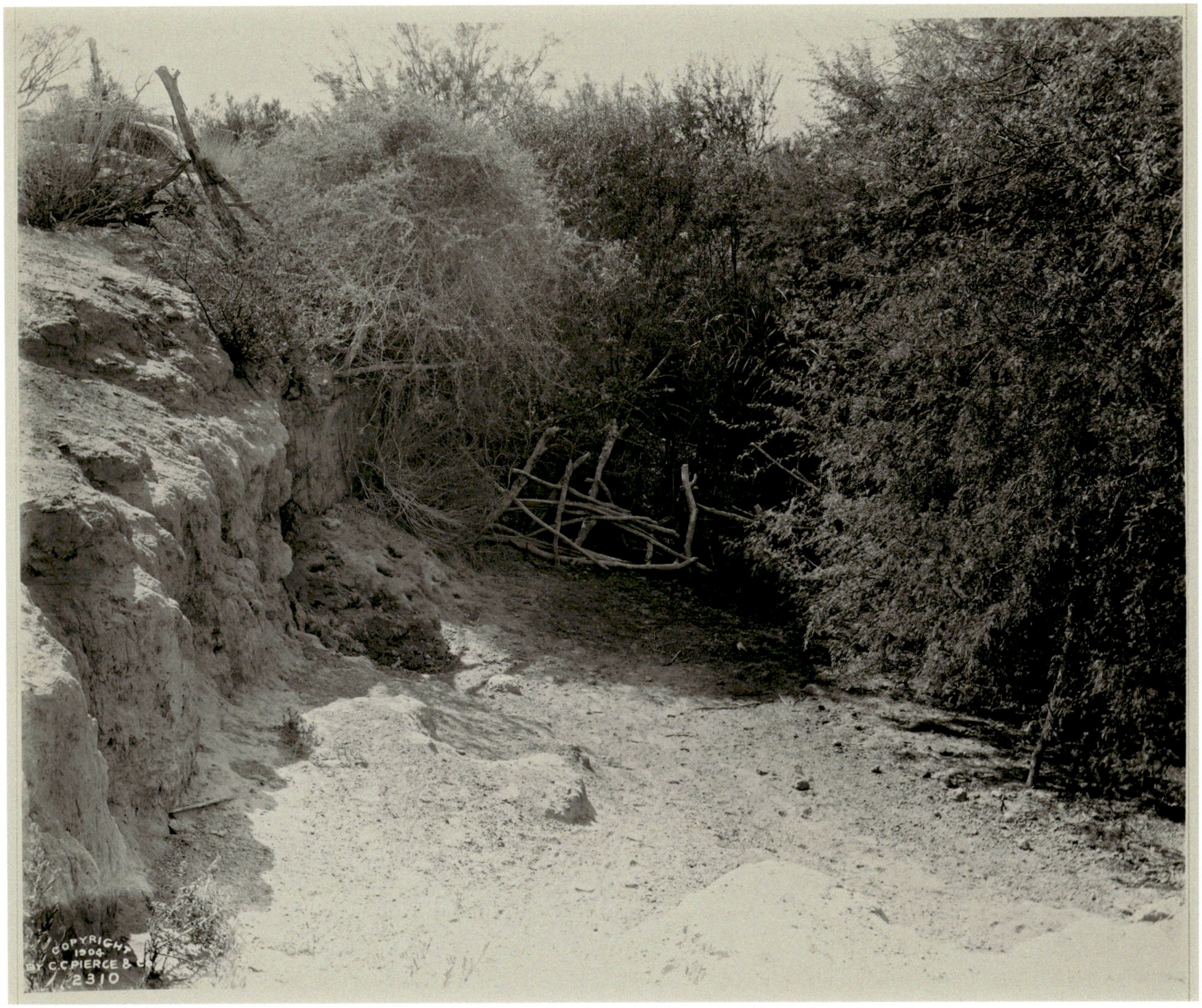

Figure 3
Mercedes Dorame, *Finding a Path—Chwiishkeshmenokre*, 2024. Inkjet print. Collection of the artist.

Figure 4
Charles C. Pierce, *Mission Indians—Coahuillas—Indian Well, Martinez*, ca. 1904. Gelatin silver print, 8 × 9⅞ in. C. C. Pierce Collection of Photographs, The Huntington, photCL Pierce 01785.

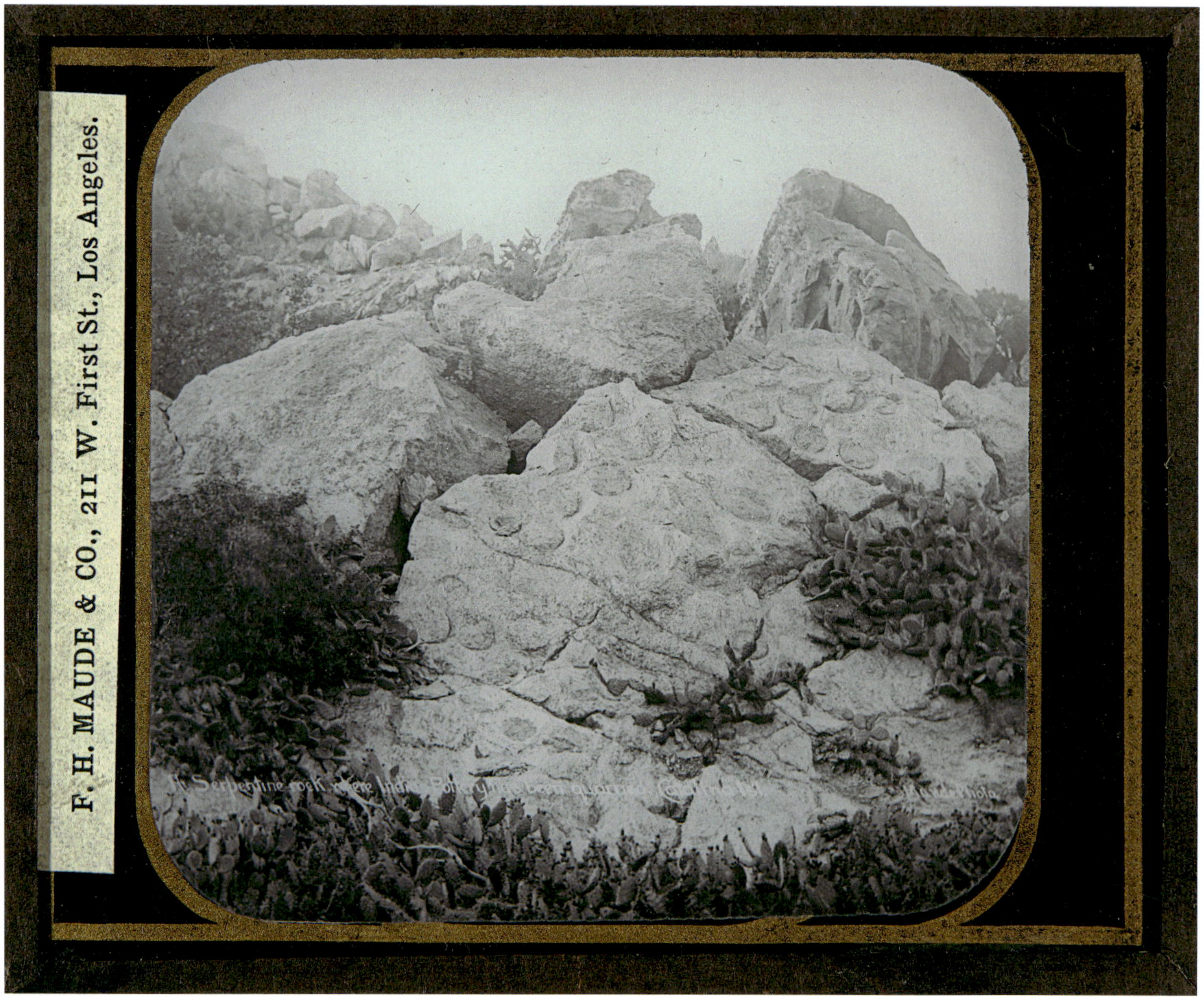

What is preserved and cared for in darkness? What does preservation imply, for what purpose, and for whom? Through the analog photographic process, the image is held, developed, and printed in the dark. This environment creates a space of safety for the delicate rendering and transformation of light into physical matter.

The missing and obscured parts of photographs work as evidence of the effects of light and time. These gaps and omissions also speak to the missing pieces of history in the narrative of the landscape of the American West.

Figure 5
F. H. Maude, *A Serpentine Rock Where Indian Pottery has been quarried, Catalina Isl.*, inscribed "Holes cut by Indian in making ollas [pottery], Catalina Island," ca. 1870–90. Lantern slide, 3¼ × 4 in. Horatio N. Rust Photograph Collection, The Huntington, photCL 11.

Figure 6
Mercedes Dorame, *Steatite Remains—'Eesey Moyookmoro*, 2022. Inkjet print. Collection of the artist.

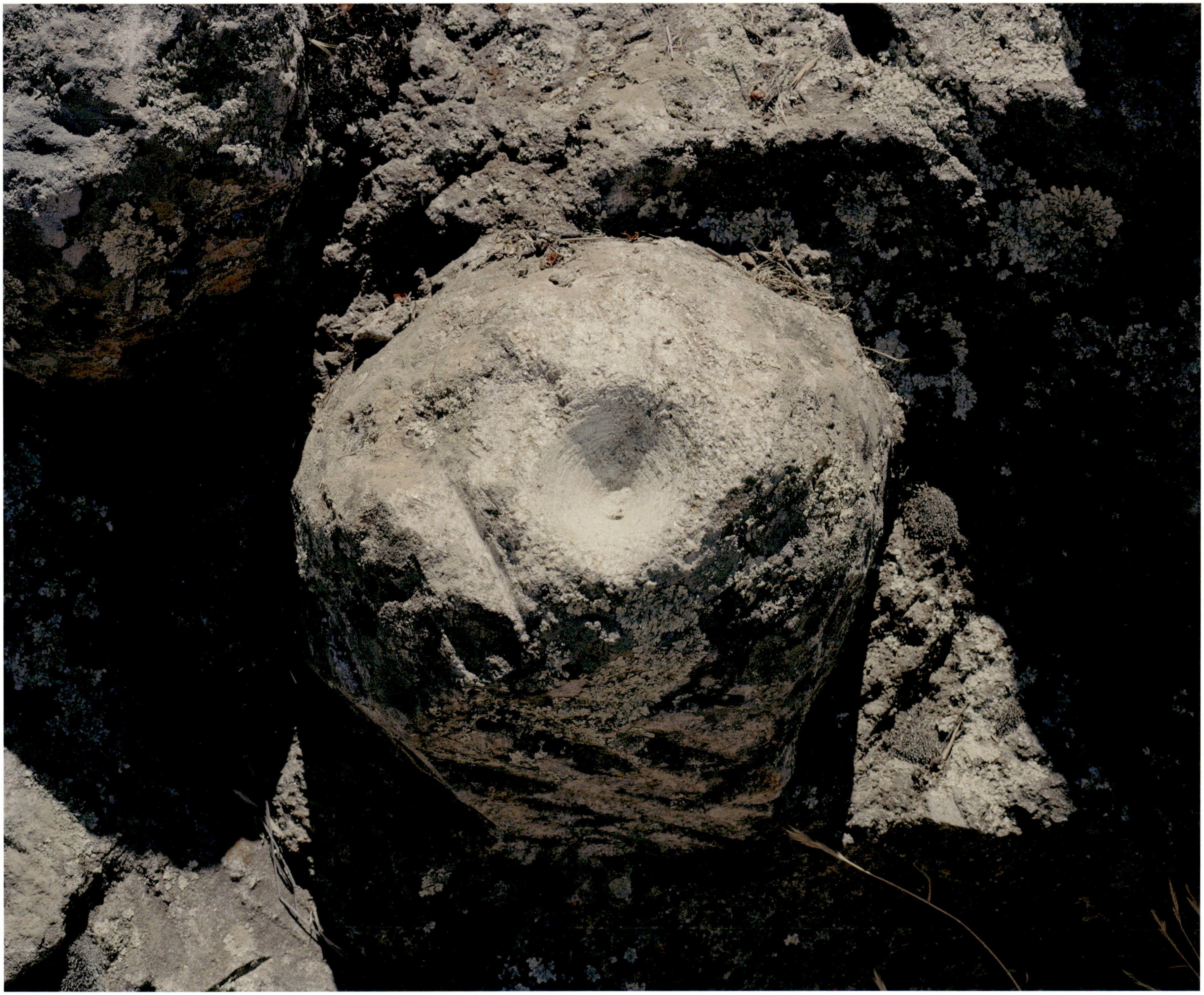

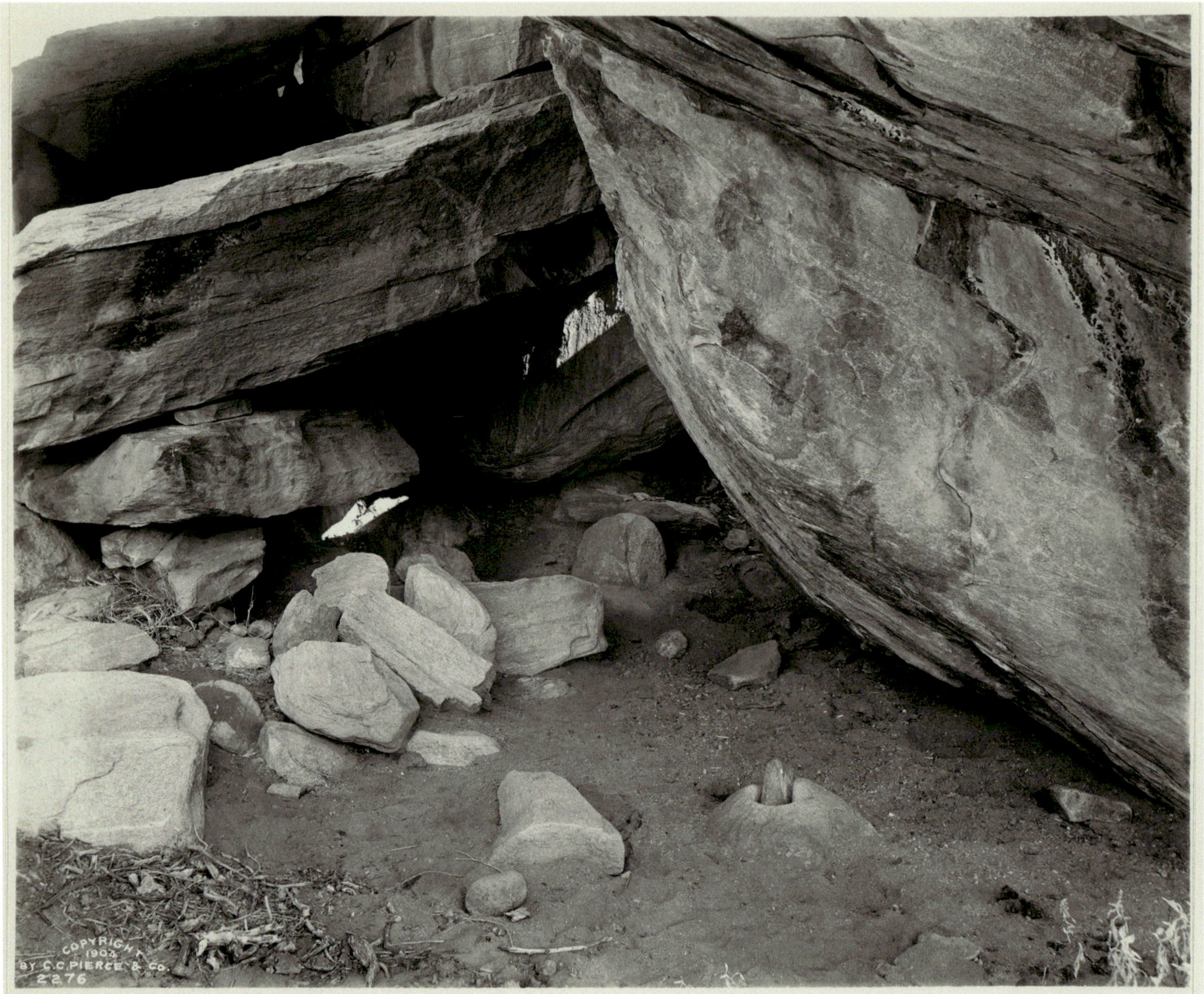

Narratives reemerge here as freshwater springs and tidal spaces reclaim their importance in connection to First Peoples' village sites, recentering water as a place of gathering, medicine, foodways, and ceremony.

Figure 7
Charles C. Pierce, *Indian Cave Dwellers, Palm Canyon, Coahuillas*, ca. 1904. Gelatin silver print, 8 × 9¾ in. The Huntington, photCL Pierce 01772.

Figure 8
Mercedes Dorame, *The Other World—'Ashoo' 'Ooxor*, 2022. Inkjet print. Collection of the artist.

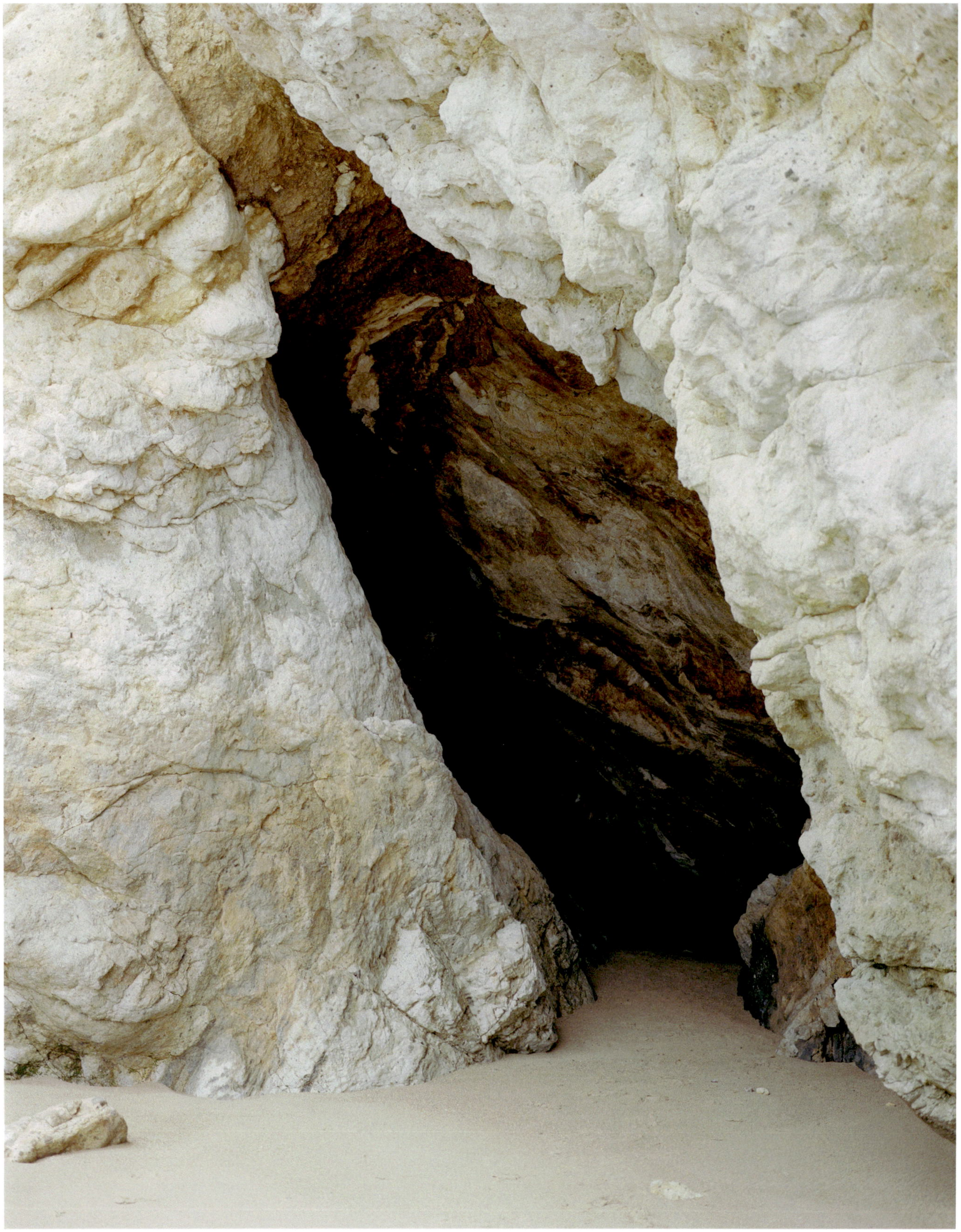

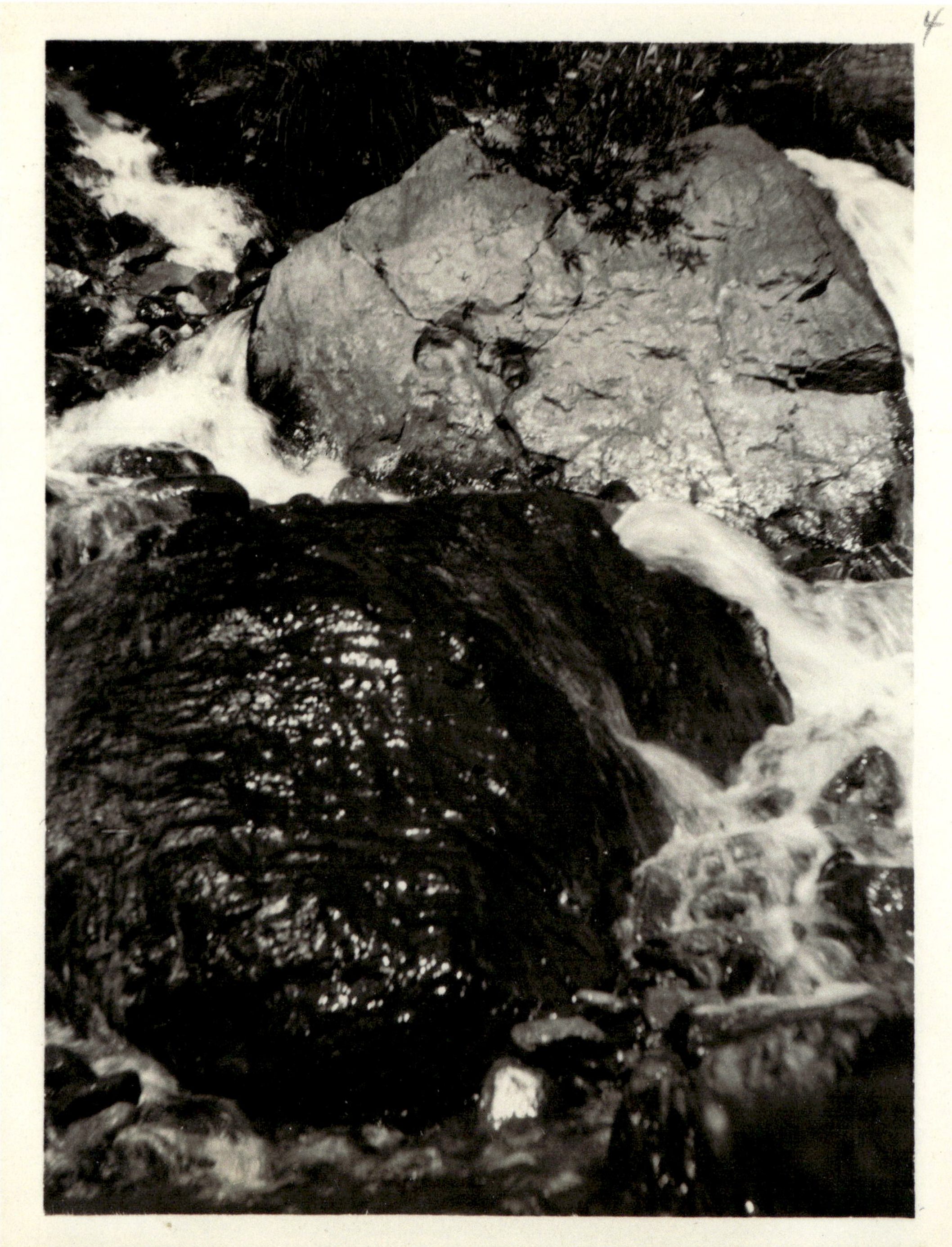

When images and histories come to the surface, either from the archive or when water courses out of the earth, this encounter questions where the surface exists and generates multiple sites of visibility through reflection and refraction; this inquiry exists both within the photograph and within a pool of water.

Figure 9
Grace Nicholson, *Waterfall on Trinity [River]* (from album page), ca. 1906. Gelatin silver print, 4¼ × 3½ in. Grace Nicholson Photograph Collection, The Huntington, photCL 56.

Figure 10
Mercedes Dorame, *Their Gathering Place—Pomooxaroochon*, 2024. Inkjet print. Collection of the artist.

Mercedes Dorame is a multidisciplinary artist from Los Angeles whose work has been exhibited internationally and throughout California. She calls on her Tongva ancestry to engage the problematics of (in)visibility and ideas of cultural construction and ancestral connection to land and sky.

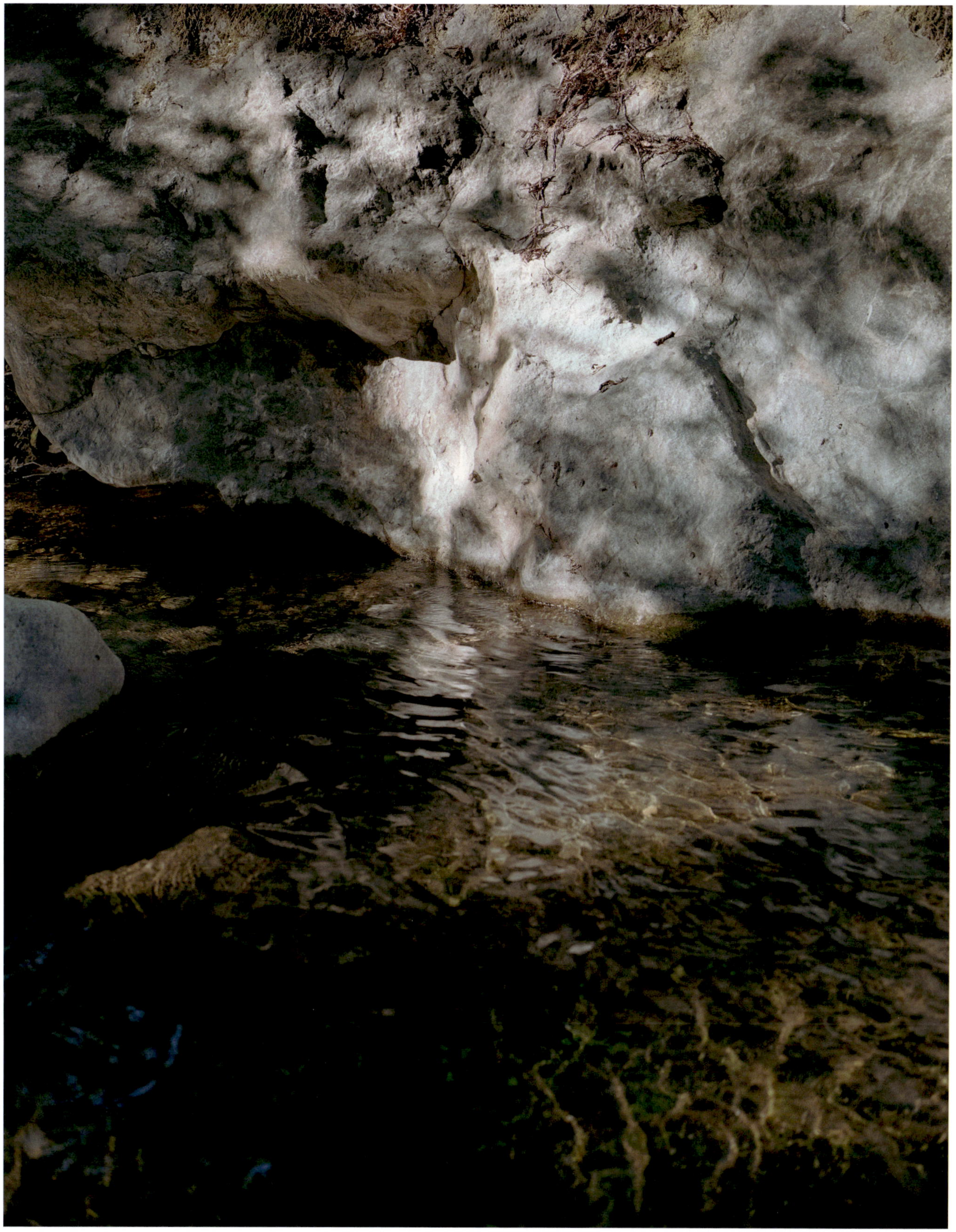

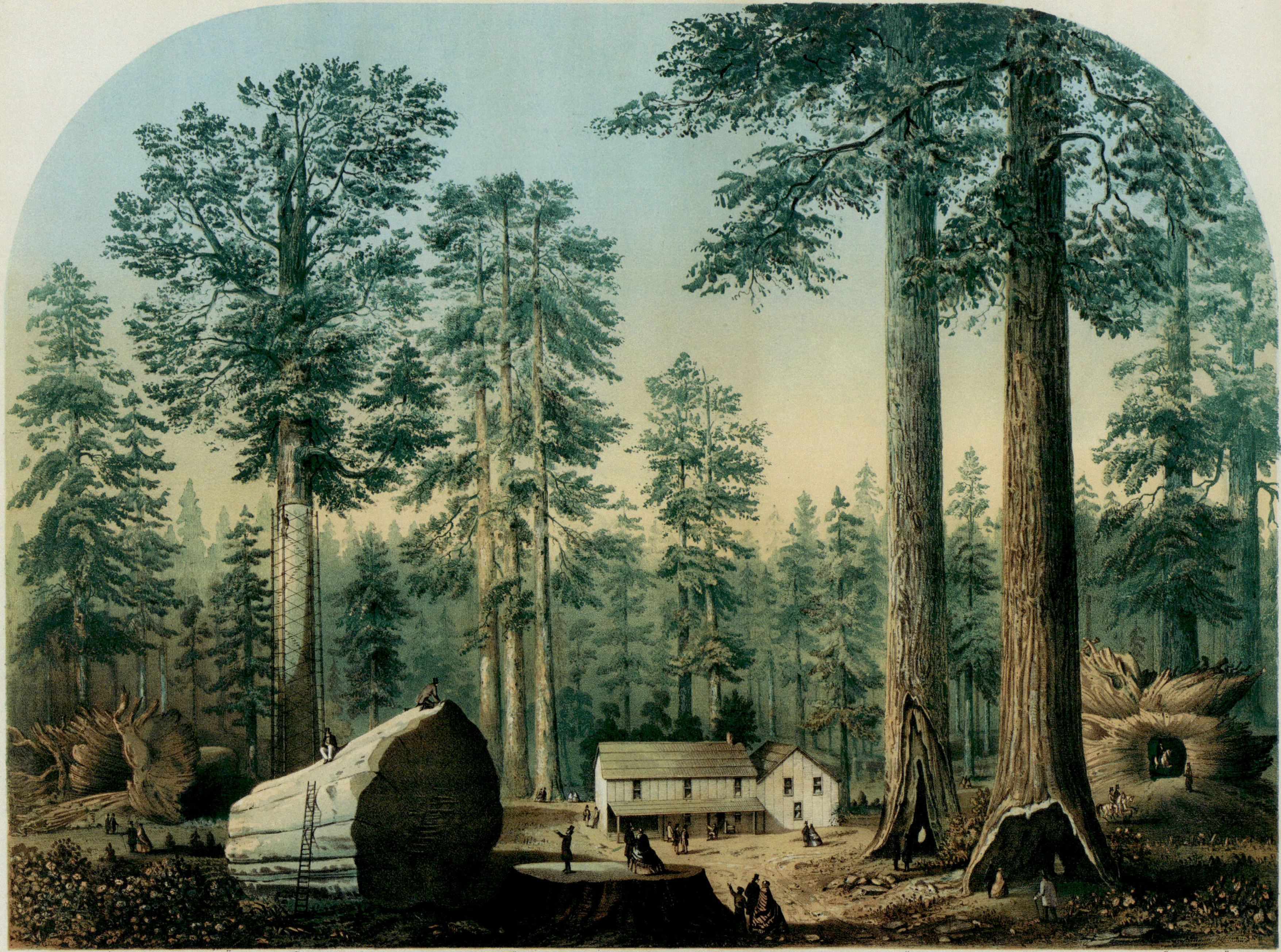

A. The Father of the Forest, 112 Feet in circumference, estimated Height when standing, 450 Feet.
B. The Mother of the Forest, 90 Feet in Cir. 327 Feet high. Bark taken off 120 Ft.
C. The Three Graces. Circum. of the Three 90 Feet, 300 Feet high.
D The Big Tree 96 Feet in Circumference 300 Feet high.

THE MAMMOTH TREE GROVE,

CALAVERAS COUNTY CALIFORNIA.

E. The Miners Cabin 80 Ft. in Cir. 300 Feet high.
F. The Pioneers Cabin 33 Feet in diameter, 150 Feet high. Top being Broken off.
G The Horseback Ride. Distance through, 75 Feet, 12 Feet in the clear.
H The Two Guardsmen.

Coda and Acknowledgments

We end this volume with two final field notes from the archive—and many notes of gratitude. An 1860 lithograph entitled *The Mammoth Tree Grove* shows one giant sequoia sawed down and another shorn of bark, destruction that paradoxically helped lead to the founding of the National Park System (fig. 1). "Let America Be America Again," a poem that Langston Hughes wrote in 1935 and sent to his friends in Los Gatos, California, spells out the nation's failures but rings with determination for the future (fig. 2). Both documents link California to national stories and offer grounds for optimism amid what Hughes called "rack and ruin."

On July 4, 1853, a group of revelers celebrated Independence Day with a band playing and thirty-two people dancing on the stump of a 1,200-year-old giant sequoia, known as the Discovery Tree or Mammoth Tree. Entrepreneurs shipped a slice of the fallen tree to display in San Francisco and New York; others stripped the bark of a neighboring tree, called the Mother of the Forest, and sent it to London to awe crowds. But some Americans, such as John Muir, expressed horror that "vandals" would exploit ancient trees and instead suggested preserving them. Eleven years later, during the Civil War, Abraham Lincoln signed the Yosemite Valley Grant Act, protecting the iconic valley and another sequoia grove, the Mariposa, for "public use, resort, and recreation." This law was the seed that, in 1872, during the era of Reconstruction, inspired the creation of the first national park at Yellowstone in the Wyoming Territory. Yosemite became a national park in 1890, and the Calaveras Big Trees are preserved in a state park, where the Mother of the Forest still stands as a dead "snag."[1]

Figure 1
A group of five men worked for twenty days, drilling holes and using wedges and saws to cut through the thirty-foot-wide trunk of the sequoia known as the Discovery Tree, Mammoth Tree, or, as named in this print, the Big Tree. For the nearby Mother of the Forest, other men built a scaffold and stripped the bark, which they shipped in pieces to be displayed in New York and in London's Crystal Palace. *The Mammoth Tree Grove, Calaveras County, California*, 1860. Lithograph, 20¼ × 26 in. Jay T. Last Collection of Views Prints and Ephemera, The Huntington, priJLC_VIEW_000718.

Langston Hughes wrote "Let America Be America Again" in October 1935 while on a train ride from New York to visit his mother in Oberlin, Ohio. Observing the shifting terrain through the window, Hughes soaked in both the beauty and the bleakness of the landscape. Using two "voices" in the poem—one reflecting the ideals of the nation and another responding through the perspective of the downtrodden—Hughes proclaimed, "Let it be the dream it used to be," but then countered with "(America never was America to me.)" Written just five years before Woody Guthrie's "This Land Is Your Land," Hughes's anthem was already part of the American ethos as words on a page as well as a song, first published in 1936, and then set to music in 1941.[2] He ended the poem with a new promise that "America will be!" underlining the word "will" in this manuscript to emphasize the future tense. For Hughes, it was not too late for America to renew its commitment to "these great green States" and to its people. Resonating as much in the twenty-first century as it did in the 1930s, its message of fracture intermingled with hope endures.

This book and the broader Huntington initiative (a special exhibition based on Library collections, new American art installations, and reimagined garden plantings) have drawn on the efforts, ideas, and expertise of many colleagues both inside and outside the institution.

In reflecting on "this land" on a 207-acre plot in San Marino, we first want to acknowledge the Gabrielino-Tongva and Kizh Nation peoples who have tended this landscape since time immemorial.

As we conceived and assembled this volume, we were deeply grateful to the publications team, Jean Patterson and Mindy Chen, and to assistant curator Armando Pulido, who all steered and refined its many pieces. Armando crafted the opening text for each section. Gina Broze, Tom Eykemans, Kestrel Rundle, Alison Keefe, Leah Finger, Dave Novacek, and Melissa Duffes at Marquand Books nurtured the book into a beautiful whole. Thanks to Walter Biggins and Jon Repetti at the University of Pennsylvania Press for aiding with distribution. The book's contributors were wonderful to work with and helped us think through the project's complex topics.

We thank those individuals and institutional partners who have supported this project with their stories and objects. Oronde Spears, Amitis Motevalli, and Karen Rapp brought Noni Olabisi's vision and legacy to light. Filmmaker Desha Dauchan, with collaborators Jerry Henry, Sushila Love, and others, created an inspiring short film about the *Troubled Island* mural; Oronde, Ami, Armando, and historian Felix Jean-Louis contributed their knowledge to the narrative. Craig and Gary Kuromi graciously shared their family history and their grandmother's wood carvings to the exhibition. Anna Canoni at Woody Guthrie Publications, and Cady Shaw, Mark Davidson, Stephanie Stewart, and Jaye McCaghren at the Woody Guthrie Center and American Song Archives all carry on Woody's good fight. Jeremy Johnson and Martina Thomas of the Delaware Tribe of Indians, and Carissa Speck and Katelyn Lucas from the staff of the Delaware Nation have informed our understandings of the Walking Purchase and the Revolutionary Era with Lenape perspectives.

We were thrilled to engage with several contemporary artists, including William Camargo and Barret Oliver and the *f/Ø* project; Mercedes Dorame; Sandy Rodriguez; Cara Romero; Samantha Morales Johnson Yang; and Tanya Aguiñiga, Natalie Godinez, and Gina Clyne of AMBOS (Art Made Between Opposite Sides). Thanks also to artist Glenn Ligon for generously lending a quilt by Rosie Lee Tompkins for the exhibition.

Many of our curatorial colleagues across the institution offered collection ideas and subject knowledge to the book and exhibition: Angélica Becerra, Dennis Carr, Erin Chase, Lauren Cross, Alanna Davey, Sarah Francis, Diego Godoy, David Mihaly, Natalie Lawler, Karla Nielsen, Olga Tsapina, Vanessa Wilkie, and Li Wei Yang. A special thank you to our predecessors, Peter Blodgett and Jennifer Watts, for their advice and moral support along the way. Our colleagues in the botanical division taught us to appreciate the many lives and histories of plants: Robert Hori, Sean Lahmeyer, Grace Lotker, Sandy Masuo, Andrew Mitchell, Ruth Siegel, and Tim Thibault. Research colleagues Brett Rushforth and Shannon McHugh, and visiting scholars Serena Zabin, Tom Martin, and others helped guide our thinking.

The related exhibition would not have been possible without the hard work and creativity of our colleagues: assistant curator Armando Pulido, who was an invaluable thought partner in the shape and organization of the show; talented exhibition designer Debi van Zyl; exhibitions team Danielle Killam, Lana Johnson, Hema Panesar, and Jesson Duller; registration team Jenny Werner, Cynthia Tovar, Chiara Barlow, Lindsey Hansen, Alexis Recto, Melissa Pankuch-Hernandez, and Melissa Mariano; Sean Kennedy, Zoe Reid, and the preparations team; and conservators Jessamy Gloor and Kristi Westberg. Likewise, we are grateful to our digital collections and imaging colleagues who fielded countless photography requests for the book and exhibition: Veronica Aguirre, Dana Barsuhn, Mario Einaudi, Travis Flack, Manuel Flores, Holly Mendenhall, and Anna Kim.

The THIS LAND IS . . . initiative has come together thanks to our leadership and administrative colleagues who enthusiastically supported the effort in all manner of ways: Karen R. Lawrence, Sandra Brooke Gordon, Christina Nielsen, Nicole Cavender, Nenette Luarca-Shoaf, Holly Moore, and Sue Juster contributed as both directors and scholars. Alice Tsay has shepherded nearly every aspect of the initiative, including substantially in this book, and in the president's office, Kathleen Stueck and Raylene Galarze have supported enormously. Mona Shulman has helped us through countless tough spots. Janet Alberti, Patty Hanna, and the rest of the finance team helped make everything possible. In information technology, Heather Hart, Stone Van Allen, and the rest of the team expertly managed digital content. The marketing and communications team worked hard to get the word out: Lori Ann Achzet, Annabel Adams, Christine Aguilera, Aric Allen, Christina Campodonico, Miranda Claxton, Kevin Durkin, Deborah Miller Marr, Arianna Muñoz, and Keisha Raines. In the education department, we have been fortunate to collaborate with Maya Abee, Anna Engstrom, Andrew Shewell, and Kim Tulipana.

We are grateful to the team in the advancement office: Randy Shulman, Sarah Basile, Brianna Anderson, Crystal Jones, Marina Kohler, and Cris Lutz, who worked closely with donors and secured several funding sources for both the exhibition and the overall initiative.

We have learned a lot from peer institutions that are also exploring important histories on this anniversary. Thank you to Amy Braden, Laura Dominguez, and Peter C. Mancall at the USC-Huntington Early Modern Studies Institute for coordinating partners from the Autry Museum of the American West, LA Plaza de Cultura y Artes and El Pueblo de Los Angeles, the Natural History Museum of Los Angeles County, Mission San Gabriel, and the USC Libraries—and to our fantastic colleagues at all those institutions. We have also been fortunate to be in dialogue with colleagues at the Japanese American National Museum, the National Center for the Preservation of Democracy, and the Smithsonian Institution.

Finally, we wish to thank our families for their constant support. Marina and Karl were our sounding boards, always providing insightful, honest feedback. Lygia and Ada will take up the next stretch of American history, and we are hopeful they will continue to work toward Langston Hughes's dream.

Figure 2 (on following spread)
Langston Hughes mailed this poem from Cleveland, Ohio, and inscribed it "to those two grand Americans," his friends the social reformers Charles Erskine Scott Wood and Sara Bard Field, who lived in a bohemian estate near Los Gatos, California, which they named The Cats. The poem was published in the July 1936 issue of *Esquire* magazine, but only the first fifty lines. It was not until 1938 that the full poem was published in *A New Song*, among other writings about the struggles of the working class. Langston Hughes, "Let America Be America Again," November 16, 1935. Typescript poem with manuscript notes. C. E. S. Wood Papers, The Huntington.

1. William C. Tweed, *King Sequoia: The Tree That Inspired a Nation, Created Our National Park System, and Changed the Way We Think About Nature* (Heyday, 2016), 3–9, 35; Andrew Chamings, "The Tragedy of California's Oldest Tourist Attraction," SFGATE, July 10, 2024, https://www.sfgate.com/travel/article/the-tragedy-california-s-oldest-tourist-19553377.php.

2. Hughes wrote in a letter to Louise Thompson Patterson dated May 8, 1941, that a friend told him he heard "Let America Be America Again" sung at Orchestra Hall in Chicago with a chorus of 150. See *Letters from Langston: From the Harlem Renaissance to the Red Scare and Beyond*, ed. Evelyn Louise Crawford and MaryLouise Patterson (University of California Press, 2016), 214.

To those two grand Americans who live on the hill at The Cats, this poem— Langston

LET AMERICA BE AMERICA AGAIN

Let America be America again.
Let it be the dream it used to be.
Let it be the pioneer on the plain
Seeking a home where he himself is free.

(America never was America to me.)

Let America be the dream the dreamers dreamed—
Let it be that great strong land of love
Where never kings connive nor tyrants scheme
That any man be crushed by one above.

(It never was America to me.)

Oh, let my land be a land where Liberty
Is crowned with no false patriotic wreath,
But opportunity is real, and life is free,
Equality is in the air we breath.

(There's never been equality for me,
Nor freedom in this "homeland of the free.")

Say, who are you that mumbles in the dark?
And who are you that draws your veil across the stars?

I am the poor white, fooled and pushed apart,
I am the Negro bearing slavery's scars.
I am the red man driven from the land,
I am the immigrant clutching the hope I seek—
And finding only the same old stupid plan
Of dog eat dog, of mighty crush the weak.

I am the young man, full of strength and hope,
Tangled in that ancient endless chain
Of profit, power, gain, of grab the land!
Of grab the gold! Of grab the ways of satisfying need!
Of work the men! Of take the pay!
Of owning everything for one's own greed!

I am the farmer, bondsman to the soil.
I am the worker sold to the machine.
I am the Negro, servant to you all.
I am the People, humble, hungry, mean—
Hungry yet today despite the dream.
Beaten yet today—O, Pioneers!
I am the man who never got ahead,
The poorest worker bartered through the years.

Yet I'm the one who dreamed our basic dream
In that old world while still a serf of kings,
Who dreamed a dream so strong, so brave, so true,
That even yet its mighty daring sings
In every brick and stone, in every furrow turned
That's made America the land it has become.
Oh, I'm the man who sailed those early seas
In search of what I meant to be my home,
For I'm the one who left dark Ireland's shore,
And Poland's plain, and England's grassy lea,
And torn from black Afric's strand I came
To build a "homeland of the free."

The free?

Who said the free? Not me?
Surely not me? The millions on relief today?
The millions shot down when we strike?
The millions who have nothing for our pay?
For all the dreams we've dreamed
And all the songs we've sung
And all the hopes we've held
And all the flags we've hung,
The millions who have nothing for our pay—
Except the dream that's almost dead today.

Oh, let America be America again—
The land that never has been yet—
And yet must be—the land where every man is free.
The land that's mine—the poor man's, Indian's, Negro's, ME—
Who made America,
Whose sweat and blood, whose faith and pain,
Whose hand at the foundry, whose plow in the rain,
Must bring back our mighty dream again.

Sure, call me any ugly name you choose—
The steel of freedom does not stain.
From those who live like leeches on the people's lives,
We must take back our land again,
America!

Oh, yes,
I say it plain,
America never was America to me,
And yet I swear this oath—
America <u>will</u> be!
Out of the rack and ruin of our gangster death,
The rape and rot of graft, and stealth, and lies,
We, the people, must redeem
The land, the mines, the plants, the rivers,
The mountains and the endless plain—
All, all the stretch of these great green States—
To make America again!

LANGSTON HUGHES
Langston Hughes
Cleveland, November 16,
1935.

Index

Page numbers in *italics* indicate illustrations.

Image Credits

Harvey Butchart Collection, Special Collections and Archives, Cline Library, Northern Arizona University (p. 8); Original handwritten lyrics to "This Land Is Your Land" by Woody Guthrie, February 23, 1940 © Woody Guthrie Publications, Inc. Courtesy of the Woody Guthrie Archives, Woody Guthrie Center, Tulsa, OK (p. 13 top left); Photo: Nathaniel Willson (p. 13 bottom left, right); *Akwesasne Notes* Courtesy of Marjorie Skidders, © Associated Press Photos: Bob Daugherty, © Washington Star Photo: John Bowden, Pete Schmick, © Daily Rag Photo: Dara Harris (p. 15); Copyright © by Octavia E. Butler. Reprinted by permission of the Octavia E. Butler Estate and Octavia E. Butler Enterprises (p. 33 right); © Cara Romero. All Rights Reserved (pp. 35–36, 93, 136); Smithsonian Gardens, Photo: Hannele Lahti (pp. 88 top, 89); Text and images Copyright © Sandy Rodriguez (pp. 94, 112, 113, 114, 116–19); Text and images Copyright © Mercedes Dorame (pp. 95, 154, 156, 159, 161, 163); © Nari Ward Studio. Courtesy the artist and Lehmann Maupin, New York, Seoul, and London, and GALLERIA CONTINUA. Photo: Matthew Herrmann (p. 104 left); Photo © Museum Associates/LACMA (p. 105 right); Copyright © Letitia Huckaby (pp. 124, 126, 127, 130–32); © Maynard L. Parker, photographer (p. 148); Copyright © The Estate of Langston Hughes. Used by permission of Harold Ober Associates and International Literary Properties LLC (pp. 168, 169).

Published in conjunction with the multiyear initiative "THIS LAND IS . . . : Reflections for America at 250," organized by The Huntington from 2025 to 2027. The initiative's anchor exhibition, *This Land Is . . .*, was on view at The Huntington, June 14, 2026–January 11, 2027.

This exhibition was generously sponsored by Hahn & Hahn LLP.

HAHN & HAHN LLP
LAWYERS

Funding for this exhibition was provided by the Douglas and Eunice Erb Goodan Endowment. Additional funding was provided by The Shapiro Center for American History and Culture, the Robert F. Erburu Exhibition Endowment, the Steinmetz Foundation, The Ahmanson Foundation Exhibition and Education Endowment, the Gladys Krieble Delmas Foundation, The Melvin R. Seiden-Janine Luke Exhibition Fund in memory of Robert F. Erburu, and the Boone Foundation.

This exhibition was part of The Huntington's "THIS LAND IS . . ." initiative, which was made possible through major support from The Fletcher Jones Foundation and Stewart R. Smith, Robin A. Ferracone, Logan Smith, and Tracy Beetler through The H. Russell Smith Foundation. Generous support for this initiative was also provided by LeeAnn and Ronald Havner through the JCS Foundation.

Library of Congress Cataloging-in-Publication Data

Names: Henry E. Huntington Library and Art Gallery issuing body host institution | Garrett-Davis, Josh editor | Lehtinen, Linde B. editor
Title: This land is... : field notes on American ground / edited by Josh Garrett-Davis and Linde B. Lehtinen.
Description: San Marino, California : The Huntington, 2026. | Published on the occasion of the exhibition This Land Is . . . Field Notes on American Ground, organized by The Huntington, June 14, 2026–January 11, 2027. | Includes bibliographical references and index.
Identifiers: LCCN 2026003601 | ISBN 9780873282741 hardcover
Subjects: LCSH: National characteristics, American | National characteristics, American, in art | Landscapes—United States—History | United States—History | LCGFT: Exhibition catalogs
Classification: LCC E169.1 .H363 2026
LC record available at https://lccn.loc.gov/2026003601

A Cataloguing-in-Publication record for this book is available from the British Library.

Published by The Huntington
1151 Oxford Road
San Marino, CA 91108
huntington.org

Project management by Jean Patterson
Publication coordination by Mindy Chen
Principal photography by Manuel Flores, Dana Barsuhn, and Anna Kim, Digital Collections and Imaging Services

Distributed by the University of Pennsylvania Press
pennpress.org

Produced by Marquand Books, Seattle
marquandbooks.com

Edited by Melissa Duffes
Designed by Thomas Eykemans
Typeset in GT America and Sentinel by Maggie Lee
Proofread by Jane Friedman
Indexed by Sherri Barnes
Color management by I/O Color, Seattle
Printed and bound in China by Artron Art Group

Details
Cover: Grafton Tyler Brown, *Ocean View Looking South West from the Residence of S.P. Pharis. Pharis District, San Mateo Co. Cal.*, ca. 1870
Frontispiece: Unidentified artist, Water tank and barracks at the Gila River Relocation Center, Arizona, 1944
p. 40: Henry Dawkins, *Liberty Triumphant; or the Downfall of Oppression*, ca. 1773
p. 56: Paris Photographic Studio, *At Hollywood, Los Angeles, CA, USA. Operated by the Kuromi Family of the Shimane Prefecture*, 1928, printed later
p. 72: James Carter Beard, *The Fifteenth Amendment*, 1870
p. 84: G. Schroeter, *Map Illustrating the Disputed Boundary Between the United States and Mexico*, 1853
p. 120: Trumbull White, *Our New Possessions: A Graphic Account, Descriptive and Historical, of the Tropic Islands of the Sea Which Have Fallen Under Our Sway* (1898)
p. 136: Cara Romero, *Evolvers*, 2019